Agency and religion play a very specific role in regulating the role and rights of women in the Mediterranean region public sphere. The possibility of women's agency to determine their own life choices finds opposing dynamics between the two shores of *Mare Nostrum*. In both secular and religious contexts, new feminist thinking and a new conception of women are emerging to redefine normative and social roles. While constitutional and private law reforms describe an arduous but successful affirmation of gender equality, a new understanding of women's agency is changing religions from within. Women's theological reflection emancipates and provides an important framework for interpreting internal dynamics, positions and roles. In external contexts, this process is also transforming religious women's participation. The Arab Springs has highlighted a new role for Muslim women as agents of political and social change. In Southern Europe, religious women have developed a new form of active participation in the social context. On both sides of the Mediterranean, gender intersects with religious identity. In this way, religion becomes an instrument of women's autonomy.

However, in their struggle to re-appropriate public discourse, women's agency faces resistance from religions. As a result, even in countries where constitutional reforms proclaim the principle of non-discrimination and equality, violence and restrictions on women's presence in the public sphere are on the rise. These two dynamics call for a discussion of the role of the law in defining the status of women in society, as well as the role of religion in achieving gender equality throughout the Mediterranean region. The legal affirmation of gender rights on both sides of the Mediterranean requires an effectiveness that depends on its ability to penetrate socio-cultural realities and traditions.

Ilaria Valenzi is a researcher in law and religion at the University of Milan and a member of the Scientific Council of the Redesm Research Centre at the University of Insubria. She is also adjunct professor at the Sapienza University of Rome, where she works on the religious factor in determining the role of politics and law in the global space. Her research focuses on post-secular freedom of religion and belief and religious minorities at the intersection of other personal and collective identity factors.

Women, Agency and Religion: Social and Legal Issues in the Mediterranean Public Space

Giappichelli-Routledge Religions, Laws and Economies in the Mediterranean Space

Book Series Direction

The Director of the Book Series is appointed by the Scientific Council of the Research Center REDESM of the University of Insubria (redesm.org).
The Editorial Board is composed of academics belonging to different scientific and disciplinary sectors of the macro-area involved by the Book Series approved by the Scientific Council of the Research Center REDESM.

Editorial Board

The Mediterranean was the cradle of many religious and political models, which transformed themselves into universal paradigms. Much has been written about this geopolitical space and its peoples, within the context of their religious and political institutions and their commercial and cultural exchanges. However it seems that this unitary vision, predominant in the past, has recently been replaced by a fragmented and partial approach; that one focuses on the individual regional actors only, neglecting the overall picture and the connections between the different parts.

This *Book Series* aims to promote an interdisciplinary analysis of the connection between the religious, social, economic, and legal aspects of the Mediterranean world. It emphasizes the role of religious beliefs and institutions as a "discursive heritage", pragmatically used in the construction of political and economic systems. Religious phenomenology will be analysed from a diachronic and dynamic perspective to highlight the interdependence between the diversified cultural forms of the Mediterranean area. The core idea is that contemporary globalization, by re-proposing old questions in new scenarios, deepens and reveals forms of osmosis between different social systems. Globalization, and the pluralism it entails, challenges the post Second World War constitutional and democratic model, which was based on the universality of human rights, with the difficulty of realizing its promises; such a challenge reactivates tensions between contemporary universalistic claims and modern nationalistic reactions. Religion, economy, state politics, international and religious rights, and soft rules are all part of this transformation, which combines in a new way modern and contemporary paradigms.
To achieve these objectives, this *Book Series* is committed to publish works produced in languages different than the English one. Exchanging methods and knowledge in one of the most important languages of globalization, along with a comparative study of the relationships between the two shores of the Mediterranean, shall constitute a further step towards the overcoming of unilateral interpretations and culturally rooted stereotypes. Moreover, the *Series* will be linked to a web platform, created to stimulate a dialogue between researchers, but also to gather and share documents.

The *Book Series* "Laws and Economies in the Mediterranean Space" is an integrated academic project, organized by the *Research Centre for Religion, Law and Economy in the Mediterranean Area* of the Insubria University, together with other Italian and foreign academic and research institutions (among others, three Universities of Milan, the Universities of Rome III, Padua, Turin, the Oriental Piedmont and, abroad, the Universities of Carthage, Tunis and Saint-Joseph, Beirut); furthermore, it is also an educational project, aimed at stimulating a cultural exchange between students, teachers, and researchers, on the one hand, and religious, social, economic and institutional actors, on the other hand.

Women, Agency and Religion: Social and Legal Issues in the Mediterranean Public Space

Edited by
Ilaria Valenzi

Routledge
Taylor & Francis Group
LONDON AND NEW YORK

G. Giappichelli Editore

First published 2025
by Routledge
4 Park Square, Milton Park, Abingdon, Oxon OX14 4RN

and by Routledge
605 Third Avenue, New York, NY 10158

Routledge is an imprint of the Taylor & Francis Group, an informa business

and by G. Giappichelli Editore
Via Po 21, Torino – Italia

British Library Cataloguing-in-Publication Data
A catalogue record for this book is available from the British Library

Library of Congress Cataloging-in-Publication Data
A catalogue record for this book has been requested

ISBN: 978-1-032-87798-3 (hbk-Routledge)
ISBN: 978-1-003-53452-5 (ebk-Routledge)
ISBN: 978-1-032-87800-3 (pbk-Routledge)
ISBN: 979-12-211-0474-5 (hbk-Giappichelli)

Typeset in Simoncini Garamond
by G. Giappichelli Editore, Turin, Italy

The manuscript has been subjected to a peer review process prior to publication.

This book has been published in the frame of the project PRIMED - Prevenzione e interazione nello spazio trans-mediterraneo thanks to the financing of the Italian Ministry of University and Research.

REDESM PriMED Ministero dell'Università e della Ricerca

CONTENTS

LIST OF FIGURES AND TABLES

CONTRIBUTORS

Biagini Erika, School of Law and Government, Dublin City University

Boussaid Leila, Algiers University

Chemaly Rita, Saint-Joseph University, Lebanon

Çuli Diana, Writer – President of the Indipendent Forum for the Albanian Woman

Ghaouti Malki Souad, Algiers University

Giorgi Alberta, Bergamo University

Lamrabet Asma, Writer and Activist – Centre d'études et de recherches féminines en Islam (Cerfi)

Limam Jinan, Tunis University

Marcou Jean, Science Po, Grenoble

Pozzo Barbara, Insubria University

Rivetti Paola, School of Law and Government, Dublin City University

Simonelli Cristina, Theological Faculty of Milan and North Italy

Spini Debora, New York University in Florence

Tauil Leïla, Geneva University

Tomassone Letizia, Waldensian Theolgical Faculty in Rome, Italy

Valenzi Ilaria, Redesm, Insubria University and Milan University

Introduction

WOMEN, RELIGIONS, AND HUMAN RIGHTS IN THE MEDITERRANEAN CONTEXT

Ilaria Valenzi

ABSTRACT: *The mutual understanding of human rights between cultural and religious roots and different conceptions of social roles is challenged by the intersection of legal, social and political aspects between the two shores of the Mediterranean.*

The perspective that this chapter will analyse is that of depolarisation between the conflicting visions of human rights on both sides, using the key of religion-post-secularisation. In this sense, the affirmation of women's rights in the Mediterranean identifies religion as a particularly relevant actor, both as a potential tool for affirming gender rights and, conversely, its limit. The space between the two shores of the Mediterranean continues to have its own specificities, even as the impact of the illiberal politics of the global right globalises the issue of women's rights and the risk of attack to which they are exposed. Seen from this perspective, women's agency within religions describes behaviours of empowerment or resistance, but also of 'doing religion'. At the same time, women's agency is also manifested in how they relate to public power, including the relationship between religion and the State. While women's rights lie in the implementation of international treaties, the effectiveness of these instruments depends on their rootedness in each country's legal and cultural consciousness. The chapter concludes by outlining the main features of the volume and the main lines of thought suggested by the authors.

1. An intersectional view on the role of Mediterranean Women

Is there a common thread linking Mediterranean women's status and emancipation? What is the role of the legal, social and political arrangements of the Mediterranean countries in achieving gender equality? Does the religious factor hinder or encourage this aspiration?

In order to analyze the role of women in the current Mediterranean context, it is necessary to adopt a cross-cutting perspective among several dimensions of study. Indeed, there is a high degree of complexity in talking about the situation of women. In fact, talking about the condition of women implies many different dimensions of investigation, both in terms of how women constantly negotiate the space of their political action and affirmation in a given context, in a word, in terms of what is commonly referred to as feminist theories and practices, and in terms of the characteristics of the contexts in which women act. That is to say, women's role in the national context is always located (Crenshaw 1991), which in our analysis does not mean ignoring the interdependent dynamic factors. This includes all the historical, social, political and legal factors that influence the protection of women, whether positively or negatively.

In this sense, the situated space in question consists of the specific area between both coasts of the Mediterranean, which historically goes beyond a physical space, expressing its religious, philosophical and cultural globalization (Ferrari 2014).

In fact, it is becoming increasingly clear that there is more than economic interdependence between the northern and southern shores of the Mediterranean. The two sides of the Mediterranean constitute a geopolitical space where different versions of human rights have to face one another.

In this sense, the mobility of borders and people, but even more the interplay between basic models of human rights protection, is highlighted by colonialism and postcolonial criticism, on the one hand, and migration, on the other. Thus, the understanding of human rights on both sides of the North-South divide is called into question.

This questioning of the mutual understanding of human rights first begins to penetrate the contexts of European countries with the stable presence of people with a migration background. It is an encounter between European principles and values on the one hand, and different understandings of social roles and the consequent recognition of rights on the other. In this respect, the idea of human rights and its connection to the cultural and religious roots of the countries of origin raise profound questions that need to be understood and that make it necessary to assess their compatibility with the legal and social substrate in which they are embedded. At a higher level, it is a question of their compatibility with the paradigm of human rights that is recognized at the international level.

But the interdependence also extends southward, with a reverse movement: The internationalization of human rights is also a yardstick for evaluating legal, political and social systems in this area. This issue has been particularly highlighted by the Arab uprisings, which have provoked a real reflection on these rights by demanding greater recognition of the protection of fundamental rights and strengthening their political-institutional arrangements, such as the role of parliaments (Biagi 2022).

The perspective that we intend to examine seeks to depolarize the view between the North and the South of the Mediterranean, also regarding the influence of religion in the relations between the two shores. Studies on the involvement of the European Union in the use of religion in international relations with the southern Mediterranean only confirm that secularism is still the main framework to which Europe refers in its foreign policy, even if it is increasingly being discussed (Wolff 2019). In the post-secularization paradigm, religion is one of the options influencing the vision of society (Habermas 2008), even in conflict with other worldviews to affirm traditional values (Stoeckl 2016).

This engagement in the religious sphere is primarily motivated by security and stability concerns, which lead Europe to prefer relations with religiously moderate partners, also through interreligious and intercultural dialogues. At the same time, the religious argument is used to reinforce the oppositions between the two sides. It is thus used by Europe as a marker of identity and culture, which stigmatizes Islam as contrary to the affirmation of individual rights, and it is used by the countries of the southern Mediterranean, which identify Europe, at the same time secular and Christian, as the perpetrator of imperialist and colonial wills.

Once again, the season of Arab uprisings represents a crucial transition. Hoffman and Jamal have already reconstructed the role of religion and the emergence of two counter-narratives. While the first argued that the uprisings were led by secular and liberal segments in rebellion against theocratic regimes, the second claimed instead that the uprising population was religious and followed a "mosque-to-square" paradigm of participation (Hoffman and Jamal 2014). These same scholars, however, concluded that individual religiosity had a far greater impact on participation in the Arab uprisings than did the communal practice of attending the mosque. That is, a picture of religious citizens far from passive emerges, as reading the Qur'an was found to be a motivator for individual political participation against social injustice. Hoffman and Jamal help us to understand that in reading the events of the Arab Springs, the religious factor should not be excluded from the demands of democracy and, consequently, that personal religiosity has a role to play in claiming social and political rights that are not the sole prerogative of secularism.

In this sense, to adopt an intersectional perspective also means to concretize the post colonial gaze of and on the Mediterranean: to identify mutual influences, it has been argued, means to think of the Mediterranean as a space to be studied beyond geographical boundaries (Proglio 2016). This means avoiding the temptation of essentialist readings on both sides of the Mediterranean, and instead seeing the Mediterranean as a space of possibility, as a space that, according to the canons of intersectional hermeneutics, is always represented by the paradigm of et/et and no longer by that of aut/aut (Collins and Binge 2016).

2. Women's rights under attack

Addressing the issue of affirming women's rights in the Mediterranean is one of the most powerful tests of what has been argued so far. Not surprisingly, the study of women's agency can demonstrate that women's rights are under attack in an overarching way, transcending territorial boundaries and linking seemingly distant contexts. In the same way, the struggles of women's movements for the affirmation of democracy and the rule of law are transversal, since they are also fundamental elements for the affirmation of rights that are more closely related to their gender dimension.

In this regard, religion plays a very specific role, according to a double binary, that of potentially affirming gender rights or, conversely, of severely restricting them.

There is certainly nothing new about the debate on the role of religions and cultures in affirming women's rights. Already in the last-1990s, Susan Moller-Okin, in her famous contribution to thinking about the legitimacy of multicultural theory, pointed out that gender and especially sexual discrimination have their roots in all cultures and religions, in all latitudes (Moller-Okin 1999). While Okin recognized a special role for the feminist movements that emerged in the West had the power to limit gender discrimination in their own legal frameworks, in other cultural contexts patriarchal, including religious, roots were prevalent against the recognition of gender rights.

In fact, in recent years, women's autonomy and rights taken for granted have come under general attack at the global level. It is also well known how this attack takes place even in Western democracies, where the religious argument is used to limit gender rights. This happens both through the use of religious actors by populist political forces, especially the so-called Global Right (Bob 2012), and through the use of the typical instruments of democratic regimes, namely the legislative and the judiciary. Several legislative interventions and court rulings have sought to limit women's rights, starting with reproductive rights. Such interventions are influenced by and reflect illiberal governmental tendencies, including patriarchal or conservative religious arguments (Mancini 2022). However, what several scholars of the gender-illiberalism nexus have argued should not be forgotten when making such arguments: Western political and legal institutions are inherently exclusionary and discriminatory towards women. In this regard, even the most liberal regimes have been associated with the difficulties women face in moving beyond the private sphere, where the recognized role of the family defined women's space for action in the world (Bogaards and Pető 2022). The question of the relationship between gender and religion is by no means secondary from this perspective either. On the contrary, the privatization of religion that is an inherent result of secularization exacerbates the gender divide, allowing the issues most closely related to sexuality and family roles to remain outside the public sphere and governed by rules that are far removed from the ideals of equality and freedom proper to liberal democracies (Mancini 2020). With the re-politicization of religion, women's bodies become a shared sacred space around which essentialist and ahistorical communities ally against perceived ultraliberal drifts (Spini 2022). In this logic of inversion of spaces and meanings, it is paradoxical how illiberal right-wingers take up the arguments about the freedom and emancipation of Western women, proper to feminist movements, in order to set them against the alleged religious and cultural discrimination proper to non-Western political regimes (Spini 2017). The instrumentalization of the fight against the Islamic headscarf in Europe is perhaps the most striking example of this (Ferrari 2022). Here, as elsewhere, the gender discrimination of non-Western women has been transformed into a cultural war on Islam.

However, even in these particular cases, we need to think about how the various anti-veiled measures implemented in the context of the European state and by the European supranational tribunal are itself an enduring feature of liberal-leaning governance (Mancini 2019).

Essentially, women's bodies and their agency constitute a battlefield uniting liberalism and illiberalism throughout time. Discussions about social and political roles and rights for women are indeed culture wars.

It is not trivial to consider that illiberal theories of anti-genderism also offer their own particular epistemology of human rights in the economy of our discourse, in which the different interpretations of human rights and, in particular, gendered ones, have been studied by the legal and political systems of both shores of the Mediterranean (Annicchino 2017). Specifically, the movements under discussion seek to refashion a new image of human rights based on natural concepts and traditional values. In the context of the movements of the illiberal religious right in the United States, the goals of Agenda Europe, a network of hundreds of organizations present in over 30 European countries, include "colonizing human rights", or imposing the ideas of ultra-conservative religious movements through the language of human rights (Walters, Kapur and Graff 2019).

In this sense, relations with the international bodies responsible for guaranteeing human rights, starting with the European Convention on Human Rights, but also including international treaties, play an essential role. In particular, due to its territorial scope and relative projection in geopolitical relations in the Mediterranean region, the Council of Europe Convention on preventing and combating violence against women and domestic violence deserves special attention.

The impact of the illiberal politics of the global right, as recently noted by Nora Fisher-Onar, affects the dichotomy of our reading of the relationship between the global North and South. Through this lens, we see one key Eurocentric assumption broken. This is the idea that religion belongs to the private sphere, while the public sphere is ruled by a pure secular logic. As this assumption collapses, the underlying bias with which systems in the Global South are viewed, where the relationship between state and religion is more porous and responding to different understandings of the role of religion in the public sphere, is also exposed (Fischer Onar 2022). In fact, the ongoing overarching attack on gender rights makes it clear that even in the West, religious references in political dynamics are more than existent, thus putting the sphere of religious presence in the public space on the agenda. This is no longer a fictional opposition between an imaginary secularized West and a religiously imprisoned global South, but rather a common theme that must be addressed universally, taking into account the different latitudes.

3. Beyond secularism, recovering the public role of religion

Adopting an intersectional view of women's agency in the Mediterranean also means assuming that women are themselves intersectional subjects. Indeed, the intersection of multiple identities and social factors is capable of restoring the multiplicity of dimensions of subjectivities and requires protection tailored to this complexity, as legal and sociological theories of intersectionality have taught. In this sense, the particular national context, which must be studied from time to time, and how it affects women's existence, cannot be ignored when analyzing women's agency between the two shores of the Mediterranean.

Similarly, the role played by religion in the social as well as the purely individual context needs to be considered. From this point of view, women are not exclusively passive subjects in their relationship with religion. Rather, they develop with and within the religious context a role that is by no means marginal. Here again, there is a historical contrast between the northern and southern Mediterranean. As Rosi Braidotti has effectively pointed out, historically, European feminism, in the study of the relationship between gender and religion, has developed a somehow agnostic, if not overtly secularized, position based on the criticism of religion as authority (Braidotti 2008). This strand of thought is historically opposed to affirmative feminist thought on religion, which also developed in the European context and was quite diverse within that context. When reconstructing it, Sabine Grenz identifies a number of streams. A first group focused on studying women's lived experiences and practices within religious groups, with an emphasis on everyday experience. The second school, emerging in reaction to the anti-Muslim policies of the 1990s and strengthened after 2001, dismantles the opposition between the secular and the religious, and thus between the secular, superior West and the religious, especially in the Muslim majority states, acknowledging the role of secularism and religiosity in defining the balance of power. A third trend is feminist theologies, which propose and use new interpretations of religious texts and theological doctrines to initiate a religious transformation from within, with implications for the vision of society at large (Grenz 2023). Overcoming the rigid binomial of religiosity and secularization seems to be the common denominator of all the cases described. Consequently, the interpenetration of these two spheres cannot be ignored when describing women's subjectivity and political and social contexts.

The revision of the religious and secular opposition for a more complex and therefore more realistic vision includes the revision of the relations between North and South. It is in this sense that the intersectional approach, which Grenz herself uses, is of great help. Indeed, Grenz argues that the secular (when not overtly anti-religious) approach is not sufficient to overcome systems of oppression of women within religions, we would add, at any latitude. In the same way, intersectional and postcolonial studies are crucial to the analysis of religions from within (Grenz 2023).

The approach just described challenges the notion of a secularized North and a religious South in our reading of this volume. The complementarity of the secular and religious spheres is essential to the dialogue between the two shores of the Mediterranean. It proposes, with an inclusive research gaze, questions that constantly cross the secular-religious border, and thus the geographical and ideal border between the two shores of the Mediterranean. This is, in turn, the new paradigm of post-secularization, postulating the juxtaposition of different options and, as in our case, forcing us to rethink both the secular and the religious realm (Spini 2017, Braidotti 2008). In this respect, the analysis of the role of women in religious contexts is of particular importance. As is often stated, religious contexts are not only the place where women are subjugated, but also the place where women assume roles that sometimes spill over outside religious contexts, directly into civil society.

Although it is not self-evident that these roles of women within religion are necessarily conducive to women's advancement (Mahmood 2005), in our case we are particularly interested in exploring those aspects of women's active participation within religion that lead to women's advancement.

4. Women's religious agency

To do so, we use the concept of agency as it applies specifically to religion, which is the thread running through all our considerations. Using agency to describe women's status within religion, especially traditional religion, has a long history. One commonly accepted definition of agency stresses the positive activation of women's agency within situations of structural discrimination or widespread cultural sanctioning (McNay 2000). In this sense, Burke highlights the importance of the use of the concept of agency specifically in the religious context. Indeed, descriptions of women belonging to religious communities generally lack the concepts of autonomy and intentionality inherent in agency (Burke 2012).

Women's agency within religions can be based on different approaches, as is the case with different strands of religiously inclusive feminism. Here, we must broadly recall Orit Avishai's reconstruction, which inspired later studies that fit our argument (Avishai 2008, Burke 2012, Granz 2023). Two opposing approaches seek a synthesis or a third path. The first approach to agency, that of religious women who seek change and challenge the religions to which they belong, can be called "resistant". The second refers to agency based on "empowerment". This is the attitude of women who seek to reinterpret religious doctrines in order to achieve a better status.

In the overall economy of the discussion, one cannot help but notice how the first type of agency again reacts on the dichotomous view of the world: North vs. south, west vs. Islam, secular vs. religious views. While we should not deny the absolute essentiality of gendered acts and behaviors of resistance, even within religions, the mere adoption of the model of resistant agency runs the risk of perpetuating non-inclusive or stigmatizing attitudes. This would have repercussions, for example, for women who adhere to traditional religious teachings. According to this view, they would lose their status as actors and we would no longer know how to read their adherence to traditional religious conceptions. Once again, we can take the example of the Islamic veil as a model. Following such a direction runs the risk of no longer understanding and reflecting on women who wear the veil. Also to describe the second approach, that of agency based on empowerment, the example of the Islamic veil can provide interesting insights.

Most useful for our purposes is the study of the use of the veil in Western contexts, where the choice to wear the veil has both a domestic political meaning, as a response to a culture of sexualizing the female body, and a foreign policy meaning, as a response to Islamophobia and the assertion of Western hegemony over the Global South (Maske 2017).

A third way is what in different contexts is called "conforming agency" (Burke 2012) or even "lived religion" (Granz 2023) or simply "active agency" (Mahmood 2005). In all these cases, the agency of religious women has to do with "doing religion" (Avishai 2008), with the practices, i.e. the everyday, that reveal the quality of women as actors in the different ways they respond to religious precepts and traditional practices. In this sense, women's agency is manifested in their ability to have formal and informal roles within the religious community; to express their knowledge and thus their authority in a field of human knowledge; and to modulate the religious meaning of things through their actions. Thus, looking at the religious and the role of women within the religious reveals something broader: the existence of multiple visions of the religious and the role of people in their definition. By influencing worldviews and relationships with power, this vision has a socially transformative effect. This is even more true in those national systems in which religion is a factor in determining personal status and liberties, whether personal, as in religious freedom, or communal, as in freedom of assembly.

Consequently, the sites of women's action cannot be ignored in this declination of agency. That is, without ignoring their contradictions, it must take into account the contexts in which they move. In this sense, if it is true that the assertion of women's rights was born and developed in the secularized West, the category of postsecularization is helpful for us in order to define a new meaning of agency.

In this sense, recovering the sphere of religion is essential for understanding the link between women's rights and subjectivity in relation to contexts where religion has particular significance for both individual and social existence. Recalling the contributions of the thinkers we have already mentioned, denying women's agency, even in religious terms, means considering the multiplicity of political grammars (Mahmood 2005, Giorgi 2016). Here we add, again using intersectional hermeneutics, that women's agency in the religious context is itself a situated concept, taking into account the intersection of different grounds. It is in this situatedness (Rebughini 2021) that the religiosity of women stands out, now experienced as an inseparable part of their cultural condition, but not necessarily as a harbinger of subalternity, now experienced as a political claim. This situatedness should address the relationship between religiosity and secularity within the political, social, and state context.

At Kelsy Burke's invitation, our analysis would not be complete without considering the areas of women's nonagency in relation to religion. By this we mean cases in which women are unable to act intentionally in religious contexts and cases in which they are unable to act as subjects with their rights recognized.

5. Women's rights at the crossroads of religion and politics

In this regard, we want to add the other side of the reflection on women's agency in relation to the religious. In addition to analyzing women's roles within religions, it is important to examine women's roles outside them, whether they belong to religious or other faith groups, or whether they have become secular. The question we want to ask, especially when the relationship between the secular and the religious in the state sphere is not clear, is how women's agency operates in relation to public power.

In that sense, the religious realm may not be an exclusive of women, but women do experience the consequences of religious influence in the public realm. Women do experience the consequences of religious influence in the public sphere, for example in relation to the universal affirmation of the principle of equality, both in the sphere of family law and in dealings with public authorities and public law. In such cases, the issues are not limited to women's rights; they are issues of democracy (Bras 2007).

Once again, and with particular caution, we must recall how much the contexts of northern Mediterranean countries have traditionally affirmed the principle of equality and parity. We know, however, how much these achievements had to struggle to become effective and how much they are still in process. We're also aware of how the West is at the center of a reverse revolution on such rights, with a new generation of conscientious objection emerging in the legal, political, and social realms (Mancini 2018).

Turning our gaze further south, we must analyze the intersection of multiple factors that give rise to the condition of gender inequality. Using a comparative approach, Lisa Hajjar identifies the interplay of at least four factors: the Shari'a, state law, domestic violence, and the struggle for women's rights. All of these factors are at the mercy of one main factor that is at the root of them all: the relationship between religion and the state. (Hajjar 2004). Although Hajjar's research focused specifically on the interaction of these factors regarding the issue of domestic violence, we believe the paradigm she identifies has universal value when applied to all women's rights issues. The problem is well known and concerns the use of Shari'a as a normative reference for family law and as a socio-cultural reference for religious values. In terms of the role of the state, the question arises of how far the legal framework can ensure appropriate forms of protection, or how far the cultural and religious environment can condition the effects of such protection.

The litmus test for the health of women's rights is the implementation of international treaties, beginning with the CEDAW, and the implementation of the 1995 Beijing Platform (Raday 2012). The effectiveness and impact of these instruments depend on their cultural legitimacy and the way they are embedded in local culture and legal consciousness, as Sally Engle Merry has pointed out (Merry 2003). While international law enshrines gender equality, social and cultural practices still differ. Thus, the conflict may take the form of the clash between the application of law and international norms, following the familiar path of the clash between the universalism of human rights and the particularism of cultural rights, among which religious traditions play a special role. (Merry 2008). This is true of all models of state-religion relations in the southern Mediterranean, with differences, whether we are talking about the communitarizing model, in which personal and family status are regulated by a system completely separate from that of the state, or the nationalizing model, in which the boundaries between religious law and state law are more fluid. The way out of the opposition between women's human rights, perceived as threatening community disintegration, and religious rights seems to follow two directions.

The first refers to the progressive involvement of women in interpreting religious norms. In this sense, depolarization comes from within, recognizing both women's own membership in the religious culture to be reformed and the need for cultural change to establish equal legal norms. Saadia Yacob's research on the feminist engagement with Islamic law (Yacob 2019) is of particular relevance in this regard. Regardless of the different approaches that have emerged since the 1970s, it is important to note that the methodologies inherent in feminism throughout the ages have contributed to the reinterpretation of Islamic law, sometimes with a typically Western view, sometimes with a view from within. In any case, the various approaches agree that the biases in the application of Islamic law to women are due in large part to the way it has been interpreted over time by political and cultural orientations. Asma Lamrabet, on the other hand, notes that once women gain access to the textual sources of the Quran, with special reference to the ethical standards, it becomes clear that it is not the spiritual message that is in question, but rather the human readings that were layered over time and fostered by social and political conditions that were hostile to the inclusion of women in the sphere of religious knowledge (Lamrabet 2015). As Dina Mansour wittily notes, the reinterpretation of personal status laws, unburdened by the bearers of political and cultural biases, opens the door to a reading of norms in light of international human rights norms (Mansour 2014).

The second relates to the political participation of women in the setting of state norms and, ultimately, in state power. The season of the Arab uprisings was marked by strong participation by women. Women, along with youth, were the unquestioned protagonists of the revolts, and their agency to claim rights and demand dramatic changes in social conditions was especially evident. The Arab Springs had the capacity to trigger a series of legislative reforms. However, as is well known, this prominence has not been followed by a political commitment at the institutional level to the same extent. On the contrary, women have been the main victims of the counter-revolutions. This has been done with the intention of re-establishing the traditionalist social and legal norms. Even in the case of post-revolution regimes, the vision to recognize women in leadership positions was missing.

This is not to say that women did not exercise their agency. On the contrary, as political and social events in the broader MENA region in recent years have shown, several authors have drawn a perspective of women's activation that began before the Arab Springs and continues well after (Stephan and Charrad 2020). It is largely a struggle that needs to continue and that is undergoing cultural change in all the contexts under consideration.

6. The contributions of the volume

This interdisciplinary volume explores the condition of women and women's agency between the two Mediterranean shores. Without neglecting the relationship between the countries and with the region as a whole, the adopted approach favors a reading of the individual contexts of the countries under examination. Identifying commonalities in the condition of women in relation to political and religious factors was the idea we wanted to pursue. From this point of view, in order to analyze the subject in its own scientific context, the authors analyzed the contexts, at national or regional level. In this sense, the volume offers a broad and epistemologically oriented perspective towards a dynamic type of intersectionality between different fields of knowledge, assuming that the female condition is the result of different factors.

Debora Spini focuses on the relationship between religious identity and women's political agency in a post-secularizing context. Drawing on postcolonial and intersectional theories that have transformed the feminist worldview, the author invites a rethinking of Western modernity. In this sense, Spini offers tools for reflecting on how to depolarize the North-South divide.

Alberta Giorgi analyses the rise of religious feminism on both sides of the Mediterranean in the wake of major political events such as the Arab Spring and the rise of a new wave of intersectional feminism in Southern Europe. In both cases, a new form of activism is emerging that involves rather than excludes religious women. Focusing specifically on Southern Europe, Giorgi's contribution analyzes the function of the migration process from the southern Mediterranean to the North Shore, focusing on the category of Muslim women. Their presence has challenged established religious practices and opened up new possibilities for activism.

Still looking to the North Shore, Barbara Pozzo focuses on the role of European private law in enabling women to participate in the multiple contexts of public space. European legal history has paid particular attention to the role of women's political rights. However, the role of private law in defining women's public status has been neglected. Pozzo draws a line between constitutionally recognized political rights and private law, which, while continuing to justify the inferior role of women in the private and family sphere, also has the potential to be used in universal feminist battles, as in the case of the right to inherit the maternal name. In the affirmation of women's agency, private and public spheres are thus interpenetrated.

As noted throughout this introduction, religious studies is also an inward look at describing female agency. Letizia Tomassone's contribution focuses on feminist theology, particularly that of Italian mainline Protestantism. She analyzes in particular the changes that queer theologies have brought to theological discourses of and about gender. As queer theology and fluid gender identities emerge, so do potential alliances in struggles against patriarchy.

Feminist theology is also making inroads into the Catholic world, beginning with the Italian world, but not exclusively. Cristina Simonelli reflects on the ongoing debate about the role of women in the Catholic Church and the perspectives it opens in related areas, such as sexual orientation and masculinity. This is especially relevant for ecclesiological considerations on the role of women and thus on ministry. In such cases, the risk of linking gender and roles is particularly high, especially when this connection is sacralized.

Another reflection of the northern coast, Albania. Diana Çuli describes the process of women's political and social liberation which accompanied the country's transition to a democratic system and a market economy. From this point of view, the author shows how the collapse of the political and social system affected the condition of women. In this transition, religion has also played a role. From a country where it had been outlawed, Albania has become a country where religion is no longer private but public. Drawing on her political experience, Çuli focuses on the struggles against gender-based violence and the long road of reforms toward gender equality that has yet to be achieved.

Leïla Tauil's contribution on *féminismes laïques*, secular feminisms and Islamic feminisms in Muslim contexts, with a focus on the Maghreb, opens the reflection on the southern shore of the Mediterranean. Starting with their historical reconstruction, the author traces the main lines of the three schools of thought and focuses on the current period after independence in Algeria, Morocco and Tunisia. The author then focuses on the current post-independence period in Algeria, Morocco, and Tunisia, analyzing specifically the movements to overturn the codified personal and family status derived from Islamic law and based on the subaltern role of women.

Erika Biagini and Paola Rivetti offer a reflection on the role of Islamic women in the Arab uprisings as an expression of their agency, focusing on Egypt, with crossovers to Tunisia and Morocco. While the Arab uprisings highlighted the role of women as agents of social change, the subsequent period is often referred to as the Arab Winter because of the role of Islamist movements in the post-revolutionary period. This has tended to overshadow the reflection on Islamic women in the uprisings, which has instead been of particular significance. The authors analyze women's agency in religious and political activism, while also highlighting Islamist women's organizational and mobilization skills.

Asma Lamrabet's reflections are based on her exceptional knowledge of the situation of women in Morocco, tracing the lines of its evolution, starting with the important family law and constitutional reforms that have taken place since the mid-2000s. Lamrabet emphasizes the necessity of a reformist view of religion in order to dismantle the instrumentalization of religious discourse, and the necessity of an evolving and progressive reading of religion in order to achieve gender equality in Moroccan society at large.

Souad Ghaouti Malki and Leila Boussaid examine the situation of women in Algeria and the difficulties encountered by the texts of public law in recognizing the principle of equality between men and women. Yet the history of women in Algeria, starting with the anti-colonial battles, is a history of participation in public life. The liberal turn that took place at the end of the 1980s also affected the economic situation of the country and the participation of women in the free economy, with an under-representation of women in economic life. To enable women's free participation in the management of the *res publica*, it is essential to overcome the obstacles created by the traditionalist approach to gender roles.

Women's political participation and gender equality are also the focus of Jinan Limam's contribution. She reflects on the situation in Libya, beginning with the marginalization of women under the Qaddafi regime and ending with women's participation in the 2011 revolution. Through a legal and political analysis, the author argues that Libya's bumpy, violent, and unfinished transition has also had an impact on gender equality in the midst of territorial fragmentation, tribalism, and the rise of religious extremism. During the transition, the situation of Libyan women deteriorated sharply, and the use of violence by militias and fundamentalist groups increased. Women's rights are indeed a dividing issue between conservative and more liberal positions. However, a debate on the status of women and their participation has become possible during the transitional period. In this regard, Libyan civil society has played a fundamental role, with advocacy for women's rights finding plenty of space, including in the process of drafting the new constitution.

The situation in Türkiye today is the focus of Jean Marcou's reflections on the role of women in the country's political life and in the life of political parties. Long considered a model for the Muslim world, Türkiye has become a country where female rights and emancipation are threatened. The religious inspiration of the policies of the Turkish leader Erdogan, according to which the relationship between men and women is not based on the principle of equality but on the principle of complementarity, limits the rights of women in the public sphere. This is particularly evident with regard to women's historically acquired rights, such as the right to vote. The future of Turkish women can therefore be seen from the perspective of religion.

Finally, Rita Chemaly addresses the impact of sociopolitical laws and practices on women's agency in Lebanon. In describing the structural discrimination faced by Lebanese women, the author analyzes the specific situation of the lack of civil codification of personal status issues. Family law, including women's rights in relation to their husbands and children, is actually based on religion with separate courts. In conclusion, the author reflects on the future of Lebanese women, beginning with recent advances in women's movements and political action.

The long journey between the two shores of the Mediterranean offers a richly articulated picture of women's agency and the status of women's rights, where social and political circumstances are conditions for the establishment of full gender equality.

The role of religions is generally perceived to be an obstacle to the implementation of these rights. A closer look, however, reveals that religious women have an essential role in the affirmation of evolutionary and progressive religious visions. Women themselves are the agents of transformation, acting thoughtfully at the intersection of private and public life, of religion and public power. Preserving this dual dimension seems to be the privileged way to affirm truly inclusive and affirmative policies.

References

Annicchino P. (2017), "The Past is Never Dead: Christian Anti-internationalism and Human Rights", in Koskenniemi M., García-Salmones Rovira M. and Amorosa P., *International Law and Religion: Historical and Contemporary Perspectives*, Oxford, Oxford University Press, 178-195.

Avishai O. (2008), "'Doing Religion' in a Secular World: Women in Conservative Religions and the Question of Agency", *Gender and Society*, 22, 409-433.

Biagi F. (2022), "I mutamenti costituzionali nell'Islam mediterraneo: riflessioni sulle dinamiche relative alla separazione dei poteri e alla forma di governo", *Alexis*, 13-19.

Bob C. (2012), *The Global Right Wing and the Clash of World Politics*, Cambridge, Cambridge University Press.

Bogaard M. and Petó A. (2022), "Gendering De-Democratization: Gender and Illiberalism in Post-Communist Europe", *Politics and Governance*, 10 (4), 1-5.

Braidotti R. (2008), "In Spite of the Times. The Postsecular Turn in Feminism", *Theory Culture and Society*, 25(6), 1-24.

Bras J. (2007), "Family Code Reform in Morocco and Algeria: What Progress for Democracy?", *Critique Internationale*, 37(4), 93-125.

Burke K. (2012), "Women's Agency in Gender – Traditional Religions: A Review of Four Approaches", *Sociology Compass*, 6(2), 122-133.

Collins P.H. and Bilge S. (2016), *Intersectionality*, Cambridge, Polity Press.

Crenshaw K. (1991), "Mapping the Margins: Intersectionality, Identity Politics and Violence Against Women of Color", *Stanford Law Review*, 43, 1241-1299.

Ferrari A. (2014), "Dove va la libertà religiosa: percorsi comuni tra le due sponde del Mediterraneo", *Stato, Chiese e pluralismo confessionale*, (5), 1-4.

Ferrari A. (2022), "Human Rights and the Osmosis between Secular and Religious Legal Systems: The Post-modern European Right to Freedom of Religion through the Prism of the Islamic Veil", in Marko J., Lakitsch M., Weirer W., Winter W., Wonisch K., *Diversity, State, and Law. National, Transnational and International Challenges*, Leiden-Boston, Brill Nijhoff.

Fischer Onar N. (2022), *A New Paradigm in Political Religion? Global Right-Wing Populism as the Greater Leveler*, available at https://berkleycenter.georgetown.edu/responses/a-new-paradigm-in-political-religion-global-right-wing-populism-as-the-great-leveler.

Giorgi A. (2016), "Gender, Religion, and Political Agency: Mapping the Field", *Revista Crítica de Ciências Sociais*, (10), 51-72.

Graff A., Kapur R. and Walters S. (2019), "Introduction: Gender and the Rise of the Global Right", *Signs*, 44 (3), 1-14.

Grenz S. (2023), "Post-Secular Feminist Research: The Concept of "Lived" Religion and Double Critique", *Interdisciplinary Journal for Religion and Transformation in Contemporary Society*, 1-23.

Habermas J. (2008), "Notes on Post-Secular Society", *New Perspective Quarterly*, 25(4), 17-29.

Hajjar L. (2004), "Religion, state power, and domestic violence in Muslim societies: A framework for comparative analysis", *Law & Society Inquiry*, 29(1), 1-38.

Hoffman M. and Jamal A. (2014), "Religion in the Arab Spring: Between Two Competive Narratives", *The Journal of Politics*, 76 (3), 593-606.

Lamrabet A. (2015), "Les Femmes et l'Islam: une vision réformiste", *Fondation pour l'innovation politique*, 1-52.

Mahmood S. (2005), *Politics of Piety: The Islamic Revival and the Feminist Subject*, Princeton, Princeton University Press.

Mancini S. (2018), "Introduction. The New Generation of Conscience Objections in Legal, Political, and Cultural Context", in Mancini S. and Rosenfeld M., *The Conscience Wars Rethinking the Balance between Religion, Identity, and Equality*, Cambridge, Cambridge University Press, 1-19.

Mancini S. (2019), "European Law and the Veil: Muslim Women from Victims to Emblems of the Enemy", in Melloni A. and Cadeddu F., *Religious Literacy, Law and History. Perspectives on European Pluralist Societies*, London-New York, Routledge, 127-136.

Mancini S. (2020), "Gender justice and religious freedom in the post-secular age", in Mancini S. (ed.)., *Constitutions and Religion*, Cheltenham, Elgar, 347-369.

Mancini S. (2022), "The Body of the Nation. Illiberalism and Gender", in Sajó A., Uitz R. and Holmes S., *Routlege Handbook of Illiberalism*, London-New York, Routledge, Taylor & Francis Group, 403-422.

Mansour D. (2014), "Women's Right in Islamic Shari'a: Between Interpretation, Culture, and Politics", *Muslim World Journal of Human Rights*, 11(1):1-24.

Maske V. (2017), "IMAN-cipation – Identity Politics of young Muslim Women within the "Muslim Youth in Germany e.V. (MJD)" between

Agency, Submission and Repression. An Analysis of the Transformation of Gender-Roles", *Interdisciplinary Journal for Religion and Transformation in Contemporary Society*, 125-156.

McNay L. (2000), *Gender and Agency: Reconfiguring the Subject in Feminist and Social Theory*, Malden, Polity Press.

Merry S. (2003), "Constructing a Global Law – Violence against Women and the Human Rights System", *Law and Social Inquiry*, 28(4), 941-977.

Merry S. (2009), *Gender Violence: a Cultural Perspective*, Malden, Wiley-Blackwell.

Moller Okin S. (1999), *Is Multiculturalism Bad for Women?*, Princeton, Princeton University Press.

Proglio G. (2016), *Decolonising the Mediterranean: European Colonial Heritages in North Africa and Middle East*, Cambridge, Cambridge Scholars Publishing.

Raday F. (2012), "Gender and democratic citizenship: the impact of CEDAW", *International Journal of Constitutional Law*, 10(2), 512-530.

Rebughini P. (2021), "Agency in intersectionality. Towards a method for studying the situatedness of action", *Socio*, 15, 189-205.

Spini D. (2017), "A call to loyalty: women's bodies, playgrounds and battlefield", *Soft Power. Revista euro-americana de teorìa e historia de la politica y del derecho*, 4 (2), 93-106.

Spini D. (2022), "Populismo e religione: risonanze e affinità", in Valenzi I. (ed.), *Il populismo religioso tra teologia e politica*, Torino, Claudiana, 21-31.

Stephan. R. and Charrad M. (2020), *Women Rising: In and Beyond the Arab Spring*, New York, NYU Press.

Stoeckl K. (2016), "Postsecular conflicts and the global struggle for traditional values", *State, Religion and Church*, 3(2): 102-116.

Wolff S. (2019), "EU religious engagement in the Southern Mediterranean: Much ado but nothing?", in Roccu R. and Voltolini B. (eds.), *The EU in the Mediterranean after Arab Uprising. Frames, selective engagement and the security-stability nexus*, London-New York, Routledge, Taylor & Francis Group.

Yacoob S. (2018), "Feminist Engagements with Legal Discourse", in Anver M. and Rumee A., *The Oxford Handbook of Islamic Law*, New York-Oxford, Oxford University Press, 75-101.

Chapter 1

GENDER, CITIZENSHIP, RELIGIOUS IDENTITY: INNOVATIVE APPROACHES TO AUTONOMY AND POLITICAL AGENCY

Debora Spini

ABSTRACT: *This chapter reacts to the contradictory, and often tragic, morphology of contemporary politics. Women's freedom and autonomy seem to be under attack on a global scale, and such attacks are often led by religious actors; more in general, religion is often invoked as the justification for oppressive policies. These challenges concern Western democracies as well. "Populism", or, to be more precise the neo-authoritarian political parties and movements, and their use and misuse of references to religious identity as well as their manipulation of women freedom play a major role. This chapter, however, wishes to respond to another "fact": that women do have a religious agency, and that religion is for many of them an important element for their self-understanding. This apparent contradiction reveals an underlying tangle of unresolved issues, and resonates with some of the key political, sociological and philosophical debates in the last years. The "fact" of women religious agency calls into question the secular/post secular dyad as well as resonating with the critical reflection on autonomy and agency; in both cases, it requires to apply the gender dimension of analysis in terms which are quite distant from those of mainstream liberal feminism. These lines of reflection point to the importance of women agency within religious communities as a crucial element in the construction of genuinely inclusive and pluralist public spheres.*

1. Backlash or new frontiers?

The nexus between religious identity and women's personal and collective autonomy musts be considered in the wider scenario of the processes often synthesised by terms such as "the return of religion" or "the crisis of secularisation". Both expressions refer to the so-called "secularisation thesis" (Bruce 2011) which has dominated social sciences for decades. According to this theory, religion was doomed to disappear, or at least to become irrelevant. This thesis is now being questioned in its diagnostic relevance: instead of waning away, religion plays a major role on the scene of global politics as well as within domestic public spheres, although in different degrees and in different forms.

The diagnosis of secularisation's process as an inevitable historical development has been questioned also for its implicit normative content, as it is indebted to a philosophy of history heralding the progress of rationalism and Enlightenment from a centre (more or less explicitly identified with the West) to a periphery (the rest of the world). This debt had important consequences on secularism as a political project, or even more, as an ideology, as in this perspective, religious belief appeared essentially as the lingering on of a pre-modern de-enlightened condition. The most recent social and political developments have made it necessary for social sciences and social theory to review well established convictions and engage in elaborating new explanatory as well as normative paradigms.

The most aggressive version of the secularisation thesis is by far not the only option available; other models give a much better account of contemporary political and social phenomena [1]. According to Taylor, in a context marked by secularisation, religious faith is no longer a component by default of social horizons, but should be considered as the result of reflexive re-assessments and re-evaluations (Taylor 2007). Religious identity, therefore, is not the legacy of a pre-modern world, but one of among the many options made possible by the rise of modernity. This view of secularizaiton goes hand in hand with an intersubjective and dialogical conception of identity; in this light, religion constitutes one of the "sources of the self" that individuals may turn to, in order to complete their journeys towards autonomous selfhood.

Just as secularisation has been conceived mostly in subtractive terms, secularism as a political project has also been too often identified exclusively with the European experience, or more specifically with only one European approach, that of French *laicité*, and with its attempt to push religion back into the private sphere [2]. This model, which originated in the need to protect citizens from being coerced into religious homogeneity, is now questioned, as it resulted in reinforcing mechanisms of exclusion. The most rigid version of secularism *à la française* in fact prevents citizens from bringing into the public sphere such an important component of their identity as religion. In the last decades, the need to recognise religiously oriented citizen for "what they are" rather than "in spite" of what they are

[1] The debate on secularisation and secularism cannot be summarised here. See at least Casanova (2013) and Costa (2009).

[2] On the different models of secularism see Srinivasan (2007), Calhoun, Juergensmeyer and Antwerpen (2011).

(Galeotti 2009) has stimulated many debates on a more difference-inclusive "postsecular" approach to democracy [3].

The discussions about the nature and scope of a postsecular society find a brutal reality check in the rise of neo-authoritarian parties and regimes claiming religion as their source of inspiration, currently taking place all over the globe. Western democracies, to begin by several European Union member States, are no exception to this trend. Equally conspicuous is the widespread *revanche* against women's rights. Tragedies such as that of Afghanistan are of such momentum as to sometimes obscure how frequently subtler and less blatant attacks to women's self-determination are taking place in many contexts, from Poland to the United States, from Asia to Latin America [4].

The connection between the two phenomena is quite deep, as policies aiming at restricting women's autonomy are almost invariably promoted by actors cloaking their political programs with the language of religion [5]. Although in Western media and political debates Islam is often indicated as primarily responsible, many Christianity-inspired parties and movements are also participating in this attack to women's autonomy.

The role of religious groups in the backlash against women's freedom does not entirely come as a surprise. Many, if not all, religious traditions have a marked patriarchal character, and actively promote the subordination of women both within religious communities as well as in society at large. The Abrahamic religions, predominant in the geopolitical area analysed by this book, surely make no exception. Both phenomena – the supposed "return" of religion as well as the backlash against women's rights – appear as part and parcel of the general crisis of democracy [6], which has been formulated in terms of "regression" or "backsliding" (Geiselberger 2017; Haggard and Kaufman 2021).

Given this contradictory scenario, the question asked by Cady and Feldessen "why questioning the secular/religious divide right now? when different religious actors seem to join forces in a generalised battle to push women back into a condition of subjection and heteronomy?" (Cady and Feldessen 2013, 6) sounds extremely appropriate.

---

[3] On this point, see the debate between Habermas and Taylor in Mendieta (2011).

[4] https://www.ingenere.it/en/research/backlash-gender-equality-and-womens-and-girls-rights.

[5] See at least Mancini and Stoeckl (2018).

[6] Economist Intelligence Unit reported that the global score of 5.7 was the lowest since the index's inception in 2006 https://www.eiu.com/n/campaigns/democracy-index-2020/.

Yet, women are even more religious than men. A study by the Pew Research Center shows that an estimated 83.4% of women around the world identify with a faith group, compared with 79.9% of men; globally, women are more devout than men by several standard measures of religious commitment (Pew Research Center 2016). This fact has raised – and still does – momentous questions as well as heated, sometimes bitter, debates among feminist theorists and activists Given the patriarchal character of most religious families, women's presence may appear as a form of willing cooperation in reinforcing introjected structures of oppression and domination. Although Muslim women are often singled out as the most evident example of these contradictions, they surely are not the only ones, as women actively participate in many Christian denominations that explicitly endorse submissive gender roles

A careful glance reveals that this representation does not account for a more complex reality. Commitment to a religious community does not necessarily and exclusively imply the passive acceptance of received rules, beliefs, and norms within it. Women have initiated a wide range of transformative practices. They have openly challenged rigid gender distinctions by performing innovative, even provocative, gestures, as in the case of Anne Soupa's candidacy to archbishopric of Lyon, or the Friday prayer led by Amina Wadud. Besides these ground-breaking statements, women's presence within religious communities expresses itself in a constant, often undercurrent, work of re-negotiations of norms and boundaries, less conspicuous although by no means less important. Women's contribution to the life of religious communities also focuses upon the dogmatic core of their respective traditions, as demonstrated by decades of scholarly production, ranging from Christian feminist theology to the wide variety of innovative approaches to Islamic theology[7]. The women's perspective in theological work follows a wide range of itineraries and strategies. In some cases, it focuses on the critical re-assessment of communities' behaviours and practices in light of the correct interpretation of foundational texts and/or application of pre-existing norms and values; in others, it goes even further, exploring alternative interpretations of those very norms and values as well as innovative, sometimes revolutionary approaches to religious texts.

The indubitable alliance between religion and gender oppression is counterbalanced by equally undisputable examples of how "being religious" becomes for women a port of entry to citizenship rather than a bar-

---

[7] For an introduction to Christian feminist theology see Parsons (2002); for a global perspective, Briggs and McClintock Fulkerson (2011). For qur'anic feminism see Hidayatullah (2014).

rier. First of all, religious identity brings women to become active part in civil society through their involvement in a wide range of grass-root organisations, from advocacy to charity. Although not explicitly "political", this form of activism does constitute a way to be present in the public sphere, and as such can be considered as an important step in view of active citizenship. In some cases, religious identity has been a stepping stone to mobilisation in political struggle in the proper sense of the world, as demonstrated, to make but one example, by the women's protest against the Citizenship Amendment Act in India (Chandhoke 2020).

Paradoxically, even membership in religious organizations re-enforcing traditional gender roles may in fact lead to political activism, as in the case of women presence in the American Christian right (Johnson 2019) or, looking beyond the Abrahamic family, in the ranks of political organisations inspired by *Hindutva* ideology, equally keen in reinforcing gender hierarchies (Sarkar 1993 and 2001).

This body of evidence, contradictory as it may be, cannot be ignored, as it opens up a new field of reflection and action for feminist practice and theory. Taking up "the challenge of a post secular turn" implies bringing up to light "a number of implicit assumptions about the feminist project itself." Braidotti 2008, 3). This challenge is all the more urgent, Saba Mahmood pointed out, for Western feminism: coming to terms with the "fact" of women's religious activism" requires a thorough reconsideration of their typical "models of agency and of subjectivity" (Mahmood 2005). This endeavour makes it necessary to critically explore the connection between secularization and women's quest for autonomy, as well as the wider question of the place of women within the overall construction process of modern individuality and selfhood.

2. Newcomers of modernity

The point of departure is quite clear: women's place in Western political modernity is far from being assured once and for all. The classics of feminist scholarship have thoroughly explored how women came to be substantially excluded from the great promise of modernity, the affirmation of individuality and autonomy. The dominant model of subject constitutes a first thematic node to be analyzed. Although the story is far more complicated than this simplified account suggests, a conception of individual as sovereign and independent has long dominated the scene; at the very least, so did the "liberal myth" (Cornell and Benhabib 1987), or "fiction of the autonomous, willing, reasoning, rights-bearing subject convened by modernity" (Brown 2001, 10). Feminist theorists also provided a thorough critical reconstruction of how profoundly the assumption regarding the modern Self moulded democratic citizenship in both its version, either in privileging a "libertarian" view of individuality or in the collective Leviathan of democratic sovereignty. (Pateman 1988 and 1989). Neither of these itineraries was open to women. Because of their "natural" difference, women remained confined within the private sphere, encapsulated within a series of hierarchies and power relationships established by "nature". Women were associated to all that was non-rational, such a passion and sentiments, as well as characterized by vulnerability and neediness (Pulcini 2001). As such, they were deemed incapable of exercising independent moral judgement, constituting the necessary requirement for political autonomy; consequently, they were destined to remain confined into the private sphere and condemned to a condition of dependence (Moller Okin 1979; Elshtein 1981, Cavarero 1992). In the hopes of first-wave egalitarian feminism, it was to be only a matter of time before the progress of modernity resolved these contradictions; yet, these expectations proved to be over-optimistic, and not only for the actual duration of the waiting time. Eventually, women did gain admission to the public space of Western democracies, but at the price of amputation and/or mimesis; they were expected to shed all aspects that did not fit into the mainstream, male-defined model of subject, taking a distance from the passional element as well as trying to hide vulnerability and neediness. In a word, women were expected to make all possible effort to be "as good as men". In fact, a mimetic approach, re-shaping the feminine subject according to the masculine model remains a constant temptation in the history of Western feminism. This a-critical assumption of existing paths to agency, as well as of the dominating model of autonomy had long-lasting effects, and have constituted a major obstacle for the elaboration of alternative approaches to citizenship and political agency.

The shortcomings of a model of autonomy shaped after a sovereign and independent self or by the most extreme versions of individualism have become evident, for reasons which are too well known to be here discussed in detail; to make but an *en passant* reference, the emergence of global risks and the impending environmental catastrophe (Pulcini 2020). Although at in the forefront a quest for alternatives, feminist scholarship[8] has not been its sole proponent. A rich philosophical debate, in the West and beyond, has engaged in an extensive redefinition of the notion of autonomy, to the point of making the separation from "classic" liberal individualism a matter of fact (Honnett and Anderson 2009; Nedelsky 2011). This reflection has

---

[8] For further analysis of the post and de colonial debates on secularisation see Spini (2021).

redefined autonomy according to a much wider range of dimensions, as relational, social, or intersubjective, situated or recognitional and considered the different meanings of t self-determination, self-government and self-authorization. The many voices participating in this debate converge in refusing a concept of autonomy as a permanent possession, identifying a sovereign, independent subject in opposition to other forms of subjectivity defined *in toto* as heteronomous or dependent. In this light, the exercise of autonomy is not an "all or nothing matter", but may be in one or more dimensions of life, permanently or only in specific circumstances (Mc Kenzie 2019, 148).

A view of autonomy which emphasizes its relational nature as well as the possibility of being exercised at various degrees, necessarily involves a dialogic and intersubjective conception of self, whereby individual identity is the result of dynamics of recognition with others, as well as of renegotiations with relevant communities and social backgrounds. Aspects long neglected or undervalued, such as dependence and vulnerability, gain new visibility and relevance. In this light, rather than claiming an ontological association, women have the chance to reflexively embrace this experience, thus challenging all the implicit or explicit assumptions which have shaped the dominant forms of political agency within the journey of Western modernity. The renewed attention on these long-undervalued aspects of subjectivity has been instrumental for many critical reflections aiming at a genuinely inclusive model of citizenship, to begin by those revolving around the political relevance of care (Tronto 2013 and 2015); along with a multidimensional notion of autonomy, it provides important resources to reassess the specific positioning of women's religious agency within the public space.

3. Is secularism bad for women?

This exploration of modernity's ambiguities and of the possible alternative itineraries within it provides useful elements to assess if and how women's quest for autonomy and self-realisation may be connected to secularisation and secularism. The nexus between secularisation and women's freedom appears at a first glance quite solid, especially if the first two are defined in reference to an implicit philosophy of history. Insofar as Enlightenment and rationalisation paved the way for the affirmation of individual rights, the arrival of secularism could in fact be expected to contribute solving once and for all "the problem of sexual difference in history" (Scott 2020). In this perspective, the fact that women could "still" be religious could not be explained in any other terms but as examples of backwardness or "false consciousness" (Reilly 2017). As a matter of fact, a strong alliance between women's liberation and secularism did exist, and for manifest and excellent reasons. In many historical contexts the interference, or influence of religious actors has strengthened male domination in the legal domain as well as in society at large; insofar as it aimed at defending citizens' equal liberty from the claims of religious institution, secular citizenship did extend its protection to women. It is therefore not surprising that for many theorists, to begin by Simone de Beauvoir, as well as for a wide range of feminist movements, secularism in its many versions appeared to be a step in the main road leading to emancipation. Sharing an account of secularisation as the retreat of religion against the necessary advancement of rationalisation and Enlightenment, secular feminists as well have considered women religiosity as a relic of the past resulting from the passive, un-reflexive loyalty to tradition.

This nexus reveals itself as far from being undisputable if considered in light of the intersection between a gender and the de- and postcolonial perspective, which helps to bring into focus the contradictory nature of modernity's supposedly universal promises of individuality, autonomy, self-determination. The subtractive model of secularisation is also intrinsically Eurocentric, and as such fit to turn into a crucial element in the colonial project (Dussel 2002, Maldonado Torres 2008). Post and de-colonial theory has highlighted how the fight against "superstition" (as such was to be considered any religion besides Christianity) thus became a marking feature of the coloniser's civilising mission, matched by a representation as the colonised as "backwards", not-yet-Enlightened[9]. The betterment of women's condition was also presented by colonial discourse as an integral part of such a mission. In reality, the emancipation of women was but a means to re-affirm the power of the colonizer over the colonized, by reducing the latter's capacity to control a most prized possession – women. The unveiling of Algerian women described by Fanon is a typical example of this double-faced mechanism (Fanon 2004). Women's freedom thus becomes a point of contention in the framework of post-colonial political conflicts; consequently, women's bodies are the symbolic battlefield between supporters and adversaries of Western top-down modernisation, a dynamic which is well evident in postcolonial societies as well as within Western democracies.

Another element must be considered in order to complete the analysis of women's position within secularist public spheres: the *vexata quaestio* of culture. The affirmation of the value of cultural difference has been instrumental in bringing up to light the intrinsic contradictions and dark side of

[9] For further analysis of the post and de colonial debates on secularisation see Spini (2021).

Western universalism, and in fostering a full inclusion of "minority" individuals and groups within the sphere of democratic citizenship (Young 1990In the last decades the reference to culture has been appropriated view of a quite different political project, to the point of becoming the pivotal notion for fully fledged cultural racism. "Cultural difference" has become the justification of policies promoting segregation and marginalization rather than inclusion and empowerment. This paradoxical result is made possible by a naturalised or reified view of culture, whereby collective identities are not conceived as resulting from historical processes but as immutable and alien from any sort of internal transformation. The specular reflection of racist appropriation is the version of multiculturalism pitting individual autonomy against the defence of group identity and groups rights. Both in fact are grounded in a "reductionist sociology" as in Benhabib words, and upon "faulty epistemic premises", first of all that "cultures are clearly delineable wholes" (Benhabib 2002, 4) [10]. "Religion" is often identified with "culture", and therefore submitted to the same operations of naturalisation and reification; just as culture, religion is defined by clear and indisputable boundaries, and isolated from historical transformations. Thus reframed, religion, just like culture, may be either mobilised to defend a supposed cultural integrity (as in the case of Europe's Christian roots) or depicted as a threat to a supposedly well-established secular tradition.

This "faulty epistemology" specifically affects women, as it forecloses from view the wide range of re-signification and negotiation practices undertaken within cultural communities (Phillips 2007). This mechanism is even stronger in the case of religious women. A reified and essentialised view of culture and religion does not permit to see and value the many expressions of women's autonomous agency within cultural and religious groups, thus resulting in further dynamics of exclusion. First of all, it enables actors that have little or no interest in fostering women's autonomy to set in motion a series of appropriation and manipulation mechanisms. The defence of "women rights" or the justified concern about the persistence of patriarchal mindset and practices within religious communities is often weaponised, in all kinds of political conflicts, from migration to foreign policy. Once again, these processes find a perfect application in the construction of the "Muslim woman", a fictional subject created by the West-

[10] Benhabib identifies two more of such premises: "(2) that cultures are congruent with population groups and that a noncontroversial description of the culture of a human group is possible; and (3) that even if cultures and groups do not stand in one-to-one correspondence, even if there is more than one culture within a human group and more than one group that may possess the same cultural traits, this poses no important problems for politics or policy" (Benhabib 2020, 4).

ern glance, described exclusively as a "victim" of her culture and therefore as in need of help and support (Abu Lughod 1996).

Furthermore, the dynamics of reification and essentialization constitute a major obstacle to genuine processes of empowerment, as they make it harder to elaborate solidarity network among women. This occurrence is all the more frequent and evident in the case of the religious practice of women which are "culturally" different (Deo 2018, 12), and replicates the typical colonial mechanisms of *reductio ad unum* so deeply ingrained within Western mainstream liberal feminism explored by Mohanty (Mohanty 1984, 351).

In light of all the issues briefly summarised above, a question comes to the forefront: is secularism bad for women? (Aune *et al.* 2017). This question, purposefully echoing the title of Moller Okin' famous book (Moller Okin 1999), appears to be absolutely opposed to the one posed by Cady and Feldessen. Cady and Feldessen themselves provide an excellent reason to question the secular-religious divide: "In part because the political exigencies of the moment work so strongly *against* seeing the limits and vulnerabilities of that divide, leaving us with distorted views and unpalatable options. [...] too strict an insistence on their separation might press us to stand *for* women and *against* religion, even at the expense of women who identify with forms of flourishing and belonging for which secularism does not allow or account". Evidently, in its most extreme forms, secularism does affect women and their possibilities for self-affirmation as well as their chances of inclusion within democratic public spaces (Toldy 2021). Insofar as it tends towards the privatisation of religion and its expulsion from civil society, secularism makes it harder for individuals – women included – to access an important "source of the self". Furthermore, deprives religiously active women them of important channels towards active citizenship rather than promoting their inclusion.

On the other hand, re-discussing the secular/religious divide is not a harmless choice, as both the historical legacy and the current events briefly sketched above remind us with dramatic urgency. The need to overcome secularism does present the danger of confining women afresh within their "traditions", and of drastically undermining their possibilities to express individual autonomy. Taking "side with religion" must not lead to reduce the options and the space for action of "those whom the religious control of gender and sexuality subject to real and growing harms" (Cady and Feldessen 2013, 8). The polarisation between secular and religious agency turns women and their autonomy into a battlefield[11]. As in the artificial

[11] "When framed as polar opposites and antagonists in struggles over gender and sexuality, moreover, religious and secular actors can often be seen to reinforce and em-

opposition with "multiculturalism" whenever forced to "take sides", women lose grounds for agency, both within the public space as well as within their own communities.

4. Alternative resources

The combination of alternatives approaches to selfhood and autonomy and a non-subtractive model of secularization provide the framework to explore a way out of these polarizations.

A rich philosophical debate, in the West and beyond, has disentangled the notion of autonomy, from a view of the Self as sovereign and independent, as well as from "classic" liberal individualism (Honnett and Anderson 2009). Feminist scholarship [12] has been at the forefront in the quest for alternatives, although by no means the sole protagonist. In the course of this reflection, autonomy has been redefined as relational, social, or intersubjective, situated or recognitional, and distinctions were drawn betweenself-determination, self-government and self-authorization.

The many voices taking part in this debate converge in refusing a concept of autonomy as a permanent possession, identifying as the marking feature of a sovereign, independent subject defined in total opposition to other forms of subjectivity, defined *en bloc* as heteronomous or dependent. In this light, the exercise of autonomy is not an "all or nothing matter", but may be in one or more dimensions of life, permanently or only in specific circumstances (Mc Kenzie 2019, 148). On the contrary, a relational view of autonomy impliesa a dialogic and intersubjective conception of self. In this case, individual identity is the result of dynamics of recognition with others, as well as the outcome of renegotiations with relevant communities and social backgrounds; aspects for a long time undervalued, such as dependence and vulnerability, thus gain new visibility and relevance [13]. This shift in perspective

---

power one another, supercharging the subject of debate and redoubling the determination of each side to prevail" (Cady and Feldessen 2013, 8).

[12] See McKenzie (2019, *Introduction*) for an excellent summary. The shortcomings of a model of autonomy shaped after a view of the Self as sovereign and independent or by the most extreme versions of individualism have become evident, for reasons which are too well known to be here discussed in detail; to make but a *en passant* reference, the emergence of global risks and the impending environmental catastrophe (Pulcini 2020).

[13] As Elena Pulcini showed with unmatched lucidity, the matter at stake is to understand how, in the present social, economic and political context of a globalising world, vulnerability and interdependence stretch across gender barriers, to the point of defining the condition of humanity and in an even broader sense, of the world (Pulcini 2012 and 2020).

may legitimately be considered a victory of feminism; yet it comes with the risk of embracing an essentialised notion of gender difference. Rather than in claiming an ontological association, women have the chance to reflexively embracing this experience, thus challenging all the implicit or explicit assumptions which have shaped the dominant forms of political agency within the journey of Western modernity. The new value assigned to this long-time neglected aspects of subjectivity has been instrumental for many critical reflections aiming at a genuinely inclusive model of citizenship, revolving around the political relevance of care (Tronto 2013 and 2015).

The potential and significance of women's religious agency in the public sphere is fully revealed when observed through the intersection between intersubjectivity, relational autonomy and a non-substractive understanding of secularization and secularism. Approaches such as Taylor's, whereby religious belief and practice are the result of a reflexive, autonomous choice reframe women religious agency in very different terms than a mere lingering of false consciousness. In light of an intersubjective and dialogical conception of identity and autonomy, religion constitutes one of the "sources" that individuals need to turn to, in order to fully realise their projects of selfhood.

The political implications are quite evident. Democratic public spaces should not simply tolerate religious difference, but concretely support their citizens' quest for individuality by ensuring that different identities find a place and a role in the public space. The wager is therefore to imagine democratic "postsecular" public spheres capable of accepting differences without reifying or essentialising culture, religion, or gender.

5. Inclusive postsecularism

The rich debate on secularisation which flourished in the past decades provides the needed resources to think of a postsecular condition as something else than "the end" of secularisation, "the defeat" of secularism and the consequent occupation *manu militari* of society by religious groups. A postsecular public space, on the contrary, must be genuinely inclusive and pluralistic; its main aim does not consist in defending the defence of "group rights" as in the shallowest version of multiculturalism, which have been, and with reason, indicted of contributing to the backlash against women's autonomy and freedom [14]. Rather, pluralism aims at providing citizens with the widest possible range of opportunities to cultivate their cultural, philosophical, and religious "sources of the self". Rather than pro-

[14] This particular point is addressed in Kymlicka (1995).

moting segmentation, a postsecular public space is a framework where meaningful exchanges take place among individual and groups, including conversation on what each of them considers as constitutive "values" [15]. These practices are essential to realise exactly that intersubjective, relational model of autonomy that has emerged as a valid alternative to many of modernity's pitfalls and as the necessary resource for a participatory model of citizenship.

Quite interestingly, the debate focussing on the possible contours of a postsecular democratic society does not feature many voices which take gender difference as a specific point of observation); an absence which gives much to reflect upon. What happens to women is not a secondary aspect in assessing whether a postsecular society in the making actually fosters genuine pluralism. Besides, women's agency within religious communities is, for the reasons briefly recalled above, a resource that should not be ignored, especially in the present circumstances. The current health state of most democratic societies around the world rises serious concerns as to the likelihood for pluralistic public spheres to emerge. Democratic public spaces worldwide seem to oscillate between indifference and apathy or the danger of precipitating into a spiral vortex of regression and extreme, divisive polarisation of identity conflicts. Under this point of view, religious women's activism in civil society and their critical praxis happening from "within" is a vital resource. The significance of their theological production and of the rich experience of renegotiations and re-signification of values, norms and beliefs goes well beyond the walls of religious families. On the contrary, it constitutes a relevant example of a immanent critical praxis rooted within cultural and social contexts [16]. The forms of critique "from within" are a necessary resource for genuine pluralism, as they prepare the ground for interactions and exchanges within the democratic public spaces rather than subscribing to divisive and confrontational identity politics. Giving appropriate recognition and voice to women's reflection and practices is therefore a crucial step in the construction of a postsecular feminism, in all its expressions from academia to activism, is the first to be called into question; in order to fill the "missing link between feminism religious activism and the post secular condition" (Braidotti 2008, 10) it must respond to the interrogation of women religious practice by engaging in a

---

[15] For a general theory of pluralism see Ferrara (2014). On the contribution of specifically religious groups to pluralistic public spheres see Dallmayr (2011); in Italian, Naso (2015).

[16] The term "immanent critique" is used here as in o Michael Walzer (1987), that is as a form of critique that moves from the unrealized normative potential of a given social praxis. For an extensive discussion of immanent critique, see Solinas 2015

necessary work of reassessment and reconsideration of implicit and explicit s assumptions.

Yehis task is by no mean exclusive to feminism theorists and activists, but concerns democratic institutions as well. A constant attention to the gender dimension is necessary in all policies that concretely shape a post secular view of society. rather than being spoken for, or cornered into choosing between apparently conflicting loyalties, women within religious communities should be granted all opportunities to fully express their individuality.

Undoubtedly this sort of such a work of gender mainstreaming is not an easy task, as it involves a host of controversial issues, from the scope of the legitimate intervention of public authorities to the claims for concrete measures of assistance to the most vulnerable members of each individual community; yet, however challenging as it might be, it must be assumed as a priority Providing appropriate recognition to the agency of religious women is not a nice addendum, but an essential element in the difficult task of revitalizing democratic public spheres.

References

Abu Lughod L. (2013), *Do Muslim Women need saving?*, Cambridge, Mass., Harvard University Press.

Anderson J. and Honneth A. (2005), "Autonomy, Vulnerability, Recognition, and Justice", in J. Christman (ed.), *Autonomy and the challenges to Liberalism*, Cambridge, Cambridge University Press, 127-149.

Aune K., Lövenheim M., Giorgi A. and Toldy T. (2017), "Is Secularism Bad for Women – La Laicité niut-elle aux femmes?", *Social Compass*, 64 (4), 449-480.

Balibar E. (2005), "La construction du racisme", *Actuel Marx*, 2 (38), 11-28.

Benhabib S. (2002), *The Claims of Culture*, Princeton, Princeton University Press.

Benhabib S. and Cornell D. (eds.) (1987), *Feminism as Critique: Essays on the Politics of Gender in Late-Capitalist Societies*, Cambridge, Polity Press.

Braidotti R. (2008), "In Spite of the Times: The Postsecular Turn in Feminism", *Theory Culture and Society*, 25 (6), 1-24.

Briggs S. and McClintock Fulkerson M. (eds.) (2011), *The Oxford Handbook of Feminist Theology*, Oxford, Oxford University Press.

Brown W. (2001), *Politics Out of History*, Princeton, Princeton University Press.

Bruce S. (2011), *In Defence of an Unfashionable Theory*, Oxford, Oxford University Press.

Cady L.E. and Feldessen T. (eds.) (2013), *Religion, the Secular, and the Politics of Sexual Difference*, New York, Columbia University Press.

Casanova J. (2013), “Exploring the Postsecular: Three Meanings of «the Secular» and their Possible Transcendence”, in Calhoun C., Mendieta E. and VanAntwerpen J. (eds.), *Habermas and Religion*, Cambridge, Polity Press.

Calhoun C., Juergensmeyer M. and Van Antwerpen J. (eds.) (2011), *Rethinking Secularism*, Oxford, Oxford University Press.

Cavarero A. (1992), *Beyond Equality and Difference*, London, Routledge.

Chandhoke N. (2020), *The strength of civil society is its spontaneity, collective mobilisation*, available at https://indianexpress.com/article/opinion/columns/indias-civil-society-moment-citizenship-act-npr-nrc-6243207/.

Dallmayr F. (2011), *Integral Pluralism. Beyond Cultural Wars*, Lexington, Kentucky University Press.

Elshtain J.B. (1993), *Public Man, Private Woman: Women in Social and Political Thought*, New York, Columbia University Press.

Fanon F. (2003), “Algeria Unveiled”, in Duara P. (ed.), *Decolonization. Perspectives from now and then,* London, Taylor and Francis.

Ferrara A. (2014), *The Democratic Horizon. Hyperpluralism and the Renewal of Political Liberalism*, Cambridge, Mass., Cambridge University Press.

Galeotti A.E., (2009), *Toleration as Recognition*, Cambridge, Mass., Cambridge University Press.

Geyselberger M. (ed.) (2017), *The Great Regression*, New York, John Wiley & Sons.

Haggard S. and Kaufman R. (2021), *Backsliding Democratic Regress in the Contemporary World*, Cambridge, Cambridge University Press.

Hidayatullah A. (2014), *Feminist Edges of the Qur'an*, Oxford, Oxford University Press.

Johnson E.S. (2019), *This Is Our Message: Women's Leadership in the New Christian Right*, Oxford, Oxford University Press.

Kriesi H. (2020), “Is There a Crisis of Democracy in Europe? Befindet sich die Demokratie in Europa in einer Krise?”, *Politische Vierteljahresschrift*, vol. 61, 237-260.

Kymlicka W. (1996), *Multicultural Citizenship: A Liberal theory of Minority Rights,* Oxford, Oxford University Press.

Mackenzie C. (2019), “Feminist Innovation in Philosophy: Relational autonomy and Social Justice”, *Women's Studies International Forum*, vol. 72, January-February, 144-151.

Mackenzie C. and Stoljar N. (eds.) (2000), *Relational autonomy: feminist perspectives on autonomy, agency, and the social self*, Oxford, Oxford University Press.
Mahmood S. (2005), *Politics of Piety. The Islamic Revival and the Feminist Subject*, Princeton, Princeton University Press.
Maldonado-Torres N. (2008), "Secularism and Religion in the Modern/ Colonial World-System: From Secular Postcoloniality to Postsecular Transmodernity", in Jáuregui C.A., Moraña M.L. and Dussel E. (eds.), *Coloniality at Large: Latin America and the Post colonial debate*, Durham N.C., Duke University Press.
Mancini S. and Stoeckl K. (2018), "Transatlantic Conversations. The Emergence of Society-Protective Antiabortion Arguments in the United States, Europe, and Russia", in Mancini S. and Rosenfeld M. (eds.), *The Conscience Wars. Rethinking the Balance between Religion, Identity, and Equality*, Cambridge, Mass., Cambridge University Press.
Mendieta E. and Vanantwerpen J. (eds.) (2011), *The Power of Religion in the Public Sphere*, New York, Columbia University Press.
Mohanty C. (1984), "Under Western Eyes. Feminist Scholarship and Colonial Discourses", *Boundary 2*, XII, 3/vol. XIII, 1 (Spring/Fall).
Moller Okin S. (1980), *Women in Western Political Thought*, Princeton, Princeton University Press.
Moller Okin S. (1999) *Is Multiculturalism Bad for Women?*, Princeton, Princeton University Press
Naso P. (2015), *L'incognita post secolare. Pluralismo religioso, fondamentalismi, laicità,* Napoli, Guida.
Nedelsky, J. (2011), Laws's Relations: A Relational Theory of the Self, Autonomy, and Law, New York Oxford University Press, 2011.
Pew Research Center (2016), *The Gender Gap in Religion around the World*, available at https://www.pewforum.org/2016/03/22/the-gender-gap-in-religion-around-the-world/.
Phillips A. (2007), *Multiculturalism without Cultures*, Princeton, Princeton University Press.
Phillips A., Porter F. and Slee N. (2017), *Researching Female Faith Qualitative Research Methods,* London-New York, Routledge.
Parson S.F. (2002), *The Cambridge Companion to Feminist Theology*, Cambridge, Cambridge University Press.
Pulcini E. (2012), *The Individual without Passions: Modern Individualism and the Loss of the Social Bond*, London, Rowman and Littlefield.
Pulcini, E. (2020), *Fra Cura e Giustizia*, Torino, Bollati Boringhieri.
Reilly N. (2017), "Secularism, Feminism, and the Public Sphere", in Zuck-

erman P. and Shook J.R. (eds.), *The Oxford Handbook of Secularism*, Oxford, Oxford University Press.

Sarkar T. (1993), "The Women of the Hindutva Brigade", *Bulletin of Concerned Asian Scholars*, 25:4, 16-24, doi: 10.1080/14672715.1993.10416135.

Sarkar T. (2001), *Hindu Wife, Hindu Nation, Community, Religion and Cultural Nationalism*, Bloomington Indiana, Indiana University Press.

Scott J.W. (2020), *The Fantasy of Feminist History,* Durham N.C., Duke University Press.

Solinas, M. (2015) "On the Forms of Immanent Critique", in Dantini M., Spini D. (eds.), *La parola, le pratiche, la cittadinanza – The Word, the Practices, the Citizenship*, Rome, Arshake, 30-39/98-106.

Toldy T.M. (2021), "Secularist Dreams and 'Women's Rights': Notes on an 'Ambiguous Relationship'", *Revista Crìtica de Ciencias Sociais*, English translation, Open edition journals available at https://doi.org/10.4000/rccsar.302 accessed October 15, 2021.

Taylor C. (2007), *The Secular Age*, Cambridge, Mass., Harvard University Press.

Tronto J. (2013), *Caring democracy: Markets, equality, and justice*, New York, New York University Press.

Tronto J. (2015), *Who Cares? How to Reshape a Democratic Politics,* Ithaca, Cornell University Press.

Walzer M. (1987), *Interpretation and Social Criticism*, Harvard, Oxford University Press.

Chapter 2
FEMINIST-RELIGIOUS INTERSECTIONS ACROSS THE MEDITERRANEAN

Alberta Giorgi

ABSTRACT: *Religious feminist positions are gaining voice and recognition on both sides of the Mediterranean, in relation to a variety of factors – including the Arab uprisings, the new wave of intersectional feminism in Southern Europe, the increase in digital activism. After contextualizing the analysis and research on religious feminist intersections on both sides of the Mediterranean, the contribution focuses on Southern Europe.*
Characterized by Christian majorities, southern European countries are experiencing a renewed women's activism, which is increasingly in dialogue with religious women too. Partly, this is related to the migration processes: the discrimination against Muslim women in Europe brought about the topic of religion, triggering complex processes of disentanglements and conceptual dissections. The contribution provides a scoping review of the studies on religious feminist encounters, campaigns, organizations and initiatives, mapping the different experiences and shedding light on the transformations in women's activism and voice across the Mediterranean.

1. Introduction

Women's and gender rights across the Mediterranean are facing increasing challenges (Giorgi et al. 2023), as demonstrated by the "anti-gender" movements in Europe (Kuhar and Paternotte 2017; Kováts and Põim 2015; Korolczuk and Graff 2018), the withdrawal of Türkiye from the Istanbul Convention and its attack against gender rights (Burul and Eslen-Ziya 2018), and the challenges to women's movements (including violence) and women's rights in the aftermath of the Arab Uprisings (Moghadam 2018). In all these cases, religion plays a significant role. Conservative religious groups constitute the backbone of the anti-gender campaign (which has its roots in the Vatican's stances against "gender", see Garbagnoli 2016), which is also embraced by right-wing populist parties; the Turkish government promotes and sponsors an "Islam of State" (Korkut and Eslen-

Ziya 2018); and the political role of Islam has grown across the Middle East and North Africa (MENA) region (Ferrero 2018). In Europe, religion is mobilized by right-wing populist actors – and, sometimes, by feminist actors too – in an anti-immigration discursive frame, according to which migrants coming from Islam-majority countries are accused of holding discriminatory attitudes toward women and thus having a culture that is incompatible with European democratic values (Norocel and Giorgi 2022). This discourse is a re-enactment of the anti-Catholic discourse of the early 1900s (see Ozzano and Giorgi 2016) and has been defined as "femonationalism" (Farris 2017).

As Aune and Nyhagen (2016) argue, it would be misleading to conclude that "religion" is "against women's rights", for many reasons. First, scholars have explored the existence of religious-feminist groups, which range from reformist to radical movements. If we consider that religion is as much an institutional reality as an embodied (Avishai 2008) and lived (Nyhagen 2017) experience, it is evident that women's activists and feminists could very well be religious and spiritual too. Moreover, research has analyzed women in religious-conservative groups, underlying their carving of spaces of autonomy in a patriarchal structure and explaining their reasons for willingly participating in such contexts (Bracke 2003; Burke 2012). Second, Aune and Nyhagen (2016) argue that opposing women's rights to religion privileges one among the many possible lenses through which inequality can be considered, and prevents the analysis of the complex intersectional forces at play in defining individual and group positions within society (Giorgi 2019).

In Europe, where the history of women's movements included the emancipation from the traditional roles enshrined in religion, mainstream feminism is prevalently understood as secular (van den Brandt 2014), although with some exceptions (e.g. van den Brandt 2015). However, many factors have contributed to increased interest in religion. First, migration and the visibility of Islam have sparked a considerable debate over how to forge alliances with religious (Muslim) women, particularly in light of the intersectional perspective that characterizes many contemporary feminist movements and campaigns (Mainardi and Giorgi 2023; Giorgi 2020; Lépinard 2014a, 2014b). Second, the changes in the socio-demographic composition of feminist movements, which increasingly include women of diverse origins variously articulating their faith, gender, and feminism (Lövheim and Lundmark 2019), are likely to trigger an internal change in European feminism, opening space to rediscuss Christian feminism – which is also gaining some public visibility (Giorgi and Palmisano 2020).

The relationships between religion and feminism are quite different in the MENA region. In North Africa and the Maghreb, as in the Middle East, women's movements and activism have a long history that is inextricably connected with colonialism (and its legacies) and with Islam. As Borrillo (2017) explains, women's public activism first developed in anti-colonial initiatives, literary production, and charities, and flourished in unions, political parties, feminist organizations, and NGOs. Particularly in the 1970s and 1980s, "feminism" was a problematic expression as it was interpreted as an "imported" concept, thus at odds with anti-colonial expectations, which included the rediscovery of Islam. The rise and thriving of conservative Islam in the MENA region further influenced women's activism and secular feminism. Islamic feminism can be interpreted as a "third way", a bridge between secular feminism and Islam that situates the sources of feminism and claim for equality and justice in faith and Islam. In her reconstruction of *Feminism in Islam*, Badran (2009) locates the emergence of Islamic feminism in the 1990s, explaining that, by the mid-1990s, the expression came to capture a composite and plural reality of actors, initiatives, movements, and positions, all based on the articulation of "principles of gender equality and social justice in Qur'anic language" (Badran 2010). The plurality of Islamic feminism and the relations between secular and religious feminisms further developed in the aftermath of the Arab uprisings, as shown for example by research in Morocco (Borrillo 2017), Egypt (Biagini 2020), Tunisia (Muhanna 2015), and North Africa more broadly (Sadiqi 2020).

This contribution focuses on feminist-religious intersections to assess the scientific and scholarly attention paid to this topic in the MENA region. More specifically, the contribution provides a scoping review of the studies on religious-feminist encounters, campaigns, organizations, and initiatives, to explore how scholars map the different experiences and shed light on the transformations in women's activism and voices.

2. Adapting the scoping review methodology

The analysis of cross-references is a first useful step in identifying intellectual networks working on similar topics. Considering the field of social sciences, an initial search in the Scopus database for the keywords feminism AND religion resulted in 352 articles. I downloaded the list of results, including their references, and analyzed the cross-references using the Bibliograph software[1]. The

[1] The software, created by Tommaso Venturini, allow the exploration of research and intellectual networks through the analysis of cross-references, host institutions, funding bodies, etc. – The software is available at: https://tommv.github.io/bibliograph/.

most cross-referenced authors are Kristin Aune[2] and Rachel Rinaldo[3], while the network of referenced works is organized in many cliques with a high number of internal cross-references, related to one another by the occasional reference to an article or book. This means that it is not possible to identify works referenced by all the authors. Among the cliques, for example, we find networks of articles considering Islamic feminism and orientalism, quoting, among others, Yegenoglu (1998), Meghissi (1999), and Ahmed (2000). Another clique considers multiculturalism, referring to, among others, Volpp (2001) or Mahmood (2001). Yet another revolves around "Western" secularism, quoting Casanova (1994), Norris and Inglehart (2004), Scott (2007), and Mohanty (1988).

To unpack the discussion on topics related to religion and feminism in the Mediterranean countries, I decided to adapt the scoping review methodology, which is used particularly in medical research (Munn *et al.* 2018). Scoping reviews have different purposes, including identifying knowledge gaps, exploring how research is conducted on a specific topic, clarifying concepts, and providing an overview of the available research about a thematic area or topic as a preliminary step toward a literature review. Also, they can be useful to answer broad questions concerning a specific field or sub-field, similar to the analysis that Avishai and Irby (2017) developed to understand whether feminist insights and concepts have penetrated research on religion and gender. They find that religion and gender are topics developed in different subfields that operate mostly separately, which partly explains the limited impact of feminist approaches.

In this case, the review aims to assess the scope of the research on the role of religion in feminist and women's movements and campaigns on the shores of the Mediterranean. Given that much research exists on religion in opposition to women's rights and feminism, particularly in Europe, and given the volume of theoretical analysis on Islamic feminism, especially in the MENA region, the analysis aimed at understanding what type of research is produced on the topic of religion in women's movements. More specifically, the review covers the analyses developed in the fields of sociology and political science.

As the scope of the review concerns the intersections between religion and feminisms (and, broadly speaking, women's activism), the selection of the journals included (1) journals covering the geographical areas, (2) journals interested in feminism and gender in both areas, and (3) journals fo-

[2] https://pureportal.coventry.ac.uk/en/persons/kristin-aune.

[3] https://www.colorado.edu/sociology/our-people/rachel-rinaldo.

cused on religion and religious issues in both areas[4]. As Avishai and Irby point out, explaining their choice of peer-reviewed journal articles to analyze whether a "feminist revolution" took place in the analysis of gender and religion: "Though not necessarily representative of the best work on a topic, the gatekeeping process of peer review means these publications are a product of negotiations between authors, referees, and editors, thereby providing insights into dominant perspectives and discourses" (Avishai and Irby 2017, 652-653).

Journals in group (1) include the International Journal of Middle East Studies (IMJES), Middle East Critique (MEC), the British Journal of Middle Eastern Studies (BJMES), European Societies (ES – the journal of the European Association of Sociology), European Journal of Political Research (EJPR – the journal of the European Consortium for Political Research), and South European Society and Politics (SESP). The first three focus on the Middle East and adjacent geo-cultural regions, ES and EJPR mostly focus on Europe, while SESP covers, as the journal website says, "both 'old' and 'new' southern Europe, focusing on Cyprus, Greece, Italy, Malta, Portugal, Spain and Turkey". Journals in group (2) include the European Journal of Women's Studies (EJWS), the Journal of Middle East Women's Studies (MEWS), Gender & Society (GS), and Kohl Journal. The first two journals cover topics broadly related to gender with a specific geographical scope, while GS, as its website says, "seeks to advance a distinctly social perspective with which to analyze gender". Kohl Journal – a Journal for Body and Gender Research[5] is comparatively new, as it started publication in 2015. The journal, which is published in open access, covers the Middle East, South West Asia, and North Africa and it is the main publication of Archives du Savoir Feministe Intersectionnel (Intersectional Knowledge Publishers). Kohl targets young academics as well as activists and independent researchers, and it is interested in challenging the "hegemony of knowledge production, and [ensuring] that our regions and communities play a central role in redefining their own intersections and challenges when it comes to feminist and sexuality research"[6]. The inclusion of this journal is thus particularly relevant to understanding how women's movements reflect on religion and religion-related issues in the area and how Islamic feminism continues to play a relevant role in Middle East-

[4] In addition to Scimago, I adopted the reputational method to select the journals. I asked expert colleagues in the three fields to name two to four top journals and then merged the resulting lists.

[5] In Arabic: كحل: مجلة لأبحاث الجسد و الجندر.

[6] https://kohljournal.press/about.

ern feminism. Journals in group (3) include Social Compass; Religion, State and Society (RSS); Muslim World (MUWO); Révue du Monde Musulman et de la Méditerranée (RMMM).

The period of publications included ranges from 2005 to (the first half of) 2021[7]. The academic attention paid to the topic of women and religion increased particularly since the mid-1990s (Giorgi 2016), in the same years during which the topic of Islamic feminism has developed (Badran 2018). Attention seems to have increased again around 2005-2006, and, particularly, some years later – see, for example, Figure 1, showing the presence of "religion and feminism" in the Scopus database.

Figure 1. Number of articles retrieved by year of publication

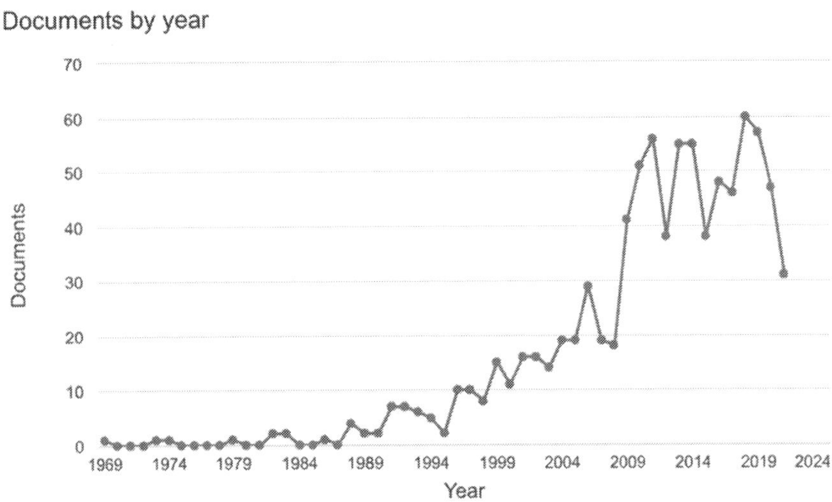

Source: Scopus.

To create a database, I searched the integral text of the articles for a list of keywords related to the topic of interest. The keywords included feminism AND religion (Islam, Catholicism, Christianity, Hinduism, Buddhism, Spirituality, Judaism[8]), women's activism, women's rights, gender rights, pious/religious women, gender AND religion. This approach aimed at inclusivity and casting a wide net. From the initial 778 results, I excluded Introductions, book reviews, and articles focusing on countries without ac-

[7] The only exception is Kohl, which was launched in 2015.

[8] And variations – e.g. Jewish, Muslim.

cess to the Mediterranean; articles covering institutions, laws, and regulations without mentioning women's activism; articles exclusively devoted to theory, with no mention of women movements' accomplishments; and articles on LGBT+ groups focusing on men only. In the end, 134 articles remained, unevenly distributed, with MEWS covering almost 40% – see Figure 2. No variation trend can be traced over time.

Figure 2. Percentage of articles from the selected journals

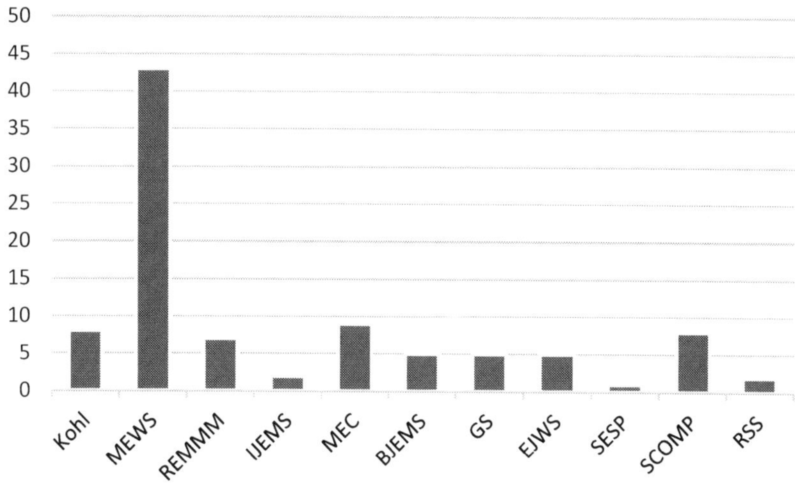

Source: Author's elaboration.

I coded the articles[9] for religious tradition, geographical area, topic, marginality or centrality of feminism-religion-gender in the overall article, and, for research articles, I recorded whether they focus on a case study or showcase comparative research.

The majority of the articles discussing the role of religion in women's activism related to Islam (82%) – with a small group of articles also considering Druze and Alevism (3%) – and Judaism (10%), while Christianity is rarely relevant (4%). The majority of the articles focus on the MENA region (12%) or on a small number of countries in the area: Türkiye (17%), Egypt (14%), and Israel (12%) (while Palestine accounts for 5%). It seems that religion is an object of observation particularly in North Africa and the Middle East – or, in other words, that religion is a matter of interest if it is Islam, while virtually no research pays attention to Christian activism (this

[9] Articles were coded on MAXQDA.

is not the case for Northern Europe – see, for example, Van den Brandt and Longman 2017). Finally, some countries were not covered by research published in the selected journals in the chosen timeframe: Croatia, Montenegro, Albania, Greece, and Libya [10].

3. Religion, feminism, and women's activism: what the discussion is about?

From the analysis, four main topics of discussion emerged that are not mutually exclusive: feminism, the religious role of women, religious women's activism, and the agency of religious women (see Figure 3). The centrality of the topic in the articles is quite balanced, as in 54% of the cases the article focuses on religious women and feminism, activism, or women's rights, and in 46% of the cases, the article only marginally touches upon them. Among the articles featuring research, 79% showcase at least a case study, while only 29% of the studies are comparative.

The discussion revolving around feminism includes two main approaches: one focuses on religious women and investigates religious feminisms, as well as religious women's attitudes toward feminism, gender equality, and women's rights; the other focuses on secular feminists, exploring the processes of othering through which they differentiate themselves from religious women. Of the two, the first approach generated more articles, while the interest in secular feminists accounts for 32% of the articles on feminism, and it is mainly located in Israel, Türkiye, or on the northern shores of the Mediterranean. Research following this approach mostly focuses on how secular feminists deal with religion and religious feminists, by exploring the processes of othering that secular feminists put in place against religious women, or analyzing the cooperation and intersections between religious and secular feminisms. Also, scholars point out the relevance of understanding and taking into account religion for secular feminism (see Nyhagen 2017). While secular feminists are the central element of the articles in some cases, they are more often a marginal aspect of research dealing primarily with other topics (such as religious women's agency).

Most of the articles about religious feminism focus on Islam and Islamic feminism, and showcase theory and research developed about the MENA region (particularly about Türkiye and, to a lesser extent, Egypt). Usually, articles focusing on this topic have it as the central argument of the analysis: authors explain what Islamic feminism is, when and how it developed,

---

[10] There is only one article on women in Libya, and it does not discuss religion.

its current relevance and how it overlaps with other concepts, and its strengths and risks. Latte-Abdallah (2010), for example, complains that knowledge of and about Islamic feminism, 10 years after the expression began to be used, was still underknown and neglected by the scientific literature. However, she also invites research on new forms of feminist engagement, which she defines as "post-Islamist". In addition, scholars explore the nuances of Islamic feminism, unpacking the different positions and describing how they have developed during subsequent conferences on the topic (e.g. Badran 2010). Authors and activists pay particular attention to positioning themselves and to discuss the concept, as well as its correct application to specific cases – see for example the interesting debate on the "Tunisian Femen", analyzed by Dakhly (2015) and El Helou (2015), or the research on women in conservative movements, developed by Ben Shitrit (2013).

In some cases, Islamic feminism is used as an analytical framework to understand women's behavior in the Middle East, or articles showcase research on Islamic feminists on both shores of the Mediterranean, exploring individual behaviors as well as movements, campaigns, organizations, and accomplishments in the Middle East (including, for example, successfully campaigning for passing favourable laws). Also, research explores women's attitudes toward "feminism" (the principles and the word), women's rights, and gender equality. Occasionally, attention has been paid to feminism and religion in the digital environment, exploring how solidarity and sisterhood are expressed and constructed online – see for example Stephan (2013), who analyzes Arab Muslim and Christian women in the diaspora.

Some of the articles also explore how state institutions and male leaders mobilized the concept of "Islamic feminism" for various purposes, for example in Morocco and Türkiye, questioning the legitimacy of adopting this expression to describe state activities or, on the contrary, questioning the legitimacy of continuing to use this expression once it has been used to describe radically different approaches. Some of the scholars whose work is featured in the selected journals argue against the use of Islamic feminism (see for example Seedat 2013). First, some contend that "Islamic feminism", while merging different approaches, risks overlooking some of the specific elements of either Islam-based or feminism-based women's struggles. In addition, the expression does not appeal to those who recognize themselves in either one of the identities that Islamic Feminism conflates. Second, others recall that Islamic conservative movements tried to undermine the concept by attacking its alleged "Western" roots, and the term sometimes remained charged even for non-conservative Muslims.

Studies show that, despite the spread of the word "feminism" particularly in the 1990s, women's theorizations and struggles for equality and emancipation are not "imported" – on the contrary, they date back to the early 1900s and cannot be understood without considering the complex intersections with colonialism, which contributed to shaping unique and context-specific feminisms, regardless of the name given to the phenomenon. In retracing the pioneering work she and Miriam Cooke have conducted, Margot Badran affirms:

> The earliest writings we found went back to the mid-nineteenth century, before the advent in most Arab countries of European colonialism, which was often associated with imposing "Western" feminism on Arab women. The feminism Arab women created, however, firmly attacked colonial intrusion. Arab women's dispersed writings displayed a cartography of feminism before a term for feminism existed in Arabic (Badran 2018, 134).

Some of the articles directly addressing "feminism" and "religious women" focus on Israel and Judaism, and a couple deal with Christian and Catholic women.

Figure 3. Percentage of articles by theme

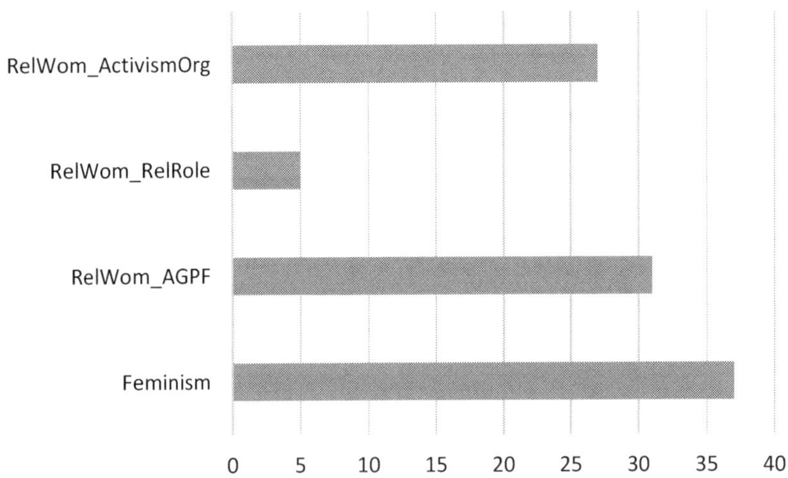

Source: Author's elaboration.

The second most relevant theme that the articles focus on is religious women, which includes exploring public figures and religious women's agency. The geographical scope is broader than in the previous category, as the showcased research covers almost all the countries (and, particularly, the ones on the southern shores of the Mediterranean). No specific trend can be traced concerning topic centrality: while in some cases the articles revolve around the theme, in others this is only a marginal aspect. Much of the analysis of public figures focuses on female intellectuals, journalists, and authors (such as poets and novelists), exploring their work under the lenses of gender and feminism, and showing their inspirational role. Shissler (2007), for example, analyzes the advice column "Cici Anne", featured in popular Turkish newspapers and magazines, authored by an outspoken champion of women's rights. Other research focuses on male and female political leaders' support for hindering women's rights.

Some of the analyses instead tackle the issue of religious women's agency, which is one of the most used concepts in discussing the relationships between women and religion (Burke 2012; Lépinard 2011; Giorgi 2019). Without specifically adopting the concept, research reflects upon the use of hijab (Al-Kazi and Gonzalez 2018) and how the visibility and invisibility of women's religiosity in the public sphere challenge our understandings of citizenship and democracy (Amiraux 2018). In some cases, articles focus on how authors or newspapers from abroad depict Arab and religious women stereotypically – see for example the comparison and contrast between novels authored by the Canadian Barbara Victor and the Algerian living in France Yasmina Kadra on the one side, and the Syrian Khaled Khalifa on the other (McManus 2013). Other scholars adopt a different perspective and analyze what and how religious women "do" religion and feminism, rather placing the spotlight on the "possibility of doing", as the concept of agency implies (Nyhagen 2017; Avishai 2008). Research explores, for example, how Muslim women negotiate intimacy and regulate public sexuality (Sehlikoglu 2016), or how men and women in the "queer" digital network in Egypt challenge heteronormativity and religious traditions (Walsh-Haines 2012). Broadly speaking, scholars pay attention to the ordinary life of religious women.

In the third and fourth categories, we find articles and research paying attention to religious women's organizations and more informal activism on the one side, and to their active role in religious organizations on the other. Much of the research covering religious women's organizations analyzes their role and stances casting a broader look on activism and exploring the relationships between religious-based activism with secular organizations, the place and relevance of religion in women's organizations and women's rights campaigns, and the role of politics in women-only networks. Otbals (2010), for example, analyzes women's associations in Andalusia, including religious associations, and explores the groups' goals and demands. Usually, the articles touching on this topic put it at the center of the analysis. In some cases, attention is paid instead to the story and development of one organization or movement – as in the case of the analysis of Orthodox Jewish women animating the conservative movement to rebuild the Third Jewish Temple on the Temple Mount/Haram al-Sharif in Jerusalem (Feldman 2017), or the "Women in Mosques" campaign in Türkiye (Alyanak 2019). In addition, analyses explore the role of international bodies and programs in advancing women's rights on the ground, particularly in the countries on the southern shores of the Mediterranean. Also, research shows women's informal activism and discusses the factors fostering public and political participation– such as in Zaatari's analysis of the culture of motherhood as an avenue for women's participation in South Lebanon (Zaatari 2006). Research on this topic has been developed in most of the countries bordering the Mediterranean.

Finally, the small group of articles pointing at women's religious role mainly focus on Islam and explore the role of female preachers in Islam in Morocco (Dirèche 2010), Syria (Kalmbach 2008), and Türkiye (e.g. Maritato 2017), and, more broadly, female religious authority. This research focus has developed mostly in the countries of the MENA region. Scholars focusing on this topic put it at the center of their analysis.

4. Conclusions

Research shows how religious women's activism to advance women's and gender rights has a long history in both Europe and the MENA region. While religious women sometimes struggle with the term "feminism", in the MENA region as well as in Europe (see Nyhagen and Halsaa 2016), it is also a word that they reclaim (Redfern and Aune 2010).

The current political changes on both the shores of the Mediterranean could indeed offer an occasion of visibility for religious women's activism. In Europe, contemporary intersectional feminist movements are likely to be less dismissive of religion than previous emancipatory movements, due to the attention they pay to the complex intersections of different dimensions of inequality. Additionally, migration has brought about the greater visibility of Islam and sparked a debate on religious women's agency and autonomy, which contributed to relaunching the feminist and feminist movement's analysis of the role of religion in feminism. Concerning migration and generational change, it is worth noting that young feminists are in fact plural – in their origins, spirituality, and religiosity – and they are likely to bring about some change. Also, the visibility of religious feminism is increasing because of its presence on the web, and due to specific initiatives (such as Mary 2.0 – see Giorgi and Palmisano 2020). In the MENA region, religiosity and religious feminism are inextricably connected with democratization and de-colonial movements – on the one side, religion is part of the regional identity proudly embodied against colonial influence, while on the other, conservative Islam is particularly active against women's rights. Islamic feminism has developed as a specific and contextual form of feminism, which is now plural and in constant transformation. The Arab uprisings and the rise of conservative religious movements contributed to challenging Islamic feminism, which is now in the process of re-shaping its forms.

Notwithstanding the factors that may contribute to increasing the visibility of religious women's feminism, scholarly attention has not similarly increased. The analysis showed that while the scientific discussion over the role of religion in feminism and women's activism is solid and well-structured, it remains circumscribed into specific subfields – which bears particular interest for some specialists. In the MENA region, Islamic feminism is the subject of feminists' and area experts' attention – they explore Islamic feminism theoretically and empirically and investigate the many other possible intersections between religion and women's activism, including the study of secular women's movements and initiatives. While the attention is mostly related to Islam, Judaism too is a focus of research. In Europe, the attention to the intersections of religion and feminism relates largely to how secular feminists deal with religion, or to migrant religious women and their feminism and/or their attitudes toward women's rights. This reflects a broader bias of an imaginary "secular Europe", for which the religion is, mostly, the religion of the other – in this case, the female other and a Europe dealing with "the Muslim question" (Selby and Beaman 2016).

References

Ahmed S. (2000), *Strange Encounters: Embodied Others in Post-Coloniality*, New York, Routledge.

Al-Kazi L.A. and Gonzalez A.L. (2018), "The veil you know: Individual and societal-level explanations for wearing the hijab in comparative perspective", *Social Compass,* 65(5), 566-590.

Alyanak O. (2019), "When Women Demand Prayer Space. Women in Mosques Campaign in Turkey", *Journal of Middle East Women's Studies,* 15(1), 125-134.

Amiraux V. (2018), "Citoyens, piété et démocratie. Réflexions sur l'occul-

tation des corps croyants, l'intimité et le droit au secret", *Social Compass*, 65(2), 168-186.
Aune K. and Nyhagen L. (2016), "Religion, politics and gender", in Haynes J. (ed.), *Routledge handbook of religion and politics*, New York, Routledge, 335-51.
Avishai O. (2008), "'Doing Religion' In a Secular World: Women in Conservative Religions and the Question of Agency", *Gender&Society*, 22(4), 409-433.
Avishai O. and Irby C.A. (2017), "Bifurcated conversations in sociological studies of religion and gender", *Gender&Society*, 31(5), 647-76.
Badran M. (2009), *Feminism in Islam. Secular and Religious Convergence*, Oxford, Oneworld.
Badran M. (2010), "An historical Overview of Conferences on Islamic Feminism: Circulations and New Challenges", *Revue des mondes musulmans et de la Méditerranée*, 128(6824).
Badran M. (2018), "Keeping the Gates Open", *Journal of Middle East Women's Studies*, 14(1), 133-136.
Ben Shitrit L. (2013), "Women, Freedom, and Agency in Religious Political Movements: Reflections from Women Activists in Shas and the Islamic Movement in Israel", *Journal of Middle East Women's Studies*, 9(3), 81-107.
Biagini E. (2020), "Islamist women's feminist subjectivities in (r)evolution: the Egyptian Muslim Sisterhood in the aftermath of the Arab uprisings", *International Feminist Journal of Politics*, 22(3), 382-402.
Borrillo S. (2017), *Femminismi e Islam in Marocco. Attiviste laiche, teologiche, predicatrici*, Roma, Edizioni Scientifiche Italiane.
Bracke S. (2003), "Author(iz)ing Agency. Feminist scholars making sense of women's involvement in religious 'fundamentalist' movements", *The European Journal of Women Studies*, 10(3), 335-346.
Burke K.C. (2012), "Women's Agency in Gender-Traditional Religions: A Review of Four Approaches", *Social Compass*, 6, 2, 122-33.
Burul Y. and Eslen-Zyia H. (2018), *Politics and Gender Identity in Turkey Centralised Islam for Socio-Economic Control*, Abingdon, Routledge.
Casanova J. (1994), *Public religions in the modern world*, Chicago, University of Chicago Press.
Dahkli L. (2015), "L'ordre des choses et le sens de l'histoire. La Tunisie après la révolution de 2010-2011", *Revue des mondes musulmans et de la Méditerranée*, 138(9256), 117-130.
Dirèche K. (2010), "The Murchidât in Morocco: Between State islam and feminist islam", *Revue des mondes musulmans et de la Méditerranée*, 128, 99-111.

El Helou L. (2015), "From Ideology to Dogma? A Discussion about Femen, Aliaa Elmahdy, and Nudity in the Arab World", *Khol: a Journal for Body and Gender Research*, 1(2), 84-92.

Farris S. (2017), *In the Name of Women's Rights: The Rise of Femonationalism*, Duhram, Duke University Press.

Feldman M.Z. (2017), "Putting Messianic Femininity into Zionist Political Action: The Race-Class and Ideological Normativity of Women for the Temple in Jerusalem", *Journal of Middle East Women's Studies*, 13(3), 395-415.

Ferrero M. (2018), "Why the Arab Spring turned Islamic: the political economy of Islam", *Constitutional Political Economy*, 29, 230-251.

Garbagnoli S. (2016), "Against the Heresy of Immanence: Vatican's 'Gender' as a New Rhetorical Device Against the Denaturalization of the Sexual Order", *Religion and Gender*, 6(2), 187-204.

Giorgi A., Garradio J. and Toldy T. (eds.) (2023), *Religion, Populism, Gender in the Mediterranean Area,* Abingdon, Routledge.

Giorgi A. (2016), "Gender, religion, and political agency: mapping the field", *Revista Crítica de Ciências Sociais*, 110, 51-72.

Giorgi A. (2019), "Feminism and Religion: queering the divide", *Rassegna Italiana di Sociologia*, LX(4), 805-826.

Giorgi A. (2020), "Religious Feminists and the Intersectional Feminist Movements – Insights from a Case Study", *European Journal of Women's Studies*, available at doi: 10.1177/1350506820931134.

Giorgi A. and Palmisano S. (2020), "Women and Gender in Contemporary European Catholic Discourse: Voices of Faith", *Religions*, 11(508), doi: 10.3390/rel11100508.

Kalmbach H. (2008), "Social and Religious Change in Damascus: One Case of Female Islamic Religious Authority", *British Journal of Middle Eastern Studies*, 35(1), 37-57.

Korolczuk E. and Graff A. (2018), "Gender as "Ebola from Brussels": The Anticolonial Frame and the Rise of Illiberal Populism", *Signs: Journal of Women in Culture and Society*, 43(4), 797-821.

Korkut U. and Eslen-Ziya H. (2018), "Understanding 'New Turkey' Through Women's Eyes: Gender Politics in Turkish Daytime Talk Shows", *Middle East Critique*, 27(2), 179-192.

Kováts E. and Põim M. (2015), *Gender as Symbolic Glue. The Position and Role Of Conservative And Far Right Parties In The Anti-Gender Mobilizations In Europe Kováts Maari Põim*, Bruxelles, Foundation for European Progressive Studies.

Kuhar R. and Paternotte D. (eds.) (2017), *Anti-gender campaigns in Europe: Mobilizing against equality*, Lanham, MD: Rowman & Littlefield.

Latte Abdallah S. (2010), "Les féminismes islamiques au tournant du XXI e siècle", *Revue des mondes musulmans et de la Méditerranée*, 128(6822).

Lépinard E. (2011), "Autonomy and the Crisis of the Feminist Subject: Revisiting Okin's Dilemma", *Constellations*, 18(2), 205-21.

Lépinard E. (2014a), "Impossible Intersectionality? French Feminists and the Struggle for Inclusion", *Politics and Gender*, 10(1), 124-130.

Lépinard E. (2014b), "Doing intersectionality. Repertoires of Feminist Practice in France and Canada", *Gender and Society*, 28(6), 877-903.

Lövheim M. and Lundmark E. (2019), "Gender, Religion and Authority in Digital Media", *ESSACHESS. Journal for Communication Studies*, 12(2(24)), 23-38.

Mahmood S. (2001), "Feminist theory, embodiment, and the docile agent: Some reflections on the Egyptian Islamic revival", *Cultural Anthropology*, 6 (2):202-236.

Mainardi A. and Giorgi A. (2023), "Re-shaping the boundaries of feminism: the case of #femminismoislamico on Instagram", *Partecipazione & Conflitto,* 16(2), 339-354.

Maritato C. (2017), "Compliance or negotiation? Diyanet's female preachers and the diffusion of a 'true' religion in Turkey", *Social Compass*, 64(4), 530-545.

McManus A. (2013), "Sentimental Terror Narratives: Gendering Violence, Dividing Sympathy", *Journal of Middle East Women's Studies*, 9(2), 80-107.

Meghissi H. (1999), *Feminism and Islamic Fundamentalism. The Limits of Postmodern Analysis*, London, Zed Books.

Mohanty C.T. (1988), "Under Western Eyes: Feminist Scholarship and Colonial Discourses", *Feminist Review*, 30, 61-88.

Moghadam M. (2018), "Explaining divergent outcomes of the Arab Spring: the significance of gender and women's mobilizations", *Politics, Groups, and Identities*, 6(4), 666-681.

Muhanna A. (2015), "Islamic and Secular Women's Activism and Discourses in Post-Uprising Tunisia", in El Said M., Meari L. and Pratt N. (eds.), *Rethinking Gender in Revolutions and Resistance: Lessons from the Arab World*, London, Zed Books, 205-231.

Norocel C. and Giorgi A. (2022), "Disentangling radical right populism, gender, and religion: an introduction", *Identities*, 29(4), 417-428.

Norris P. and Inglehart R. (2004), *Sacred and Secular: Religion and Politics Worldwide*, New York, Cambridge University Press.

Nyhagen L. (2017), "The lived religion approach in the sociology of religion and its implications for secular feminist analyses of religion", *Social Compass*, 64(4), 495-511.

Nyhagen L. and Halsaa B. (2016), *Religion, gender and citizenship: faithful women, gender equality and Feminism*, London, Palgrave Macmillan.

Ortbals C.D. (2010), "The Potential of Local Women's Associations in Andalusia: Pursuing Culture, Enriching Lives and Constructing Equality", *South European Society and Politics*, 15(2), 203-223.

Ozzano L. and Giorgi A. (2016), *European Culture Wars and The Italian Case: Which Side Are You On?,* London, Routledge.

Redfern C. and Aune K. (2010), *Reclaiming the F Word: The New Feminist Movement*, London, Zed Books.

Sadiqi F. (ed.) (2020), *Women's Movements in Post-"Arab Spring" North Africa*, London, Palgrave MacMillan.

Scott J.W. (2007), *The Politics of the Veil*, Princeton, Princeton University Press.

Sedaat F. (2013), "When Islam and Feminism Converge", *The Muslim World*, doi: 10.1111/muwo.12022.

Selby J.A. and Beaman L.G. (2016), "Re-posing the 'Muslim question'", *Critical Research of Religion*, 4(1), 8-20.

Shelikoglu S. (2013), "Exercising in Comfort: Islamicate Culture of Mahremiyet in Everyday Istanbul", *Journal of Middle East Women's Studies*, 12(2), 143-165.

Stephan R. (2013), "Creating Solidarity in Cyberspace: The Case of Arab Women's Solidarity Association United", *Journal of Middle East Women's Studies*, 9(1), 81-109.

van den Brandt N. (2014), "Secular Feminisms and Attitudes Towards Religion in the Context of a West-European Society. Flanders, Belgium", *Women's Studies International Forum*, 44, 35-45.

van den Brandt N. (2015), "Feminist Practice and Solidarity in Secular Societies: Case Studies on Feminists Crossing Religious. Secular Divides in Politics and Practice in Antwerp, Belgium", *Social Movement Studies*, 14(4), 493-508.

van den Brandt N. and Longman C. (2017), "Working against many grains: Rethinking difference, emancipation and agency in the counter-discourse of an ethnic minority women's organisation in Belgium", *Social Compass*, 64(4), 1-18.

Volpp L. (2001), "Feminism Versus Multiculturalism", *Columbia Law Review*, 101(5), 1181-1218.

Yegenoglu M. (1998), *Colonial Fantasies. Towards a Feminist Reading of Orientalism*, Cambridge, Cambridge University Press.

Walsh-Haynes G. (2012), "The Egyptian Blogosphere: Policing Gender and Sexuality and the Consequences for Queer Emancipation", *Journal of Middle East Women's Studies*, 8(3), 41-62.

Zaatari Z. (2006), "The Culture of Motherhood: An Avenue for Women's Civil Participation in South Lebanon", *Journal of Middle East Women's Studies*, 2(1), 33.

Chapter 3

THE ROLE OF EUROPEAN PRIVATE LAW IN RENDERING WOMEN'S PARTICIPATION TO PUBLIC SPACE EFFECTIVE

Barbara Pozzo

ABSTRACT: *During the last centuries, women's political rights in Europe have been at the core of a wide debate and found their recognition in constitutional texts that were introduced, with different times and methods, in all European countries.*

Nonetheless, women's participation in the public space does not depend solely on the formal recognition of political rights in constitutional texts, but also from the role of private law in shaping women's status in society.

There has always been a biunivocal relationship between private law rules concerning the status of women and the reforms that introduced female suffrage and the equality principle at constitutional level.

On the one side, private law was able to uphold "gendered rules of conduct" – even after the introduction of political rights in the constitution – that were challenged, and eventually changed, by the legislative branch, by the courts, and by legal doctrines that adapted the law to new social demands.

On the other side, private law has a potential to render the fight against women's discrimination mainstreaming, like in the questions concerning matters related to the patrimonial consequences of divorce, the right to maintain the maiden name, or – finally – in the case concerning mothers' rights in establishing relationships by descent and the legal consequences thereof, including the passing on of the mother's surname to her children.

1. Introduction

In the *public space* of the 19th century and of the first half of the 20th century, men and women were situated at the two extremities of the scale of values. They opposed each other like day and night [1]. The *public man*, invested with an official function, played an important and highly regarded role in society: he is responsible for political decisions, he fights in war for the honour and values of the fatherland, he holds the reins of the family and decides on the fate of the children.

Women found their place at home: fate has reserved them a role as mothers and wives, guardians of the domestic space. The house is their temple. A *public woman* was the most despicable thing there can be. If the language is the mirror of the culture and values of a society at a given historical moment [2], we might observe that the meaning of a "public woman", in English, but also in French ("*une femme publique*"), in Italian ("*una donna pubblica*"), in Spanish ("*una mujer public*") always corresponds to the concept of a *prostitute*: depraved, debauched, lustful, venal [3].

The place of women in the public space has always been problematic in the Western world since ancient Greece, having thought and constructed politics as the heart of decision-making and power [4]. Not to underestimate is the crucial role that religious aspects have played in this regard. We have in fact to remember that in the most ancient stage of development of religious rules, the interpretation of sources considered of divine origin was certainly influenced by the social, cultural, and legal context of those societies that were predominantly patriarchal.

But the division of roles and of spaces has even more ancient roots, to which anthropologists have paid more attention in recent times, shedding light on various aspects that contribute to explain the ancestral origin of a

---

[1] I take this metaphor from Perrot M., *La place des femmes. Une difficile conquête de l'espace public*, Paris, Les Éditions Textuel, 2020, 5.

[2] White J.B., *When Words Lose Their Meaning: Constitutions and Reconstitutions of Language, Character, and Community*, Chicago, The University of Chicago Press, 1984.

[3] Landes J.B., *Women and the Public Sphere in the Age of the French Revolution,* Ithaca-London, Cornell University Press, 1988, 3.

[4] Elshtain J.B., *Public Man, Private Woman: Women in Social and Political Thought.* 2nd ed., Oxford, Princeton University Press, 1981, where the Author traces the evolution of the binomial public man/private woman in the history of political philosophy from Plato to Marx, highlighting the forms and ways in which a separation between the public/male and private/female spheres has been established, which opens an abyss between the world of domestic, family, daily relationships and the world governed by political, abstract and institutionalized relationships.

different specialization of the sexes[5]. This literature, which has at times abandoned the academic character to become popular[6], has induced a new awareness on historical data that most of us had studied in elementary school and then forgotten forever. All of us have been taught that at some point in evolution, humans have taken a bipedal stance. We have been told that to walk upright on two legs had a lot of advantages: we can see farther, and we can carry objects with us, as well as weapons that help us hunt and defend our neighbours. But it had also a lot of disadvantages and women paid an extra price for that, as it had a lot of consequences on their role in society. An upright gait required narrower hips, constricting the birth canal at the same moment when babies' heads were getting bigger, as they had to contain our human brain which became more and more voluminous. Consequently, death in childbirth became a major hazard for human females and women who gave birth earlier, when the baby's head was still relatively small, had more chances to survive the delivery. Natural selection played here an important role, favouring earlier births. The result is that, in comparison with other mammals, humans – being born prematurely – need much more care and for a longer time, which implied specific choices on the side of the whole group to survive. Lone mothers could hardly forage enough food for their offspring and themselves having to treat children at the same time. This favoured social ties, but also a specialization of roles: someone, the nursing mother, had to remain "home" to look after the newborns, while someone else, the one that seemed best suited to fighting wild animals, had "to go out" in search for food[7]. It is incredible that this specialization of roles still maintains its importance in times where the only peril that we must face to get our food is to go to the supermarket.

"Private" and "public", as the separate realms for women and for men[8], have been described and offered different explanations and grounds in history, none of which appear completely satisfactory[9], also since the history of women is increasingly recognized as a chapter yet to be written[10]. It is

---

[5] Héritier F., *Masculin/Féminin. La pensée de la différence*, Paris, Éditions Odile Jacob, 1996.

[6] Compare Harari Y.N., *Sapiens: a brief history of humankind,* London, Harvill Secker, Random House, 2014, which has been translated in numerous languages and has reached the top of the charts around the world.

[7] The example is taken from Harari Y.N., *Sapiens: a brief history of humankind,* cit., 20.

[8] Sartori D., "Donne e uomini tra pubblico e private", *Annali di studi religiosi*, 5, 2004, 367.

[9] de Beauvoir S., *Le deuxième sexe,* t. I, Paris, Éditions Gallimard, 1949, 79 ff.

[10] For a general overview see Lerner G., *The Creation of Feminist Consciousness, From Middle Ages to Eighteen-seventy,* Oxford, Oxford University Press, 1993, 247 ff.

only in recent years that we became aware that women's contribution to human history has often been overlooked[11], and that research aimed at highlighting the role of women in society has multiplied. Various studies have focused on women's position in Western society over the centuries[12], or have investigated a more limited historical period[13] or their contribution to a historically important movement[14], or in various disciplines[15]. Others have focused on their access to education[16] or to a professional life[17].

It is not then by chance that Carole Pateman has argued that: "*The dichotomy between the private and the public is central to almost two centuries*

---

[11] Patou-Mathis M., *L'homme préhistorique est aussi une femme. Une histoire de l'invisibilité des femmes,* Paris, Allary Editions, 2020; Criado Perez C., *Invisible Women: Exposing Data Bias in a World Designed for Men*, London, Chatto & Windus, 2019; Perrot M., *Les Femmes ou les silences de l'Histoire,* Paris, Flammarion, 1998; Fraisse G., *Les Femmes et leur histoire,* Paris, Gallimard, Collection Folio Histoire, 1998; Thalmann R., "L'oubli des femmes dans l'historiographie de la Résistance", *Clio. Femmes, Genre, Histoire,* 1, 1995.

[12] Perrot M. and Duby G. (eds.), *Histoire des femmes en Occident*, 5 voll., Paris, Pion, 1990-1991; Allen A.T., *Women in twentieth-century Europe*, London, Macmillan International Higher Education, 2007.

[13] Wiesner-Hanks M., *Women and Gender in Early Modern Europe, New Approaches to European History*, Cambridge, Cambridge University Press, 2019; Hunt M., *Women in eighteenth century Europe*, London, Routledge, 2014; Zancarini-Fournel M., *Histoire des femmes en France: XIXe-XXe siècle*, Rennes, Presses Universitaires de Rennes, 2005; Leyser H., *Medieval Women: Social History Of Women In England 450-1500,* London, Hachette UK, 2013.

[14] Bartolo B., *Donne del Risorgimento – Le eroine invisibili dell'unità d'Italia,* Torino, Ananke, 2011; Capeda Fuentes M., *Sorelle d'Italia, Le donne che hanno fatto il Risorgimento*, Peveragno, Blu Edizioni, 2011.

[15] For anthropology, see the essays collected by Reiter R.R., *Toward an Anthropology of Women*, New York-London, Monthly Review Press, 1975; for art, see Butler R., *Hidden in the Shadow of the Master, The Model-Wifes of Cézanne, Monet & Rodin,* New Haven-London, Yale University Press, 2008; Colonelli L., *Le muse nascoste – Protagoniste dimenticate di grandi opera d'arte*, Firenze, Giunti, 2020; for Music see Pendle K. (ed.), *Women and Music: A History*, 2nd ed., Bloomington, Indiana University Press, 2001.

[16] Jacobi J., *Mädchen- und Frauenbildung in Europa. Von 1500 bis zur Gegenwart,* Frankfurt-New York, Campus Verlag, 2013; Lirosi A., *Libere di sapere. Il diritto delle donne all'istruzione dal Cinquecento al mondo contemporaneo*, Roma, Edizioni di Storia e Letteratura, 2015; Soldani S. (ed.), *L'educazione delle donne: scuole e modelli di vita femminile nell'Italia dell'Ottocento,* Milano, Franco Angeli, 1989.

[17] Schweitzer S., *Femmes de pouvoir. Une histoire de l'égalité professionnelle en Europe (XIXe-XXIe siècle),* Paris, Payot, 2010; Zolesio E., "Des femmes dans un métier d'hommes: l'apprentissage de la chirurgie", *Travail, genre et sociétés*, 2, 2009, 117-133; Cordes O., *Frauen als Wegbereiter des Rechts. Die ersten deutschen Juristinnen und ihre Reformforderungen in der Weimarer Republik*, Hamburg, Diplomica® Verlag GmbH, 2012; Krontiris T., *Oppositional Voices: Women as writers and translators of literature in the English Renaissance*, London, Routledge, 1997.

of feminist writing and political struggle; it is, ultimately, what the feminist movement is about" [18].

The pivotal role of the access to the public sphere has remained central in the Feminist debate for decades, as pointed out by another eminent representative of this movement, Catharine MacKinnon: "*For women the measure of the intimacy has been the measure of oppression. This is why feminism has had to explode the private. This is why feminism has seen the personal as the political. The private is public for those for whom the personal is political. In this sense, for women there is no private, either normatively or empirically*" [19].

As lawyers, it seems important to analyze how legal rules have crystallized these social roles, how law has played an important part in maintaining them and how – at the same time – law has become, over the last two centuries, the tool to dismantle them.

2. From the Old Regime to the Revolution

To trace the history of women in the public space in contemporary history, it seems an obligatory step to begin our reconstruction with that period of profound renewal which was the passage from the *Ancien Régime* to the Revolution.

The French Revolution took place at the resounding call to recognize women's rights that Olympe de Gouges' "*Déclaration des droits de la femme et de la citoyenne*" launched in 1791 [20].

The historical context in which this claim took place is characterized by liberal ideas of individualism and equality, that found their cradle in the seventeenth century. These ideas required the overcoming of traditional societal structures embedded in "natural" hierarchies and inequalities but neglected to give a rational response to women's claims to equal rights.

The historical passage from French absolutism to bourgeois society is crucial to the understanding of women's role in XIXth century society [21].

---

[18] Pateman C., "Feminist Critiques of the Public/Private Dichotomy", in Benn S.I. and Gaus G.F. (eds.), *Public and Private in Social Life*, New York, St. Martin's Press, 1983, 281.

[19] Mackinnon C.A., *Toward A Feminist Theory of The State*, Cambridge, MA, Harvard University Press, 1989, 191.

[20] Mousset S., *Women's Rights and the French Revolution: A Biography of Olympe de Gouges,* London, Routledge, 2007, 63-79; Riva J., "The Radical Novelty of Olympe De Gouges", *Nottingham French Studies*, 53.3, 2014, 345-358.

[21] See Landes J.B., *Women and the Public Sphere in the Age of the French Revolution,* cit., 2.

We must recall that under the *Ancien Régime*, women had a subjugated role in society and were generally excluded from the exercise of power[22]. On the other side, this was not considered particularly exceptional as they shared this situation with most men of that period: the hierarchical structure of society deprived many subjects, men and women, of fundamental rights and to the possibility to participate in public debate.

Nonetheless, and despite the patriarchal structure of the society of that time, it is also true that women belonging to upper classes and to the aristocracy took part in and influenced political events and public language[23], while women of urban artisanal classes participated to a series of public activities, sharing work settings with men[24].

To understand the role that women could play in the *public* sphere under the Old Regime it is important to recall the tradition of *Salons*, as *private* spaces opened to intellectuals and artists to debate or converse on topics related to cultural or political current events[25].

From the 16th century onwards, the *Salon* took the organizational form of the modern era and, during the Enlightenment, their role was decisive in spreading culture outside the circles of power (secular or ecclesiastical) and the figure of the organizer or host, who was often a woman, was established.

The Parisian literary *Salons* excelled in fame in this era in which, beyond the figure of the patron, the meetings were often characterized by the presence of a prominent personality through whom they filtered discussions and forged new ideas, arriving then also at dealing with philosophical, religious, and political problems. The fortune of this type of aggregation is explained by the traditional immobility and the refractoriness of the official institutions towards the new demands of culture and with the increased

---

22 Edmond and Jules De Goncourt, who devoted their attention to women's situation in the XVIII century (*La femme au XVIIIe siècle,* last ed., Paris, Editions Flammarion, 2021) give a quite sad portrait of the birth of a girl in this period: "*Quand au dix-huitième siècle la femme naît, elle n'est pas reçue dans la vie par la joie d'une famille. Le foyer n'est pas en fête à sa venue; sa naissance ne donne point au cœur des parents l'ivresse d'un triomphe: elle est une bénédiction qu'ils acceptent comme une déception. Ce n'est point l'enfant desire par l'orgueil, appelé par les espérances des pères et des mères dans cette société gouvernée par des lois saliques; ce n'est point l'héritier prédestiné à toutes les continuations et à toutes les survivances du nom, des charges, de la fortune d'une maison; le nouveau-né n'est rien qu'une fille et, devant ce berceau où il n'y a que l'avenir d'une femme, le père reste froid, la mère souffre comme une Reine qui attendait un Dauphin*".

23 Landes J.B., *op. cit.*, 17.

24 Landes J.B., *op. cit.*, 21.

25 von der Heyden-Rynsch V., *Europäische Salons, Höhepunkte einer versunkenen weiblichen Kultur,* München, Artemis & Winkler, 1992.

demand for comparison between different positions of thought and experience[26].

Despite the presence of various configurations of *Salons*, in every form of meeting some constant characteristics were nevertheless found: the meetings were free, spontaneous and informal; the participants had a socio-cultural contiguity; the meetings had an intellectual interest, which prevailed over other purposes; in the debate an equal intellectual capacity of the participants was implicitly recognized, even in the presence of a prominent personality.

The *Salonnières*[27] were the protagonists of these unique institution of the early modern period, where women could rise to a certain social prominence, so to gain the attention of a vast public[28].

In these "private" settings, women could participate in conversations on an equal basis with guests. Very often favoured by their rank or their social position, the *Salonnières* became a point of reference for the intellectuals who frequented them[29].

The *Salon* hinged on the central figure of a woman, the landlady: married, sometimes widowed, or separated, never single; elegant, intelligent and cultured (even if as a woman she had not received a thorough education), she spoke in an easy and witty way, had refined manners and knew European languages.

The *Salonnières* indifferently welcomed male and female representatives, nobles, or bourgeois as long as they were educated; they opened up a space for conversation, favouring relationships between guests; they promoted young talents and could make them known to the public.

Between the seventeenth and eighteenth centuries the *Salon* thus became an important space for female emancipation, where – in contrast to her own submissive and silent family role – an educated woman could

---

[26] Kale S., *French salons: high society and political sociability from the Old Regime to the Revolution of 1848*, Baltimore, John Hopkins University Press, 2004; Lilti A., *Le Monde des salons. Sociabilité et mondanité à Paris au XVIIIe siècle,* Paris, Fayard, 2005.

[27] Duggan A.E., *Salonnières, furies, and fairies: the politics of gender and cultural change in absolutist France*, 2nd ed., Newark, University of Delaware Press, 2005, 2021; Pekacz J.T., "The salonnières and the philosophes in Old Regime France: The authority of aesthetic judgment", *Journal of the History of Ideas*, 1999, 277-297; Brown H. and Dow G., *Readers, writers, salonnières: female networks in Europe, 1700-1900*, New York, Peter Lang, 2011.

[28] Craveri B., *La civiltà della conversazione,* Milano, Adelphi, 2001 (English translation: *The age of conversation*, New York, New York Review Books, 2005). References to this book are to the Italian version.

[29] One of the most famous Salons, and most probably the first to open in Paris, was the one of Madame de Rambouillet. Compare Craveri B., *op. cit.*, 55 ff.

make music, discuss philosophy, literature, or science by asking questions and manifesting openly their own opinions. Landes outlines in this respect that "*women functioned as adjuncts, then, of a system of advancement for merit. Circles at court and salons in the city became centers of female power brokers*" [30]. In other words, *noblesse de sang* and *noblesse de l'âme* were considered on an equal footing.

The phenomenon, and in particular its excesses, was not without criticism and attracted the mockery of Molière, who in the *Femmes savantes* exercised all his satire on academic pretension and female education. In his other work "*Les Précieuses ridicules*" the French playwright attacks the new fashion of using hyperbolic paraphrases and elaborate metaphors, as the ones employed by Madeleine de Scudéry, *femme de lettres,* whose works mark the apogee of this movement [31].

According to a certain historical reconstruction, salon sociability is then presented as an important tool for women to gain importance in the public sphere during the 18th century [32].

Following Jürgen Habermas's conception of the "public sphere" [33], this situation faded away with the emergence of the new *bourgeois* society of the nineteenth century. Just as the public sphere eroded in the nineteenth century, according to Habermas, the salon culture, with women at its centre, disappeared in the 1780s because it was incompatible with the new, masculine, political culture that developed during and after the Revolution [34].

That this reconstruction is correct, is now subjected to scrutiny by historians who emphasize how S*alons* not only survived but flourished after the Revolution, proliferating in nineteenth-century France [35]. Independently from this historical *querelle,* it is important to analyze which is the status of women that descends from the legislation that was adopted after the Revolution and that frames the new patriarchal bourgeois family.

---

[30] Landes J.B., *op. cit.*, 24.

[31] Denis D. and Spica A.-E. (eds.), *Madeleine de Scudéry: une femme de lettres au XVIIe siècle*, Arras, Artois Presses Université, 2019.

[32] Landes J.B., *op. cit.*, 39 ff.

[33] Habermas J., *Strukturwandel der Öffentlichkeit. Untersuchungen zu einer Kategorie der bürgerlichen Gesellschaft,* Frankfurt am Main, Suhrkamp, 1962; an English translation appeared under the title, *The Structural Transformation of the Public Sphere: An Inquiry Into a Category of Bourgeois Society,* Cambridge, Polity Press, 1992.

[34] Pekacz J.T., "Les Amies des philosophes: The making of Enlightenment salons in nineteenth-century France", *French History and Civilization*, 5, 2014, 53-61.

[35] Pekacz J.T., *op. cit.*

3. Equality... but not for all

With the *Déclaration des Droits de l'Homme* adopted in August 1789 the fundamental principle of equality was pronounced: "*Men are born and remain free and equal in rights. Social distinctions can only be based on common utility*" [36]. By 1791, new articles extended civil and political rights to Protestants, Jews, and other categories of people that previously had none, but the situation of women did not improve much [37].

During those times of freedom for all, *Sans-culottes* and *Jacobins* both affirm that women must stay at home, next to their lord, their husband. But many women do not admit this proposal and claim a fighting position alongside men and are present on the streets on July 14th [38].

In the *Treatise on the authority of the husband* by Pothier, the influential lawyer, whose work was incorporated almost textually in the French *Code Civil*, we read: "*Le mariage, en formant une société entre le mari et la femme, dont le mari est le chef, donne au mari, en la qualité qu'il a de chef de cette société, un droit de puissance sur la personne de la femme, qui s'étend aussi sur ses biens*" [39].

Notwithstanding this subjugated position, women benefited from some changes during the Revolution, such as equal inheritance between children, although they still had very few opportunities for education or training, followed by the near impossibility for them to work and earn a decent income [40].

In this context, some women stand out for their claims of rights that put

---

[36] The original version of Art. 2 of the Declaration stated: "*Les hommes naissent et demeurent libres et égaux en droits. Les distinctions sociales ne peuvent être fondées que sur l'utilité commune*".

[37] Pédron A., "'Nous aussi nous sommes citoyennes': Female Activism during the French Revolution", *Women in French Studies Special Conference Issue*, 2019, 71.

[38] Bertaud J.P., *La vie quotidienne en France au temps de la Révolution (1789-1795)*, Paris, Hachette, 1983, It. trans.: *La vita in Francia ai tempi della Rivoluzione*, Milano, Mondadori, 2022, 217. References to this book are to the Italian edition.

[39] Pothier R.J., *Traité de la puissance du mari sur la personne et les biens de la femme*, in *Oeuvres de Pothier, contenant les Traités du droit français, Nouvelle édition mise en meilleur ordre et publiée par les soins de M. Dupin, Avocat a la Cour royale de Paris*, t. VI, Paris, Chasseriau, 1825, 1. The text goes on stating: "*La puissance du mari sur la personne de la femme, consiste, par le droit naturel, dans le droit, qu'a le mari, d'exiger d'elle tous les devoirs de soumission qui sont dus à un supérieur. Un de ses principaux effets, est un droit, qu'a le mari, d'obliger sa femme à le suivre partout où il juge à propos d'aller demeurer ou résider, pourvu néanmoins que ce ne soit pas hors du royaume et en pays étranger: car si le mari, en abjurant sa patrie, voulait s'y établir, la femme, qui doit encore plus à sa patrie q'à son mari, ne serait pas obligée de l'y suivre, et d'imiter l'abjuration que son mari fait de sa patrie*".

[40] Pédron A., *op. cit.*, 72.

them on an equal footing with men: Théroigne de Méricourt[41] who played an active role in the Revolution, Marie Madeleine Jodin[42] who published *Vues législatives pour les femmes* in 1790, and the most famous Olympe de Gouges[43] with her *Déclaration des Droits de la Femme.*

Although the important role played by women during the Revolution, the legislation that was passed defining the status of women for the next century was far from being listening to their claims.

The French Civil Code of 1804, often presented as a "revolutionary" code, introducing the principle of equality of all citizens before the law, codified the subjugated role of women inside and outside the family.

Even from a first view of the main rules of the Code civil, it is understood that the role of the woman had no autonomy and therefore no possibility of determining her destiny alone.

The wife owed obedience to the husband (Art. 213 Code civil), was obliged to live with him and to follow him wherever he considered fit to reside (Art. 214 Code civil). The husband alone administered the assets belonging to the family. He could sell and mortgage them without the wife's consent (Art. 1421 Code civil). The husband also had the administration of the wife's personal property. He could exercise alone all the movable and possessory actions belonging to the woman (Art. 1428 Code civil). Once the woman was married, even the dowry was administered by the husband alone (Art. 1531 Code civil). Although marriage was conceived as a contract, based on mutual consent (Art. 144 ff. Code civil), a wife's adultery was sufficient to allow the husband to obtain divorce (Art. 229 Code civil), while she was able to get divorce on account of the husband's adultery only if he kept his concubine in the common house (Art. 230 Code civil). Women could not be witnesses in all procedures concerning civil status documents (Art. 37 Code civil), nor before a notary public for last will dispositions (Art. 980 Code civil). Special rules applied to unmarried women of age, namely the only ones who could sue in court without the permission of a male member of the family.

The image we get is that of a woman who depends on her husband in all respects, confined to the home, since in the absence of a specific marital authorization she could neither move nor work, and therefore was unable to become independent.

---

[41] Roudinesco E., *Théroigne de Méricourt: Une femme mélancolique sous la Révolution,* Paris, Albin Michel, 2013.

[42] Gordon F. and Furbank P.N., *Marie Madeleine Jodin 1741-1790 – Actress, Philosophe and Feminist,* London, Routledge, 2001.

[43] Faucheux M., *Olympe de Gouges*, Paris, Gallimard, 2018; Ravera C., *Olympe de Gouges*, Roma, Elemento 115, 2019; Mousset S., *Women's Rights and the French Revolution: A Biography of Olympe de Gouges,* London, Routledge, 2007.

The myth of the "mistress of the house" was not only framed by the *Code civil*. Under the insistence of political and religious authorities, the responsibility for domestic tasks became the "natural" role of women: "*every true woman knows that her place is in the house [...], since that is what nature has ordered*" [44].

Not that the private spaces of the house were in the complete domain of the wife. Far from it! The father/husband dominated the house as well. He has his own places: the smoking room and the billiard room, where the men retire to chat after social dinners; the library, because books remain men's affairs; the office, where the children enter only trembling [45].

This is rendered particularly evident in the writing of a famous French literate woman of that period: George Sand, *nom de plume* of Aurore Dupin [46]. Aurore Dupin married when she was only 19 Casimir Dudevant, the illegitimate son of Baron Jean-François Dudevant, a French military officer, and soon had two children. Bored by her family life in the provinces, she moved to Paris and in order to gain access to public spaces, she began to dress in men's clothes. She soon became famous as writer with the success of her novel *Indiana*. It is interesting to underline how in her autobiography, Sand describes how she felt dispossessed of her home after her marriage, although she inherited the house and property of Nohant from her grandmother. It was in fact her husband, who increasingly managed and dominated the household [47].

While living in a house of her own, to escape from her husband's dominance, she hides herself in the smallest room, which becomes her refuge and where she can write and at the same time stay close to her children:

> "*My room at that time was my grandmother's old dressing room because it had only one door and passage for one person only under any circumstances. My two children occupied the adjoining room. I heard their breathing, and I could watch over them without disturbing their sleep. This dressing room was so small that with my books, my herbaria, my butterflies, and my rocks ... there was no space for a bed. I made do with a*

---

[44] Després C., "De la maison bourgeoise à la maison moderne. Univers domestique, esthétique et sensibilité féminine", *Recherches féministes*, 1989, 2(1), 3-18; Bauhain C., "Masculin et féminin, les habitations bourgeoises au XIXe siècle", *Les Annales de la recherche urbaine, Familles et patrimoines*, 41, 1989, 15-26.

[45] Perrot M., *La vie de famille au XIXe siècle*, cit., 47 ff.

[46] Walton W., "Literary Production and the Rearticulation of Home Space in the works of George Sand, Marie d'Agoult and Hortense Allart", *Women's History Review*, 6:1, 1997, 115-132.

[47] Walton W., *op. cit.*, 120.

hammock. I made my desk out of an armoire that opened into a secretary" [48].

This image does not correspond to the "mistress of the house" that is usually portrayed in popular literature. In a story that immediately brings to mind Virginia Woolf's *A Room of One's Own*, that will only be published many years later, Sand describes herself as seeking privacy within a space – the home – that was only supposedly constructed to be private and 'feminine': "*Sand presents herself as an interloper in her own home because the marriage laws accorded husbands authority over their wives, children, and joint property*" [49].

If this is a picture of bourgeois women, other contexts provide differentiated situations. In the rural society of France, recent historiography has highlighted how husband and wife had complementary tasks, in a work environment that established a continuity between private and public spaces. The impression one gets from this is that all in all, there was a harmonious balance between the two sexes, in which the wife held the purse strings most of the time [50].

4. The evolution along the 19th century

The appropriation of public spaces by women took place gradually, through those openings that society allowed them. Charity, the ancient duty of Christian women, had long led women out of their homes on permitted itineraries: to visit the poor, the prisoners, the sick. The importance of social problems during the 19th century transformed this custom into a need. And it is precisely in philanthropy, and therefore in the private management of the social sector, that women are recognized as having a first important role outside of domestic spaces. It was an unpaid job, as it was the one at home, but philanthropy has meant an important experience for women that changed their perception of the external world and contributed to their insertion into the public sphere [51].

Associationism soon developed from this philanthropic work, first with male leadership and then also with exclusively female leadership. Methods and objectives developed over time and while initially these associations'

---

[48] I take this quotation from Walton W., *op. cit.,* 120.

[49] Walton W., *op. cit.,* 120.

[50] Perrot M., *La vie de famille au XIXe siècle,* Paris, Éditions du Seuil, 2015, 62.

[51] Duby G. and Perrot M., *Histoire des femmes en Occident,* IV, *Le XIXe siècle*, dir. by Fraisse G. and Perrot M., Paris, Librairie Académique Perrin, 2002, 540 ff.

aim was simply "charity", later expanded to include moralization and hygiene.

In this regard, one, among the many examples that are worth remembering, concerns the activity at the Saint Lazare prison for women. Founded as an institution for lepers in the Middle Age, it was transformed in 1794 into a prison for women. It became soon the abode of all sorts of women convicts: criminals, thieves, spies, prostitutes, etc. Among them there were so many infected with venereal disease that a special infirmary became indispensable[52]. Here the women's association called "*Oeuvre des libérées de Saint Lazare*" was active with the view of "*preserving women in danger to get lost and providing to the released, without distinction of religion or nationality, the means of rehabilitation*"[53].

Philanthropy slowly turned into social work, into experiences of social education that take place especially in the most proletarian neighbourhoods. In France there are emblematic examples in Charonne developed by Marie Gahéry with the "*Union Familiale*"[54].

Through their activity, women are over the course of time recognized a competence that legitimizes their desire for managerial autonomy in these associations devoted to social affairs.

On the other side, with the development of industrialization, women left their homes in search of a salary that could provide a better income for the family[55]. But we also must remember that the valorization, abusive but significant, of productive work in the 19th century erected as the only workers the salaried employees, while relegating in the shadow of marital support shopkeepers and peasants, later called "family helpers".

The growing separation between the workplace and the private home, had different consequences: on one side, the "*salariées*" gained a place outside the house and were paid, even if they received by law a wage lower than that of man; on the other side, housewives suffered of the fact that, following the regression of domestic work and industrial concentration, household work was economically devalued because it could not be quanti-

---

[52] Blum P., "The Hôpital Saint-Lazare in Paris: Its Past and Present History", *British Journal of Venereal Diseases*, 24(4), 1948 Dec., 151-152.

[53] Valette A., *Oeuvre des libérées de Saint-Lazare, fondée en 1870, reconnue d'utilité publique par décret du 26 janvier 1885,* Alençon, Imprimerie de F. Guy, 1889, 10.

[54] Fayet-Scribe S., *Associations féminines et catholicisme. De la charité à l'action sociale,* Paris, Editions Ouvrières, 1990; Eloy J., "Les Maisons sociales et les Résidences sociales ou le développement collectif par les reconnaissances mutuelles", *Vie sociale*, 2, 2, 2012, 53-66.

[55] Perrot M., *De la nourrice à l'employée. Travaux de femmes dans la France du XIXe siècle, Le mouvement social*, 1978, 3-10.

fied. This far too simple a dichotomous vision which led to concealing the problem of the reproduction and maintenance of the labour force and to denying the immense unpaid work of housewives[56].

As far as the admission to schools was concerned, education in the 19th century was characterized by social and gender inequality. The current idea then was that education should be as adapted as possible to the future of everyone. Thus, a girl of the people had to be satisfied at best with the first notions of elementary education. Brought up for the house, the hearth, women had to learn about domestic work. The woman was made for the family, hence the scandal caused after 1848 by the first professional schools for women.

The education of young girls of a higher social category did not bring them closer to their brothers. The role played by religion was essential. Since the Catholic Reformation, the Church, which has the supervision of education, marks a particular solicitude for that of girls. The woman is felt as a factor of rechristianization through the influence she was able to play in the family. For reasons of morality, the education of girls had to remain separated from that of the boys and, in fact, during the 19th century girls' schools was subject to separate regulations. The "Loi Falloux" of 1850[57] imposed to municipalities with more than 800 inhabitants to open a primary school for girls. It further established financial restrictions for female education: lightly loaded of instruction, but rich in domestic apprenticeships, the education of girls had to be much cheaper than that of boys[58].

Girls' education was not foreseeing Latin or philosophy, as they should not compete with boys, even if the century develops the theme of the "*mère éducatrice*"[59]. Having come to power in 1877, the Republicans, developed higher primary education for girls which opened to them the inferior employments of commerce and the public service. The law of 1880[60], which created secondary education for young girls, still shows several gaps: classical humanities and philosophy, gateway to *baccalauréat* and higher educa-

---

[56] Duby G. and Perrot M., *Histoire des femmes en Occident,* cit., 547.

[57] *Loi du 15 mars 1850 relative à l'enseignement*, called "*Loi Falloux*" after the name of Minister who proposed it.

[58] Mayeur F., "Garçons et filles du XIXe au XXe siècle: une éducation différente", *Enfance*, 33, 4-5, 1980, numéro thématique: *Congrès international de psychologie de l'enfant,* 153.

[59] Mayeur F., "Garçons et filles du XIXe au XXe siècle: une éducation différente", cit., 154.

[60] *Loi sur l'enseignement secondaire des jeunes filles* 21 décembre 1880, called "*Loi Camille Sée*" after the name of Minister who proposed it.

tion, are still absent. The high school system of young girls is still inspired by the ideal woman, who will be a wife and mother, guardian of family and social order [61].

French universities gradually opened their courses to women in the second half of the XIXth century, but it is only in 1880 [62], when the admission of girls to high schools and the possibility to get a *baccalauréat* was established by law [63], that women began to gradually flow to universities [64].

So, while there were only 965 women enrolled at French universities in the academic year 1899-1900 (that is to say 3.2% of total student numbers), by the eve of the First World War, their number had increased considerably, becoming about the 10% of the total.

Although formally admitted to universities, their presence, especially in some faculties, met with much resistance. Female students were finally accepted even in the most traditional universities, but they had to cope with a sexist school system which did not prepare them adequately to university. In most cases, women's success depended, therefore, on a considerable amount of personal work to achieve the required level. Further, from a social point of view, female students were often considered under a negative light: they were named *«cervelines»*, women capable to go against nature and social order, rejecting their primary mission of wives and mothers [65].

It is interesting to note that some faculties, like the law school, were considered utmost unfeminine, even more than other professions full of responsibilities, like the study of medicine [66]. As it has been suggested by a French commentator, in continental Europe, the faculty of law remained for a long

---

[61] Lécuyer C., "Une nouvelle figure de la jeune fille sous la IIIe République: l'étudiante", *Clio. Histoire, femmes et sociétés,* online since January 1, 2005, accessed April 19, 2019, available at: http://journals.openedition.org/clio/437; doi: 10.4000/clio.437; Tikhonov Sigrist N., "Les femmes et l'université en France, 1860-1914", *Histoire de l'éducation*, online since January 1, 2014, accessed May 20, 2021, available at: http://journals.openedition.org/histoire-education/1940; doi: https://doi.org/10.4000/histoire-education.

[62] Tikhonov Sigrist N., *op. cit.*, 53; Lécuyer C., *op. cit.*, 166; Condette J.-F., "Les "cervelines" ou les femmes indésirables: l'étudiante dans la France des années 1880-1914", *Carrefours de l'éducation*, 15, 2003, 39-61.

[63] *Loi sur l'enseignement secondaire des jeunes filles*, 21 December 1880.

[64] Christen-Lécuyer C., "Les premières étudiantes de l'Université de Paris", *Travail, genre et sociétés,* 2000/2, 4, 35-50, who points out that the *Loi Camille Sée* was aimed more to train cultured wives and mothers than future college students.

[65] Condette J.-F., "Les Cervelines» ou les femmes indésirables", cit.

[66] Corcos C.A., "Portia Goes to Parliament: Women and Their Admission to Membership in the English Legal Profession", *Denver University Law Review*, 75, 2, 1998, 307, 319.

time "*a territory reserved for men*"[67]. In most European countries, women gained access to medical schools before they could study law, in some case several decades earlier[68]. Most likely it was believed that women were – by their very nature – capable of *caring* for other human beings, especially if they were other women or children. The society of the time, on the other hand, was much less inclined to consider that women had that rationality and that capacity for abstract logic, required for the legal profession.

5. The first reforms

Hand in hand with access to higher education, some reforms granted women new forms of independence also in the professional field. A law passed in 1895[69], established that married women, regardless of their matrimonial regime, could open a savings bank book and freely withdraw sums without the assistance of their husband, unless expressly opposed by him.

In 1897[70] a reform of the Civil Code of 1804 granted women the right to be witnesses in acts of civil status and instrumental acts in general.

In quick succession, other provisions come into force, allowing women to register on the electoral lists of commercial judges, though they still cannot be eligible for the function of judge[71], or to create mutual benefit societies, establishing that even married women can exercise this right without the assistance of their husbands[72].

With the new century, women with a law degree were finally allowed to take the oath of lawyer and to exercise this profession[73].

Further laws established that women could be eligible for Chambers of Commerce and Chambers of Arts and Manufactures[74].

---

[67] Christen-Lécuyer C., *Les premières étudiantes de l'Université de Paris*, cit., 35: "*Certaines facultés s'ouvrent plus facilement aux femmes que d'autres: le droit demeure longtemps un territoire réservé aux hommes*".

[68] Albisetti, J.C. "Portia Ante Portas: Women and the Legal Profession in Europe, ca. 1870-1925", *Journal of Social History*, 33(4), 2000, p. 825.

[69] *Loi sur les caisses d'épargne* n. 29946, 20 July 1895.

[70] *Loi accordant aux femmes le droit d'être témoins dans les actes de l'état civil et les actes instrumentaires en general* n. 33663, 7 December 1897.

[71] *Loi ayant pour objet de conférer l'Electorat aux femmes pour l'élection au Tribunaux des commerces,* n. 34007, 23 January 1898.

[72] *Loi relative aux Sociétés de secours mutuels*, n. 34303, 1 April 1898.

[73] *Loi du 1 décembre 1900 ayant pour objet de permettre aux femmes munies des diplômes de licencié en droit de prêter le serment d'avocat et d'exercer cette profession.*

[74] Décret portant réorganisation du Conseil supérieur du travail, 14 March 1903.

Another important reform passed in 1907, concerning the salary of married women. With this new law, married women, whatever their matrimonial regime, could freely collect and administer their salary. The law further specified that married women had the same rights of administration on the salary than the wife separated, on the condition that she exercises a profession distinct from that of her husband. This included the right to sue, without marital authorization, for all disputes relating to her right of administration [75].

In addition, as far as access to the professions concerns, new laws began to introduce specific guarantees that would have made the working mother more confident that she would be able to keep her job even after childbirth [76], and maternity leave [77].

6. The status of women according to the English Common Law in the 19th century

This portrait of the "*femme bourgoise*" and her place in French society of the 19th century, enshrined in the Code civil of 1804, is not very far from the one that we find in a different context with a different set of rules.

According to the English Common Law, the legal status of married women was governed by the *doctrine of coverture*, or doctrine of *spousal unity*, as set out in Blackstone's "*Commentaries on the Laws of England*" (1765) [78]: "*if husband and wife were «one body» before God, they were «one person» in the law, and that person was represented by the husband*" [79].

---

[75] *Loi relative au libre salaire de la femme mariée et à la contribution des époux aux charges du ménage,* n. 49537, du 13 July1907.

[76] *Loi garantissant leur travail ou leur emploi aux femmes en couches,* n. 972, 27 September 1909.

[77] *Loi sur le repos des femmes en couches,* n.5699, 17 June1913.

[78] William Blackstone was appointed as the first Vinerian Professor of English Law at Oxford in 1758. His most prestigious work, *The Commentaries on the Laws of England,* in four volumes, was published after resigning from the Chair in 1765, but taking advantage of the lectures that he had collected during those years of teaching. The first volume was published in the same year. The second was published in 1766 and the third in 1768. The fourth volume, dealing with Criminal Law, was finally published in 1770. Blackstone's treatise had an enormous success non only in England, where it was often republished until the 1870s, but also in the American Colonies. The first American edition was produced in 1772.

[79] Rodriguez-Ruiz B. and Rubio-Marin R., "Transition to Modernity, the Achievement of Female Suffrage and Women's Citizenship", in Rodriguez-Ruiz B. and Rubio-

More in detail, this doctrine suspended the rights of married women: "*By marriage, the husband and wife are one person in law: that is, the very being or legal existence of the woman is suspended during the marriage, or at least is incorporated and consolidated into that of the husband; under whose wing, protection, and cover, she performs everything; and is therefore called in our law-french a «femme-coverte» under the protection and influence of her husband, her baron, or lord; and her condition during her marriage is called her coverture...*" [80].

Femme coverte o *feme covert*, was then the legal status of a married woman whose legal rights and obligations were subsumed by those of her husband, while an unmarried woman, or *feme sole*, had the right to own property and make contracts in her own name.

This theory was usually given as a reason to deny women any public role, under the assumption that a married woman would be represented in society and at political level already by her husband. This doctrine also had an enormous impact on the evolution of common law rules in the private sphere [81]. In fact, it held that a married woman had no legal identity distinct from the identity of her husband, this doctrine denied her independent legal existence.

Not unlike what happened in France, at the beginning of the 19th century, under the common law, married women could not have private property. According to Blackstone "*the sole and absolute property rests in the husband, to be disposed at his pleasure, if he chooses to take possession of them*" [82]. As far as clothing, money, household goods and furniture were concerned, "*the husband hath therein an immediate and absolute property devolved to him by the marriage...which can never revert to the wife*" [83].

The only exception to these rules concerned the wife's "paraphernalia", the apparel, and ornaments of the wife suitable to her rank and degree [84].

Finally, married women could not sue alone, on their own behalf.

From another point of view, married women could not oppose sexual intercourse requested by the husband, nor report him for violence. Lord

---

Marin R. (eds.), *The Struggle for Female Suffrage in Europe, Voting to Become Citizens*, Leiden-Boston, Brill, 2012, 6.

[80] Blackstone W., *Commentaries on the Laws of England*, vol. II, pt. 2, cit., 433.

[81] Zaher C., "When a Woman's Marital Status Determined Her Legal Status: A Research Guide on the Common Law Doctrine of Coverture", 94 *Law Libr. J.* 459, 2002.

[82] Blackstone W., *Commentaries on the Laws of England*, vol. II, pt. 2, cit., 435.

[83] Blackstone, *op. loc. cit.*

[84] MacFarlane A., *Marriage and Love in England, 1300-1840*, Oxford, Blackwell, 1986, 272.

Hale's doctrine on marital rape that granted an immunity to the perpetrator[85] displayed an influence well into to the twentieth century[86].

In 1753, the Parliament passed the '*Act for the better preventing of clandestine Marriages*', also known as the 'Hardwicke's Marriage Act', after the name of Lord Hardwicke, who defended the bill in the Houses of Parliament.

The Act, that was introduced to try to bring control into the many irregular marriages that were taking place all over Britain, often involving seduction, bigamy, and fraud, was considered one of the most controversial and divisive measures that passed into law during the eighteenth century[87].

Although some Historians[88] point out that the eighteenth century should be interpreted as a period when affective individualism and 'the companionate family' were triumphing over patriarchy and parental control, the 'Hardwicke's Marriage Act' seems to have represented the authoritarian assertion of the economic and political interests of parents over children[89]. It had become increasingly difficult for the upper class to "marry down", thus decreeing the immobility of the social classes.

Since its very inception, the Act was further denounced of being "*the most dangerous consequence to the female sex*"[90], as increased formalities would mean less protection for women[91]. The novelty of the Act was in fact to render compliance with certain formalities essential to the validity of a marriage, while before, according to canon law, the exchange of promises to marry was considered sufficient to constitute a marriage[92]. Further, if the couple promises were expressed in words of the future tense, the mar-

---

[85] Sir Matthew Hale, *Historia placitorum coronæ. The history of the pleas of the crown,* published from the original manuscripts by Sollom Emlyn. With additional notes and references to modern cases concerning the pleas of the crown, printed by Ez. Rider, London 1800, 629.

[86] As shown in the case R v. Miller [1952] 2 All E.R. 529. Compare Adamo S.A., "The Injustice of the Marital Rape Exemption: A Survey of Common Law Countries", *American University International Law Review*, 4, 3, 1989, 555-589.

[87] Lemmings D., "Marriage and the Law in the Eighteenth Century: Hardwicke's Marriage Act of 1753", *The Historical Journal*, 39, 2, Jun., 1996, 339-360.

[88] Stone L., *The family, Sex and Marriage in England 1500-1800*, London, Penguin, 1990; Trumbach R., *The rise of the egalitarian family: aristocratic kinship and domestic relations in eighteenth-century England*, New York, Academic Press, 1978.

[89] Lemmings D., "Marriage and the Law in the Eighteenth Century", cit., 341.

[90] Hansard's Parliamentary History, vol. XV, col. 69.

[91] Probert R., "The Impact of the Marriage Act of 1753: Was It Really "A Most Cruel Law for the Fair Sex"?", *Eighteenth-Century Studies*, 38, 2, Winter, 2005, 247-262.

[92] Probert R., "The Impact of the Marriage Act of 1753", cit., p. 247.

riage became binding as soon as sexual intercourse occurred[93]. It was therefore believed that with the new law, many women who had been seduced because of a marriage promise, would no longer be able to claim any rights against the father of the child.

As far as adultery was concerned, it is important to recall that under English law, all children born of a marriage, were automatically the legitimate offspring of the couple, regardless of who the real father was. Men was recognized a wider sexual freedom, before and after the marriage, while women were taught the value of virginity before getting married and the pursuit of chastity after marriage. It should not come as a surprise if – in this context – adultery was taken into consideration under a "*double standard*" test, whereby adultery by a woman was regarded as worse than adultery by a man[94].

Nonetheless, as it has been noted: "*if society was to allow men comparative sexual freedom and at the same time keep single women virgin and married women chaste then a solution had to be found which would gratify the former without sacrificing the latter. The answer lay in prostitution and the widespread view that a class of fallen women was needed to keep the rest of the world pure*"[95].

This double standard was playing its role also in law of divorce[96]. Until 1857, only an Act of Parliament could legally end a marriage. After the Reformation, the Roman Catholic Church could no longer regulate English marriages, while Parliament had not transferred jurisdiction in matrimonial cases to secular courts. The courts of the Church of England were still applying the medieval canonical principles, according to which marriage was indissoluble and would not grant divorce. In conclusion, ecclesiastical courts would not dissolve marriage, while secular courts had no jurisdiction[97].

However, the upper classes, who could afford to enlist lawyers, began to petition the Parliament for a Private Act to end a marriage. Historical research has pointed out that this practice became increasingly common in the 18th and early 19th centuries[98], and that while most of husband's re-

---

[93] Tavor Bannet E., "The Marriage Act of 1753: 'A Most Cruel Law for the Fair Sex'", *Eighteenth-Century Studies,* 30, 3, Spring, 1997, 233-254.

[94] MacFarlane A., *Marriage and Love in England, 1300-1840*, cit., 242.

[95] Thomas K., "The Double Standard", *Journal of the History of Ideas*, 20, 2, Apr., 1959, 195-216, in particular 197.

[96] Holmes A.S., "The Double Standard in the English Divorce Laws, 1857-1923", *Law & Social Inquiry*, 20, 2, Spring, 1995, 601-620.

[97] Holmes A.S., "The Double Standard in the English Divorce Laws, 1857-1923", cit., 604.

[98] Holmes A.S., *op. loc. cit.*: "*before 1714, Parliament granted only 10 such divorces; during the remainder of the 18t century 123 Private Acts were passed. The number of*

quests were based of wife's adultery, "*no woman obtained such a divorce before 1801, and in 150 years only four acts were passed at the behest of the wife. None of the wives based her petition on the commission of adultery alone. The four divorces granted to women by Parliament included two cases of incestuous adultery and two cases involving bigamy, in one of which the adultery had been aggravated by cruelty*" [99].

Finally, in the event of divorce, the offspring were generally entrusted to the husband, not to the wife.

7. The first vindications of women's rights

In Britain, as well as in France, there was no lack of voices that since the 19th century rose in favor of the emancipation of women, first of all Mary Wollstonecraft [100], who published *A Vindication of the Rights of Woman: with Strictures on Political and Moral Subjects* in 1792 [101]. Wollstonecraft's political thought is strongly linked with her critique of female education models and the proposal to rethink education to allow women to be independent and rational [102]. As she herself reports in her work's *Dedication to M. Talleyrand-Périgord*:

> "*Contending for the rights of woman, my main argument is built on this simple principle, that if she be not prepared by education to become the companion of man, she will stop the progress of knowledge and virtue; for truth must be common to all, or it will be inefficacious with respect to its influence on general practice. And how can woman be expected to co–operate unless she knows why she ought to be virtuous? Unless freedom strengthen her reason till she comprehend her duty, and see in what manner it is connected with her real good? If children are to be educated to understand the true principle of patriotism, their mother must be a patriot; and the love of man-*

these divorces increased during the first half of the 19th century; between 1800 and 18 Parliament passed 184 Private Acts".

99 Holmes A.S., *op. loc. cit.*

100 On the life of Mary Wollstonecraft, see William Godwin's biography of his late wife Mary Wollstonecraft: *Memoirs of the Author of «A Vindication of the Rights of Woman»,* published in London, J. Johnson, n° 71, St. Paul's Church Yard, 1798. The book has been recently published in Italian: *Mary Wollstonecraft* (translated into Italian by S. Bellavista), Roma, Castelvecchi, 2014.

101 Wollstonecraft M., *A Vindication of the Rights of Woman,* London, printed for J. Johnson, n° 71, St. Paul's Church Yard, 1792, available now in Classic Reprint, London, Forgotten Books, Paperback, March 29, 2018.

102 Cossutta C., "Educare come gesto politico. La riflessione di Mary Wollstonecraft", *Storia del pensiero politico*, 2, May-August, 2017.

kind, from which an orderly train of virtues spring, can only be produced by considering the moral and civil interest of mankind; but the education and situation of woman, at present, shuts her out from such investigations".

In Wollstonecraft's view, education would free women from ignorance and would have the immense advantage of estranging them from the art of *coquetry* [103], superstition and sensual egoism [104]. But at that time formal schooling for girls was very poor. The private schools that existed, were more inclined to provide middle-class girls with girlish manners for a competitive marriage market, than promoting intellectual achievement. Notwithstanding the wide spreading ideals of the Enlightenment, that stigmatized the prejudices concerning the female mind, no institutions of higher education admitted women at that time [105].

8. The doctrine of separate spheres

The Victorian age has been strongly characterized by an ideological divide between the public sphere and the private sphere: the first viewed as a masculine domain concerned with paid work and political life, the second interpreted as a female domain related to domesticity and family [106]. Even here, as in France, the transitional period of the late eighteenth and early nineteenth centuries is very important to define the role of men and women in the public sphere.

According to Catherine Hall, it was in this period that "*gender divisions were reworked*" and "*men placed firmly in the newly defined public world of business, commerce, and politics: women were placed in the private world of home and family*" [107].

This perspective was strongly emphasized, although sometimes in a critical way, also by novels and poems published already since beginning of the century, which pointed out the codified rules of behaviour of men and women. Reading Jane Austen or the Bronte sisters, the role of absolute subjugation of women in the society of the time and the difficulties in receiving the

---

[103] Taylor B., *Mary Wollstonecraft and the Feminist Imagination*, Cambridge, Cambridge University Press, 2003, 13.

[104] Taylor B., *Mary Wollstonecraft and the Feminist Imagination,* cit., 15.

[105] Taylor B., *Mary Wollstonecraft and the Feminist Imagination,* cit., 44.

[106] Digby A., "Victorian values and women in public and private", *Proceedings of the British Academy*, 78, 1992.

[107] Hall C., "Private Persons versus Public Someones: Class, Gender and Politics in England, 1780-1850", in Lovell T. (ed.), *British Feminist Thought. A Reader*, Oxford, UK-Cambridge, Mass., USA, Wiley-Blackwell, 1990, 52.

adequate education that Wollstonecraft was revindicating, appears evident.

In a well-known dialogue of *Pride and Prejudice,* that takes place between Elizabeth Bennet and Mr. Darcy, with the complicity of Miss Bingley, this is the portrait of an "*accomplished woman*" that is presented [108]:

> *"Then"*, observed Elizabeth, *"you must comprehend a great deal in your idea of an accomplished woman".*
>
> *"Yes; I do comprehend a great deal in it".*
>
> *"Oh! Certainly",* cried his faithful assistant (Miss Bingley) *"no one can be really esteemed accomplished, who does not greatly surpass what is usually met with. A woman must have a thorough knowledge of music, singing, drawing, dancing, and the modern languages, to deserve the word; and besides all this, she must possess a certain something in her air and manner of walking, the tone of her voice, her address and expressions, or the word will be but half-deserved".*
>
> *"All this she must possess"* added Darcy, *"and to all this she must yet add something more substantial, in the improvement of her mind by extensive reading".*
>
> *"I am no longer surprized at your knowing* only *six accomplished women. I rather wonder now at your knowing* any".

Among the poems, an important place was played by the "*Angel in the House*", published by Coventry Patmore in 1854, which marked the classic stereotype of the ideal woman during the Victorian era: chaste, pure, devoted to her husband and to the education of children, with no desires of her own.

> "*Man must be pleased; but him to please*
> *Is woman's pleasure; down the gulf*
> *Of his condoled necessities*
> *She casts her best, she flings herself.*
> *How often flings for nought! and yokes*
> *Her heart to an icicle or whim,*
> *Whose each impatient word provokes*
> *Another, not from her, but him;*
> *While she, too gentle even to force*
> *His penitence by kind replies,*
> *Waits by, expecting his remorse,*
> *With pardon in her pitying eyes*" [109].

---

[108] The citation is taken from Jane Austen, *Pride and Prejudice* (first published in 1813), London, Harper Press, 2010, 36 f.

[109] The quotation is taken from Patmore C., *The Angel in the House*, Part I, Book I, Canto IX: I.1-I.12, London-Cambridge, Macmillian & Co., 1863, 109.

The poem was not particularly reputed for its literary value, but it serves from an historical point of view to get a look at the common life of middle-class lifestyles in Victorian England. Useless to say that this stereotype was at the center of harsh critiques at the end of the century [110] and that Virginia Woolf referred to it as a phantom to get rid of: "*Killing the Angel in the House was part of the occupation of a woman writer*" [111].

The doctrine of separate spheres was also at the core of John Ruskin's essay '*Of Queen's Gardens*', that was originally given as a public lecture before being published in his two-essay collection *Sesame and Lilies* [112]. Ruskin presents the question of superiority of one sex to the other as something foolish "*as if they could be compared in similar things. Each has what the other has not: each completes the other and is completed by the other: they are in nothing alike, and the happiness and perfection of both depends on each asking and receiving from the other what the other only can give*" [113]. At the same time, he presents the virtues and characteristics of both sexes, thus codifying the rationale for the separation of spheres:

> "*Now their separate characters are briefly these. The man's power is active, progressive, defensive. He is eminently the doer, the creator, the discoverer, the defender. His intellect is for speculation and invention; his energy for adventure, for war, and for conquest, wherever war is just, wherever conquest necessary. But the woman's power is for rule, not for battle, and her intellect is not for invention or creation, but for sweet ordering, arrangement, and decision. She sees the qualities of things, their claims, and their places. Her great function is Praise; she enters into no contest, but infallibly adjudges the crown of contest. By her office, and place, she is protected from all danger and temptation*" [114].

In his essay, Ruskin addresses question about "*the woman's true place*

[110] Moore N., "The Realism of "The Angel in the House": Coventry Patmore's poem reconsidered", *Victorian Literature and Culture*, 43, 1, 2015, 41; Showalter E., "Killing the Angel in the House: The Autonomy of Women Writers", *The Antioch Review*, 50, 1/2, 50th Anniversary Issue, Winter-Spring, 1992, 207.

[111] Virginia Woolf, *Professions for Women*, an abbreviated version of the speech Virginia Woolf delivered before a branch of the National Society for Women's Service on January 21, 1931, was published posthumously in *The Death of the Moth and Other Essays,* London, Hogarth Press, 1945.

[112] Ruskin J., *Sesame and Lilies, Two Lectures delivered in Manchester in 1864, 1. Of King's Treasuries; 2. Of Queen's Gardens,* London, Smith, Elder & Co., 1865.

[113] Ruskin J., *Of Queen's Gardens*, cit. All the citations are taken from [Etext #1293], The Project Gutenberg Etext of Sesame and Lilies, by John Ruskin.

[114] Ruskin J., *Of Queen's Gardens*, cit.

and power" in society, recognizing that women have many positive qualities, but are still flawed through human nature [115]. The kind of education for her, should therefore recognize her limits and take into consideration her office:

> "*The first of our duties to her – no thoughtful persons now doubt this, – is to secure for her such physical training and exercise as may confirm her health, and perfect her beauty; the highest refinement of that beauty being unattainable without splendour of activity and of delicate strength. To perfect her beauty, I say, and increase its power; it cannot be too powerful, nor shed its sacred light too far: only remember that all physical freedom is vain to produce beauty without a corresponding freedom of heart*" [116].

After having molded her physical frame, it will be necessary "*to fill and temper her mind with all knowledge and thoughts which tend to confirm its natural instincts of justice, and refine its natural tact of love*". But in Ruskin's perspective, "*all such knowledge should be given her as may enable her to understand, and even to aid, the work of men*", and not for women's own advancement in society, what will set him against the opposite view disclosed by John Stuart Mill [117].

9. The Angel "*out*" of the house

Notwithstanding the vast echo that the Victorian ideal of woman enclosed within the domestic walls spread out along the 19th century, women's presence in some sectors of social life demonstrated their ability in gaining a role in the public space [118].

One of the first fields where women were active outside their homes – was in France – was philanthropy, developed out of parochial charity that was initially considered part of the private sphere, as it was where women relied mostly on personal ties [119]. Charity implied the possibility for women to

---

[115] Austin L.M., "Ruskin and the Ideal Woman", *South Central Review*, 4, 4, Winter, 1987, 28-39.

[116] Ruskin J., *Of Queen's Gardens*.

[117] See further in this chapter. Millett K., "The Debate over Women: Ruskin versus Mill", *Victorian Studies*, 14, 1, *The Victorian Woman*, Sep., 1970, 63-82.

[118] Williams Elliott D., *The Angel out of the House, Philanthropy and Gender in Nineteenth-Century England,* Chapel Hill, University of Virginia Press, 2002. See further *Histoire des femmes en Occident,* IV, *Le XIXe siècle*, cit., 542 ff.

[119] Prochaska F.K., *Women and philanthropy in nineteenth-century England,* Oxford, Oxford University Press, 1980.

expand a working activity in the community, outside the house, as fund-raising for these initiatives often implied the organization of public bazaars where women were very active: "*The charitable bazaar thus bridged the public and the private, but in what we might call a socially acceptable borderland*" [120].

Among the prominent figures in this ambit, we must recall Octavia Hill [121] and her role in promoting social housing [122], who elaborated a conception of philanthropy as a science intended to promote individual responsibility; her book *Our Common Land* [123] imbued with liberal ideology, expressed an optimistic faith in private initiative which she preferred to state intervention [124].

So, while philanthropy became the more and more "womanized" [125], women's presence in this area was used also to gain a new role in the political arena. This is mostly evidenced by the events that characterized the anti-slavery movement [126], where the involvement of women implied the overcoming of a gender-based boundary, that separated the private circles of homes and families from the one of the public and political, but that was "accepted" as this was conceived as a borderland between philanthropy (private sphere) and politics (public sphere) [127].

Another area where women succeeded in gaining ground in the public sphere was local government [128], regarded as an extension of housekeeping:

---

[120] Digby A., "Victorian values and women in public and private", cit., 201; see further *Histoire des femmes en Occident,* IV, *Le XIXe siècle*, cit., 542.

[121] Whelan R. (ed.), *Octavia Hill and the Social Housing Debate, Essays and Letters by Octavia Hill*, London, Civitas, 1998.

[122] Wohl A.S., "Octavia Hill and the Homes of the London Poor", *Journal of British Studies*, 10, 2 (May, 1971), 105-131; Bremner R.H., "'An Iron Scepter Twined with Roses': The Octavia Hill System of Housing Management", *Social Service Review,* 39, 2, Jun., 1965, 222-231.

[123] Hill O., *Our Common Land (and other Short Essays),* London, Macmillan and Co., 1877 available at: https://en.wikisource.org/wiki/Our_Common_Land_(and_other_short_essays.

[124] *Histoire des femmes en Occident,* IV, *Le XIXe siècle*, cit., 541.

[125] Prochaska F.K., *Women and philanthropy in nineteenth-century England,* cit., 223.

[126] This was true for England as well as for the United States. As far as the role of women in the antislavery movement in the United States is concerned, see Taylor C., *Women of the anti-slavery movement: the Weston sisters*, London, Macmillian, 1994. For England, see Midgley C., *Women against slavery: the British campaigns, 1780-1870*, London, Routledge, 2004.

[127] Midgley C., "Anti-Slavery and Feminism in Nineteenth-Century Britain", *Gender & History*, 5.3, 1993, 343; Digby A., "Victorian values and women in public and private", cit., 202.

[128] Hollis P., *Ladies Elect: Women in English Local Government, 1865-1914*, Oxford, Oxford University Press, Clarendon Press, 1987.

"*The government of the village is but the government of the home, only at a larger scale*" [129].

Finally, with the development of industrialization, women gained a new dimension in the public sphere [130], although this new situation was full of lights and shadows. On the one side, working women constituted a challenge to the traditional pattern as they were earning money, which allowed them to rise to a new rank in the public sphere and to a new consideration at political level, as suffrage during the Victorian age was based in property [131]. Nonetheless, women's paid work remained subsidiary to female work in the home, being characterized by lower wages in comparison to men and an important component of seasonal and part-time work [132].

Historical research developed in the last twenty years of the past century [133], points out that for the lower working class, the role of women might have been different, referring to a hidden matriarchy that existed behind "*a facade of male dominance, separation of the sexes and female inferiority*" [134]. Unlike what happened in the bourgeoisie, in the less well-off classes women were considered not only "*arbiters of their own and their families' lives*" and "*dominant influences within their own communities*" [135].

On the other side, Historians [136] have also pointed out a different perspective, that working-class women's status within the family declined in the 19th century as a result of industrialization and urbanization [137].

---

[129] Fordham E.O., "Why women are Needed as Parish Councillors", *Parish Councils Journal*, 1 March 1896, cited in Digby A., "Victorian values and women in public and private", cit., 203.

[130] Scott J.W. and Tilly L.A., "Women's work and the family in nineteenth-century Europe", *Comparative Studies in Society and History*, 17.1, 1975, 36-64.

[131] Digby A., "Victorian values and women in public and private", cit., 204.

[132] See Walby S., *Patriarchy at work: patriarchal and capitalist relations in employment, 1880-1984,* Hoboken (New Jersey), Wiley, 1986.

[133] Digby A., "Victorian values and women in public and private", cit., 207, refers in particular to Chinn C., *They worked all their lives, women of the Urban Poor, 1880-1939*, Manchester, Manchester University Press, New York, distributed by St. Martin's University Press, 1988.

[134] Chinn C., *They worked all their lives, women of the Urban Poor,* cit. 13.

[135] Chinn C., *They worked all their lives, women of the Urban Poor,* cit., 16-17.

[136] Scott J.W. and Tilly L.A., "Women's work and the family in nineteenth-century Europe", cit.; Oren L., "The Welfare of Women in Laboring Families", in Hartman M. and Banner L. (eds.), *Clio's Consciousness Raised,* New York, Joanna Cotler Books, 1974, 226-244; Stearns P., "Working-Class Women in Britain, 1890-1914", in Vicinus M. (ed.), *Suffer and Be Still*, Bloomington-Indiana-London, Indiana University Press, 1972, 100-120.

10. The emancipation movement and the first reforms during the 19th century

Along with the first forerunners of English Feminism, who contributed to an awareness raising of the women's legal conditions, arrived the first reforms. The works of Harriet Taylor [138] and his husband John Stuart Mill [139], certainly contributed to this aim. In her *The Enfranchisement of Women* [140] Taylor Mill points out that "*women have as good a claim as men have, in point of personal right, to the suffrage*", and that they have been excluded from the public sphere not on the ground of women's intellectual gaps, but much more because of the relations of force that had come to establish between the two sexes in the course of the history. According to Taylor Mill: "*That those who were physically weaker should have been made legally inferior, is quite conformable to the mode in which the world has been governed. Until very lately, the rule of physical strength was the general law of human affairs*" [141].

Harriet Taylor Mill deplored the lack of formal education for women that along with the restrictions on women's social experience, constituted a dire restriction on their cultural education [142]. In her perspective, education of women became even more critical because of their special role as teachers of children, and therefore of the whole community. That is why women should study subjects like mathematics for the same reason that men do: to improve their overall intelligence, not merely to solve mathematical problems [143].

This line of argument is also to find in John Stuart Mill's *The Subjection of Women* [144], where the Author underlines that the condition of the wom-

---

[137] A complete and careful analysis is conducted by Tomes N., "A "Torrent of Abuse": Crimes of Violence between Working-Class Men and Women in London, 1840-1875", Journal of Social History, 11, 3, Spring, 1978, 328-345.

[138] Jacobs J.O. (ed.), *The Complete Works of Harriet Taylor Mill,* Bloomington, Indiana University Press, 1998. See further: Seiz J.A. and Pujol M.A., "Harriet Taylor Mill", *The American Economic Review,* 90, 2, *Papers and Proceedings of the One Hundred Twelfth Annual Meeting of the American Economic Association*, May, 2000, 476.

[139] Collected Works of Mill J.S., *XXI Essays on Equality, Law, and Education,* Robson J.M. (ed.), London, Routledge, 2014.

[140] *The Enfranchisement of Women* was published in the Westminster Review (July 1851): 295-96, under the name of John Stuart Mill. An on-line version is available at https://www.laits.utexas.edu/poltheory/jsmill/diss-disc/eow.html.

[141] *The Enfranchisement of Women,* available at https://www.laits.utexas.edu/pol theory/jsmill/diss-disc/eow.html.

[142] Jacobs J.O. (ed.), *The Complete Works of Harriet Taylor Mill,* cit., 4 ff.

[143] Jacobs J.O. (ed.), *The Complete Works of Harriet Taylor Mill,* cit., 5.

[144] Mill J.S., *The Subjection of Women,* London, Longmans, Green, Reader, And Dyer, 1869, EBook #27083, Project Gutenberg, https://library.um.edu.mo/ebooks/

an, her subordination, and her emancipation, depend on the marriage relationship. In his view, women were educated according to a particular goal: the transition from the family of origin to that of the husband [145]. He campaigned for women's suffrage, in particular during the debate on the *Second Reform Act*, that took place in the British Parliament in 1867. The aim of the Act was to include working men in the towns and cities among eligible voters, while agricultural workers were not taken into consideration as far as voting rights were concerned. On June 5, 1867, John Stuart Mill delivered a speech defending a special amendment to the *Second Reform Act,* aimed at recognizing women the right to vote [146]. The Second Reform Act passed, but Mill was defeated, and his amendment did not pass.

The first legislative reforms that came into being during the 19th century, sheds light on the fact that private law slowly began to adapt to a new role for women in society, along with a new perception of her attitudes.

The *Custody of Infants Act*, that came into force in 1839 after a long debate promoted by Caroline Norton, who published several pamphlets arguing for the natural right of mothers to have custody of their children [147], changed the law related to the custody of the children after divorce. Before 1839, the child custody was generally awarded to the father, but the new Act allowed mothers to petition the courts for custody of her children up to the age of seven, and for access in respect of older children [148].

The *Act for the Better Prevention and Punishment of Aggravated Assaults upon Women and Children*, which was passed in 1853, was enhancing the protection of women from violent assaults which were happening in the marriage [149]. The law was aimed at limiting the legal implications of Cover-

---

b32202945.pdf. The essay is also included in Robson J.M. (ed.), *Essays on Equality, Law, and Education,* cit., 259.

[145] Smith E.S., "John Stuart Mill's "The Subjection of Women": A Re-Examination", *Polity*, 34, 2 (Winter, 2001), 181-203; Lyndon Shanley M., "Marital Slavery and Friendship: John Stuart Mill's The Subjection of Women", 9 *Pol. Theory* 229, 1981.

[146] Pugh E.L., "John Stuart Mill and the Women's Question in Parliament, 1865-1868", *The Historian,* 42, 3, May, 1980, 399-418.

[147] Norton C., *The Separation of Mother and Child by the Law of "Custody of Infants" Considered,* London, Roake and Varty, 31, Strand, 1838; see further McGough L.S., "Protecting Children in Divorce: Lessons from Caroline Norton", Edward S. Godfrey Scholar-in-Residence Lecture, 57 *Main Law Review*, 13, 2005.

[148] The Act was further replaced by the *Custody of Infants Act of 1873,* whose Section 1 allowed the Court of Chancery to order that a mother would have access to, or custody of, any infants under sixteen years of age; or to order that any such infants in her custody were to remain so subject to any regulations for the access of the father or guardian.

[149] Tomes N., "A "Torrent of Abuse": Crimes of Violence between Working-Class Men and Women in London, 1840-1875", cit.

ture, that implied women had no weapon against their husbands as they were considered property with no legal protection from beating, assault, or rape[150]. The initiative must be considered the result of campaigning by feminists and activists, who denounced marital violence as an *evil* that was *rapidly growing*[151]. Arguing that cruelty to animals was more severely penalised than cruelty to wives, underlying "*the startling principle of English law that women are of less value than Poodle dogs and Skye terriers*", activists were able to convince Mr. Fitzroy, Member of the Parliament for Lewes, to pick up women's cause and lead the initiative for new legislation[152]. The *Act for the Better Prevention and Punishment of Aggravated Assaults* did not ban a man's violence against his family; it only instituted a legal limit on the amount of force that could be inflicted before it was labelled as brutality and was therefore considered a progress.

In 1857, the English Parliament voted the *Matrimonial Causes Act*[153]. The law made the competence of the ecclesiastical courts, which were still applying canon law, and the principle of indissolubility of marriage disappear. The new law recognized only adultery as grounds for divorce. However, a husband merely had to prove simple adultery, while a wife had to prove adultery compounded by some other marital offense such as incest, bigamy, cruelty, or desertion[154]. The statute of 1857 further recognized the divorced woman as a *femme sole,* a legal status which gave her complete control over her own property.

But the Act which gave married women the right to own and control property was the *Married Women's Property Act* of 1870, further reformed in 1882[155]. Considered the most important of all the legal reforms won by

[150] Surridge L., "Dogs' Bodies, Women's Bodies: Wives as Pets in Mid-Nineteenth-Century Narratives of Domestic Violence", *Victorian Review*, 20.1, 1994), 1-34.

[151] Foyster E., *Marital Violence: An English Family History, 1660–1857,* Cambridge, Cambridge University Press, 2005, 239 f.

[152] Foyster E., *Marital Violence: An English Family History, 1660-1857,* cit., 239.

[153] On the historical context in which the Law was introduced, see Maddox P., "The Background of, and Contemporary Reaction to, the Matrimonial Causes Act, 1857", 18 *Cambrian L. Rev.,* 62, 1987.

[154] Savage G.L., "The Operation of the 1857 Divorce Act, 1860-1910 a Research Note", *Journal of Social History*, 164, Summer, 1983, 103-110.

[155] Barrett-Lennard T., *The Position in Law of Women: A Concise and Comprehensive Treatise on the Position of Women at Common Law as Modified by the Doctrines of Equity and by Recent Legislation: Together with the Married Women's Property Acts, 1870, 1874, 1882, the Rules of the Supreme Court, 1883, Relating to Taking Acknowledgements, and the Postal Regulations, 1883, Affecting Married Women,* London, Waterlow and Sons, 1883. See further Beth Combs M., "A measure of legal independence: The 1870 Married Women's Property Act and the portfolio allocations of British wives", *The Journal of Economic History*, 65.4, 2005, 1028-1057.

feminists in the nineteenth century[156], the 1870 and 1882 *Married Women's Property Acts'* passage constituted a significant change in married women's legal status in Britain. The *Property Acts* granted married women independent property rights, finally overturning much of the English common law of *coverture* that had characterized all the 19th century[157].

11. The principle of equality and the reforms in the 20th century

Women's rights evolution in the French legal system and the English common law during the 19th century show a development of private law that was able to be transplanted in many other parts of Europe and of the entire world, defining a model for all those countries that were put either under the French or British political or colonial influence[158].

It was through private law reforms connected with their personal status that women slowly gained a voice to speak in the public space during the 19th century, while it was only with the turning of the century that debate around female suffrage and women's emancipation became part of the debate that led to the formulation of constitutional principles affirming equality between the two sexes.

In English common law, in the absence of a written Constitution, a series of judicial decisions dating back to *Kruse v Johnson* ([1898] 2 QB 91) established the existence of a '*common law principle of equality*' as a part of

---

[156] Griffin B., "Class, Gender, and Liberalism in Parliament, 1868-1882: The Case of the Married Women's Property Acts", *The Historical Journal,* 46.1, 2003, 59-87, points out that "*The most striking feature of the debates on the Married Women's Property Bills is how little time was spent discussing the principle of sexual equality, and how much time was spent discussing the idea that giving married women property rights would cause discord in the home*" (p. 62).

[157] Griffith J.R., *The Married Women's Property Act, 1870: And the Married Women's Property Act, 1870, Amendment Act, 1874. Its Relations to the Doctrine of Separate Use. With Appendix of Cases, Statutes and Forms*, London, Stevens & Haynes, 1875.

[158] The notion of legal transplant is crucial in comparative law research. See Sacco R., "Legal Formants: A Dynamic Approach to Comparative Law" (Installment II of II), *The American Journal of Comparative Law*, 39, 2, Spring, 1991, 343-401. To mark the topical relevance of the issue, at its Washington Conference in 2010, the International Academy of Comparative Law dedicated an entire session to the issue of "*Legal Cultures and Legal Transplants*", published in *Isaidat Law Review*, 1 – Special Issue 1, 2011. More recently, on the notion of legal transplant, compare Graziadei M., "Comparative Law as the Study of Transplants and Receptions", in Reimann M. and Zimmermann R. (eds.), *The Oxford Handbook of Comparative Law*, Oxford, Oxford University Press, 2007, 441; Id., "Legal Transplants and the Frontiers of Legal Knowledge", *Theoretical Inquiries in Law*, 10, 2, 2009, 723.

the wider public law doctrine of rationality and prohibited unequal treatment based on 'distinctions which were not properly justified'.

As we have seen, during the last two decades of the 19th century, Parliament reformed the property rights of married women, allowing them to own and control property in their own right. It was anyway only with a series of reforms that took place throughout the 20th century that the principle of equality became effective.

The Sex Disqualification (Removal) Act of 1919 enabled women to join the professions and professional bodies, to sit on juries and be awarded degrees. In 1920, *The Sex Discrimination Removal Act* allowed women access to the legal profession and accountancy. The Law of Property Act of 1922 allowed both husband and wife to inherit property equally.

As far as divorce is concerned, the Matrimonial Causes Act of 1937 allowed women to petition for divorce on the same terms of men for the first time, although, it retained the requirement for adultery, cruelty or desertion to be demonstrated[159]. The 1937 Act did not include financial provision, while Courts decided claims for periodical payments on "*a one-third approach*", meaning one-third of the joint incomes of the parties, although this was often dependent upon who was at fault for the breakdown of the marriage. With the Matrimonial Causes Act 1973, reasons for divorce were expanded to include "*behaviour which makes it unreasonable to expect the petitioner to live with the respondent*", allowing people to divorce without having to prove an objective failing. Finally, the law was recently reformed with the *Divorce, Dissolution and Separation Act 2020* that allows no-fault divorce in England and Wales. Eventually, the Human Rights Act 1998 partially incorporated the European Convention on Human Rights (ECHR) into domestic law, and by so doing the probation of sex discrimination obtained quasi-constitutional force.

In France, the evolution took another path. It was only with a Law of 18th of February 1938 that married women were granted civil capacity, finally deleting Art. 213 of the Code Civil, and it was only a law of 1965 that

[159] The *Matrimonial Causes Act* of 1857 remained the basis for divorce in England until 1937. A Royal Commission appointed in 1909 to investigate the operation of the 1857 Act did recommend various changes and reforms, but Parliament did not act upon those immediately. The Matrimonial Causes Act of 1923 made wives and husbands equal before the law regarding the grounds for divorce, and changes in administrative procedure in 1914, 1920 and 1926 made divorce more available to the poor by decentralizing the court and by providing for financial aid.3 Yet the grounds for divorce remained the same until the Divorce Act of 1937 broadened them to include desertion and insanity. Cf. Savage G.L., *The Operation of the 1857 Divorce Act, 1860-1910 a Research Note,* cit., 103.

gave women the right to manage their own property and engage in professional activity without the consent of their husbands [160].

As far as women's suffrage is concerned, French women obtained the right to vote in 1944, while the equality principle was introduced in the *Préambule* of the 1946 Constitution [161].

Beyond what happened in France and in the English Common law, during the first half of the 20th century, Western countries recognized women the right to vote, while the principle of equality was enshrined in most national Constitutions [162]. Equal universal suffrage was reached in Finland in 1906, in Germany, Austria and Poland in 1918, in Sweden in 1919, in Ireland in 1922, in in Spain in 1931, and in Italy only in 1946.

The equality principle was introduced at the constitutional level in different moments across these jurisdictions. However, this principle did not alter the applicable rules until the introduction of reforms shaped by the tools of private law. Although with different degrees, when constitutional norms came into force providing for equality between men and women, they were often in contradiction with private law regimes. Constitutional principles formed a second and higher-order level of legislation that set the goal to be pursued through private law rules. This started a process of profound reforms of private law rules to put the principle of equality into effect that have characterized the whole 20th century.

Already in 1919, the Constitution of Weimar introduced the equality principle between men and women in all contexts (Art. 109 of the Weimarer Verfassung: "*Männer und Frauen haben grundsätzlich dieselben staatsbürgerlichen Rechte und Pflichten*"). Legal equality between men and women was at least basically given, and marriage was based on "equality between the two genders". Nonetheless, the Civil Code of 1900 (Bürgerliches Gesetzbuch) at Paragraph 1354 dealt with the relationship between husband and wife in legal matters as follows: "*The man is entitled to the decision in all matters relating to community life*". The so-called "Obedience paragraph" (Gehorsamsparagraph) remained in force until 1957, when the *Law on the Equality of Men and Women in the Field of Civil Law* (Gesetz über die Gleichberechtigung von Mann und Frau auf dem Gebiet des bürgerlichen Rechts) came into force, but it was not until 1977 with the *Reform of*

---

[160] Loi n. 65-570 du 13 juillet 1965.

[161] Chaperon S., "The difficult struggle for Women's Political Rights in France", in Rodriguez-Ruiz B. and Rubio-Marin R. (eds.), *The Struggle for Female Suffrage in Europe, Voting to Become Citizens*, cit., 305.

[162] With an important exception given by the American Constitution. See Sullivan K.M., "Constitutionalizing Women's Equality", 90 *Calif. L. Rev.*, 735, 2002.

marriage and family law (Reform des Ehe- und Familienrechts) that the so-called housewives' marriage was replaced with the partnership principle. Until 1977, under the law in force in West Germany, a married woman's right to work was recognized only insofar it was compatible with her marriage and family duties.

In Poland, the Constitution of 1921 stated in its Art. 96 that "*All citizens are equal before the law. Public offices are equally accessible to all, according to the provision of the law*". Some Reforms, based on the equality principle, were undertaken in the private law sphere immediately after the enactment of the Constitution. A Polish Statute of 1921 granted married women the right to live separately from their husbands, to manage their own funds, and to bring action before the courts. Nevertheless, the formulation of the equality principle in the Constitution, which subjected it to "*the provisions of the law*", resulted in broad legal discretion that allowed Prussian, Austrian and Russian law counter to equality to remain in force. After the Second World War, the change in the political system brought with it a new Constitution in 1952. Its article 66 stipulated that "*Women in the Polish People's Republic have equal rights with men in all spheres of public, political, economic, social and cultural life*". The Private Law Reform entered into force in 1946, introduced the same principles in all private law domains, although in recent times the International press highlights the limitations that women's rights suffer in Poland as a consequence of the revival of the traditional dimension of the family [163].

In Italy, the evolution was even slower [164]. The principle of gender equality was introduced at the constitutional level in 1948. Before the Constitution of 1948, while the country was still a kingdom, Parliament passed Law 17 July 1919, n. 1176, concerning the legal capacity of women in 1919. This Act abrogated articles 134 to 137 of the Civil Code of 1865 related to the *autorità maritale*. The same law had a very important provision for the professional future of Italian women because it enabled them to exercise all the professions and to hold jobs in the public administration. Although this reform could have had an impact on the emancipation of women in Italy, with the rise of Fascism the role of men remained predominant in all professional sectors and in public life. The movements supporting women's right to vote failed until the end of World War II. With the introduction of

[163] Fuszara M., "Between Feminism and the Catholic Church: The Women's Movement in Poland", *Sociologický časopis / Czech Sociological Review*, 41(6), 2005, 1057-1075, available at https://nbn-resolving.org/urn:nbn:de:0168-ssoar-54867; Id., Polish Women's Fight for Suffrage, in Rodriguez-Ruiz B. and Rubio-Marin R. (eds.), *The Struggle for Female Suffrage in Europe, Voting to Become Citizens*, cit., 143-157.

[164] Pozzo B., "Masculinity Italian Style", *Nev. LJ*, 13, 2012, 585-618.

women's suffrage in 1946 and of the principle of equality in the 1948 Constitution a new path towards the recognition of women's rights was opened. Yet, very little happened in the following decades as far as private law was concerned. Only between the end of the '60s and the first half of the '90s reforms were passed to render the equality principle more broadly effective in this sphere too.

12. Working women and the first legislation aimed at protecting them in the public sphere

Parallel to the development of a movement that granted the vote to women along with the principle of equality, with the development of industrialization and the gradual entry of women into the public sphere, legislation was developed to manage the presence of women in the workplace.

In Victorian Britain, where industrialization developed his presence and impact first, the Government introduced a protective legislation, aimed to secure either a reduced presence or a total absence of women from specific areas of work [165]. For example, the Mines Regulation Act of 1842 excluded all women and girls and all boys under the age of 10 from underground coal mine employment [166]. On the other side, the Factory Acts Victorian Age, which were passed in 1847, 1850, 1867, 1874 and 1878, raised a lively debate encountering the opposition of those female associations who were fighting for the enfranchisement of women. In particular, those who resisted legal regulation of women's labor usually declared that their objection is to special legislation applying only to women. The way these laws operated was regarded as unfair, because they hampered women's power to compete in the labor market, introducing restrictions, apparently aimed at the protection of women, that finally resulted in the lowering of women's wages, and in diminishing the aggregate demand for women's work [167]. Further, the critique against this kind of "protective legislation" was focusing on the fact that it generally put on the same ground women and children, highlighting the different legal situation of men and women. At the end, these legislative interventions made clear how labour policies and political citizenship were intimately connected, as they were working on the assump-

---

[165] Levine P., "Consistent Contradictions: Prostitution and Protective Labour Legislation in Nineteenth-Century England", *Social History*, 19, 1, Jan., 1994, 17-35.

[166] Humphries J., "Protective Legislation, the Capitalist State, and Working Class Men: The Case of the 1842 Mines Regulation Act", *Feminist Review*, 7, Spring, 1981, 1-33.

[167] Webb S., *Women and the Factory Acts*, London, Fabian Society, 1896, 3.

tion that women needed protection particularly in the interests of their potential motherhood [168].

This resistance against law reforms that introduced special norms for working women was widespread in Western countries [169]. In France, in 1892, a law was passed [170] that introduced a limitation of the working day, the prohibition of night work and dangerous work, a compulsory weekly rest. This law is always presented as an important turning point for women workers, who seem, at least on paper, to be favoured over men, in the name of the necessary protection of the weaker sex [171]. In reality, the law is not well applied and leads to perverse effects, excluding women from certain jobs, not necessarily the most arduous [172].

In Italy, an organic intervention only came in 1902 with the *Carcano Law*, entitled: *Disposizioni circa il lavoro delle donne e dei fanciulli* (Provisions concerning the work of women and children) [173], and soon renamed the '*protective law*' for women.

With this law, the Italian legislator placed itself – albeit somewhat belatedly – in the wake of European initiatives, which had imposed restrictions on the working hours of children and women since the early 19th century [174]. The 1902 law, strongly supported by the socialists and in particular by Anna Kuliscioff, nevertheless followed a paternalistic approach: like children, women were considered in a condition of minority and fragility, to be used as a residual workforce compared to the male workforce, also in order to preserve the traditional structure of the family, actually limiting their entrance in the public space.

---

[168] Levine P., "Consistent Contradictions", cit., 18.

[169] Jenson J., "Paradigms and Political Discourse: Protective Legislation in France and the United States before 1914", *Canadian Journal of Political Science / Revue canadienne de science politique,* 22, 2, Jun., 1989, 235-258.

[170] Loi du 2 novembre 1892 sur le travail des enfants, des filles et de femmes dans les établissements industriels.

[171] Dubesset M., Zancarini-Fournel M. and Chapitre V., "Lois et légitimité du travail féminin, débats et réalités", in *Parcours de femmes: Réalités et représentations*, 1880-1950, Lyon, Presses universitaires de Lyon, 1993, 80.

[172] Dubesset M., Zancarini-Fournel M. and Chapitre V., *op. cit.*, 81.

[173] Legge 19 giugno 1902, n. 242, *Disposizioni circa il lavoro delle donne e dei fanciulli,* in GU n. 157 of 7 July 1902.

[174] Passaniti P., "La legislazione sul lavoro delle donne e dei minori. L'Italia e l'Europa", in Minesso M. (ed.), *Welfare e giovani in Italia e in Europa nei secoli XIX-XX,* Milano, Franco Angeli, 2015, 78 ff.; Sileo G., "La legislazione europea sul lavoro femminile e minorile di inizio secolo: un quadro comparator", in *Lavoro e cittadinanza femminile, Anna Kuliscioff e la prima legge sul lavoro delle donne*, Milano, Franco Angeli, 2016, 60 ff.

According to the new legislation, women of any age and children up to the age of 15 were granted a full day's rest each week, as well as an intermediate rest during the working day. Night work was also forbidden for males under the age of 15 and for underage women, with a number of exceptions.

The Italian Law of 1902 is also of considerable importance for having introduced 'maternity leave' of one month after childbirth, exceptionally reducible to three weeks. During the post-natal rest period, however, the woman was not guaranteed any pay, let alone the preservation of her job. It was also guaranteed that in factories in which at least 50 female workers worked, it was obligatory to set up a breast-feeding room, and in any case breast-feeding had to be permitted both in the room attached to the factory and by allowing the nursing mothers to leave the factory in the manner and at the times established by the internal regulations.

But even in Italy, like in other countries, this kind of legislation that in theory should have accompanied women in their entrance into the public sphere, was criticized. The Carcano Law saw the light at a time when the movements for the emancipation of women in Italy were consolidating [175] and where the debate on the law saw the positions of Anna Maria Mozzoni, deeply critical of the protective policies adopted by the law, which – in her perspective – would have constituted a real obstacle to women's independence, contrast with those of Kuliscioff herself, a debate that also led to the pages of *L'Avanti!* [176].

To conclude, the rationale behind the first national measures regulating female work in factories, adopted between the last quarter of the nineteenth century and the beginning of the twentieth, was that women together with children belonged to a specific category of factory workers needing special protection because they were physically weaker than men and more susceptible to exploitation. At the same time, this protective legislation pursued in maintaining the symbolic functioning of the separate spheres for it crystallised traditional conceptions of gender roles.

---

[175] Weber M., "La partecipazione politica femminile in Italia: evoluzione, determinanti, caratteristiche", *Italian Political Science Review/Rivista Italiana Di Scienza Politica,* 11, 1981, 281.

[176] Ballestrero M.V., "La legge Carcano sul lavoro delle donne e dei Fanciulli", in Passaniti P. (ed.), Lav*oro e cittadinanza femminile, Anna Kuliscioff e la prima legge sul lavoro delle donne*, Milano, FrancoAngeli, 44, in particular 50 ff.

13. The introduction of the gender equality principle into the International Agenda

In line with these national interventions, the first steps were taken to establish interstate agreements on conditions of work, through the creation of the International Association for Labour Legislation (IALL) in 1900. In 1905, the IALL successfully convened an international meeting of experts, which laid down the basis of two international Conventions, adopted at a conference in Berne in 1906. One of these prohibited nights work for women in industry, and the second prohibited the use of white phosphorus in the manufacture of matches. As many as 41 states or colonies adhered to the international Convention prohibiting the use of white phosphorous, and 25 to that prohibiting night work for women [177].

Over the twentieth century, the International Labour Organsation elaborated further Conventions concerning the prohibition of night work for women in industry [178]: although at the beginning they were conceived as memorable achievements for the protection of female workers, they were finally considered to being an embarrassment to the Organization's commitment to promote gender equality and nondiscrimination at work [179].

The idea to protect women in the public space, as vulnerable subjects, has been at the center of a long debate that developed relentlessly, especially since the end of World War II, when the question of gender equality entered the International Agenda. It is in fact in 1946 that the United Nations Commission on the Status of Women (UNCSW) was established as a mechanism to promote, report on, and monitor issues relating to the political, economic, civil, social and educational rights of women. As declared during its first session, the Commission proclaimed as one of its guiding principles: "*to raise the status of women, irrespective of nationality, race, language or religion, to equality with men in all fields of human enterprise, and to eliminate all discrimination against women in the provisions of statutory law, in legal maxims or rules, or in interpretation of customary law*".

Since then, many international legal instruments have been introduced

[177] Rodgers G., Lee E., Swepston L. and Van Daele J., *The International Labour Organization and the quest for social justice, 1919-2009,* Geneva, ILR Press an imprint of Cornell University Press, Ithaca and International Labour Office, 2009.

[178] These are: the Night Work (Women) Convention, 1919 (No. 4), the Night Work (Women) Convention (Revised), 1934 (No. 41), the Night Work (Women) Convention (Revised), 1948 (No. 89) and the Protocol of 1990 to the Night Work (Women) Convention (Revised), 1948.

[179] Politakis G.P., "Night Work of Women in Industry: Standards and Sensibility", 140 *Int'l Lab. Rev.*, 403, 2001.

or modified to deal specifically with women's rights [180]. Among these, international law doctrine has identified different paths to deal with gender issues, that characterize the approach concerning the entrance of women into the public sphere.

A first path is the one followed by so-called *protective conventions* [181], that deal with specific economic issues that women had to face moving beyond the domestic sphere, but – at the same time – implicitly accept the traditional social definition of a woman as wife and mother. Among these conventions we find the already mentioned conventions concerning the prohibition of night work for women in industry [182] and the ILO for the *Convention Concerning the Employment of Women on Underground Work in Mines of All Kinds* [183]. This first approach did not treat women as equal to men since women are generally treated as subordinates when they act outside their traditional domestic sphere. International laws aiming at protecting women could therefore authorize permanent inferiority and facilitate the maintenance of this situation [184].

A second path, following a *corrective approach*, assumes that women are not treated equally in certain areas and that therefore the law must intervene to introduce corrective mechanisms. Among the conventions that followed this approach were the ones that attempted to regulate prostitution at an international level through prohibitions on the transporting of women and children for immoral purposes [185]. A second example worth mention-

---

180 Kaufman Hevener N., "International Law and the Status of Women: An Analysis of International Legal Instruments Related to the Treatment of Women", 1 *Harv. Women's L.J.*, 131, 1978.

181 Kaufman Hevener N., "International Law and the Status of Women", cit., 134.

182 See *supra*.

183 Adopted by the General Conference of the International Labour Organization June 21, 1935, as modified by the Final Articles Revisions Conventions, 1946, 40 U.N.T.S. 63.

184 As Kaufman Hevener N. ("International Law and the Status of Women", cit., 135) pointed out: "*Under the protective approach, the identity of the woman who moves beyond the domestic sphere does not alter, and she continues to be treated by the law with regard to this primary role. The focus of legislative attention is not on her actual activity but rather remains on her domestic role, and it is the perceived characteristics of this role that the law allegedly seeks to protect*".

185 Kaufman Hevener N., "International Law and the Status of Women", cit., 138: conventions on this matter were established already in 1910, 1921, 1933, while in 1949, the United Nations adopted the *Convention for the Suppression of the Traffic in Persons and of the Exploitation of the Prostitution of Others* (Approved by General Assembly resolution 317 (IV) of 2 December 1949), which entered into force on the 25 July 1951.

ing is the *Convention concerning the nationality of married women*[186] that intervened to correct a situation where no legislation existed to protect married women's right to retain or renounce national citizenship in the way that men could.

Finally, a third path is the one that is adopting a *nondiscriminatory approach,* which is based on the principle that whatever difference may exist between the sexes should not become the ground for differential treatment. Among the Conventions that adopt this approach there are the general conventions like the *United Nations Charter*, the founding document of the United Nations, that was signed on 26 June 1945. The principle of non-discrimination receives various formulations in the Charter, as in the Preamble it is stated that the United Nations are determined, among others, "to reaffirm faith in fundamental human rights, in the dignity and worth of the human person, in the equal rights of men and women…". Further Art. 1, among the Purposes of the UN includes the promotion of respect for human rights and fundamental freedoms "*for all without distinction as to race, sex, language, or religion*"[187].

Another important acknowledgment of the principle of non-discrimination is to find in the *Universal Declaration of Human Rights*, adopted by the General Assembly in 1948, which in Art. 2 establishes that: "*Everyone is entitled to all the rights and freedoms set forth in this Declaration, without distinction of any kind, such as race, colour, sex, language, religion, political or other opinion, national or social origin, property, birth or other status*". The Universal Declaration of Human Rights further dictates principles that impact directly also on the private law dimension, introducing the equality principle in the marriage and family law dimension. In particular, Art. 16 establishes:

> 1. *Men and women of full age, without any limitation due to race, nationality or religion, have the right to marry and to found a family. They are entitled to equal rights as to marriage, during marriage and at its dissolution.*
>
> 2. *Marriage shall be entered into only with the free and full consent of the intending spouses.*

---

[186] The *Convention on the Nationality of Married Women* was adopted on 20 February 1957 and entered into force in 1958.

[187] Other references to the non-discriminatory theme appear in Articles 13(1)(b), 55(c), 56, 62(2) and 76(c) of the Charter, in which members of the Organization pledge to take separate and cooperative action to promote universal respect for human rights and fundamental freedoms of all without regard to sex or other distinctions. See Kaufman Hevener N., "International Law and the Status of Women", cit., 141.

To further boost the application of the Universal Declaration of Human Rights, two covenants on human rights were drafted and opened for ratification in 1966, both reinforcing the principle of equal rights [188].

Other international conventions of a nondiscriminatory nature, which focus specifically on gender issue were further adopted [189].

Finally, in 1979 the United Nations adopted the *Convention on the Elimination of all Forms of Discrimination Against Women* (CEDAW), which is generally referred to as the International Bill of Rights for women [190]. The Convention aims to reach three aims: to ensure full equality of women before the law and protection against discrimination in the public as well as the private sphere; to improve the de facto position of women; and to address prevailing gender relations and the persistence of gender-based stereotypes. In particular, CEDAW recognizes the full equality of women and men under the law and proscribes discrimination against women in education, employment, political participation, healthcare, and economic life. It further affirms the right of women to vote and to stand for elected office; to receive equal pay for equal work; to own and dispose of property; to obtain loans, mortgages, and other forms of credit independently of husbands or male relatives; to enter into or dissolve marriage

---

[188] The International Covenant on Civil and Political Rights foresees in Art. 2, 1, that "*Each State Party to the present Covenant undertakes to respect and to ensure to all individuals within its territory and subject to its jurisdiction the rights recognized in the present Covenant, without distinction of any kind, such as race, colour, sex, language, religion, political or other opinion, national or social origin, property, birth or other status*". Art. 3 further stipulates that "*The States Parties to the present Covenant undertake to ensure the equal right of men and women to the enjoyment of all civil and political rights set forth in the present Covenant*". In an analogous way, The International Covenant on Economic, Social and Cultural Rights establishes at Art. 2 the following principle: "*The States Parties to the present Covenant undertake to ensure the equal right of men and women to the enjoyment of all economic, social and cultural rights set forth in the present Covenant*".

[189] These are: The ILO Convention Concerning Equal Remuneration for Men and Women Workers for Work of Equal Value adopted in 1951; the UN Convention on the Political Rights of Women adopted in 1953; The UN Convention Against Discrimination in Education adopted in 1960; the UN Convention on the Consent to Marriage, Minimum Age for Marriage and Registration of Marriages adopted in 1962.

[190] Facio A. and Morgan M.I., "Equity or Equality for Women - Understanding CEDAW's Equality Principles", 60 *Ala. L. Rev.*, 1133, 2009; Holtmaat H.M.T., "CEDAW: A holistic approach to women's equality and freedom", in Sinding-Assen H. and Hellum A. (eds.), *Women's Human Rights: CEDAW in International, Regional and National Law*, Leiden, Leiden University Scholarly Publications, 2013, 95-124; Cole W.M., "Convention on the Elimination of All Forms of Discrimination against Women (CEDAW)", in Naples N.A. (ed.), *The Wiley Blackwell Encyclopedia of Gender and Sexuality Studies*, 1st ed., Hoboken, New Jersey, John Wiley & Sons, 2016, 1.

freely and with full consent; and to exercise equal parental rights. State parties are obligated, among other things, to provide equal educational opportunities, paid maternity leave, and access to family planning services, and to suppress prostitution and the trafficking of women.

An important step taken to achieve substantive equality in all spheres is that CEDAW requires two types of actions by the State: (1) actions to achieve equality of opportunity between men and women, and (2) actions to correct the inequalities of power between men and women. This means measures that eliminate the inequalities of power between the sexes. CEDAW addresses the issue of special measures, indicating that States Parties may adopt temporary special measures aimed at accelerating *de facto* equality between men and women that shall be discontinued when the objectives of equality of opportunity and treatment have been achieved.

Abandoning a *law in the books* approach to adopt a *law in action* approach, CEDAW foresees that the basis for evaluating whether a state is providing women equal opportunities to those of men is equality of results. This means that according to CEDAW, the indicators of equality are not in policies, law, or institutions that have been created to give opportunities to women, but in what all these laws and policies have achieved.

Art. 17 of the CEDAW established a *Committee on the Elimination of Discrimination Against Women,* that was formed on 3 September 1981 after the CEDAW received the 20 ratifications required for it to enter into force. According to article 18, States must report to the Committee on the progress they have made in implementing the CEDAW and the Committee issue general recommendations that elaborate on its views of the obligations imposed by CEDAW.

With this Convention, that has been adopted by 189 Parties [191], it would seem that women's right to be a vital part of the public sphere should now be fully recognized.

Nonetheless, the Committee often referred to barriers that still exist in order to give full accomplishment to this goal. In particular, in a Recommendation of 1997 concerning the availability of special measures [192], the Committee referred that "*In order, however, to overcome centuries of male domination of the public sphere, women also require the encouragement and support of all sectors of society to achieve full and effective participation, en-*

---

[191] United States and Palau have signed, but not ratified the treaty. The Holy See, Iran, Somalia, Sudan, and Tonga are not signatories to CEDAW.

[192] Comm. on the Elimination of Discrimination Against Women, *Report of the Committee on the Elimination of Discrimination against Women,* 15, UN Doc. A/52/38 (July 7-25, 1997).

couragement which must be led by States parties to the Convention, as well as by political parties and public officials".

In the 1990s, the Council of Europe has undertaken a series of initiatives in line with those of the United Nations and with the aim of eliminating violence and in particular domestic violence against women. The first steps were taken in 2002 with the adoption of a specific Recommendation [193], while in following years the Council launched a "*Campaign to Combat Violence against Women, including domestic violence (2006-2008)*".

The awareness that harmonized legal standards for the victims were needed, in order to offer the same level of protection everywhere in Europe, led the Ministers of Justice of Council of Europe member states to take steps in order to achieve a general framework. In 2008, the Committee of Ministers set up an expert group mandated to prepare a draft convention in this field [194], that was finally produced in December 2010.

The Council of Europe *Convention on preventing and combating violence against women and domestic violence*, so-called *Istanbul Convention*, is the first instrument in Europe to set legally binding standards specifically to prevent gender-based violence, protect victims of violence and punish perpetrators.

The EU signed the Convention in June 2017, and the implementation of the Istanbul Convention has now become one of the priorities in the EU 2020-2025 gender equality strategy. Unfortunately, this Convention, that had Türkiye as the first signatory also saw this country become the first to withdraw its accession. A sign, perhaps, that the condition of women raises new challenges today and consequently still remains a very open question in the Mediterranean scenario.

14. Conclusions

Recent research has emphasized that notwithstanding the important role that the law has played to allow women to embrace the public sphere, the association of women with private spaces and men with public ones continues today in western industrialized society.

In particular, some writers have emphasized the still existing physical

---

[193] Recommendation Rec (2002)5 of the Committee of Ministers to member states on the protection of women against violence". Council of Europe Committee of Ministers. Archived from the original on 28 July 2020. Retrieved 18 December 2012.

[194] The *Ad Hoc Committee for preventing and combating violence against women and domestic violence*, CAHVIO.

and psychological vulnerability of women when they enter public spaces unaccompanied by men [195], while others [196] have questioned the validity and the usefulness of this emphasis, suggesting that it is inconsistent with women's frequent use of urban public spaces and their enjoyment of urban public life. Nonetheless, it still appears to be a common opinion that women do not enjoy the same *freedom of the streets* that men do [197].

It is not by chance, that the United Nations have focus their most recent initiatives on the various kinds of violence that women and girls experience in public spaces, from unwelcome sexual remarks and touching to rape and femicide. This situation reduces women's and girls' freedom of movement and their ability to participate in school, work and public life. This violence further limits their access to important services and their enjoyment of cultural and recreational activities, and finally negatively impacts their health and well-being. For these reasons, the United Nations launched in 2011 the "Safe Cities Free of Violence against Women and Girls" Global Programme, while in 2013, the Global Flagship Initiative "Safe Cities and Safe Public Spaces for Women and Girls" was created, to support local and national governments to address multiple sustainable development goal targets across multiple goals.

In 2019, the United Nations published an *International Compendium* that addresses local authorities, policy makers, women's rights organizations, researchers and other practitioners committed to creating safe and sustainable cities and public spaces for women and girls across the world [198]. The compendium illustrates in a practical way some practices, strategies, and tools from women's safety partnerships in cities.

This is a sign that beyond the principles, which are fundamental and indispensable, private law may still play an important role in shaping, through the instrument of the voluntary agreement, forms of cooperation

---

[195] Boys J., "Women and public space", in Matrix Book Group, *Making space,* 37-54, London, Pluto Press, 1984; Enjeu C. and Save E., "The City: Off limits to women", *Liberation*, July/August, 1974, 9-13; Wekerle G., "Women and the urban environment", in Stimpson C.R., Dixler E., Nelson M.J. and Yatrakis K.B. (eds.), *Women and the American city,* Chicago, University of Chicago Press, 1981, 185-211.

[196] Lofland L., "Women and urban public space", *Women and Environments,* 6, (1984) 12-14.

[197] Franck K. A. and Paxson L., "Women and urban public space", in *Public places and spaces*, Boston, MA, Springer, 1989, 121-146.

[198] UN WOMEN, *Safe Cities and Safe Public Spaces for Women and Girls – Global Flagship Initiative: International Compendium of Practices,* New York, UN WOMEN, 2019. Prepared by the Ending Violence against Women Section in UN Women Coordination and Production: Lizzette Soria, Technical Specialist, in collaboration with Laura Capobianco, Advisor, Safe Public Spaces.

that can render effective the possibility for women to participate and enjoy the public sphere.

References

Adamo S.A. (1989), "The Injustice of the Marital Rape Exemption: A Survey of Common Law Countries", *American University International Law Review*, 4, 3, 555-589.

Albisetti, J.C. (2000), "Portia Ante Portas: Women and the Legal Profession in Europe, ca. 1870-1925", *Journal of Social History*, vol. 33, no. 4, 825.

Allen A.T. (2007), *Women in twentieth-century Europe*, London, Macmillan International Higher Education.

Austen J. (2010), *Pride and Prejudice* (first published in 1813), London, Harper Press.

Austin L.M., "Ruskin and the Ideal Woman", *South Central Review*, 4, 4, Winter, 1987, 28-39.

Ballestrero M.V. (2016), "La legge Carcano sul lavoro delle donne e dei Fanciulli", in Passaniti P. (ed.), *Lavoro e cittadinanza femminile, Anna Kuliscioff e la prima legge sul lavoro delle donne*, Milano, FrancoAngeli, 44.

Barrett-Lennard T. (1883), *The Position in Law of Women: A Concise and Comprehensive Treatise on the Position of Women at Common Law as Modified by the Doctrines of Equity and by Recent Legislation: Together with the Married Women's Property Acts, 1870, 1874, 1882, the Rules of the Supreme Court, 1883, Relating to Taking Acknowledgements, and the Postal Regulations, 1883, Affecting Married Women*, London, Waterlow and Sons.

Bartolo B. (2011), *Donne del Risorgimento – Le eroine invisibili dell'unità d'Italia*, Torino, Ananke.

Bauhain C. (1989), "Masculin et féminin, les habitations bourgeoises au XIXe siècle", *Les Annales de la recherche urbaine, Familles et patrimoines*, 41, 15-26.

Bertaud J.P. (1983), La vie quotidienne en France au temps de la Révolution (1789-1795), Paris, Hachette.

Beth Combs M. (2005), "A measure of legal independence: The 1870 Married Women's Property Act and the portfolio allocations of British wives", *The Journal of Economic History*, 65.4, 1028-1057.

Boys J. (1984), "Women and public space", in Matrix Book Group, *Making space,* 37-54, London, Pluto Press.

Blum P. (1948), "The Hôpital Saint-Lazare in Paris: Its Past and Present History", *British Journal of Venereal Diseases*, 24(4), Dec., 151-152.

Bremner R.H. (1965), "'An Iron Scepter Twined with Roses': The Octavia Hill System of Housing Management", *Social Service Review,* 39, 2, Jun., 222-231.

Brown H. and Dow G. (2011), *Readers, writers, salonnières: female networks in Europe, 1700-1900*, New York, Peter Lang.

Butler R. (2008), *Hidden in the Shadow of the Master, The Model-Wifes of Cézanne, Monet & Rodin,* New Haven-London, Yale University Press.

Capeda Fuentes M. (2011), *Sorelle d'Italia, Le donne che hanno fatto il Risorgimento*, Peveragno, Blu Edizioni.

Chinn C. (1988), *They worked all their lives, women of the Urban Poor, 1880-1939*, Manchester, Manchester University Press, New York, distributed by St. Martin's University Press.

Christen-Lécuyer C. (2000), "Les premières étudiantes de l'Université de Paris", *Travail, genre et sociétés,* 2, 4, 35-50.

Criado Perez C. (2019), *Invisible Women: Exposing Data Bias in a World Designed for Men*, London, Chatto & Windus.

Colonelli L. (2020), *Le muse nascoste – Protagoniste dimenticate di grandi opera d'arte*, Firenze, Giunti.

Condette J.-F. (2003), "Les "cervelines" ou les femmes indésirables: l'étudiante dans la France des années 1880-1914", *Carrefours de l'éducation*, 15, 39-61.

Corcos C.A. (1998), "Portia Goes to Parliament: Women and Their Admission to Membership in the English Legal Profession", *Denver University Law Review*, vol. 75, 2, 307, 319.

Cordes O. (2012), *Frauen als Wegbereiter des Rechts. Die ersten deutschen Juristinnen und ihre Reformforderungen in der Weimarer Republik*, Hamburg, Diplomica® Verlag GmbH.

Cossutta C. (2017), "Educare come gesto politico. La riflessione di Mary Wollstonecraft", *Storia del pensiero politico*, 2, May-August.

Craveri B. (2001), *La civiltà della conversazione,* Milano, Adelphi (English trans.: *The age of conversation*, New York, New York Review Books, 2005).

De Beauvoir S. (1949), *Le deuxième sexe,* t. I, Paris, Éditions Gallimard.

De Goncourt, E. and J. (2021), *La femme au XVIII*[e] *siècle,* last ed., Paris, Editions Flammarion.

Denis D. and Spica A.-E. (eds.) (2019), *Madeleine de Scudéry: une femme de lettres au XVIIe siècle*, Arras, Artois Presses Université.

Després C. (1989), "De la maison bourgeoise à la maison moderne. Univers domestique, esthétique et sensibilité féminine", *Recherches féministes*, 2(1)3-18.

Digby A. (1992), "Victorian values and women in public and private", *Proceedings of the British Academy*, 78.

Duby G. and Perrot M. (2002), *Histoire des femmes en Occident,* IV, *Le XIXe siècle*, dir. by Fraisse G. and Perrot M., Paris, Librairie Académique Perrin.
Duggan A.E. (2005), *Salonnières, furies, and fairies: the politics of gender and cultural change in absolutist France*, 2nd ed., Newark, University of Delaware Press.
Enjeu C. and Save E. (1974), "The City: Off limits to women", in *Liberation*, July/August, 9-13.
Eloy J. (2012), "Les Maisons sociales et les Résidences sociales ou le développement collectif par les reconnaissances mutuelles", *Vie sociale*, 2, 2, 53-66.
Elshtain J.B. (1981), *Public Man, Private Woman: Women in Social and Political Thought.* 2nd ed., Oxford, Princeton University Press.
Facio A. and Morgan M.I. (2009), "Equity or Equality for Women - Understanding CEDAW's Equality Principles", 60 *Ala. L. Rev.*, 1133.
Faucheux M. (2018), *Olympe de Gouges*, Paris, Gallimard.
Fayet-Scribe S. (1990), *Associations féminines et catholicisme. De la charité à l'action sociale,* Paris, Editions Ouvrières.
Foyster E. (2005), *Marital Violence: An English Family History, 1660–1857,* Cambridge, Cambridge University Press, 239.
Fraisse G. (1998), *Les Femmes et leur histoire,* Paris, Gallimard, Collection Folio Histoire.
Franck K. A. and Paxson L. (1989), "Women and urban public space", in *Public places and spaces*, Boston, MA, Springer, 121-146.
Fuszara M. (2005), "Between Feminism and the Catholic Church: The Women's Movement in Poland", *Sociologický časopis / Czech Sociological Review*, 41(6), 1057-1075, available at https://nbn-resolving.org/urn:nbn:de:0168-ssoar-54867.
Godwin W. (1798), *Memoirs of the Author of «A Vindication of the Rights of Woman»,* published in London, J. Johnson, n. 71, St. Paul's Church Yard.
Gordon F. and Furbank P.N. (2001), *Marie Madeleine Jodin 1741-1790 – Actress, Philosophe and Feminist,* London, Routledge.
Graziadei M. (2007), "Comparative Law as the Study of Transplants and Receptions", in Reimann M. and Zimmermann R. (eds.), *The Oxford Handbook of Comparative Law*, Oxford, Oxford University Press, 441.
Graziadei M. (2009), "Legal Transplants and the Frontiers of Legal Knowledge", *Theoretical Inquiries in Law*, 10, 2, 723.
Griffin B. (2003), "Class, Gender, and Liberalism in Parliament, 1868-1882: The Case of the Married Women's Property Acts", *The Historical Journal,* 46.1, 59-87.

Habermas J. (1962), *Strukturwandel der Öffentlichkeit. Untersuchungen zu einer Kategorie der bürgerlichen Gesellschaft,* Frankfurt am Main, Suhrkamp (*The Structural Transformation of the Public Sphere: An Inquiry Into a Category of Bourgeois Society,* Cambridge, Polity Press, 1992).

Hall C. (1990), "Private Persons versus Public Someones: Class, Gender and Politics in England, 1780-1850", in Lovell T. (ed.), *British Feminist Thought. A Reader*, Oxford, UK-Cambridge, Mass., USA, Wiley-Blackwell, 52.

Harari Y.N. (2014), *Sapiens: a brief history of humankind,* London, Harvill Secker, Random House.

Héritier F. (1996), *Masculin/Féminin. La pensée de la différence*, Paris, Éditions Odile Jacob, 1996.

Hill O., *Our Common Land (and other Short Essays)* (1877), London, Macmillan and Co., available at: https://en.wikisource.org/wiki/Our_Common_Land_(and_other_short_essays.

Hollis P. (1987), *Ladies Elect: Women in English Local Government, 1865-1914*, Oxford, Oxford University Press, Clarendon Press.

Holmes A.S. (1995), "The Double Standard in the English Divorce Laws, 1857-1923", *Law & Social Inquiry*, 20, 2, Spring, 601-620.

Holtmaat H.M.T. (2013), "CEDAW: A holistic approach to women's equality and freedom", in Sinding-Assen H. and Hellum A. (eds.), *Women's Human Rights: CEDAW in International, Regional and National Law*, Leiden, Leiden University Scholarly Publications, 95-124.

Humphries J. (1981), "Protective Legislation, the Capitalist State, and Working Class Men: The Case of the 1842 Mines Regulation Act", *Feminist Review,* 7, Spring, 1-33.

Hunt M. (2014), *Women in eighteenth century Europe*, London, Routledge.

Jacobi J. (2013), *Mädchen- und Frauenbildung in Europa. Von 1500 bis zur Gegenwart,* Frankfurt-New York, Campus Verlag.

Jacobs J.O. (ed.) (1998), *The Complete Works of Harriet Taylor Mill,* Bloomington, Indiana University Press.

Jenson J. (1989), "Paradigms and Political Discourse: Protective Legislation in France and the United States before 1914", *Canadian Journal of Political Science / Revue canadienne de science politique,* 22, 2, Jun., 235-258.

Kale S., *French salons: high society and political sociability from the Old Regime to the Revolution of 1848*, Baltimore, John Hopkins University Press, 2004.

Kaufman Hevener N. (1978), "International Law and the Status of Women: An Analysis of International Legal Instruments Related to the Treatment of Women", 1 *Harv. Women's L.J.,* 131.

Krontiris T. (1997), *Oppositional Voices: Women as writers and translators of literature in the English Renaissance*, London, Routledge.

Landes J.B. (1988), *Women and the Public Sphere in the Age of the French Revolution,* Ithaca-London, Cornell University Press, 3.

Lécuyer C. (2005), "Une nouvelle figure de la jeune fille sous la IIIe République: l'étudiante", *Clio. Histoire, femmes et sociétés,* online since January 1, accessed April 19, available at: http://journals.openedition.org/clio/437; doi: 10.4000/clio.437.

Lemmings D. (1996), "Marriage and the Law in the Eighteenth Century: Hardwicke's Marriage Act of 1753", *The Historical Journal*, 39, 2, Jun., 339-360.

Lerner G. (1993), *The Creation of Feminist Consciousness, From Middle Ages to Eighteen-seventy,* Oxford, Oxford University Press, 247 ff.

Leyser H. (2013), *Medieval Women: Social History of Women in England 450-1500*, London, Hachette UK.

Levine P. (1994), "Consistent Contradictions: Prostitution and Protective Labour Legislation in Nineteenth-Century England", *Social History*, 19, 1, Jan., 17-35.

Lofland L. (1984), "Women and urban public space", *Women and Environments,* 6, 12-14.

Lilti A. (2005), *Le Monde des salons. Sociabilité et mondanité à Paris au XVIIIe siècle,* Paris, Fayard.

Lirosi A. (2015), *Libere di sapere. Il diritto delle donne all'istruzione dal Cinquecento al mondo contemporaneo*, Roma, Edizioni di Storia e Letteratura.

Lyndon Shanley M. (1981), "Marital Slavery and Friendship: John Stuart Mill's The Subjection of Women", 9 *Pol. Theory*, 229.

McGough L.S. (2005), "Protecting Children in Divorce: Lessons from Caroline Norton", Edward S. Godfrey Scholar-in-Residence Lecture, 57 *Main Law Review*, 13.

MacFarlane A. (1986), *Marriage and Love in England, 1300-1840*, Oxford, Blackwell, 272.

Mackinnon C.A. (1989), *Toward A Feminist Theory of The State*, Cambridge, MA, Harvard University Press.

Maddox P. (1987), "The Background of, and Contemporary Reaction to, the Matrimonial Causes Act, 1857", 18 *Cambrian L. Rev.,* 62.

Mayeur F. (1980), "Garçons et filles du XIXe au XXe siècle: une éducation différente", *Enfance*, t. 33, 4-5, numéro thématique: *Congrès international de psychologie de l'enfant,* 153.

Midgley C. (2005), *Women against slavery: the British campaigns, 1780-1870*, London, Routledge.

Midgley C. (1993), "Anti-Slavery and Feminism in Nineteenth-Century Britain", *Gender & History*, 5.3, 343.

Mill J.S. (1869), *The Subjection of Women,* London, Longmans, Green, Reader, And Dyer, EBook #27083, Project Gutenberg, https://library.um.edu.mo/ebooks/b32202945.pdf.

Millett K. (1970), "The Debate over Women: Ruskin versus Mill", *Victorian Studies*, 14, 1, *The Victorian Woman*, Sep., 63-82.

Moore N. (2015), "The Realism of "The Angel in the House": Coventry Patmore's poem reconsidered", *Victorian Literature and Culture*, 43, 1, 41.

Mousset S. (2007), *Women's Rights and the French Revolution: A Biography of Olympe de Gouges,* London, Routledge.

Norton C. (1838), *The Separation of Mother and Child by the Law of "Custody of Infants" Considered,* London, Roake and Varty, 31, Strand.

Oren L. (1974), "The Welfare of Women in Laboring Families", in Hartman M. and Banner L. (eds.), *Clio's Consciousness Raised,* New York, Joanna Cotler Books, 226-244.

Passaniti P. (2015), "La legislazione sul lavoro delle donne e dei minori. L'Italia e l'Europa", in Minesso M. (ed.), *Welfare e giovani in Italia e in Europa nei secoli XIX-XX,* Milano, Franco Angeli, 78.

Pateman C. (1983), "Feminist Critiques of the Public/Private Dichotomy", in Benn S.I. and Gaus G.F. (eds.), *Public and Private in Social Life*, New York, St. Martin's Press, 281.

Patmore C. (1863), *The Angel in the House*, Part I, Book I, Canto IX: I.1-I.12, London-Cambridge, Macmillian & Co., 1863, 109.

Patou-Mathis M. (2020), *L'homme préhistorique est aussi une femme. Une histoire de l'invisibilité des femmes,* Paris, Allary Editions.

Pédron A. (2019), "'Nous aussi nous sommes citoyennes': Female Activism during the French Revolution", *Women in French Studies Special Conference Issue*, 71.

Pekacz J.T. (1999), "The salonnières and the philosophes in Old Regime France: The authority of aesthetic judgment", *Journal of the History of Ideas*, 277-297.

Pekacz J.T. (2014), "Les Amies des philosophes: The making of Enlightenment salons in nineteenth-century France", *French History and Civilization*, 5, 53-61.

Pendle K. (ed.) (2001), *Women and Music: A History*, 2nd ed., Bloomington, Indiana University Press.

Perrot M. (1978), *De la nourrice à l'employée. Travaux de femmes dans la France du XIXe siècle*, in *Le mouvement social*, 3-10.

Perrot M. (1998), *Les Femmes ou les silences de l'Histoire,* Paris, Flammarion.

Perrot M. (2015), *La vie de famille au XIXᵉ siècle,* Paris, Éditions du Seuil, 62.
Perrot M. (2020), *La place des femmes. Une difficile conquête de l'espace public*, Paris, Les Éditions Textuel.
Perrot M. and Duby G. (eds.) (1990-1991), *Histoire des femmes en Occident*, 5 volumes, Paris, Pion.
Politakis G.P. (2001), "Night Work of Women in Industry: Standards and Sensibility", 140 *Int'l Lab. Rev.*, 403.
Pothier R.J. (1825), *Traité de la puissance du mari sur la personne et les biens de la femme*, in *Oeuvres de Pothier, contenant les Traités du droit français, Nouvelle édition mise en meilleur ordre et publiée par les soins de M. Dupin, Avocat a la Cour royale de Paris*, t. VI, Paris, Chasseriau.
Pozzo B. (2012), "Masculinity Italian Style", in *Nev. LJ,* 13, 585-618.
Prochaska F.K. (1980), *Women and philanthropy in nineteenth-century England,* Oxford, Oxford University Press.
Probert R. (2005), "The Impact of the Marriage Act of 1753: Was It Really "A Most Cruel Law for the Fair Sex"?", *Eighteenth-Century Studies*, 38, 2, Winter, 247-262.
Pugh E.L. (1980), "John Stuart Mill and the Women's Question in Parliament, 1865-1868", *The Historian,* 42, 3, May, 399-418.
Ravera C. (2019), *Olympe de Gouges*, Roma, Elemento 115.
Reiter R.R. (1975), *Toward an Anthropology of Women*, New York-London, Monthly Review Press.
Riva J. (2014), "The Radical Novelty of Olympe De Gouges", *Nottingham French Studies*, 53.3.
Rodgers G., Lee E., Swepston L. and Van Daele J. (2009), *The International Labour Organization and the quest for social justice, 1919-2009,* Geneva, ILR Press an imprint of Cornell University Press, Ithaca and International Labour Office.
Rodriguez-Ruiz B. and Rubio-Marin R. (eds.) (2012), *The Struggle for Female Suffrage in Europe, Voting to Become Citizens*, Leiden-Boston, Brill.
Roudinesco E. (2013), *Théroigne de Méricourt: Une femme mélancolique sous la Révolution,* Paris, Albin Michel.
Ruskin J. (1865), *Sesame and Lilies, Two Lectures delivered in Manchester in 1864, 1. Of King's Treasuries; 2. Of Queen's Gardens,* London, Smith, Elder & Co.
Sacco R. (1991), "Legal Formants: A Dynamic Approach to Comparative Law" (Installment II of II), *The American Journal of Comparative Law*, 39, 2, Spring, 343-401.
Sartori D. (2004), "Donne e uomini tra pubblico e private", *Annali di studi religiosi*, 5, 367.

Savage G.L. (1983), "The Operation of the 1857 Divorce Act, 1860-1910 a Research Note", *Journal of Social History*, 164, Summer, 103-110.

Schweitzer S. (2010), *Femmes de pouvoir. Une histoire de l'égalité professionnelle en Europe (XIXe-XXIe siècle),* Paris, Payot.

Scott J.W. and Tilly L.A. (1975), "Women's work and the family in nineteenth-century Europe", *Comparative Studies in Society and History*, 17.1, 36-64.

Seiz J.A. and Pujol M.A. (2000), "Harriet Taylor Mill", *The American Economic Review,* 90, 2, *Papers and Proceedings of the One Hundred Twelfth Annual Meeting of the American Economic Association*, May, 476.

Showalter E. (1992), "Killing the Angel in the House: The Autonomy of Women Writers", *The Antioch Review*, 50, 1/2, 50th Anniversary Issue, Winter-Spring, 207.

Sileo G. (2016), "La legislazione europea sul lavoro femminile e minorile di inizio secolo: un quadro comparator", in *Lavoro e cittadinanza femminile, Anna Kuliscioff e la prima legge sul lavoro delle donne*, Milano, Franco Angeli, 60 ff.

Smith E.S. (2001), "John Stuart Mill's "The Subjection of Women": A Re-Examination", *Polity*, 34, 2 (Winter), 181-203.

Soldani S. (ed.) (1989), *L'educazione delle donne: scuole e modelli di vita femminile nell'Italia dell'Ottocento,* Milano, Franco Angeli.

Stearns P., (1972) "Working-Class Women in Britain, 1890-1914", in Vicinus M. (ed.), *Suffer and Be Still*, Bloomington-Indiana-London, Indiana University Press, 100-120.

Stone L. (1990), *The family, Sex and Marriage in England 1500-1800*, London, Penguin.

Sullivan K.M. (2002), "Constitutionalizing Women's Equality", 90 *Calif. L. Rev.*, 735.

Surridge L. (1994), "Dogs' Bodies, Women's Bodies: Wives as Pets in Mid-Nineteenth-Century Narratives of Domestic Violence", *Victorian Review*, 20.1, 1-34.

Tavor Bannet E. (1997), "The Marriage Act of 1753: 'A Most Cruel Law for the Fair Sex'", *Eighteenth-Century Studies,* 30, 3, Spring, 233-254.

Taylor B. (2003), *Mary Wollstonecraft and the Feminist Imagination*, Cambridge, Cambridge University Press, 13.

Taylor C. (1994), *Women of the anti-slavery movement: the Weston sisters*, London, Macmillian.

Thalmann R. (1995), "L'oubli des femmes dans l'historiographie de la Résistance", *Clio. Femmes, Genre, Histoire,* 1.

Thomas K. (1959), "The Double Standard", *Journal of the History of Ideas*, 20, 2, Apr., 195-216

Tikhonov Sigrist N. (2014), "Les femmes et l'université en France, 1860-1914", *Histoire de l'éducation*, online since January 1, accessed May 20, 2021, available at: http://journals.openedition.org/histoire-education/1940; doi: https://doi.org/10.4000/histoire-education.

Tomes N. (1978), "A "Torrent of Abuse": Crimes of Violence between Working-Class Men and Women in London, 1840-1875", Journal of Social History, 11, 3, Spring, 328-345.

Trumbach R. (1978), *The rise of the egalitarian family: aristocratic kinship and domestic relations in eighteenth-century England*, New York, Academic Press.

Valette A. (1889), *Oeuvre des libérées de Saint-Lazare, fondée en 1870, reconnue d'utilité publique par décret du 26 janvier 1885,* Alençon, Imprimerie de F. Guy, 10.

Von der Heyden-Rynsch V. (1992), *Europäische Salons, Höhepunkte einer versunkenen weiblichen Kultur,* München, Artemis & Winkler.

Walby S. (1986), *Patriarchy at work: patriarchal and capitalist relations in employment, 1880-1984,* Hoboken (NJ), Wiley.

Walton W. (1997), "Literary Production and the Rearticulation of Home Space in the works of George Sand, Marie d'Agoult and Hortense Allart", *Women's History Review*, 6:1, 115-132.

Webb S. (1896), *Women and the Factory Acts,* London, Fabian Society, 3.

Weber M. (1981), "La partecipazione politica femminile in Italia: evoluzione, determinanti, caratteristiche", *Italian Political Science Review/Rivista Italiana Di Scienza Politica,* 11, 281.

Wekerle G. (1981), "Women and the urban environment", in Stimpson C.R., Dixler E., Nelson M.J. and Yatrakis K.B. (eds.), *Women and the American city,* Chicago, University of Chicago Press, 185-211.

Whelan R. (ed.) (1998), *Octavia Hill and the Social Housing Debate, Essays and Letters by Octavia Hill*, London, Civitas.

White J.B. (1984), *When Words Lose Their Meaning: Constitutions and Reconstitutions of Language, Character, and Community*, Chicago, The University of Chicago Press.

Wiesner-Hanks M. (2019), *Women and Gender in Early Modern Europe, New Approaches to European History*, Cambridge, Cambridge University Press.

Williams Elliott D. (2002), *The Angel out of the House, Philanthropy and Gender in Nineteenth-Century England,* Chapel Hill, University of Virginia Press.

Wohl A.S. (1971), "Octavia Hill and the Homes of the London Poor", *Journal of British Studies*, 10, 2 (May), 105-131.

Wollstonecraft M. (1792), *A Vindication of the Rights of Woman,* London, printed for J. Johnson, n. 71, St. Paul's Church Yard, available now in Classic Reprint, London, Forgotten Books, Paperback, March 29, 2018.

Zaher C. (2002), "When a Woman's Marital Status Determined Her Legal Status: A Research Guide on the Common Law Doctrine of Coverture", *Law Libr. J.*, 94, 459.

Zancarini-Fournel M. (2005), *Histoire des femmes en France: XIXe-XXe siècle*, Rennes, Presses Universitaires de Rennes.

Zolesio E. (2009), "Des femmes dans un métier d'hommes: l'apprentissage de la chirurgie", *Travail, genre et sociétés*, 2, 117-133.

Chapter 4
QUEER AS A LESSON IN REALITY

Letizia Tomassone

ABSTRACT: *Italy is the country where a large part of thought is influenced by Catholic culture. This is also the case within the feminist debate, where there is a polarization between essentialist feminism, of difference, which is reluctant to confront queer issues, and radical feminism. This also has consequences for the Italian legislation. The fiercest clashes take place precisely between women of different components of the movement. How does feminist theology and in particular Protestant theology fit into this debate? Certainly, it is not an option for us to ontologize the two genders and legitimize dualism.*
Furthermore, queer theologies have opened the doors to the expression of the younger generations, bearers of fluid and transitory identities. However, the question of gender justice, which still has its basis in the painful struggle to get out of patriarchy, must always be tied to this thought open to the most radical expressions. Women, LGBTQ people and gender fluid people can build on these alliances of thought and meeting practices that to a large extent are still to be discovered.

Italy is the country where a large part of thought is influenced by Catholic culture. This is also the case within the feminist debate, where there is a polarization between the feminism of sexual difference and radical feminism intertwined with the LGBTQ+ movement.

This has consequences for the legislation in our country, where unexpected alliances are created with conservative political parties that support traditional family values and gender roles. The most bitter clashes take place precisely between women of the different components of the movement. How does feminist theology and in particular Protestant theology fit into this debate?

Certainly, for us Protestants it is not an option to ontologize the two genders and legitimize dualism. In fact, the "thought of sexual difference" practiced by the Italian feminist philosophical community called "Diotima", which today I judge as essentialist, expresses in secular terms the same Catholic natural theology which has given strength and nourishment to the unequal and complementary duality between man and woman. A theology expressed in texts such as the "Mulieris Dignitatem", which proposes the Petrine principle for men and the Marian principle for women: the first a public and proactive function, the second an intimate and welcoming function. (Apostolic Letter 1988).

The search for a free sense of difference obviously did not look to these alliances, but somehow that feminist thought was captured to legitimize the Catholic theology of difference, which likes to use the Marian model.

The political practice of sexual difference was "born from the simple desire to be in the world with the body and thought of women", rooting itself in the body and in the relationship between women with the free expression of oneself at the center (De Perini 2021). This is why it contrasts with the queer instances of the fluid subject, somehow detached from the body, and with the idea of gender as a social construction.

I found the Diotima group's attempt to listen to queer requests interesting, as expressed in an article by Sandra De Perini, which also talks about the totally new, unexpected question of a queer God.

The free sense of self and spirituality go together. In the political practice of sexual difference a dimension of spirituality came about through the female genealogy open to a dimension other than oneself ("the mother or whoever for her") (Muraro 2006) and the seminal "divine feminine" in the writings of Luce Irigaray (Irigaray 2007). In the queer movement, on the other hand, the reference to a "divine other" has become established, divergent, disobedient to the rules of heterosexuality, fluid, source of all differences and devoid of patriarchal power. The exponent who most clearly elaborated this thought was the Argentine theologian Marcela Althaus-Reid (2003), and today in Europe the Catholic theologian Teresa Forcades carries forward this divine naming of non-dual and non-heteronormative difference (Forcades 2019).

It should be noted that queer theologies have opened the doors also in Italy to the younger generations, bearers of fluid and transitory identities, less interested in sexual difference, even if this disinterest runs the risk of no longer focusing attention on questions of gender justice, in a country where inequalities at work and femicides are still the raw background on which we move.

Sandra De Perini therefore affirms the need for historical feminists of difference, to allow themselves to be questioned by the queer demands of the new generations, even to allow themselves to be "used" to "further clarify and radicalize our politics", making it clear that "sexual difference crosses all differences".

However, this is precisely the point at which the clash, and the intertwining with a Catholic theology anchored to the biblical narratives of the creation of man and woman takes place. Although decades of feminist exegesis, and not only, have highlighted that the Genesis account does not lay the foundations for an ontology of gender dualism, but rather for the conception of a human being created from the beginning in relationship.

The debate therefore continues, and it will be important not to close the channels of communication by importing the Anglo-Saxon controversy on exclusivist feminism, which does not recognize trans-women as women, as until now it doesn't in Italy.

1. Roots in the body

A common feature of the feminism of difference and of political feminism in Italy was precisely the awareness of being rooted in one's own body as a woman and of starting from herself.

Today, the impact with the current harsh reality of denied rights relating to women's freedom over procreation and abortion in the US has led to a debate on feminist practices and writings that brings us to revisit some moments of history of the past fifty years of the movement in Italy.

The struggle for free, gratuitous, and safe abortion has given form and experiential basis to the feminist struggle to define themselves as free women, active subjects capable of making decisions. In fact, maintaining the prohibition of abortion and consequently the practice of clandestine abortions, held women in a position of subordination and isolation, in an instrumental function to the family, on the one hand, and to exploited work, on the other.

Therefore, the struggles for the legalization of abortion have been part of the women's movement against patriarchy. Carla Lonzi wrote in a letter to Pasolini dated January 21, 1975: "Our goal was not to deny the freedom of abortion, but to change its meaning in the conscience of those who will continue to suffer it, even free, the woman, and to impose it, a culture, if we don't mean man". Otherwise said: it is the woman who is forced to undergo an abortion, even though allowed by law; it is the culture, or should we say man, that imposes it, whether a law exists or not.

In the Manifesto of Female Revolt, which dates to 1970, she also wrote in this regard: "The denial of the freedom of abortion is part of the global veto that is put on the autonomy of women" (Manifesto 2017).

The struggle for freedom and female difference then materialized in the path taken by the "Libreria delle donne" in Milano and the Diotima philosophical community, around the leading figure of Luisa Muraro (Libreria 1987). Muraro talks about the construction of the free sense of sexual difference, which brought out the truth that

> "*Humanity is made up of women and men. Using the word men for women too was patriarchal bullying. Women are a human being, they are humanity. There must be a free sense of sexual difference. However, the difference between men and women has been transformed into stereotypes*" (Columba 2018).

It is precisely on these stereotypes that both the bourgeois proposal of man-woman complementarity, which in any case maintains the subordination of woman to man, and, more recently, the discussion around queer and transgender identities are shattered. In the first case, Carla Lonzi's choice of separatist feminism offers the space of feminine identities conceived as starting from herself, and of a free sexuality not subjected to male needs or control. Maria Luisa Boccia writes: "Shared by all is the discovery that emancipation is a broken promise. Because it does not really put an end to traditional destiny, but above all because in equality or parity with men a woman does not find existential, political, and cultural answers to the sense of self" (Boccia 2010).

In the second case, however, the same feminists faced with fluid identities that are no longer marked by sexual difference, become unyielding in their refusal to recognize transgender M to F in the collective of women. I agree on the fact that, since gender is also a cultural and social construction, as Judith Butler teaches (Butler 2006), men who become women through transition are still bearers of an imposed identity, built on patriarchal heterosexual codes.

The sexual binarism that is denounced by queer thought, as exposed for example in a bill, then rejected by the Italian Parliament, such as D.D.L. Zan, does not correspond to sexual difference. This, in fact, is a process of differentiating oneself, not from the male model, but starting from one's own body, in which one is rooted as a woman, no longer condemned to being inferior. The act of deferring begins with an act of disobedience to this destiny, to start from oneself and from there learn to speak about oneself. The feminism of difference has worked for a long time, and continues to do so, in a collective way, in the sharing between women, because the gaze of the other mutually authorizes freedom. However, the rooting of this path remains essential in the female body that she is, that she becomes. Here because it is difficult to meet the demands of those who undertake the transition, thus rejecting their body, in a paradoxical exaltation of individual freedom. This analysis is already investigated in an Anglican theologian's article on the queer question as a search for the status of the subject (Gugliermetto 2013).

Today we see that even feminism can become a commodity, a brand that fits into the market system, instead of unhinging it as the founders of the women's revolution wanted. Feminism has also entered the sphere of the demand for individual freedom, it has become a good that can be bought and sold, but no longer the activator of a collective process, no longer capable of questioning revolutionary practices such as Marxism, starting with issues related to female domestic work and gender issues (Oliveri 2018). Perhaps, however, by changing the forms of transformative social communication, we can recognize the potential of revolutionary, albeit branded, gestures: internal-external to the system of commodification, from which nothing seems to escape, if not the real experiences of people who live humiliations but also fulfillment with their body and soul.

In Italy, collective female subjects have joined forces to make of the feminist re-elaboration of theology their road to liberation. Therefore, they do not only address questions relating to gender in the churches, but open their eyes to the whole historical, dogmatic, and theological construction that has shaped the various Christian churches, leading them to be what they are today.

Among these collective subjects are the groups of women of the dissident Christian communities in Italy, which recognize as their founding moment the Eucharist celebrated by women in the national assembly of Brescia in 1988 (Visitazioni 2021).

There are also the associate theologians in the Coordination of Italian Women Theologians which now has more than a decade of very productive history: publications, seminars and a focused attention on the present in the major Italian theological magazines.

Regarding the Zan bill, the National Council on CTI expressed itself in favor of it, saying that it cannot be rejected because "there are stories that are insulted, despised and raped" (CTI 2021). Therefore "any frontal resistance to this bill signed by Zan reveals itself as a form of inhospitality towards lives. For this reason, it can only sound anti-evangelical". However, the same document points out the critical aspect of the bill, which seems to separate the bodies from people's lives. Let us therefore return here to the central point also emphasized by the philosophers of difference, namely that there cannot be a separation between body and self-expression, or there is the risk of again introducing a dualistic anthropology, and women do not fit this pattern. Thus, they write carrying forward the urgency of a hermeneutic work on experience rooted in the body.

> "*It is as if one fails to grasp that the bodily experience is already psychic from the very beginning and that the interpretative experience, personal and social at the same time, is somehow rooted in the body from the very beginning. We should know – women usually know – that sexual difference is the sign of the finitude of every life that comes into the*

world, and that this difference is at the same time biological, psychic, symbolic and social and that with all these traits it becomes history" (Coordinamento Teologhe Italiane 2021).

2. Gender Justice

Certainly, queer theologies have opened the doors to the expression of the younger generations, bearers of fluid and transitory identities. However, the question of gender justice, which still has its basis in the painful struggle to get out of patriarchy, must always be tied to this thought open to the most radical expressions.

The work done in the evangelical field in Italy is very important in this regard. The Lutheran Synod, prompted by the LWF and the Lutheran Italian Women's Network, drafted an important document on gender justice in churches. (Chiesa Luterana 2021). Also the FDEI (Federation of Evangelical Women in Italy) is working through a long-term project on violence against women, a project that has also involved help desks in evangelical hospitals dedicated to women in need and the training of workers at all levels, in churches and diaconal structures. Evangelical churches in general are also active in organizing training and reflection on homo-transphobia issues, preparing and participating in ecumenical vigils, to foster awareness in faith communities.

3. Inclusion and new subjects

Women, LGBTQ+ and gender-fluid people have so far been able to build alliances and interconnected practices, and will still have a lot to develop together.

The fact that today some churches and some Christian movements are completely open to the LGBTQ people presence and to gay and lesbian ministers cannot suddenly erase the terrible history of exclusion and persecution that homosexual people have suffered from Christianity. The roots of these persecutions are found in some (few) biblical texts and in the sexophobia developed by the Christian church in the first millennium. The stories of repression in society are accompanied by the silent homosexuality lived in convents and churches.

Today we range from the development of pastoral care for homosexuals, in the Catholic and evangelical fields (in the latter context often pastoral care is aimed at prior transforming, reconditioning and "healing" in the direction of heterosexual normativity), to the blessing of same sex couples adopted by some European and American Protestant churches (actually aimed at the transformation of the heteronormative morality, as in the "More Light" churches in the USA).

What is called into question, also thanks to the important theological work carried out by women theologians, is the patriarchal manipulation of the image of God, presented as the apex of a *Kuriarchal* structure that becomes a reference even for access to God's forgiveness and grace, which works with dynamics of domination and submission of women but also of those who find themselves in social positions of slavery, submission to colonialism and poverty.

The real news is that in the last few decades women and men with LGBTQ+ orientations have spoken and come out in churches. They have thus become authors of their history and their search for a God who liberates. This is the most significant result of a hitherto hidden path: the desire to show oneself and to be there, overcoming every concealment and every shame. Visibility does not in itself mean inclusion or acceptance but implies that there is no room for the strategy of silence on the different sexual identities that churches have used in modern times.

At the same time, categories codified by health regulations and legal indications tend to classify sexual identities in an ever more detailed way, both to allow people access to healthcare pathways, for example, of sex change, and to de-pathologize the different identities. But this creates a distortion that details identities in an almost mechanical way, forgetting that identities are processes and narratives, movements, and cannot be defined once and for all. The same mistake was made in the aforementioned D.D.L. Zan that wanted to crystallize the definitions instead of taking note of the transformative processes of life in constant motion.

More than the surgical transition, also underestimated is the great impact created by the social transition, which transforms both the person and the environment around him/her. This does not only concern trans people but all situations in which a non-cisgender or non-binary identity is made explicit.

Bodies have always been more fluid and tender than moral rules – Marcela Althaus-Reid defines the body as "incorrigible, rude, libertine" – and the queer gaze helps us to see it.

But even before that, it is the word of faith that de-legitimizes every construction of human identity which offers an illusory way of salvation; it is the word of faith that instead proposes the grace of God that reaches us in our being in pieces, in the fragmentation of our identity. The queer God is inclusive of all diversity experienced, suffered, or enjoyed by human beings.

4. Intersectionality

Gender identity has to do with the sense of self and the manner of intertwining relationships; we can say that it derives both from the sexual gender with which one is born and from the cultural and social construction of the gender to which one is assigned.

An integrated approach is needed between nature, culture, and education, which also considers intersectionality. The fluid body also collides with its limits, with the partiality that develops in the relationship with the other.

A young evangelical trans writes that today transexual people would have greater strength to identify themselves and tell the truth about themselves if they had retraced the path of women of "starting from oneself" and seeking community among women, without exposing themselves to constant comparison with the other from itself in the patriarchal world which creates only disparity and repression.

Porpora Marcasciano writes in the introduction to the book "Elements of trans criticism":

> "*When there is no self-narration, the sense of things escapes us, and awareness is not created. Transsexuality was defined by the old patriarchy which, through religion, science, and politics, established the codes to represent it and to talk about it. The unavoidable and essential practice of starting from oneself, a precious heritage of the women's movement, would have allowed the gathering of the complexity of one's own experience that the external gaze and its interpretation have scattered in a thousand fragments*" (Marcasciano 2010).

But what do we mean by intersectionality?

Intersectionality is an approach introduced in sociology and jurisprudence by Crenshaw in the 1980s to describe the intersection of different social identities and their possible particular discrimination, oppression, or domination and as a critique of black feminism against anti-discrimination doctrine, feminist theory and anti-racist policies (Crenshaw 1989).

We are therefore dealing with humans in their complexity, with the environment or communities in which they develop, with the oppressions and freedoms they experience, and with the divine image that the religious community around them perceives and transmits.

Often the religious community is an obstacle to the development of individuals, instead of offering a space for their spiritual and human growth. This is because it stops at past acquisitions and does not react with a lively dynamic to changes in identities and situations.

Experience tells us, for example, that local churches, even in the

Protestant sphere, are happier to welcome a male pastor with wife and children, thus still creating a barrier of prejudice and distrust towards people who live a non-binary sexuality. Furthermore, in this way the communities of faith express the erroneous belief that sexual identity is determined once and for all and is fixed, while today we see a great fluidity in people's lives, which is accompanied by work mobility and the broadening of horizons through globalization.

Thus, the communities of faith remain firm in a bourgeois understanding of the world, of identities and of love and family relationships, and find it difficult to open to the transformations taking place today. This even though they believe in a God who makes all things new and who expresses him/her/itself in the plurality of relationships. A Trinitarian God involved in the plurality and multiplicity of relationships in motion, never fixed on a single definition of her/him/itself.

5. Languages about the divine

However, glimpses of freedom can also be found starting from religious communities and this reveals the hope that a path is possible. For example, it is present in the work of revisiting language that feminists have been carrying out for decades, both in biblical hermeneutics and in the liturgical and pastoral fields.

It is now clear that there is a close connection between authoritarian theology and patriarchal images of God, liturgies and language models, on the one hand, and cisgender violence and normativity in churches, communities, families and politics, on the other. Churches and congregations around the world are clearly called to address these problems.

In Christian theology the principle of the "imago Dei" is affirmed, that is, that every human being is created in the image of God, and this gives them full dignity and the right to exist as they are; on the other hand, an eschatological perspective of inclusion in Christ overthrows the hierarchies and relationships of domination and subordination based on differences: Gal 3:28 "there is no male and female in Christ, neither slave nor free, neither Jew nor Greek".

Creation and redemption are seen as the two references to an inclusive, welcoming, and plural divine presence. Both from the point of view of the original creation, and from that of the transformation that moves towards the messianic time of fulfilment; the plurality of human identities is welcomed and blessed.

Nicole Ashwood from Jamaica, head of the World Council of Churches' "A Just Community of Women and Men" program, made a passionate appeal to take more seriously the radicality of the Biblical claim that God created human beings in her/his/its image assigning to them the charge of taking care of the whole creation. For her, God is an equalizer of all inequalities. All differences between people are secondary. And the dignity of every human being and of all creation must be protected from destruction (Building 2013).

"There can be no discriminating hierarchy in a theology that places at the center of its faith the belief that all human beings are in the image of God. All these hierarchies and forms of discrimination are a challenge to overcome with theology, spirituality, and the practice of nonviolence – and therefore also a challenge for the Church and for peace", concluded President Antje Heider-Rottwilm at the end of the conference of the European network of Churches of Peace. (Heider-Rottwilm 2013).

6. The LGBTQ+ issue among refugees in Italy

The issue of the image of God also has an impact on Muslim understanding. I report the experience of a Muslim trans person, which I found in a degree thesis based on research among refugees in Italy with LGBTQ+ identity.

It is an example of divergent thinking of its own kind compared to the dominant thought of Islam in Pakistan, which allows one to live one's spirituality in a positive way, regardless of the tradition received, and reinventing the relationship of intimacy with God. It is that of Amina (20 years old, M to F woman of Pakistani origin, of Islamic religion), who in this way managed to reconcile her Muslim identity with her transition:

> "*Yes, in sura, and it is written, it talks about people, God said I can do what I want, I can give him a son as a daughter, and a daughter as a son. These mean he is talking about transgender people. A son is born becomes a daughter. So he talks about these things, then if people don't understand the problem is theirs.*
>
> *But there are some people who think 'to change sex is a sin, we should remain as God made us, we cannot make physical changes.' I think that this is not a sin, so this is a natural thing. God made us like this and put us to the test because if it was a sin, why would God put a woman in our body, in my body? If this was a sin, then I would not be like this. If I am like this there is a reason. For this thing, if God made me like this there is a reason. For this I am like this and I do not think this is a sin*" (*sic*) (Coletta 2021).

Thus, a critical homosexual and lesbian community has also developed in Islamic Ummah, which takes up the legacy of criticism of women, of a Koran freed from the misogynistic and patriarchal tradition. Thus, being created by God also means being accepted in one's gender transition and does not involve the obligation to adhere to compulsory heterosexuality.

7. A changing divine

Now we come to the biblical images of a multiple and unfixed divine.

In the Bible God is not sexuated, even if many images represent him/her/it in an anthropomorphic way, sometimes masculine, sometimes feminine. As examples we can refer to the mother eagle as an icon of the God who takes her little ones out of Egypt, the Lord of the celestial world who makes the stars and the mountains sing, or even the multifaceted presence in three men who let themselves be hosted by Abraham and Sarah in their desert tent.

The First Testament's way of describing God does not create a hierarchy between female and male images, between anthropomorphic and inanimate images (rock, fire, spring, trees, to name but a few).

The Jewish authors of the first millennium BC knew that an image of God cannot and must not be made, and that the divine escapes any attempt to classify or manage it. This is also the meaning of the second of the ten words entrusted to Moses: "Do not make yourself a sculpture, nor an image of the things that are in heaven above or on earth below or in the waters under the earth" (Exodus 20:4 and Deuteronomy 5:8). From this flows the complete freedom of God from human religious forms, and this has a powerful consequence also on human action in history: it ensures that it is not possible to legitimize a violent and identity-based action using God's name.

Thus writes the theologian John McNeill, somewhat simplifying:

> "*Whether we are gay, and therefore imagine a male God, or lesbians, and therefore imagine a female God, in our relationship of prayer with God there is in any case a necessary homoerotic dimension […]. For most gays and lesbians, it is precisely the human experience of homosexual love that opens the way to hope for a possible passionate relationship of love with God*" (McNeill 2016).

8. A lesson in reality

The theology and practice of the churches must allow themselves to be accompanied and questioned starting from the emerging queer subjects, those who do not find themselves in the anthropological and "natural" categories imposed by the dominant narratives. With a look also to neuroscience, as well as to the social sciences, a fruitful dialogue can emerge unless one demand to establish a new natural determinism over neuroscience.

For this reason, it is important to put the topic of gender identities in the dialogue between theology and neuroscience. Here some conclusions.

1. In the first place, theology is founded on the datum of creation, those narratives of Genesis 1 and 2-3 which restore human identity conceived since the beginning in relation. The relationship does not, however, imply male-female otherness as the norm for all differences. On the one hand, it is precisely neuroscience that show us how sexual identity is a process that lies in a fluid line of continuity between hyper-feminine and hyper-masculine. On the other hand, philosophical and theological reflection tells us that when two subjects are in relationship, there is a third, which is their "being-between": a relational whole that also refers to the Trinitarian image of the divine. (Irigaray 1996) This relational whole is spread into a network that also involves our being animals and "companions among species", as Donna Haraway writes. This is a field in which eco-feminisms are also developing practices aimed at broadening the sense of identity as the belonging of the human subject to the whole world of the living, to the community of creation. (Johnson 2018).
2. The second criterion at stake is being in the image of the divine, an element that in theology has two poles, as stated above: the act of creation of the human being, which is founded and is constitutive of the radical equality of every single person in the social body; and the Christological event of a promised fullness, which overcomes, or integrates, or brings to fulfilment the different gender identities. In the resurrection, even the androcentric culture that influences our identities so strongly appears to be superseded. This observation is already part of classical Christian theology, even if in the past it led to postponing the promise of fullness to a future that does not belong to the historical sphere, while today it is claimed as a possibility of reinventing the present.
   In the same way, female resistance to patriarchal hierarchies does not lose value in eschatological realization; on the contrary it finds an answer already in the present, in creating liberated spaces, separatist or not, depending on whether one follows the elaboration and theological practice of Mary Daly, rigidly separatist also in imagining the future, (Daly 1999) or the Christological elaboration of E. Schuessler Fiorenza, (Schuessler-Fiorenza 1983) which proposes the church of Wo-Man,

which includes in a post-patriarchal space all the people crushed by the *kuriarchy* and who seek freedom in the community of equals.

3. The resistance of bodies is the third element that theology must face. They are those bodies that resist the normative definitions dictated by natural or cultural determinisms. But they are also souls and self-understandings that resist bodies perceived as "other than oneself", as in gender dysphoria. All queer subjects stand out today thanks to that persistence that alone can make room for their full dignity. The balance between amazement and suffering must be seen from a theology that wants to reaffirm that identity is be called to live by God, and not a destiny tied to a body. The permanence of our ego is a being pulled out of any determinism, a work of the divine that is other than us, a voice that resounds and sets us on the road. Then the subjects become nomadic, not because they wander in the void, but because in the encounter with that voice they recognize their own being as a gift, and at the same time as a conquest, always fluid, never final, always in transit.

References

Althaus-Reid M. (2003), *The Queer God*, New York-London, Routledge.

Apostolic Letter Mulieris Dignitatem of the Supreme Pontiff John Paul II on the Dignity and Vocation of Women on the occasion of the Marian year (1988), available at https://www.vatican.va/content/john-paul-ii/en/apost_letters/1988/documents/hf_jp-ii_apl_19880815_mulieris-dignitatem.html.

Boccia M.L. (2010), "Carla Lonzi, il congedo dal patriarcato – Fare differenza", *Il Manifesto*, 4 March 2010 available at https://www.libreriadelledonne.it/_oldsite/news/articoli/Manif040310.htm.

Butler J. (2006), *Gender Trouble: Feminism and the Subversion of Identity*, New York-London, Routledge.

Chiesa luterana (2021), *Giustizia di genere. La presa di posizione del XXIII Sinodo sulla giustizia di genere*, https://www.chiesaluterana.it/giustizia-di-genere/.

Chunakara M.G. (ed.) (2013), *Building Peace on Earth. Report of the International Ecumenical Peace Convocation*, Geneva, WCC publications, https://www.oikoumene.org/sites/default/files/Document/IEPCreport_EN.pdf.

Coletta V. (2021), "Experiences of Life and Intersectionality of Transgender Refugees Living in Italy: A Qualitative Approach", *International Journal of Environmental Research and Public Health*, 18.

Columba P. (2018), *Il femminismo è superato. Falso!* [Feminism is outdated. False!], Bari, Laterza, 8.

Coordinamento Teologhe Italiane (2021), *A proposito del ddl Zan*, available at https://www.teologhe.org/newsletters/comunicazioni-dal-cti-3/.

Crenshaw K. (1989), "Demarginalizing the Intersection of Race and Sex: A Black Feminist Critique of Antidiscrimination Doctrine, Feminist Theory and Antiracist Politics", *University of Chicago Legal Forum*, 139, https://scholarship.law.columbia.edu/faculty_scholarship/3007/.

Daly M. (1999), *Quintessence... Realizing the Archaic Future: A Radical Elemental Feminist Manifesto*, Boston, Beacon Press.

De Clercq E. (2018), *Etica del gender*, Brescia, Morcelliana.

De Perini A. (2021), "Pensiero queer e femminismo radicale", *Viottoli*, 2, 89-93.

Forcades T. (2019), *Siamo tutti diversi! Per una teologia queer*, Roma, Castelvecchi.

Forcades T. (2020), Il *corpo gioia di Dio*, San Pietro in Cariano (VR), Gabrielli.

Gugliermetto G. (2013), "Le teologie queer e la ricerca del soggetto" [Queer theologies and the search for the subject], *Protestantesimo*, 68:2013, 261-272.

Heider-Rottwilm A. (2013), "Violence against Women", in Dorn C. (ed.), *Peace in Christian Thought and Life. An Anthology*, Geneva, WCC Publications, 252-257.

Irigaray L. (1996), *I Love to You: Sketch of A Possible Felicity in History*, New York-London, Routledge.

Irigaray L. (2007), "Donne divine", in Irigagary L., *Sessi e genealogie*, Milano, Dalai.

Kao Y.G. (2023), My *Body, Their Baby. A Progressive Christian Vision for Surrogacy*, Stanford, CA, Stanford Universtity Press.

Johnson E. (2018), *Creation and the Cross: The Mercy of God for a Planet in Peril*, Maryknoll, N.Y., Orbis Books.

Libreria delle donne di Milano (1987), *Non credere di avere dei diritti. La generazione della libertà femminile nell'idea e nelle vicende di un gruppo di donne*, Torino, Rosenberg & Sellier.

Manifesto di Rivolta Femminile (Roma, luglio 1970), available at https://www.internazionale.it/notizie/2017/03/08/manifesto-di-rivolta-femminile.

Marcasciano P. (2010), *Elementi di critica trans*, Roma, Manifestolibri.

McNeill J. (2016), *Freedom, glorious freedom. The Spiritual Journey to the Fullness of Life for Gays, Lesbians, and Everybody Else*, Maple Shade, NJ, Lethe Press.

Muraro L. (2006), *L'ordine simbolico della madre*, Roma, Editori Riuniti.

Muraro L. (2016), *L'anima del corpo. Contro l'utero in affitto*, Milano, ed. La Scuola.

Oliveri A. (2018), "Il manifesto di Rivolta Femminile ha cambiato l'Italia. Per questo dovremmo leggerlo tutte", *The Vision*, 3 August 2018, available at https://thevision.com/attualita/manifesto-femminista/.

Pazé V. (2023)., Libertà in vendita. Il corpo fra scelta e mercato, Torino, Bollati Boringhieri.

Schuessler F.E. (1983), *In Memory of Her: A Feminist Theological Reconstruction of Christian Origins*, New York, Crossroad.

Visitazioni. I gruppi donne delle comunità di base e le molte altre si raccontano (2021), available at https://www.cdbitalia.it/gruppi-donne/visitazioni/.

Chapter 5
WOMEN IN THE CATHOLIC CHURCH: (DE)SACRALISING BOUNDARIES

Cristina Simonelli

ABSTRACT: *Even in the Catholic Church, and even in traditionally more moderate countries of the Latin tradition, there is a considerable debate going on around the roles played by women. The issue actually brings with it other related perspectives, such as gender perspectives, reflection on masculinity, ongoing debates around sexual orientation and, from an ecclesiological point of view, the theology of ministry and consideration of synodal praxis and the transformations that affect both. The general assumption, also expressed in the title, is to investigate the connection between gender/role models and their sacralization even in the third millennium.*

1. External boundaries and internal fault lines

Christian thought, even in its version of pastoral and journalistic dissemination, has a kind of congenital difficulty in relating its assumptions to the respective projects and cultural anthropology, extending at best to sociological investigations [1]. In these notes I will attempt to do so, albeit in non-specialist terms, starting with the question of boundaries, as posed by Mary Douglas in a classic of the last century:

> "*The concept of society is a powerful image: it is powerful in its very right to control or drive men to action. This image is endowed with form, with external boundaries, with margins, with an internal structure. Its pattern has the power to reward conformity and repel attack.*

---

[1] Morra S. and Ronconi M., *Incantare le sirene. Chiesa, teologia e cultura in scena*, Bologna, EDB, 2019, 196-219.

> *There is energy in its margins and unstructured spaces. Every experience man has of structure, margins or boundaries is ready to be used as a symbol of society'*[2].

This way of organising societies – whether they are clan-structured and therefore extended family groups, or are presumed to be free from similar patterns and therefore evolved – touches deep elements that are in a certain sense always also connected to a general idea of the sacred, through the mechanism clean/pure/inside *versus* dirty/impure/outside. It is no coincidence that the anthropologist devotes ample space in that same essay to the so-called 'code of sanctity' of Leviticus, in which the identification of boundaries is functional to identity understood as separation from everything else[3]. A particularly eloquent example is the prohibition (Lev 19:19) of wearing clothes made from two different yarns, animal (wool) and vegetable (linen). As Gianluca Carrega[4] suggests, the prohibition is multifactorial and refers to different interpretations: cosmological (creation occurred by separation, it should not be remixed), socio-political (preserving the group from exogamy) and cultic (only priests could wear such clothes). In any case, its symbolic significance is evident: it draws boundaries by means of a very fragile line, but to this line it attributes an identity and sacral significance. In the same way, in the myth of Rome's foundation, the *pomerio* functions, which extends over the furrow traced by Romulus' plough, but immediately becomes so powerful as to cause the death of Remus, the transgressor who crossed and profaned it. In the same direction, the *pomerio* becomes the sign of the right of asylum – regulated in a social and sacred sense – and the *limes of* citizenship, extended ideally and effectively as the territory expands, with different levels of belonging.

If it is pointless, therefore, to multiply the examples, which are also found in the modern era in the *sacredness of patriarchal boundaries*, it is not idle to observe that the Christian and especially Catholic declination of this dimension doubles the stakes, carrying over to the third millennium a version in which belonging, roles and doctrines are controlled by an equally sacralised leadership, moreover with a masculine and celibate reserve, which is not found in the same way in the other places of *governance* that

---

[2] Douglas L., *Purity and Danger. An analysis of the concepts of pollution and taboo,* London, Routledge & Kegan Paul, 1970, 185 (It. ed.: Bologna, Il Mulino).

[3] Douglas L., *Purity and Danger,* cit., 85-105.

[4] Carrega G., *The wool mixture and other abominations of Leviticus*, 2022, available at https://www.gionata.org/6-aprile-2022-incontro-on-line-su-lomosessualita-e-altri-delitti-del-levitico-con-carrega. Cf. Douglas M., *Leviticus as Literature*, London, Oxford University Press, 1999.

were traditionally homogenous and separate, such as political leadership groups, intellectual elites, armies, the judiciary.

Obviously in such a reconstruction I am the first not to fully recognise myself, at the very moment in which I am convincingly painting it: there are in fact theological, perhaps even simply religious, and historical reasons for affirming it and at the same time relativising it. From a historical point of view, in fact, women and gender studies have long shown not only the exclusion of women and the construction of symbolic cages relating to roles, but also unsuspected spaces of presence and speaking out: the rhetoric of consensus and unanimity in Christian historiography tends to conceal the counter/narratives and dissonances, brought to light instead by the subjects concerned. In Italy, a particular and virtuous space in this sense is occupied by the studies of Adriana Valerio[5] and what can in a certain sense be called her school. Within this collective horizon, it is worth showing the workings of this kind of investigation through a recent publication aimed at bringing to the attention of a potentially vast public a phenomenon of dissent, also largely female, at the heart of a critical moment for the Catholic Church such as the Pontificate of Pius IX and the First Vatican Council, interrupted by the Italian conquest of the city of Rome. In what was significantly called the Anti-Council[6] the women's question, linked to civil emancipation but also to the status in the Catholic Church, had a significant space:

> "*If the adherences of the stronger sex are much to be valued, the adherences of the gentler sex are of far greater value, for it is vain to hope for the triumph of truth and reason as long as half of mankind continues to be completely obedient to those who call themselves the ministers of God, when they are but impostors and natural allies of all tyrannies. For some time now there has been much talk in the world of the emancipation of women, who are to be granted the same rights as men, and that is all very well; but how would her moral condition be improved by the acquisition of these rights, if she had not first been subjected to another yoke, that of superstition and the priest? The latter will then be master of society as a whole, as long as he has the woman's soul, the very soul of the family*"[7].

[5] Valerio A., *Donne e Chiesa. Una storia di genere*, Roma, Carocci, 2016; Ead., *Il potere delle donne nella Chiesa. Giuditta, Chiara e le altre*, Roma-Bari, Laterza, 2016.

[6] Valerio A. (ed.), *L'Anticoncilio del 1869. Donne contro il Vaticano I,* Roma, Carocci, 2021.

[7] Ricciardi G., *L'Anticoncilio di Napoli del 1869,* Stabilimento tipografico Strada S. Pietro a Majella 31, Napoli, 1870, cited in Valerio A. (ed.), *L'Anticoncilio del 1869*, cit., 13.

The event, little known to ecclesiastical historiography, is also significant in the light of the outcome of Vatican I and the resistance to the ecclesiological aspects of its pronouncements, which also took on an ecumenical significance: there was in fact a dissent that, inflamed also by excommunications, in part would recognise itself in the (Vetero)Catholic Church, while to another extent would undertake what Angela Berlis indicates as "internal migration" [8]. This broad communion of saints responds to the *exodal perspective*, as suggested by a document of the Ecumenical Group of Dombes in the 1990s, but also to that Church of Christ, the foundation and goal of the different denominations, to which Vatican II also refers. In commenting on that event, I take up what has already been expressed, noting "how there are people who yearn for the same evangelical freedom, for a similar spiritual depth precisely while choosing or accepting to belong to different denominations: their way of inhabiting them has an *exodal* root, that is, it tends to denounce boundaries, in a certain sense dilating them for all. We have thus identified a people of women and men who, leaving the Churches or remaining in them, nonetheless aspire to something deeper, yearn for a Beyond, by whatever name they know or wish to indicate it" [9].

What has just been illustrated may be an example of an infringement of the rhetoric of uniformity from a historiographical and theological point of view. Also significant is the reflection carried out on the side of interreligious dialogue, in a manner in which it is the very statute of depth and seriousness of the individual implantations that allows for a relativisation of boundaries, rendered diaphanous and subtle by thickness and depth:

> "*Time and space become more generous when we explore fundamental truths in the presence of the other. 'Subtle places' open up. In its highest form, prolonged interaction between people of different faiths offers a glimmer of the Transcendent and an awareness of the Divine, whose presence is elusive. However, 'thin' times and places require 'thick' religiosity. Feminist theologies and serious interfaith engagement are ways to "thicken" our religious understanding because they require the onerous task of reweaving religious identity*" [10].

---

[8] Berlis A., "'In My Modest Cell I am not a Rebel': Lady Charlote Blennerhasset (1843-1917) and Her Desire or Spiritual Renewal Following the First Vatican Council", *Religion &Teology*, 24, 3, 2017, 1-31.

[9] Simonelli C., *Per la testimonianza del Vangelo. L'opposizione al Vaticano I come fedeltà alla tradizione,* in Valerio A. (ed.), *L'Anticoncilio del 1869*, cit., 83-107.

[10] Boys M., "Learning in the Presence of the Other", in Trible P. and Lipsett D., *Faith and Feminism*, Roma, Aracne, 2017, 171-172.

In this regard, Morra, already cited above, shows how it is possible to apply the point of view of communities of practice, elaborated by Étienne Wenger, in the context of social learning theories to the shared subjectivity of the ecclesial community, in a broad sense, thus across and beyond the different confessions [11]. In the community of practice, the legitimacy of "peripheral participation", the "negotiability of meanings", ambiguity taken as an opportunity and the "unsaturated density of reifications", i.e. the possibility of "finding the words to say what needs to be said, without the discourse being saturated, complete, incapable of accepting anything else" are fundamental [12].

In all the reported perspectives, women occupy a not inconsiderable space. indeed, they stand, albeit not alone, precisely in those internal faults, those unstructured spaces, of which Douglas spoke, that interfere with the group as a whole.

2. What's not obvious: intersections and gender gaps

As can be seen, therefore, the gender issue runs through, often unacknowledged, the entire horizon, in which a sort of invisibility of gender differences prevails, which makes one review, for example, the absence of women from top roles as natural or accidental or linked to a lack of competence *versus* a male supremacy passed off in some respects as natural, in others as the result of competence and merit.

From this point of view, unfortunately, discrimination against women extends far beyond the ecclesiastical sphere and touches, albeit not equally, so many aspects of social and political life. An example from this point of view is the experience of the pandemic in Italy in recent years: in 2020, the Technical Scientific Committee assisting the government was composed of 20 people, all men [13]. At a press conference at which a journalist pointed this out, the head of the Civil Protection Department candidly explained that this was not deliberate discrimination, but a matter of fact, because each of the participants was only there because he was already in charge of a specific sector. This made the mechanism even more evident: not only in that body, but in all those that belonged to it, management roles were held by men [14].

---

[11] Morra S. and Ronconi M., *Incantare le sirene*, cit., 196-219. The terms in inverted commas in this section refer to this section.

[12] Morra S. and Ronconi M., *Incantare le sirene*, cit., 207.

[13] https://www.repubblica.it/politica/2020/04/30/news/donne_task_force_catena_di_comando_covid19-255273362/.

[14] https://www.openpolis.it/gestione-covid19-poche-donne-e-non-nei-ruoli-chiave/.

Other factors, such as social and ethnic ones, interfere in this what can be referred to as the 'power map', but gender discrimination works its way through all the others, increasing the gap: this is why we prefer to speak today of an intersectional perspective [15] or, sometimes, in the theological sphere, of kyriarchy [16]. It is easy to refer to overseas contexts and to the protest called *Back Lives Matter*, but Italy too, despite the romantic self-image that often dwells in many Italians, is far from being exempt from ethnic discrimination and from widening social gaps, which can be seen as multiple gaps in terms of income, housing, health, education, and access to digital tools.

In this complex horizon, to be fruitful, reflection is called upon to move in multiple directions, overcoming/without/abandoning, if one may so express it according to a sort of Hegelian *aufhebung*, the simpler plan of *women studies*, becoming *gender studies* and integrating a critical reflection on masculinity. I say assuming without abandoning, because the risk, dreaded by many feminists, could be that of returning to a universal that ultimately conceals male preeminence once again. However, this is not an ineluctable fate, but a risk that can be avoided. The absence of such a path would, on the contrary, risk confining reflection to a separatism of little theoretical lucidity and even less practical relevance.

Italy, traditionally less equipped in this perspective, is gaining ground perhaps not too quickly, but with hermeneutic finesse. Particular credit is due to Stefano Ciccone [17] and the collective work of *Maschile plurale*, which points out that "men's studies are not the studies in which men talk about themselves – which is certainly nothing new – but those in which they do so 'from themselves'" [18]. A collective work, by female theologians, has recently joined the all-Catholic proclamation of a year dedicated to Saint Joseph to extend reflection to religious models, from theological to devotional [19], while a doctoral dissertation at the Waldensian Faculty has produced its own specific study that moves from the feminist practice of "starting from

---

[15] Crenshaw K., "Mapping the margins. Intersectionality, identity politics and violence against women of colour", *Stanford law review*, 43/6(1991), 1241-1299. Schüssler Fiorenza E. (ed.), *L'esegesi femminista del XX secolo*, Trapani, Il Pozzo di Giacobbe, 2016.

[16] Schüssler Fiorenza E., *Gesù, figlio di Miriam, profeta della Sofía. Questioni critiche di cristologia femministe*, Torino, Claudiana, 1996.

[17] Ciccone S., *Essere maschi: tra potere e libertà*, Roma, Rosenberg & Sellier, 2009.

[18] Vedovati C., "La riflessione maschile in Italia tra men's studies, genere e storia", available at https://www.maschileplurale.it/2007-i-mens-studies-in-italia/, 2007.

[19] Autiero A. and Perroni M. (eds.), *Maschilità in questione. Sguardi sulla figura di san Giuseppe*, Brescia, Queriniana, 2021.

oneself" and develops the reflection on the plural and relational aspect of masculinity already highlighted by the Australian sociologist Raewynn Connel[20] and by Rhiannon Graybill's hypothesis of the "unstable masculinity of the prophets"[21]. Thus expresses its author, Gabriele Bertin:

> "*The starting point for understanding the meaning of the masculine and its 'being in the world' starts precisely from recognising the paradox that the neutral discourse of the masculine, which has invaded and permeated the whole of society, has at the same time led to a silence on men themselves: they have become addicted to their own invisibility, made tangible only by the force of opposition born of the women's freedom movement, and have never had the chance to develop a language to speak about themselves with consciousness and partiality: "To stop being a phenomenon and pose as a subjectivity means to build the basis for a new confrontation and a new dimension of conflict: with the different positions of women, with other men, with other male paths of critical reflection, with political cultures". Recognising the partiality of male thinking is articulated in that path of history that has become the norm and that the style of patriarchy, as a system of expectations, customs and powers, has imposed over time, altering the perception of self*"[22].

As we have seen, therefore, cultural and political processes are closely intertwined and experience persistence – which tends to be justified on the basis of hypostatised boundaries, whether in the philosophical-scientific form of *nature* or the archaic form of sacredness – but also transitions and changes. What makes the difference in ecclesial dress, however, is that the sacral form identified in the previous paragraph, often attributed exclusively to pre-critical and pre-modern societies, is not only present in the Catholic Church, but is even enhanced there by the specific form that its hierarchical roles play and its dogmatic pronouncements exhibit. This can be observed by focusing precisely on the ordained roles, with male reserve and celibate majority. Not, however, without unstructured fault lines!

---

[20] http://www.raewynconnell.net/p/masculinities_20.html. Italian translation of her study: *Maschilità: Identità e trasformazioni del maschio occidentale*, Milano, Feltrinelli, 1996.

[21] "Elisha's Body and the Queer Touch of Prophecy", *Biblical Theology Bulletin*, 49, 1, 2019, 32-40.

[22] Bertin G., *Mosè: mito di un uomo racconto di un maschio Provare a rileggere la maschilità del profeta per eccellenza,* Torino, Claudiana, 2021, 12: the quote is from Vedovati C., "La riflessione maschile in Italia tra men's studies, genere e storia", cit.

3. Order and disorder: the ministries debate

If we compare in diachronic terms the socio-political and ecclesial indicators, especially those relating to the apex positions, we can see that in the Protestant Churches, of different denominations, the trend has followed the general trend of society, whereas in the Catholic and Orthodox Churches this has not been the case, at least as far as the ordained spheres are concerned. Before going into the specifics of the issue, however, I will explain where the binomial order/disorder that is the subject of this paragraph comes from. I exemplify this by referring to an interesting text prepared by the women of the *Synod Network* and presented to the Secretariat of the Synod of the Catholic Church. In it, also accepting a plurality of opinions that it is necessary to keep open, it speaks of calling for the diaconal and priestly ordination of women, but not without demanding a *de-clericalisation* of the entire community and also of male ordained roles. What is desired, therefore, is a dis/order, in the sense of welcoming the common lay trait, of leaving behind hypothetical practices that are no longer sustainable. Order for women, therefore, and at the same time dis/order of leading roles, for all and everyone. There will be a way to return to this, after presenting the state of the Catholic debate on the subject, briefly compared with the situation of the other Churches.

3.1. Reformation Churches: women of the Word

It must be acknowledged that not even the secular and modern structure of the Churches born of the Reformation in the 16th century sheltered them completely from gender asymmetry, because pastoral roles were long performed by men. However, the presence of women in the workplace and the suffragist demand for the vote brought an increasing awareness of women, who began to demand a critical interpretation of the Scriptures, an essential element of the process we are about to describe. One cannot fail to mention at least the meeting organised in 1848 by some women (*Seneca Falls Convention*) and their *Declaration of Rights and Sentiments.* The most famous name is that of Elizabeth Cady Stanton who, on that occasion, coordinated a collective Bible work (26 contributors) finished many years later under the title *The Woman's Bible*[23].

---

[23] However, one should also remember the similar endeavours of the Methodist F. Willard (1839-1898) and the Catholic Elisa Salerno who was equally active for women's rights, especially in the workplace, and author of *Commenti critici alle note bibliche antifemministe* (1926), Centro Documentazione e Studi Presenza Donna (ed.), San Pietro In Cariano (VR), Gabrielli, 2020.

In fact, the first pastors belong to the North American world and the Congregationalist churches, in which each community makes legitimate choices, without the need for approval by a central body. This is how Serena Noceti picks up the story:

> "*On 15 September 1853, Luther Lee, a Wesleyan Methodist pastor who was very committed to the cause of women, ordained Antoinette Brown as pastor. Brown was then 28 years old; she was a staunch supporter of the anti-slavery campaign and was involved in movements for the recognition of women's rights. Having felt the call to preach the gospel, in the late 1840s she began attending advanced theological courses at Oberlin College, a university institution that allowed equal access to men and women. [...] In reality, after her, for many decades there would be very few women ordained as pastors (always in Congregationalist churches): in 1889 there were 4, in 1899 there were 49, in 1920 109, an extremely limited number compared to the approximately 5,600 pastors registered in the* Unitarian Churches *in the same year*" [24].

Europe followed at a distance: in the Reformed Church the first consecration was celebrated in Zurich in 1918, but until 1963 there was no full recognition of the role. In Italy, the churches of the Protestant area opened up to the female pastorate with increasing determination from the 1960s onwards: in 1962 the Waldensian Synod decided to recognise women's participation in the pastorate and in 1967 Carmen Trobia and Gianna Scicolone were consecrated pastors. The Assembly of the Italian Baptist Church (UCEBI) decided in the same direction in 1982.

A path that therefore required time and discernment processes, but which today already allows us to take stock. A collective book in the Italian area – *Donne di Parola. Pastore, diacone e predicatrici nel Protestantesimo italiano* – takes stock of the female pastorate in our country, starting from its historical roots – already pointed out in Noceti's contribution just cited and to which we refer for a detailed analysis of the theological models involved – reviewing the media echoes (wittily traced by Di Carlo), and the hermeneutical and theological framework (Green, Maggi, Tomassone). The volume also includes articles by Catholic women authors, showing how different affiliations, realisations and opinions can give rise to a collective subject of women's theology, strong, mobile and differentiated: one of those faults that allow positive transitions, mentioned above.

---

[24] Noceti S., *Donne pastore. Storie, teologie, confronti ecumenici* in Tomassone L (ed.), *Donne di Parola. Pastore, diacone e predicatrici nel Protestantesimo italiano,* [Teologhe e Teologie 5], Firenze, Nerbini, 2020, 47.

In fact, Tomassone, introducing the volume, places its genesis in an external and an internal question. The first 'starts from the journey of friends, sisters, colleagues, of the other Churches. In particular, the journey of Catholic women theologians questions the meaning and richness of our experience, the fragilities experienced and the obstacles encountered [...] The external question also comes from secularised society and looks at the visibility of women pastors and women appointed in the government of the Church: *moderator, president, bishop*. The woman who expresses her authority from the top of a pulpit or a pew creates curiosity and questions about the role of women in religions'.

The internal question, Tomassone continues, is 'more complex': 'as women pastors or deacons we ask ourselves whether and how changes have taken place in the Churches as a result of our presence [...] Have forty years and more of women's ministries in the Protestant Churches changed the heart of the Churches?'[25].

3.2. The double game of tradition: comparing the old Catholic and Roman Catholic churches

One aspect that begs to be picked up before the state of the matter in the strictly Catholic sphere is that which concerns the idea of Tradition. Its historical and theological treatment would risk overloading the pages and blurring its development. I will limit myself to a consideration and then to a comparison between two experiences. The consideration already introduces us to the next point and concerns the reiterated Catholic claim to move so much within the Apostolic experience alone that it cannot change its forms. Obviously it is easy to see how in this horizon the questions of boundaries return, in the sense that it is all too evident that on many things instead we have moved in the direction of development, eliminating the practices of prophetesses and deaconesses and introducing, to name but a few macro issues, a territorial State, an obligation to celibacy for the clergy or the thesis of the Infallibility of the Roman Pontiff, albeit with many limitations (understandable only to insiders, moreover, in the face of a term that in the current language has an all too clear meaning).

It is precisely on this last aspect, linked to that Vatican I of which we have already spoken, that we can educate the comparison I mentioned: in the rejection of the infallibilist thesis, canonists and historians were especially active, considering it a pernicious innovation contrary to tradition. All

[25] I have excerpted from the *Introduction* (full contribution: 5-14]. In the volume also contributions by Cavallari, Pons, E. Tomassone, Sfredda, Galapon, Trotta.

of this had certain junctures specifically related to the question of women and especially the roles they can/must play in the Church: those who have most written about the possibility of the development of tradition, up to and including conspicuous changes in ecclesiastical discipline (compulsory celibacy for the clergy, unknown in the first centuries) and doctrine, up to and including the definition of Papal Infallibility – i.e. the Roman Catholic Church – wields Tradition to deny the development of ministerial discipline and thus reject the ordination of women, even diaconal (already present in the early Church, however). The Evangelical Churches, as we have seen, have taken a very different path, just as the Old-Catholic Church has taken a different path: not without scrutinising the signs of the times and the Scriptures, also rethinking the relationship between individual ministerial roles and the community (synodal) dimension of the entire church. Angela Berlis, a deacon since 1988 and presbyter since 1996, traces the stages of this journey[26].

Unfortunately, the issue is in such a critical area that it appears where one could least imagine, as in the short-circuit – hopefully now resolved, at least with a formal apology – that was produced in a speech by Pope Francis who, on the basis of his rejection of a Council, compared the Vetero-Catholics to the Traditionalists and saw proof of the alleged heresy of the former precisely in the fact that they ordain women[27].

3.3. Catholic Church: state of the art. Diaconate between history and contemporary debate

Already during the Second Vatican Council, Paul VI removed the question of women's ordination from the debate, claiming it to himself (along with that on the compulsory celibacy of the Latin clergy and on contraception, let it be said in passing, not exactly incidental). Silencing the

[26] Berlis A., *La rinascita del diaconato femminile. La via delle chiese vetero-cattoliche dell'Unione di Utrecht*, in Noceti S. (ed.), *Diacone. Quale ministero per quale Chiesa?*, Brescia, Queriniana, 2017, 269-288. and the recent interview on the occasion of his twenty-fifth priestly ordination: https://www.herder.de/cig/cig-ausgaben/archiv/2021/21-2021/ich-war-oft-die-erste-frau. See also Berlis A., "Katholisch ohne Rom", *Katholisches Bistum der Alt-Katholiken in Deutschland*, https://www.alt-katholisch.de/katholisch-ohnerom-vortrag-von-angela-berlis/ [27.10.21]; and Tosatti T, "La donna nella Chiesa Cristiana vetero-cattolica", *Adista Documenti*, 39, 2020. The Italian Old Catholic Mission corresponds to the Italian Old Catholic Church – Italian Catholic Christian Mission.

[27] https://www.chiesacristianaveterocattolica.org/images/comunicati/Dichiarazioni_Papa_Francesco_sui_vetero_cattolici.doc.

conciliar debate was easy, but it was certainly unthinkable to do the same outside of it. As the number of requests and the proliferation of interventions, of various contexts and tenor, increased, it was not long before two very harsh documents arrived, which focused on the affirmation of the impossibility of priestly ordination (frequently named, with an exhumed pre-conciliar lexicon, *sacerdotal*) for women: *Inter Insignores* of 1976 by the Congregation for the Doctrine of the Faith, which was followed in 1996 by John Paul II's *Ordinatio sacerdotalis.* The modality became more and more impositional, while the argumentative basis became less and less[28]. As Grillo-Horak significantly argue in *Le istituzioni ecclesiali alla prova del genere* the "non possumus" can be understood in the sense of "it does not depend on us", so the question can be considered far from closed[29]. Beyond this, in any case, the exclusion from the presbyteral role, and also the prohibition of public debate, had a flywheel effect on the question of diaconal ordination, for which an argument of tradition could certainly not be made, given that, beyond Phoebe in Corinth and other New Testament passages with over-extended masculinity, there are well-documented rites of deacon ordination with the laying on of hands and epiclesis, elements of the rite considered fundamental by Catholic liturgical-sacramental doctrine. In this temperament in 2016, the Major Superiors of women's religious congregations met, as is their practice, with the Pope, who had been Francis for three years, asking some questions, visible to all on the Vatican website.

The set of questions was wide-ranging and covered different aspects, including the use of money in the church and the relationship between prayer and action for justice, but the second of them was specifically about the diaconate for women:

> "*Consecrated women already do so much work with the poor and marginalised, they teach catechesis, accompany the sick and dying, distribute communion, in many countries lead communal prayers in the absence of priests and in those circumstances deliver the homily. In the Church there is the office of the permanent diaconate, but it is only open to men, married or not. What prevents the Church from including women among the permanent deacons, just as it did in the early Church? Why not set up an official*

[28] In the transition from the former to the latter, there is a narrowing of the argumentative basis (biblical arguments are reduced and those relating to the necessarily masculine symbolic representation of Christ are omitted, while denial focuses on "the eternal divine design" and "unbroken tradition") but a raising of the level of cogency of the claim is produced.

[29] Grillo A. and Horak D., *Le istituzioni ecclesiali alla prova del genere. Liturgia, sacramenti e diritto*, Cinisello Balsamo, San Paolo, 2019, 160-168.

commission to study the matter? Can you give us some examples of where you see the possibility of a better inclusion of women and consecrated women in the life of the Church" [30]?

The question is straightforward and disarming: it starts from the observation of what women already do, from practices of solidarity and closeness to people in situations of fragility and poverty, to pastoral and liturgical service, including leading the assembly with the homily. Finally, the conclusion is ingenious, because it asks not on what basis women could be included in the diaconal role, but more wittily 'what it prevents'. And she calls for the establishment of a commission.

Francis' response is affable and encouraging, first of all with respect to the possible changes to the Code: despite the fact that it is often brandished like a barbed wire fence, it is enough to know just a little about its historical events, both remote and recent, to realise that it is a living instrument, with a non-trivial evolution and with some revolutions, such as that of 1983 that conformed the legislative instrument to the perspective of Vatican II. Moreover, following a *Motu proprio* by Benedict XVI [31] some canons relating to the ordained ministry have changed, in the sense of a more articulate distinction between the different degrees of the sacrament of order, with particular reference to the diaconate. In fact, it is specified that deacons, unlike bishops and presbyters, do not act 'in the person of Christ the Head' but 'are empowered to serve the people of God in the diaconia of the liturgy, of the word and of charity' (canon 1009, § 3). Most recently, then, the elimination by another *Motu Proprio* of the term *viri* from can 230, § 1, which made it possible to institute female readers and acolytes, roles that women used to perform by proclaiming the Scriptures, doing catechesis and distributing the Eucharist in an 'extraordinary' way, but not in a recognised and recognisable form, i.e. 'instituted'.

The Commission on the diaconate – certainly not the first one, by the way – was convened, worked for a while and then delivered a brief document, still unpublished, to Francis in which, it is reported, reasons for and against are briefly stated, but it is affirmed that it cannot be a commission to decide. Suspended, therefore, without the document being made public,

---

[30] https://www.vatican.va/content/francesco/en/speeches/2016/may/documents/papa-francesco_20160512_uisg.html.

[31] The *Motu proprio in* question is *Omnium in mentem* of 26 October 2009: https://www.vatican.va/content/benedict-xvi/en/apost_letters/documents/hf_ben-xvi_apl_20091026_codex-iuris-canonici.html.

another one was set up, of which only the composition is known at the moment[32], completely renewed.

4. Voices that become choir: synod multiplied

Also driven by specific initiatives, such as the Synodal *Way of the German Catholic Church* and the *Amazon Synod*, the entire Catholic Church has been convened in synod, with the main and declared purpose of reflecting on ecclesial processes, on the ways in which decisions are made, and on their transparency. It is in fact a synod on synodality, on the wave of the expression of Chrysostom repeatedly relaunched also by Pope Francis, *Church and synod are synonyms*[33] resourceful issue for the transformation of the synod "from an event" to a "process", set by the apostolic exhortation *Episcopalis communio*[34]. Our theme is present here in chiastic form: from the point of view of the theme of leadership roles, which is advanced everywhere but partly silenced as it would not be on the agenda, and from the point of view of the subjects involved as locutors. Thus, at every step, it emerges, arousing hope in some and stiffening in others: it would suffice to point out the reform of Book VI of the Code, signed by Francis on 8 December 2021, which has included among the *delicta graviora* alongside child abuse also the act of attempting the ordination of women, without specifying the degree (i.e. diaconate, presbyterate, episcopate)[35].

Desire for reform and fear of certain aspects of it intersect and redraw provisional boundaries, which are even more significant when observed from the other point of view, that of the subjects involved, as the *Vademecum* that accompanies the synod process well illustrates. In a framework such as the one outlined, if no subject is excluded in preference to methodological ones, so is no interlocutor excluded in principle. Obviously these are the chances: the execution then depends on so many variables and so

---

[32] https://press.vatican.va/content/salastampa/it/bollettino/pubblico/2020/04/08/0210/00474.html.

[33] On the patristic dimension of this and other recurring expressions, I refer to Simonelli C., "Memoriale del futuro. Il ricorso alle fonti come principio dinamico", in Coda P. and R. Repole (eds.), *La sinodalità nella vita e nella missione della Chiesa. Multi-voice commentary on the Document of the International Theological Commission,* Bologna, EDB, 2019, 29-37.

[34] https://www.vatican.va/content/francesco/it/apost_constitutions/documents/papa-francesco_costituzione-ap_20180915_episcopalis-communio.html.

[35] https://www.vatican.va/content/francesco/en/apost_constitutions/documents/papa-francesco_costituzione-ap_20210523_pascite-gregem-dei.html.

many differences, even if the possibility of sending summaries and materials also through computer channels, as happened in the last synods of bishops, does indeed make a difference; indeed, as some of the initiatives of the Italian Synod Network[36] show, it is often the "unexpected" subjects[37] who are the most eager to enter into the dynamics of dialogue and to get active for it.

There is also a novelty, not absolute, but extensive compared to previous editions, and it is the presence of Sister Nathalie Becquart, as Under-Secretary of the Synod with voting rights[38], as well as four women among the eighteen *Consultors* (Alessandra Smerilli, M. Luisa Berzosa Gonzales, Cecilia Costa and Myriam Wijlens)[39]. Both elements – the breadth of the listening process and the non-homogeneity of the Secretariat and the *Consultatories* – are a novelty, the extent of which will have to be assessed over time, to see whether they are minor changes or the beginning of a real process of change. Undoubtedly, however, the inclusion of these women in the apex structures of the Synod of the Catholic Church performs a revelatory function. Their mere presence, in fact, even before the interesting things they are already saying and will continue to say and do, makes clear and acutely denounces the scandal of previous homogeneity.

5. Alliances: disambiguate

After this long *excursus* on ministries and the synod, to return to the subject of sacred borders also brings with it the theme of alliances, not without an all too easy reference to the movement of connection between throne and altar in the so-called Restoration after Napoleon's defeat in 1815, which bears the very name of the *Holy Alliance*: in that case the collaboration was political, cultural and religious, and even in name sanctioned an anti-modern and conservative bond in which Churches and States bound and

---

[36] https://www.viandanti.org/website/wp-content/uploads/2021/02/2.Lettera-aperta-ai-Vescovi-13.10.2021_DEF.pdf; the Cati worked in the period 2019-2021 on the topic of the Reformation, focusing on synodality: http://www.teologiacati.it/wordpress/?p=384.

[37] See the significant process of a French intervention, which started with the abuses and extended to FT and the synod: Légrand H. and Camdessus M., *Una Chiesa trasformata in popolo,* Milano, Paoline, 2021; and also https://www.gionata.org/papa-francesco-ringrazia-suor-jeannine-per-il-suoi-anni-di-ministero-con-le-persone-lgbt/.

[38] http://secretariat.synod.va/content/synod/it/attualita/interviste-a-suor-nathalie-becquart.html.

[39] http://secretariat.synod.va/content/synod/it/la-segreteria-del-sinodo-dei-vescovi/elenco-dei-consultori-della-segreteria-generale-del-sinodo-dei-v.html.

strengthened each other. On many occasions this horizon, albeit in a similar, certainly not identical manner, has reappeared: I am thinking of the connections between conservative, racist and homophobic policies that supported the no-gender campaign, lucidly highlighted, among others, by Massimo Prearo's research on the *Neo-Catholic Hypothesis*[40]. On the other hand, if Roman Catholicism as a whole owes to Francis' affable and tending mode of shifting reform from the institutional to the inner level, it is also easy to see how in some more conservative contexts even acquisitions that seemed to be already underway are being put into shape: I am thinking, for example, of the meeting in Cuba, precisely with that Patriarch of Moscow Kirill who never ceases to accuse the West of excessive 'openness' towards homosexuality, but also of the very un-women-friendly manner used in the dialogue with the Imam of Al kazar. Or to the fact that scandalously the Vatican, as a state, has not signed the Istanbul Convention against gender violence, despite having been repeatedly asked to do so.

In the modalities just exemplified, the alliance confirms in a sacred sense, and thus tightens gender boundaries, in all the possible extension of the concept. However, other forms of covenant are in place that also concern the Catholic Church in its real form as an inclusive community, albeit imperfectly so. One can point thus to the profound relationship between professions of faith and lay *confidants*, the collaborations for the protection of the ecosystem and peace in the interconnectedness of life, the increasingly broad and stable discourse around the queer reality, in the awareness that every life is a sacred story. In this sense I would like to point out a book recently translated into Italian, through an excerpt from the preface:

> "*The few words that we spend again are meant to be a collected and at the same time open space from which to approach the voices of these twenty-three women, without overpowering them. Their narratives are strong but also tenuous, they make present among us people who have suffered so much, yet have also spoken out, have raised a voice that could still be ignored or censored. As before the bush that sends flashes of fire into the wilderness (Ex 3:2-5), to gather that revelation we must remove our shoes and bend our knees: we place our feet on holy ground. They flow before us first of all lives and proper names – sometimes still protected by pseudonyms, so strong are still the negative judgements and insults*"[41]

---

[40] Prearo M., *L'ipotesi Neo-cattolica. Politologia dei movimenti anti-gender*, Milano-Udine, Mimesis, 2020.

[41] Simonelli C., "Preface" to the Italian edition of *Love Tenderly*, Grace Surdoveled, in Simonelli C. and Scarmoncin L. (eds.), *Nella Giustizia e nella tenerezza. Storie sacre di religiose lesbiche e queer*, Cantalupa (TO), Effatà, 2022, 6.

The holiness that characterizes this permanently provisional and inclusive community is deep, dynamic, porous and welcoming.

6. A conclusion: the house and the fortress

Therefore, resuming the path taken, it seems to me that I can pick it up again through the idea of boundaries, more mobile, however, than what their official representation and the related rhetoric of consensus would have us think: shifted continuously by alliances, by breaches, by unstructured and often unexpected internal spaces. In support of this hypothesis, I like to cite a figure who certainly does not occupy a dissident space in the Catholic imagination: Chiara Lubich. In a 1989 testimony, she recalls an experience she had sixty years earlier, when little more than an adolescent, she went on a pilgrimage to the Marian Sanctuary of Loreto:

> "*It was 1939 and I had travelled to Loreto for a conference of Catholic schoolgirls. It was my first long trip. I still did not know what the Lord would want of me and I did not worry about it. The first time I entered the little house in Loreto, guarded by the fortress-church, I was seized with great emotion*" [42].

Certainly at a distance of many years Lubich re-reads what would become the Focolare. However, the evocative power of that memory is great, and in a certain sense its anticipatory force: the experience of churches as houses, as roads, as "field hospitals", scattered and capable of making themselves welcome space contrasts with that of a "church-fortress". The latter, described in that text I think without bitterness, but with great realism, is crumbling with the rubble of a system. The hypothesis, I might even dare to believe, is that there is a persistence of the little house network just as the fortress system is collapsing: put in biblical terms, a little bit bold and a little bit visionary, one might believe that the promise of a life "that hell is not" is addressed precisely to that little house encroaching on the road.

---

[42] Lubich L., "Testimonianza del 18 Maggio 1989", in Del Nero E., *Cose antiche e cose nuove. Il profilo laicale in Chiara Lubich alla soglia del Concilio Vaticano II*, Roma, Città Nuova, 2021, 150.

References

Berlis A. (2017), "'In My Modest Cell I am not a Rebel': Lady Charlote Blennerhasset (1843-1917) and Her Desire or Spiritual Renewal Following the First Vatican Council", *Religion &Teology*, 24, 3, 1-31.

Berlis A. (2017b), "La rinascita del diaconato femminile. La via delle chiese vetero-cattoliche dell'Unione di Utrecht", in Noceti S. (ed.), *Diacone. Quale ministero per quale Chiesa?,* Brescia, Queriniana, 269-288.

Bertin G. (2021), *Mosè: mito di un uomo racconto di un maschio Provare a rileggere la maschilità del profeta per eccellenza,* Torino, Claudiana.

Boys M. (2017), "Learning in the Presence of the Other", in Trible P. and Lipsett D. (eds.), *Fede e femminismo,* Roma, Aracne, 171-172.

Canobbio G. (2023), *Un nuovo volto della Chiesa? Teologia del Sinodo*, Brescia, Morcelliana.

Carrega G. (2022), *Prefazione*, in Enns P., *Come funziona davvero la Bibbia*, Cantalupa (TO), Effatà, 7-8.

Carrega G. (2022b), *The wool mixture and other abominations of Leviticus,* https://www.gionata.org/don-carrega-e-lomosessualita-e-altri-delitti-del-levitico/.

Ciccone S. (2009), *Essere maschi: tra potere e libertà*, Roma, Rosenberg & Sellier.

Ciccone S. (2019), *Maschi in crisi? Oltre la frustrazione e il rancore*, Torino, Rosenberg &Sellier.

Crenshaw K. (1991), "Mapping the margins. Intersectionality, identity politics and violence against women of colour", *Stanford law review*, 43/6, 1241-1299.

Del Nero E. (2021), *Cose antiche e cose nuove. Il profilo laicale in Chiara Lubich alla soglia del Concilio Vaticano II*, Roma, Città Nuova.

Douglas M. (1970), *Purity and Danger. An analysis of the concepts of pollution and taboo,* London, Routledge & Kegan Paul.

Douglas M. (1999), *Leviticus as Literature*, London, Oxford University Press.

Green E. and Simonelli C. (2019), *Incontri. Memorie e prospettive della teologia femminista*, Cinisello Balsamo, San Paolo.

Green E. (2023), *Dio, il vuoto, il genere*, Torino, Claudiana.

Grillo A. and Horak D. (2019), *Le istituzioni ecclesiali alla prova del genere. Liturgia, sacramenti e diritto*, Cinisello Balsamo, San Paolo.

Légrand H. and Camdessus M. (2021), *Una Chiesa trasformata in popolo,* Milano, Paoline.

Morra S. and Ronconi M. (2019), *Incantare le sirene. Chiesa, teologia e cultura in scena*, Bologna, EDB.

Noceti S. (2020), *Donne pastore. Storie, teologie, confronti ecumenici* in Tomassone L. (ed.), *Donne di Parola. Pastore, diacone e predicatrici nel Protestantesimo italiano* [Teologhe e Teologie 5], Firenze, Nerbini, 18-30.

Noceti S. (2017), *Diacone. Quale ministero per quale Chiesa?,* Brescia, Queriniana.

Perroni M. (ed.) (2023), *Leadership religiose: la parola alle donne. Sette testimonianze*, Roma, Carocci.

Prearo M. (2020), *L'ipotesi Neo-cattolica. Politologia dei movimenti anti-gender*, Milano-Udine, Mimesis.

Schüssler Fiorenza E. (ed.) (2016), *L'esegesi femminista del XX secolo*, Trapani, Il Pozzo di Giacobbe.

Schüssler Fiorenza E. (1996), *Gesù, figlio di Miriam, profeta della Sofía. Questioni critiche di cristologia femministe*, Torino, Claudiana.

Simonelli C. (2016), *Dio patrie famiglie. Le traiettorie plurali dell'amore*, Milano, Piemme.

Simonelli C. (2019), "Memoriale del futuro. Il ricorso alle fonti come principio dinamico", in Coda P. and R. Repole (eds.), *La sinodalità nella vita e nella missione della Chiesa. Multi-voice commentary on the Document of the International Theological Commission,* Bologna, EDB, 29-37.

Simonelli C. (2021), *Per la testimonianza del Vangelo. L'opposizione al Vaticano I come fedeltà alla tradizione,* in Valerio A. (ed.), *L'Anticoncilio del 1869, L'Anticoncilio del 1869. Donne contro il Vaticano I,* Roma, Carocci, 83-107.

Simonelli C. and Scarmoncin L. (eds.) (2020), *Nella Giustizia e nella tenerezza. Storie sacre di religiose lesbiche e queer*, Cantalupa (TO), Effatà, 2022 [Italian edition of Surdovel G (ed.) *Love Tenderly. Sacred Stories of Lesbian and Queer Religious*, Mount Rainier, New Ways Ministry.

Tintori C. (ed.) (2022), *Adesso tocca a noi. Donne, leadership e altri misfatti, Milano*, Edizioni terra Santa.

Tomassone L. (ed.) (2020), *Donne di Parola. Pastore, diacone e predicatrici nel Protestantesimo italiano,* [Teologhe e Teologie 5], Firenze, Nerbini.

Valerio A. (2016), *Donne e Chiesa. Una storia di genere*, Roma, Carocci.

Valerio A. (2016b), *Il potere delle donne nella Chiesa. Giuditta, Chiara e le altre*, Roma-Bari, Laterza.

Valerio A. (ed.) (2021), *L'Anticoncilio del 1869. Donne contro il Vaticano I,* Roma, Carocci.

Chapter 6

COMMITMENT TO GENDER EQUALITY AND HUMAN RIGHTS – AN IDEALISTIC PASSION?

Diana Çuli

ABSTRACT: *In the last thirty years of Albania's transition from a closed political system with a centralised state economy to a democratic system and a market economy, the position of women has changed significantly in many ways, and has been accompanied by a number of issues that may also be relevant to gender studies in order to understand more clearly how the overthrow of political and social systems affects women's lives in a substantial way.*
Women, as well as Albanian society itself, were suddenly faced with problems of political decision-making and unemployment. Religions also play a central role after the communist regime. This has had an impact on women's freedom of choice and on society as a whole.
The creation of a women's movement in Albania is crucial for their rights and for legislative achievements. Nevertheless, obstacles remain. Current and future priorities must be to improve the status of women, to strengthen women's leadership and equal opportunities in all areas, to combat violence and media stereotypes.

Yes, I think that commitment to gender equality and human rights as well as for equal access to opportunities and justice may seem an idealistic passion and a long-life dream. I think also that it is a process, maybe not revolutionary, but surely evolutionary.

In the last thirty years of Albania's "transition period", which passed from a closed political system, with a centralized state economy to a democratic system and a market economy, the position of women changed significantly in many ways and was accompanied by a number of issues, which may also be valid for gender studies, to understand more clearly how the overthrow of political and social systems affects the lives of women in a substantial way.

To better understand what happened during these three decades after the above-mentioned changes and how is the situation today it is necessary a short view in our history and especially in the period of communist regime.

The second half of the last century has seen two ways of emancipation for women in the world. These two different ways met each other in beginning of 1990's and exchanged their experiences: the occidental way and the one of the ex-East countries, which has been under a communist regime.

With the arrival in Albania of various groups of women from many western countries and non-governmental organizations, mainly from Italy and France, which dealt with gender and human rights, also with the problems of building a civil society and helping in the process of restoring first elements of democracy in our country, we noticed that the main and it is OKItessential differences between the women emancipation's way in the ex-socialist countries and that of the occidental ones consisted in some fundamental actions: the socialist states (Albania, URSS, Bulgaria, Romania, etc.), since the first days of their established power declared, by Constitution, many important rights equal to men and women: the right of vote, of work, the right of education, equal salaries, etc. Surely, all this existed in the total lack of freedom of speech and real human rights. While the women in the western countries have won their rights through their struggles, not as gifts by the government. So, in the beginning of the 90's the two groups met and began to learn the history of each other. The women in Albania haven't had the possibility to fight for themselves, consequently, the long and rich experience of the struggles for equality of women from Europe and US was a great support and a great lesson.

1. A short history

The Albanians, as all the ancient peoples of the Balkans, being one of the peoples living near the Hellenes, with their fascinating mythology, have, as all the inhabitants of the peninsula, very similar believing. Some time it is difficult to understand and to discover the real origins of multiple branches of these mythologies. The fatalism, for example, the malediction that lasts till the seventh generation! The tragedy of Agamemnon or of Clytemnestra seems to have yet its roots in the Epirot and Illyrian land. The sacrifice of Iphigenia has its echo at the revenge and the cruel rules towards women expressed by the Albanians in their most hard model, the Kanun (the laws of a part of Albania inherited in centuries). Even today, we may listen some old women saying in a fatalistic way that the life is directed by Destiny, that the revenge, the war, the death, the woman's bad fate is written by Destiny once and for ever. Fortunately, this is not any more a general thinking. But historically the Albanian women thought that they were cursed, because they were not born males, but females. As women, they had not the right to judge their destiny, that, in the case of women, was not directed by God. Their life was directed by the chance, as the Ariadne's yarn untangled once and for ever and no one could do anything against it.

Historically, in the Albanian society the sacrifice has been always a concept related mostly to the women. In the Illyrian-Albanian mythology the mothers sacrifice their life for the children the sisters help and support their brave brothers that go to the war and this narrative continued for centuries. According to the Kanun, for example, if in a family there are no more males (being killed or dead, or simply not being born) one of the sisters, or the only sister was obliged to deny her female life, to be dressed as a man and to behave like a man in order to take part in the masculine life of the village till the end.

Till the 1930's the roles of women in the Albanian theatre were played by men. No woman has ever been in a state position. No woman has ever participated in the men-gatherings in the rural zones, that had the authority to decide the main issues of the communities. The women rarely were honoured, and they were *brave* only in cases when they were united with men, with arms in hand, against the occupations. Till 1938, many researchers or travellers were astonished and shocked to see that, in some regions, the graves of the women were dig deeper than those of the men, because their sins were bigger!

2. Religion

We often ask: why this turning back deep in history? To understand ourselves, to understand the others and to find, maybe, what does it mean to be a Christian Albanian or a Muslim Albanian, a Balkan inhabitant, Christian or Muslim one? In this context what is the role of the women, during our long history of wars and during the period of anti-religion regime? In this long history of lances, shields, infinite wars, assassins, the woman manifests herself like a meteor only in the clear sky of popular poetry, where she is honoured, adored, described as a marvellous human being. Only there, maybe the rude men expressed their secret dreams! Or, in the dream of the poets, that are another race. Otherwise, it would be very difficult to explain the strong discriminative behaviour that they have demonstrated towards women in the centuries. In the Northern regions of Albania, the Kanun dominated over Muslims and Christians. Its versions ruled also in the Southern regions. Its origins have the roots deep in history, but it was reinforced during the ottoman occupation, acting as a non-official internal

Constitution of the Albanians under ottomans, through which they regulated the relations between themselves, against the Osman rules. This non-official law, that exercised it power during many centuries was hardly condemned under the communist regime, which did not permit other laws and banned it by law. In the 90's when this state did not exist anymore, in different places the Kanun and some of its forgotten rules reappeared again, after many decades. Mainly, the rules related to *vendetta* and to the position and status of women, which were extremely oppressive, discriminatory, and violent. At those moments the democratic state was weak, without experience and with a series of social and economic problems to solve.

The Kanun considers the woman as an instrument of work, only to give birth to children, a servant of the husband, family and house. According to its articles, she has not any right, not of the property, heritage, no right to express her opinions. Nothing.

The Muslims in the central Albania and those crossed with the orthodox people of the South present another situation. The Muslims tried to apply the Sharia in some cities, where the women covered their faces when they went out (Elbasan, Tirana, Kavaja, etc.) In the villages the women had to work on the fields and, for that very practice and important reason, the men's rules were not so rigid. The orthodox population was not very different in its attitude towards women. They also had to work hard in the fields and in the housekeeping and have also been in the same way as oppressed as the Muslim women. Shortly, women under the three main religions of Albania, Islam and Bektashi, Catholic and Orthodox, in centuries, suffered the same lack of rights and had no social or political position in the society.

There is an opinion that tries to explain the dramatic and tragic events in Albania related to their violence towards women, for example, that the Albanians have not a strong faith, independently of the numerous churches and mosques that they construct now everywhere in the country. Maybe there is an objective truth in it. Naturally, the lack of a true consecration towards the Christianity or the Islam in Albania – the opposite of what was happening in neighbouring countries – and the lack of a religious spirit produced different effects related with the responsibilities in this world. Because of its history, especially because of the ottoman occupation, a long period of terror and of the sufferings for five centuries, the country was transformed in a tunnel without a light in the end of it. A big part of the population was obliged to emigrate in Greece and in Italy. All the country, its culture, its traditions were ravaged, impoverished. It was also an odd period, when people went to the mosques with Christian names, signed with half-Muslim and half-Christian names, turned back home and prayed another God, not the official one. As a result, because of these huge sacrifices, a nationalistic spirit began to show up, like a little ray of light in the obscurity of the Middle Age, when they declared a national slogan: *The religion of the Albanians is to be Albanian*. That calmed down the troubled conscience because of the undesired conversion to another religion and expressed the dream of an independent state. The continuous wars to save their territory and the different conversions in different religions never gave them the possibility to meditate and to reflect on the lessons of the religion, on its knowledge, its secrets, its mysticism. They have always lived with the alarming sensation of the new occupations and prayed God with arms in hands. So, during that terrible period, when the Albanians were impoverished, killed, massacred, alienated in their culture and their traditions, was born that main idea of being always an Albanian. This historic fact is clearer in our days, when the Albanians, independently of their religious origins, marry each other and frequent the saint places of each other without problem. The communist regime post Second World War found a fertile land to plant the atheism. It was a real preoccupation for the intellectuals who feared the lack of the spiritual life and understood quickly what it means to lose the respect for the individual human being. And they were right: the life of the Albanians, men and women together was more suppressed, more oppressed. Paradoxically, all this complicated religious situation and the period of imposed atheism had, as a consequence, lack of religious hate and struggles, but good and praiseworthy religious co-existence, one of the few nations that saved and protected the Hebrews during the Nazis occupations of Albania.

The post-communist period returned the freedom of religion and the situation during these 30 years has been quite different, even for women. The context is completely another one and the women's rights, status and position do not depend especially on their religious relevance, but on the state legislation and the culture of the modern Albanian society.

3. The socialist period

Turning back to the socialist system and to its attitude towards women, it is right to say that this period helps us to better understand the complexity of the strategy it elaborated, inside a demagogic narrative about liberation of human beings from the slavery and their total equality in everything.

The communist system in Albania assigned to women equal rights with men, but, at the same time it denied the rights of men and women in general. It obliged the women to work, as well as men – nobody could stay unemployed and everybody was nominated in a certain work by the state. Work created for women a possibility to have a social life, to be a subject in the Albanian society. This system attacked with all its ideological, juridical, cultural means and by severe sanctions the prejudices, the old patriarchal mentalities, and the cruel rules of Kanun related to women. We may say that the regime attacked in general all the discriminative sentiments towards women. For example, in a divorce, the tribunal supported *quasi* always the woman and punished hardly the man, if the "fault" for the divorce was his. In all the films, plays, spectacles of that time the women were presented always as the positive personages, while the men were the patriarchal, the violent, the bad guys. The regime insisted so much in this direction, that the women couldn't bear any more this 'perfect' representation of themselves. And not any men dared to be publicly against this official taboo subject of women.

The women profited of this space that constituted a new favoured situation in comparison with all the past systems in the history of Albania. In these new conditions the Albanian women were everywhere, in the education and health system, in the culture, also in politics. This is true. But, it is also true that the communist regime never did anything for the real *libération,* that liberation related to the social relations of the women with the others and inside the family, limiting in the level of the social life and not of the individual life. Individualism was something to be condemned in a regime like that. Things, thoughts, opinions, attitudes had to be collective. The communist state was very determined not to tolerate its citizens to be developed as individuals.

Women were engineers, doctors, journalists, sometime presidents of agricultural cooperatives, where they gave orders to the men! But in the moment they returned home, the doors were closed and they were alone, slaves of their husbands, doing the household as their grand-mothers did once upon a time. The equality had a high price: they had to work three times more than men to have the possibility to continue their carrier. The only women organization in Albania of that period, had not any link or relation with the European women movement or of other countries in the world. It defined and condemned the feminism as a struggle between sexes. It declared that the women emancipation and the equality between men and women was completely realized in a communist country as Albania and women had no need to fight for their rights, always "protected by the regime". The Albanian communist regime, not as the other ex-communist states, banned by law the abortion or the reproductive rights. This sanction was not based on the socialist ideas and Marxist theories that supposed it as a women's right, but on the demographic policy of the birth rate. According to this policy, Albanian state considered the abortion as an obstacle to the question of the raising of the population, that was an emergency to make face to the possible enemies (imperialist countries, as the regime justified its rules) who, as the communist propaganda declared, were preparing to occupy Albania. The contraceptives were also not permitted, and the policy of family planning did not exist. But, the Albanian women, as all the women in world history, realized clandestine abortions, under terrible conditions, because of poverty, lack of possibilities to raise many children, because of other difficult situations, etc., putting in danger their life.

There was no communication between couples, families or young people about the sexual issues; the social control supported this style and concept of life. The young people married each other without preparation about sexual life and they experienced a lot of perpetual contradictions. This is our destiny, said sadly the young women, disappointed of their life. Think of your children, said to them their mothers and grandmothers, it's your destiny, as it was ours. Always, even when the women worked as professors of the universities, as journalists or doctors, the general conception towards them was that their primary role was to be a mother and a wife. All the departments of the ministries related to the women position in society had nominations such as: "Mother and children", "Woman and the family", "The health care of mother and children"! Even in the 2000's, when the women associations were now in contact with a lot of women movements in the world and were able to convince the government to create an important commission on gender issues, it was nominated "The Commission of Woman and the Family"! Many other years passed till the moment when this discriminative phrase was cancelled and changed to "The Commission on gender equality".

One of the most known strategies of the ex-regime in Albania was its perseverance on a "clean and honest moral of the people", based on the patriarchal reminiscences of the society. This was a trick to enforce the power of the dictature that used every instrument – even from the most remote past. In the Albanian artistic films of that time does not exist a scene of kisses between two people in love, because it was against the good morality of Albanian society. The love scenes were realized only in the degenerated movies of the capitalist countries, said the regime propaganda!

During the socialist system we may say that women were part of the social life, but their freedom was false and contradictory. The Albanian society became accustomed to see women everywhere: in the ministries, in the municipalities, but very rarely they were in higher posts. In the education system where 80% of professors were women, rarely they were in the posts of the dean, the president, the director of the high schools. In the parliament, where women and men were almost in equal number, they all raised the hand to vote *yes* or *no* for the proposed laws, but it was also a false vote, because it was a commanded vote and not a free one.

The Albanian closed system of the real socialism tried to change the patriarchal heredity and to reduce the level of the masculine culture, but it acted unilaterally and without any contact with the outside world, stopping, in this way, the process of the natural development of the society. In the Politburo, the highest decision-making party instrument that stood above the government and parliament, where were decided the *real decisions* on policies and the economy of the country, the enthusiastic achievement of the equality of men and women did not exist. In 12 members there was elected always only one woman. In short, the declaration of Albanian communists that came in power with the strong promise that they would give total equality to all people, the same to men and to the women, was complicated and insidious. They declared that applied the Marxist theories on the gender equality, but they never wanted to go straight in its real essence. There, in the Politburo, they did not desire any more to have women to decide together with them on important questions of the society. There, the old rules, those that helped them to avoid the presence of women, were very necessary.

4. The progress of women movement and the situation of gender equality in Albania after the 1990 and today

In the beginning of the 90's apart the enthusiasm of the big political changes, which pushed the Albanians to go on and to reconstruct a very impoverished and exhausted country, we began to think what was going to happen with the situation of women, due to the fact that a new and completely different legislation was being prepared. At that time Albanian women learned a lot by the international groups of women movements: Italian, European and US, who supported them to follow this process and, on the other hand, to create in Albania a free women movement, new organizations, independent by the state, that became later very strong and influential in the Albanian society. At that time, in 1992, was founded the *Independent Forum for the Albanian Woman*, one of the first women NGO-s in the country, that had 15 branches in different regions and many members. Its activity still goes on, working as always on women empowerment, gender equality, leadership of women, following social and cultural processes.

During these decades, as in all countries where the difficulties for women are bigger, they organize themselves easier and quicker, even in societies dominated by poverty and discriminatory behaviours. This was verified in Albania too. Women demonstrated strong will and determination in many difficult moments, especially in the first decade after 90's. In 1997, when in Albania, because of wrong, unexperienced and corrupted policies exploded large insurrections and there existed even the danger of a civil war, when men attacked and opened the magazines of arms and began to shot in air, proud to possess two or three guns, women were organized to save what was possible to save. In that period of total absurdity, when the state, the police and the army did not exist anymore, the women associations did a non-stop activity against the arms, leading all the civil society. Of course, there were also many men that followed these groups and fought to establish the public order in the country. During that terrible year, women from all ages, social status, old ones, peasant ones, did everything to get away arms form the hands of their men.

Today, after 30 years, after a long way of struggles to obtain equality, against the violence towards women, after many efforts for a legislation in favour of gender equality in all fields we may say that Albanian women have achieved a great progress.

5. Work force

The number of women in workforce is increasing, very rapidly, especially in last years. It is surprisingly increasing in agriculture, where now women are not only most workers, but also owners of land, of the agritourist activities, agri-business, etc.

6. Violence

According to a study performed by the Swedish government, UNDP and UN Women, more than 50% of Albanian women have been victims of some form of "sexual, physical or psychological violence". As in many other countries, the situation created by COVID 19 has increased the number of reported cases of domestic violence on women. The women movement, international organizations in the country as UN, etc., mass media institutions, social media, protection shelters, etc., work hard on raising awareness. During the pandemic period the parliament voted other reinforcing laws related to the violence against women in general and especially on domestic violence.

7. Decision-making women participation

As a result of many effort of the women organizations, parliamentary groups of women, of the civil society in general and the self-consciousness of women in general, today many of them have successfully run for office

According to the Monitor Report on the representation of women in the parliamentary elections, April 2021 of AWEN – *Albanian Women Empowering Network*, in 2017, for the first time in the history of the democratic transition in Albania, women had 28% of parliamentary seats. This representation is a very important achievement of the women lobbies for the quota of 30% in the parliament and a very inspiring experience for the raising of the equal representation of women in all the decision-making policies. For the first time Albania had a vice-prime minister in the government. For the first time in the history of Albania now we have the highest number of women ministers: 9 women ministers in a government with 16 ministers (2021). The trend for women party-leaders is positive, as well as the number of women local councillors (35%), of women mayors (9 in 61), etc. In general, the initiatives by the Albanian Parliament are encouraging women to run for various political offices, according to the 2020 report of the *Center for Legal and Civic Initiatives* in Albania.

8. Turning back at the reproduction rights

Women organizations in 1996 proposed to the first Albanian parliament elected by free democratic vote, the law on Reproductive Rights, after consultations with local and international experts, especially with IPPF – International Planned Parenthood Federation. It was not an easy struggle. Living for decades in a dictatorial regime, which used also the patriarchal traditions to oppress the people, this proposal seemed not very pleasant to a parliament dominated by men – there were only three or four women in 140 men. But, in the end, the pressure of the society did it possible. Now, in a very different situation, according to the 2020 Report of the *Center for Legal and Civic Initiatives in Albania*, the Albanian law severely limits access to abortion. Coupled with restricted access to healthcare due to the COVID-19 10 outbreak, many women find it impossible to receive access to safe abortion care. Referring to the Amnesty International reports, governments in the region deem abortion care as an inessential health service. Leah Hoctor, the Regional Director for Europe's Center for Reproductive Rights, has called on many governments, including the Albanian government, to intervene. She states that "European governments must act urgently to guarantee safe and timely access to abortion care during the COVID-19 pandemic".

9. The women problems are so universal!

In some meetings with women in difficult situations in Albania it happens that they sob deeply and say: no woman in the world has such an impossible life...! And then begins a discussion related to the world women situation, to the sexist laws – not only the sexist cultural behaviours – that we may see everywhere. In Us where rapists can claim parental rights, in Russia where domestic violence isn't necessarily a crime, in Sudan where girls as young as 10 can get married, in Iran where wives need permission to travel abroad, in Belarus where women can't become truck drivers, in Saudi Arabia where women aren't allowed to drive, in India where husbands can rape their wives, with no consequences... and more and more!

Things are never perfect and sometimes we feel turning back in the past. Nevertheless, even that there exist cultural norms that may influence the sexist laws and weakening women's rights in Albania, prevent them to achieve equality in health, safety and prosperity, the will and the struggles never end.

A very positive fact is that the new generation of Albanian women organizations and women movement in general, are very prepared to affront the new challenges. Their main references are *UN Convention of all Forms of Discrimination against women, The Beijing Declaration, the Platform for Action* and the *UN 5 Global Goals* – achieve gender equality and empower all women and girls – goals that today for the Albanian gender equity activists are as main pillars in their everyday work.

10. Gender sensivity in media operators

Very important in the work of the women movement in Albania is also its attention towards the gender sensitive indicators for media. (UNESCO framework of indicators to gauge gender sensitivity in media operations and content). It exists a clear relationship between the empowerment of women and the development of Media. While the mentalities and the gender stereotypes exist in the social structures and in the minds of people, media has the potential to distribute or to ameliorate them. In Albania one of the worries of the gender equity activists is the gender equality in the content in the editorials of information – written, visual or online, private or public. Many studies and research have pointed out that to women journalists are committed a higher number of violations, compared with their male colleagues. According to the study of Fredrich Ebert Stiftung, Tirana, 2020, there are verified the following phenomena: sexual harassment in workplace, degrading, insulting language towards women journalists, lower salaries for women, exclusion from leading positions. "When asked about on this topic, 25% of women journalists said that they feel under pressure from male superiors. Meanwhile 31% of them expressed that they know cases where their colleagues have been harassed sexually in the workplace.

A last study showed that in TV shows, approx. 73% of the guests are men, while only 27% of them are women. Study conducted by the Pro-LGTB organization in cooperation with the German Embassy in Tirana monitored 109 TV shows and 293 articles print media in the period March-August 2020. Other studies have confirmed the same trend. There is a market lack of women in political television debate, with rare exceptions, reinforcing the widespread stereotype that 'politics is a job for men'. The involvement of women journalists in talk shows is a tendency, which significantly alleviates the imbalance of the guests from a gender perspective also on topics such as economics, security, justice".

We may say that during many years these issues and others as narrative in the media, issues of gender portraying, for example women as victims and not as strong figures, the language of hate/ misogyny, etc., are topics continuously discussed by the UN Media Forum in Tirana, by the Forum of professionals Women Journalists of Albania and by AWA- Albanian Woman Association in Audiovisual. These groups are some of the last initiatives that women journalists in Albania have realized.

11. Legislation situation

Regarding the legislation about women position in society it is important to underline that institutional framework related to gender equality, violence based on gender and domestic violence extends to the level national and local. The main national authority in charge with these issues is the ministry in charge of gender equality. According to Law no. 9970/2008 "On Equality Gender in Society", each line ministry has a focal point. Even at the local level, there are gender employees in every municipality, which further also enclose the role of local coordinators against domestic violence. Even the Parliament has some structures in support of gender equality. Subcommittee on *Gender Equality and Prevention of Violence against Women*, which was set up in 2017, is part of the Standing Parliamentary Committee for Work, Social Affairs, and health. The purpose of this subcommittee is to oversee the implementation of the strategy of National Center for Gender

Equality, to report on situation of domestic violence and discrimination against women and to hold hearings with stakeholders and various institutional actors. In addition, it is also "Alliance of Women MP's, founded in 2013 to promote gender equality in parliament and to include the gender perspective in legislation. Also, the Commissioner for Protection from Discrimination is an independent structure, set up in 2010, which protects individuals from discrimination, including gender discrimination. The Commissioner is appointed by parliament and reviews complaints of discrimination against individuals or groups, acting on their behalf or defending their interests. In his jurisdiction, he may undertake administrative investigations, issue decisions, make recommendations, impose sanctions and represent plaintiffs in court with their consent.

Albania has ratified in 1993 the Convention on the Elimination of all Forms of Discrimination against Women (CEDAW) as well as Council of Europe Convention on Prevention and Control against Violence against Women and Domestic Violence (Convention of Istanbul) ratified in 2012. Albania is a member state of the Beijing Platform for Action (1995) and of United Nations Security Council Resolution 1325 for Women, Peace and Security. Prepares reports regularly on its commitments and on the implementation of recommendations of international instruments. The government of Albania has submitted to the GREVIO Committee in 2017 its report on the implementation of the Istanbul Convention. Also, an action plan, which reflects the recommendations received. Albania has submitted its report to fourth periodic CEDAW Committee in 2014, for which received recommendations in 2016, as well as shadow reports from the People's Advocate and by civil society organizations. The National Implementation Report of the Beijing Platform +25 was presented at May 2019. Reporting on the Beijing Platform for Action is every five years. For the first time, civil society prepared and presented a shadow report on the Beijing Platform for Action. Consultations are held for the compilations of the international report and meetings with civil society, international partners, Alliance of Women, deputies, etc.

It is a long list and a high number of data – that is impossible to enumerate here – that give clear views on the active presence of Albanian women in society, the progressive process towards the gender equality in all fields of life and the achievements that the Albanian society has realized during these 30 years. There are, of course, many problems, contradictions, still violence, stereotypes, discriminatory attitudes, but there is completely another situation, where the antique rules and traditions, the barriers of dictatorship are learned in the schoolbooks.

The patriarchal families, that are as pyramids, with a man commanding everybody in the top of it, today cannot exist anymore: young people are gone away, in the open world of the country or elsewhere, without listening to the old orders and I feel a great pleasure. Because the foundation of this century pyramid is crumbled down in a few years – a dream that infinite generations of wretched women have dreamed in terrible nights, wailing and hoping to see this scary building destroyed. It has not been easy, but it is realized!

There are people – sociologists, analysts that are very much alarmed: the family in Albania is going to be destroyed! Our wonderful traditions to respect the clan of the family is not the same anymore! 70% of the divorces (horrible!) are required by the women!

I read these apocalyptic titles and a feeling of liberation overwhelms me. I imagine those young women that face the violence and denounce it! They have no fear, they do not think that that was their destiny! They are courageous and they can face the prejudices, the pressures of the parents, everything! They want to be free and independent and to live a dignified life. I feel better in such days. According to the data, mostly these divorces are required by women, because of the violence exercised upon them. During communism almost never women dared to denounce the domestic violence, even with the promises, laws, courts and women as positive personages in theatre. During these 30 last years the issue of non-denouncing the violence is almost exceeded, at least in 80% of cases.

Some months before writing this contribution I read some short stories written by young high school students in Tirana. The theme was the gender equality.

I remained astound.

I thought that sometimes we do not see clearly in the reality, that the stereotypes and prejudices do not permit us to have a clear idea of the quick development of the new generations.

I think that the questions that we had difficulties to articulate thirty years before in front of an auditorium dominated by men, even that the women speakers were well-known professionals, today are issues discussed very freely by young people not yet in the age of university, in a large spectre of interpretation and reflection.

And I think that everything that aims the progress of the society, every sacrifice consciously accepted, every struggle in this direction, no matter how difficult or impossible it seems, does not go in vain. The Albanian society is a providential one, because it has such wonderful young boys and girls with so progressist ideas for the society, for the future world they want to live, for the humanity in the middle of which they will work and that will have their own struggles. They have very clear ideas about the history of the gender relations, about the infinite barriers and discriminations towards women, but they are also very convinced that the time to continue with this separating and hierarchic culture of society is finishing. Because, when boys and girls together think the same way on these questions, it means that this culture will be not easy to survive.

And, yes, the commitment to gender equality and human rights may seem an idealistic passion and a long-life dream, but it happens that it is also realizable!

References

AWA (2024), UNDP Campain *"Unë tregoj – I speak",* Tirana, 6 March.

AWEN Network (AWEN – a network of 10 women organizations from different regions of Albania) (2021), *Raport monitorimi: përfaqësimi I grave në gjedhjet parlamentare*, April Raport monitorimi, April: *Gratë në programet politike gjatë zgjedhjeve parlamentare. Dhuna seksuale dhe ngacmimi seksual – Një analizë e situatës,* Tirane.

Caka E. (2015), *The role and the rights of Albanian women during XVII-XVIII centuries*, Tirane, Studime Historike.

Commissioner for Protection from Discrimination (2019), UN Women: *Barazia Gjinore dhe siskriminimi në organet e emëruara të pushtetit vendor*, Tianë, available at https://portavendore.al/wp-content/uploads/2019/06/Barazia-gjinore-dhe-diskriminimi-ne-organet-e-meruara-te-pushtetit-vendor.pdf

EU/UN *Women Report of Civil Society Organizations for Implementation of the Beijing Platform for Action in Albania* (2019), Beijing + 25, available at https://rrjetikunderdhunesgjinore-monitorime.al/wp-content/uploads/2020/01/Albanian-CSOs-report-on-the-implementation-of-BPfA.pdf.

Fushatat e suksesshme në Shqipëri kundër dhunës ndaj grave dhe vajzave, dhunës n ëfamilje dhe barazisë gjinore (2020), Programi Funded by the European Union, Observatori për të drejtat e fëmijëve dhe të rinjve, Albania, UN Women.

INSTAT (2020), *Indeksi I Barazisë Gjinore në Republikën e Shqipërisë*, Supporters: EU, World bank, Minisria e Shëndetsisë dhe Mbrojtjes Sociale.

INSTAT (2020), *UN Women, Women Count: Burrat dhe gratë në Shqipëri, Women and Men in Albania*, Tirana.

Ministria e Shendetsise dhe Mbrojtjes Sociale (2021), *Strategjia Kombëtare për barazinë Gjinore 2021-2030*. Approved 30.06.2021.

Ministria e Shendetsise dhe Mbrojtjes Sociale, Ministria për Evropë ndhe

Punët e Jashtëme (2019), *National Review for Implementation of the Beijing Platform for Action*, Beijing + 25-Tiranë, April.

Poni M. and Xheka S. (2023), *Report. Sexual Harassment in The Workplace: A National Study*. Published by *Together for Life*, within the project "Synergy for the empowerment of Girls and Women". Tirana, October.

Puto A. (2015), "Gruaja në kinemanë shqiptare të pasluftës", ("The Woman in the Albanian Cinematography of the post-War"), *JAVANEWS*.

"Rrjeti I monitorimit kundër dhunës me bazë gjinore": Thirrje publike: Të ndalohet urgjenitsht dhuna verbal ndaj grave candidate në zgjedhje! (2021), Tirana, March.

Shehu A., Danaj E., Kocaqi M. and Sulçe V. (2022-2023), Programi *Democracia dhe të drejtat e njeriut. Studim për gratë në Republikën e Shqipërisë*, Tiranë, Friedrich-Ebert-Stiftung.

Sinani G. (2020), *Burri dhe gruaja ne fete monoteiste* (The Man and the Woman in the Monotheist religions), Tirana, Zani i Naltë, January, 26.

Sulçe V. (2020), *Changing the narrative of women in the media, Fridrich Echbert Stifung Study*, November 2020, Tirana, https://www.fes-tirana.org/al/pub.

Susan E. (1998), *Pritchett Post: Women in Modern Albania*, Jefferson, North Carolina-London, McFarland&Company Publishers.

World Bank Report: Women, Bussiness and the Law (2022), Albania. Gratë, biznesi dhe ligji në Shqipëri.

Chapter 7

FÈMINISMES LAÏQUES, SECULAR FEMINISTS AND ISLAMIC FEMINISMS IN MUSLIM COUNTRIES: EXPERIENCES IN THE MAGHREB

Leïla Tauil

ABSTRACT: *This chapter aims to deal with lay feminisms (*féminismes laïques*), secular feminisms and Islamic feminisms in Muslim contexts, focusing on the Maghreb, with a view to proposing a reading grid that will allow us to grasp the logics underlying these three feminist expressions. To do this, we begin by providing some historical references relating to the emergence, from the 1920s onwards, of the first women's associations in favor of gender equality in the Arab world, and then we focus on the contemporary feminist movements of the post-independence period in the Maghreb (Algeria, Morocco and Tunisia). The latter mobilize primarily around demands for egalitarian reform or abolition of the Personal Status and Family Codes, derived from "Islamic law" (*Shari'a*), which ratify the hierarchical relationship between the sexes (marital authority, repudiation, polygamy, etc.).*

1. Introduction

The purpose of this article is to address the issue of laical feminists, secular feminists and Islamic feminists within Muslim countries, focusing in particular on the Maghreb, with a view to establishing a framework for appreciating the dynamics underlying these three feminist expressions. Before doing so, we shall start by discussing some of the key moments in history, starting from the 1920s and the emergence of the first women's associations campaigning for gender equality in the Arab world, after which we shall focus on contemporary post-independence movements in the Maghreb (Algeria, Morocco and Tunisia). These have mobilised primarily around calls for egalitarian reforms and the abolition of personal status and family codes adopted under "Islamic law" (Sharia), which provide for hierarchical relations between the sexes (husband's authority, repudiation, polygamy, etc.).

2. The emergence of laical and secular Arab feminism during the colonial period

Feminism within the Arab world, "both as an explicit discourse and as an organised public movement" [1], started to emerge during the 1920s against the backdrop of colonisation, with feminist pioneers both making claims to gender equality and also participating in anti-colonial combat. In Egypt, Huda Sharawi founded the "Egyptian Feminist Union" in 1923, which campaigned for access by girls and women to education, the workplace and politics. She committed a subversive act in the same year by no longer wearing a veil in public following her return from the International Alliance of Women congress [2]. In addition, all of the founding figures within Arab feminism discarded their veil – progressively resulting in wide-scale abandonment of the veil – as they considered the place of women's bodies within the public sphere to be at stake, and thus decided to call for equality with men, who were not subject either to a requirement to wear a veil or to any controls over their sexuality [3]. These initial Arab feminist movements, which involved in particular Coptic and Muslim women, are considered to be laical and secular as they mobilised "a discourse concerning rights, citizenship and nationalism" [4], whilst claiming equality between all citizens, both men and women, protecting in particular their respective religious affiliations.

Leading figures in the Maghreb included in particular the Algerian Hassiba Ben Bouali, a militant and fighter in the National Liberation Front, the Tunisian Bchira Ben Mrad and the Moroccan Malika Al Fassi, each of

---

[1] Glacier O., "Le féminisme arabe", *revue relation*, September 2007, http://www.cjf.qc.ca/fr/relations/article.php?ida=664.

[2] Dayan-Herzbrun S., "Féministe et nationaliste égyptienne: Huda Shaarawi", *Figures d'intellectuelles, Mil neuf cent*, 16, 1998.

[3] "Leïla Tauil revient sur le siècle de combat des féminismes arabes", interview with Mounira Elbouti, *Le Monde arabe*, October 2018, https://lemonde-arabe.fr/15/10/2018/leila-tauil-feminisme-arabe-maroc-tunisie/.

[4] Glacier O., *op. cit.*

whom set up major women's movements during the 1930s, which were committed both to emancipating women as well as liberating their countries from the colonial yoke.

It is important to stress that, following the emergence of political Islam, towards the end of the 1970s rhetoric started to be used that sought to disqualify laical feminists, within Muslim contexts, by dismissing them as a "pure product" of the "imperialist West" [5]. However, this was a historical misinterpretation in two senses in that, on the one hand, all of the initial Arab feminist organisations systematically associated themselves with anti-colonial liberation movements, whilst remaining true to the world feminist movement. On the other hand, a "deconstruction of the colonial discourse on 'traditional women'" [6], who needed to be saved from the misogyny of "indigenous" men, shows that in actual fact the colonial protectorate ended up reinforcing local patriarchal relations by maintaining male domination at the family, social, economic and legal levels, and failing to achieve any improvement in the status of "indigenous" women.

3. Laical and secular feminisms after independence: experiences in the Maghreb

After Arab countries had gained their independence, authoritarian governments emerged and adopted modernisation policies, driven by left-wing pan-Arabism, although without any democratisation. As far as the status of women was concerned, a genuine paradox prevailed throughout the Arab and Muslim world whereby equality between men and women was proclaimed within the texts of constitutions and in the public sphere, whilst at the same time legalising a sacred inequality between the sexes, within the private sphere, through the adoption of personal status and family codes. These codes were essentially inspired by "Islamic law" (the Sharia), which sacralised stipulations set out in the Koran (husband's authority, polygamy, inequality in relation to inheritance, etc.) when it was formalised during the 8th and 9th centuries of the common era, establishing the legal minority – as all pre-modern legal systems did – of women.

In Algeria, the Family Code was only adopted by the National Popular Assembly in 1984, which replicates women's inferior status as sacralised

---

[5] Chafiq C., "Le piège du féminisme islamique", ed. by Clara Domingues, *Clara magazine,* 9 February 2011.

[6] Barkaoui A. and Bouasria L., "Les paradoxes de l'indigène. La voix d'une femme est une révolution", *Printemps arabes, Printemps durables, revue des femmes philosophes,* 2-3, May 2013.

within the Sharia along with a variety of male privileges. From this point onwards, feminists started to organise and to mobilise, setting up associations most of which called for the repeal of the Family Code. Pressure from Islamist environments certainly played a key role in the adoption of this patriarchal code; however, this violence against women "was already firmly rooted in political institutions. This happened before the creation of the Islamic Salvation Front which, once it had been legalised, not only sought to defend this code but also called for its full application" [7].

In Morocco, the Personal Status Code was enacted in 1957 shortly after independence, and placed on a legal footing rules contained within the Sharia that discriminated against women. Malika Al Fassi, a pioneer of Moroccan feminism, and her fellow campaigners publicly denounced this Code as soon as it was adopted, objecting to its fundamentally patriarchal nature and calling for a reform based on the principle of gender equality (equality in relation to succession, abolition of polygamy, etc.) [8]. Mindful of the broad swath of political parties for which women's questions were not a priority, Moroccan feminists – most of whom hailed from the political left – broke ranks from the 1980s onwards to invest in large networks of associations, prioritising their battles around the need to reform the Personal Status Code [9]. They were also confronted with a rising Islamist force, which systematically opposed its demands for equality.

In Tunisia, President Habib Bourguiba pursued a genuine "state feminism" involving the post-independence adoption in 1956 of a revolutionary Personal Status Code, which amongst other things abolished polygamy and replaced repudiation with judicial divorce. This placed Tunisian women in a more privileged position compared to other women throughout the Arab and Muslim world. However, the Personal Status Code did not completely move beyond the inequalities sacralised within the Sharia. In addition, H. Bourguiba, who established an authoritarian regime in spite of his pro-women policies, increasingly displayed a desire "to crush the Marxist intellectual left" [10]. In order to do so, he provided support to

---

[7] Lalami F., "L'enjeu du statut des femmes durant la période coloniale en Algérie", *Nouvelles Questions Féministes*, 27, 3, 2008, 16-27.

[8] El Bouhsini L., "Le féminisme au Maroc: histoire d'une évolution difficile", in Benradi M. (ed.), *Le Féminisme face aux défis du Multiculturalisme*, Université Mohammed V Rabat-Agdal, Faculté des Sciences Juridiques, Economiques et Sociales Rabat-Agdal, AFARD, 2009, pp.48-59.

[9] Alami M'chichi H., *Le féminisme d'État au Maroc: jeux et enjeux politiques*, Paris, Ed. L'Harmattan, 2010.

[10] Bessis S., "Le féminisme institutionnel en Tunisie", *Clio. Histoire, femmes et sociétés,* 1999.

more conservative views by encouraging "the creation of associations 'to safeguard the Koran', which form the front line of the Islamist movement" [11] – a strategy pursued by various non-democratic Arab states, which largely accounts for Islamism and re-Islamisation. This political approach had direct consequences for the status of women as in 1974 H. Bourguiba eventually gave up his project concerning the amendment of the law of succession to ensure greater equality. Confronted with this dangerous situation for women, feminists from civil society mobilised from the end of the 1970s onwards, creating a vast network of associations with a view to preserving their acquired rights and to reclaiming full equality throughout all areas.

During the 1980s, feminist movements in the Maghreb based their egalitarian claims essentially on the universal principle of human rights and international conventions – including in particular the CEDAW [12]. However, from the end of the 1980s, in line with changes in the Islamist paradigm [13], a number of feminist associations also developed religious arguments in favour of equality, based on the theories of reformist theologians from the Arab renaissance intellectual and cultural movement (*Nahda*) [14].

In effect, Islamist proponents and the supporters of re-Islamisation, who called for the mandatory covering of the female body and the allocation of women to their "primary roles" in the private sphere as wives and mothers, made the battles of Arab feminists more complicated. As well as "engaging with universal feminist problems, such as unequal rights between men and women" [15], they were forced to "address the de-legitimisation of Arab feminism on the pretext that it was a Western phenomenon that threatened religion" [16]. However, historical research shows that the appearance of Arab feminisms from the 1920s onwards came as "a clear

---

[11] Bessis S., *op. cit.*

[12] For example, he Convention on the Elimination of All Forms of Discrimination against Women, adopted on 18 December 1979 by the United Nations General Assembly, was ratified by Morocco in 1993.

[13] From the 1980s onwards, throughout all majority Muslim societies, Islamist actors gained ground by becoming active within civil society (associations, trade unions, universities, politics, charitable work, etc.). The Muslim Brotherhood, followed later by the Salafists, became the main actors on the market "offering an explication for Islam". Cf. in particular Maréchal B., *Les Frères musulmans en Europe, racines et discours*, Paris, PUF, 2009, 275.

[14] Tauil L., *Féminismes arabes: un siècle de combat. Les cas du Maroc et de la Tunisie*, Paris, Ed. L'Harmattan, 2018, 50-51.

[15] Glacier O., *op. cit.,* 2007.

[16] *Ibidem.*

Arab response to women's conditions of subordination within their social environment" [17].

The creation of Collective 95 Maghreb-Equality ["*Collectif 95 Maghreb-Egalité*] in 1992 with a view to participating in the World Conference on Women held in Beijing in 1995 was a highly significant development for feminism in the Maghreb. This collective's President, Wassyla Tamzali, provided nuanced clarification concerning the condition of women in the Maghreb, who were stuck between a state Islam that had been treating them as second-class citizens since independence, through the adoption of the Personal Status Code and the Family Code inspired by the Sharia, and religious Islamism that sought to maintain them in a state of subjection, coupled with societal sexual morals that placed constraints on their bodies and a lack of freedom, reflecting the political priorities of the ruling oligarchies.

> "*We are developing feminist thought, and we are dealing with the various problems that have arisen. Our biggest problem concerns the current interpretation of Islam within Maghreb societies. In Tunis, we have seen that one of the problems has been how to shape our answers to Islamism. In 1995, we thus developed a response to Islam, but not to Islamism. Today, the real danger is political Islam, which implies the major subjection of women. (…) However, if one analyses the situation, one can see that, in actual fact, women's bodies have become the real issue of political debate and that there will be no progress in Algeria until men and women have been freed from these sexual morals. (…) Freeing women means calling for freedoms that call into question political power, the only interest of which is to perpetuate itself in order to control the country's wealth*" [18].

4. A shared historic experience of Algerian, Moroccan and Tunisian feminists: the "Collective 95 Maghreb-Equality"

The creation in 1992 of Collective 95 Maghreb-Equality [*Collectif 95 Maghreb-Egalité*], which is comprised of laical and secular Maghreb feminist associations, such as the Association for the Promotion of Women's Rights [*Association pour la Promotion des Droits des Femmes*] based in Algeria, the Democratic Association of Women in Morocco [*Association Démocratique des Femmes du Maroc*] and the Tunisian Association of Democratic Wom-

---

[17] *Ibidem.*

[18] Morsi S., "Entretien avec Wassyla Tamzali", e-mujeres.net, https://e-mujeres.net/entretien-avec-wassyla-tamzali/.

en [*Association Tunisienne des Femmes Démocrates*], was a highly significant shared experience.

Specifically, Algerian, Moroccan and Tunisian feminists from this Collective resolutely committed themselves to achieving legal recognition for full and complete equality within both public and private spheres. The work carried out by them sought to achieve harmonisation between national legal rules and international law (CEDAW, etc.). In order to do so, the Collective rooted in civil society – also including jurists and judges from Algeria, Morocco and Tunisia – published a historic draft law, *The Guide to Equality within the Family in the Maghreb* [*Le Guide de l'égalité dans la famille au Maghreb*], proposing "*One hundred measures and provisions to achieve egalitarian codification within the Maghreb of personal status law and family law*"[19], which was essentially based on universal principles of human rights[20]. This Guide, a genuine pedagogical tool seeking to promote gender equality both under the law and culturally, reproduced the various discriminatory articles from the respective personal status codes and family codes (legal age of marriage, matrimonial guardian, repudiation, polygamy, inequality in relation to succession, etc.)[21] from the three Maghreb countries. It developed a systematic argument based on the contextualisation of Islamic legal doctrines, along with a sociological argument that took account of social changes, as well as a legal argument in favour of gender equality based on universal human rights and international conventions.

For example, the Guide mentions articles providing for inequality in relation to succession from the personal status codes and family codes of Algeria, Morocco[22] and Tunisia, which thus refer to the Sharia and are based

[19] Collectif 95 Maghreb-Egalité, *Guide to Equality in the Family in the Maghreb,* ed. by Women's Learning Partnership for Rights, Development and Peace (WLP), 2005.

[20] Rhiwi L., "Revendications collectives des femmes du Maghreb/Cent mesures et dispositions pour une codification maghrébine égalitaire du statut personnel et du droit de la famille", in Preiswerk Y. and Thorndahl M. (eds.), *Créativité, femmes et développement,* Geneva, Ed. IUED, 1997.

[21] The Guide covers eleven issues accompanied by eleven objects, specifically: "1. harmonising the minimum legal age for marriage; 2. consent to marriage; 3. freedom to choose one's spouse; 4. prohibition of polygamy; 5. abolition of the duty of obedience; 6. shared responsibility for maintaining the family; 7. equality in relation to the dissolution of marriages; 8. the allocation of the house to the person with custody of the children; 9. the right of divorced mothers to remarry; 10. sharing parental responsibilities; 11. equality in relation to inheritance. " cf. Rhiwi L., *op. cit.*

[22] For example, the Moroccan Family Code promulgated in 2004 includes in particular Art. 351, which provides that "(...) the daughter, in the presence of the sons; (...) the sisters (...) in the presence of the brothers (...). In such cases, the estate shall be shared in such a manner that the male heir inherits twice the share of the female heir".

on the following verse from the Koran as justification for this discrimination against women:

> "*Allah charges you concerning (the provision for) your children: to the male the equivalent of the portion of two females. (...)*" (verse 11, chapter 4).

The Guide develops a religious argument, which demonstrates that the stance taken within the Koran in relation to inheritance is not absolute as the Koran also contains verses that suggest that equal shares should be given to men and women, citing in particular the following verse:

> "*Unto the men (of a family) belonges a share of that which parents and near kindred leave, and unto the women a share of that which parents and near kindred leave, whether it be little or much – a legal share*" (verse 7, chapter 4).

Again pursuing a religious line of argumentation the authors cite the reformist theologian Tahar Haddad (who died in 1935), who argued that inequality in relation to succession was not a dogma as the Koran also contains verses mandating equality, whilst defending a reinterpretation of the Sharia with a view to promoting equality between women and men [23]. In sociological terms, the Guide casts light in particular on the evolution of Maghreb families, which have largely become nuclear families, with numerous women in work in order to support the needs of their families, including a significant number who now classed as householders. Finally, as regards the law, the Guide recalls that discrimination in relation to inheritance violates all principles of equality between the sexes which have been asserted at international level within declarations, treaties and agreements concerning universal human rights, referring explicitly to the Fourth World Conference on Women held in Beijing in 1995 [24].

As regards the issue of inheritance in particular, as with the 100 articles of the law proposed, full equality was called for.

> Article 87: "*The female and male descendants of a deceased person shall be vested with equal rights over the estate*".

---

[23] Haddad T., *Notre femme, la législation islamique et la société*, Maison tunisienne de l'édition, 1930 (translated into French in 1978).

[24] Collectif 95 Maghreb-Egalité, *Guide to Equality in the Family in the Maghreb, Ed.* Women's Learning Partnership for Rights, Development and Peace (WLP), 2005, 132-139.

Article 88: "*Women and men who are related to the same degree (...) shall have equal rights over the estate*".

Article 89: "*The wife and the husband shall be vested with the same rights over the estate of the deceased spouse*".

Feminists from the Collective 95 Maghreb-Equality are fully aware that in the Maghreb, as is moreover the case in all majority Muslim societies, the question of gender equality at all levels of society is intrinsically related to the fundamental problem of the secularisation of family law, which is still rooted in the Sharia, which legalises and sacralises male domination in all areas. Legalised inequality within the first locus of socialisation, the family, effectively cannot in any way further gender equality within the public sphere. These authors of this document thus refer as a priority matter to human rights as a frame of reference and the UN Convention on the Elimination of All Forms of Discrimination against Women (CEDAW). However, as the personal status codes and family codes are still rooted in the Sharia, they strategically develop a religious argumentation – this is the case in particular for Moroccan secular feminists living in a kingdom that invokes religion as a basis for its legitimacy – that draws on the approach taken by reformist theologians. According to these theologians, this approach seeks to adapt Islamic law in line with the requirements of modernity and democracy, without however "calling Islam into question as a religion, as an element of cultural heritage (...) within a secular state" [25]. As is demonstrated by *The Guide to Equality within the Family in the Maghreb*, laical and secular feminists rely on religious and sociological arguments in support of full and undifferentiated equality. In our view, the difference between laical feminists and secular feminists lies in the fact that the former endorse a religious justification (Sharia) whereas the latter justify calls for reform with reference to religion only on a secondary basis.

5. Laical feminists and secular feminists: should the codes of personal status and family codes be secularised or reformed?

When addressing the issue concerning codes of personal status and family codes in the Maghreb, feminists position themselves with reference to their respective histories and socio-political contexts, thanks to their long respective struggles in obtaining reforms to improve their legal status, without however ever achieving a fully egalitarian family law.

In Algeria, secular feminists have historically only called for reforms and

[25] Rhiwi L., *op. cit.*

amendments to the Family Code, thus accepting its foundation in the Sharia, whereas laical feminists have demanded its outright repeal. At present, a majority of secular and laical feminists are calling for the repeal of the Family Code and its replacement with an egalitarian Civil Code that is compliant with the CEDAW, as mentioned by feminist Fatma Boufenik, the founder of the association *Fard*:

> "*Historically, the Family Code has been objected to on the grounds that it is unconstitutional, and that it does not enable Algeria to comply with its commitments under the Convention on the Elimination of All Forms of Discrimination against Women, the CEDAW. There were two positions, one that called simply for the amendment of the Family Code, and the other that demanded its repeal, followed by its replacement by an egalitarian Civil Code. At present, the entire feminist movement favours the repeal of the Family Code and the enactment of a Civil Code rooted in equality*" [26].

In contrast to the Algerian and Tunisian republics, Morocco is a monarchy in which the King, who claims to be a descendant of the prophet Mohammed, is known as the "Commander of the Faithful". The political system is thus based on religious legitimacy, which has led all secular feminists (most of whom favour a secularised Family Code) to make their peace with this state of affairs by publicly calling for egalitarian reforms based primarily on human rights as a universal frame of reference, and on a secondary basis on "egalitarian jihad". In March 1992 Latifa Jbabdi, a major feminist figure who was a driving force in particular behind the petition "A million signatures to reform the *Moudawana*", fully endorsed a project for a democratic and egalitarian society – against a backdrop marked by Islamism, which promotes a conservative view of society based on hierarchical gender roles – whilst reconciling with the religious dimension to Moroccan royalty, as is clear from this extract from a speech given in 2003, shortly before significant reforms to the Family Code in 2004:

> "*It's about choosing what sort of society we should live in. This choice cannot under any circumstances be held hostage to politicians' games and bidding contests. It is clear that the outcome to the works of the advisory commission charged with the reform of the law on personal status will depend on factors related both to its composition as well as the wider political context, which is characterised by head-on clashes between modernisers and conservatives. Conservatives will not hesitate to exploit Islam for political*

---

[26] Source: https://www.liberte-algerie.com/actualite/pour-labrogation-du-code-de-la-famille-330768.

ends, including by demonstrations of force and a systematic rejection of the entire process of change embarked upon by the country. Nadia Yassine solemnly recognised this. But we are still optimistic. The political will of His Highness King Mohammed VI is clear. The Royal Directives have called for jihad, for the implementation of the universal values of human rights, and for consideration to be given to social reality and the spirit of the day" [27].

Moreover, the new Family Code was promulgated in 2004, marking genuine progress in the rights of Moroccan women [28], after a speech given by Mohamed VI which perfectly illustrated his role as "Commander of the Faithful" (*Amîr al mu'minîn*) by drawing on scriptural sources as justification for the egalitarian reforms:

"By addressing our High Directives to this Commission, and pronouncing on the draft Family Code, we understand that the following substantive reforms will be introduced: 1. The adoption of a modern formulation to replace concepts that violate the dignity and humanity of women, placing the family under the joint responsibility of husband and wife. In this regard, my ancestor the Prophet Sidna Mohammed – peace and blessing be upon him – said: "women are equal to men before the law". It is moreover reported that he said: "he who honours the family is worthy, whilst he who humiliates it is ignoble". (…) I cannot, in my capacity as Commander of the Faithful, authorise what God has prohibited, nor can I prohibit what the Almighty has authorised".

Feminists are as a whole laical in Tunisia, and one of the first feminist associations to emerge out of civil society, the powerful Tunisian Association of Democratic Women [*Association Tunisienne des Femmes Démocrates*] explicitly refers to positive law in its statutes, calling for a clear separation between religion and the state. In the extract from the speech below given in 2012, the great feminist Sana Ben Achour explains the challenge of laicity in Arab countries where laical feminists are opposed not only to Islamist forces that consider women to be inferior, but also to "Islam as a state religion". This is effectively the main obstacle to the achievement of full equality throughout all Arab and Muslim states which, in the name of

---

[27] "Latifa Jbabdi, présidente de l'UAF, "'Nous ne devons plus tolérer le terrorisme intellectuel'", interview by Khadija Ridouane, *Le Matin*, Casablanca, 15 July 2003.

[28] The 2004 reforms concerned in particular an increase in the age of marriage for girls to 18, the abolition of paternal protection for marriage, equal rights and duties for men and women within the family, and the woman's right to apply for a divorce and to obtain custody of the children. However, the Family Code is not entirely egalitarian as it still incorporates, amongst other things, inequality in relation to succession.

this principle, have stated reservations in relation to those egalitarian provisions contained in CEDAW that are deemed to be contrary to the Sharia. For this reason, laical feminists openly defend a "laical conception of the law, the state and rights", refusing to be dragged into the field of culturalist and religious discourses that ascribe them subordinate status.

> "*It is a fact that laical feminism emerged in these Muslim countries during the 1980s – at the same time as Islamist movements – in opposition to 'Islam as a state religion', which was brandished by omnipotent governments as a barrier against international human rights instruments such as the Convention on the Elimination of All Forms of Discrimination against Women (…). Across the Arab world, out of the 22 states comprising the League of Arab States, 16 have adhered to it, although almost of them have imposed substantial reservations, in some cases general and in some cases specific, in relation to various fundamental provisions in the Convention*[29]*. Under these circumstances, it can be appreciated that, as part of their fight for equality and rights, feminists have mobilised in relation to public policies against institutionalised discrimination and discrepancies between universal rights and national laws. Refusing to be dragged into the minefield of culturalist discourses, they have made a choice – not without difficulty – in favour of the laical conception of the law, the state and rights. (…) This approach is taken within the Founding Charter of the ATFD, which states that 'this struggle can only be successful within the context of a society governed by positive law that enshrines principles of non-discrimination and gender equality*" (ATFD Charter, 1989)[30].

It is important to stress that these laical and secular feminist movements have remained very active through to the present day, but are often – in our view – marginalised both within academia and within the media, in contrast with Islamic feminists, who have gained visibility through numerous investigations. However, historically Islamic feminists appeared on the scene much later and in sociological terms they are infinitely smaller in the Maghreb than laical and secular feminists. An enlightening example of their

[29] "General reservations, such as those applied by Saudi Arabia and Mauritania, are rare. However, specific reservations, accompanied in some cases by interpretative reservations according to which the States declare that they "will not take any action that runs contrary to the articles of their constitution concerning Islam as a state religion", are more common. These have been applied by Algeria, Bahrein, The Comoros, Egypt, the United Arab Emirates, Iraq, Libya, Jordan, Kuwait, Lebanon, Morocco, Oman, Syria and Tunisia" cf. Ben Achour S., "Féminismes laïcs en pays d'islam", *La diversité dans le droit*, Tunis, 2012 (document provided by the author).

[30] Ben Achour S., "Féminismes laïcs en pays d'islam", cit.

agency during the "Arab Spring" was "the call of 8 March for dignity and equality", which was symbolically drafted by eight leading feminist figures and submitted on 8 March 2012 to the Secretary-General of the League of Arab States, and called for the establishment of full equality between the sexes in all new constitutions[31].

6. The emergence of the concept of "Islamic feminism"; experiences in Morocco

The concept of "Islamic feminism"[32] arose during the 1990s based on experiences in Iran where Islamist women called for an improvement in women's status in accordance with the Sharia, whilst defending the political and ideological Islam of the Iranian government. Islamic feminism has manifested itself in various different forms, such as the Malaysian *Sisters in Islam*, which acts as a social force of opposition to Islamism. Since the 1980s it has turned into an extremely important socio-political force, in Malaysia as throughout the rest of the Arab and Muslim world, which targets women and ascribes them inferior status in the name of the Sharia. Islamic feminists – who in our view should be distinguished from the numerous Islamist women who defend a view of the Sharia that sees the sexes as complementary and hierarchical – mainly call for an egalitarian reinterpretation of verses that discriminate against women by attempting to deconstruct patriarchal interpretations. They dig out female figures from the dawn of Islam, such as the prophet's wives, then elevating them as models to be identified with in order to achieve the emancipation of all Muslim women. Islamic feminists thus explicitly endorse a project of society that is grounded on "a retrospective utopia"[33] drawing on religious reference points that can in some cases take second place to the universal reference of human rights.

In the Maghreb, although a large number of Islamist women are opposed to secular and laical feminists, arguing that their legal status can be

[31] http://www.mesopinions.com/petition/droits-homme/appel-8-mars-dignite-egalite/5909.

[32] This section incorporates some passages from the author's publication *Féminismes arabes: un siècle de combat. Les cas du Maroc et de la Tunisie*, Paris, Ed. L'Harmattan, 2018, 126-130.

[33] Dassetto F., "Le drame de l'islam contemporain", *La Libre Belgique*, 10 September 2014, https://www.lalibre.be/debats/opinions/2014/09/10/le-drame-de-lislam-contemporain-ENDU57VWNVASJIJPSD6ZMOVOJI/?fbclid=IwAR0P7WG6ID-ucmMdegWcVT5akPnAaazkb2Dgpt3fDz0srjUnm39ySHRfYIY.

improved within the strict framework of the Sharia, a very small number of women in the public eye identify themselves with Islamic feminism. They are moreover absent in Algeria and Tunisia, as it is specifically in Morocco that the concept of Islamic feminism started to appear within public discourse from 2005 onwards. These Islamic feminists have not participated in the battles fought by Moroccan secular feminists, who have been involved for decades in associations, the law, academia and politics, constantly campaigning for egalitarian reforms to the Family Code and full gender equality throughout all areas. Islamic feminism in Morocco has operated alongside a secular feminism, with which it seeks to compete by mobilising the primacy of religion as a basis for legitimising feminist claims. This Islamic feminism in search of legitimacy has been operating within a context where Islam is the official state religion[34], and within a society characterised – as is the case in many Muslim countries – by pressures for re-Islamisation originating from social actors as well as an Islamic movement that advocates a return to religious orthodoxy and political Islam. In Morocco, the network of secular feminist associations, which is based on the primacy of the universal values of human rights and only secondly on religious arguments in favour of equality, is careful of this new expression of Islamic feminism, and is vigilant in seeking to preserve the recent legal gains resulting from the reform of the Family Code in 2004. In effect, by calling for the abolition of polygamy and repudiation, and for its replacement by judicial divorce, Moroccan secular feminists "are running counter to the spirit and letter of religious texts"[35].

The relatively recent phenomenon in Morocco of Islamic feminism, which was initially marginalised, has gained ground thanks to the electoral win by Islamists in November 2011, enabling it to officially mark out its position within political debate and within power structures. Islamic feminism denounces patriarchal readings of scripture and demands in particular women's rights to education and participation in society, systematically rooting its claims in rigorous dogma. This Islamic feminism sees itself as having greater legitimacy than secular feminism as it calls for an Islamic equality, acting in the name "of Islam, the religion of all Moroccans, both women and men"[36]. A debate is therefore ongoing between the ideas of

---

[34] Chikhaoui N., "Féminisme islamique au Maroc", *Paroles de féministes musulmanes*, *L'autre parole*, no. 121, Rabat, March 2009: http://www.lautreparole.org/articles/298.

[35] *Ibidem*.

[36] Alami M'chichi H., "Les féminismes marocains contemporains. Pluralité et nouveaux défis", *Nouvelles Questions Féministes*, 33, 2, 2014, 65-79.

secular feminists and Islamic feminists, which may have an impact on the future of women in Morocco in terms of the weight of religion or laicity within the very definition of their role within society. But "what is Islamic women's project for Moroccan women?"[37], question as was aptly asked by Naïma Chikhaoui, and what is the basis for their commitment? The arguments made by Moroccan Islamic feminists in an attempt to elaborate the bases for a theory make two main claims: first, the right to a female or rather feminist reinterpretation of scripture – which according to an apologetical approach is considered to be fundamentally egalitarian – whilst at the same time denouncing patriarchal interpretations; secondly, the need to reveal the women who are glorified within the Koran along with the prophet's female companions, who consolidate this image of an egalitarian Islam. The objectives of these Islamic feminists also extend to the religious domain, in particular at institutional level and in terms of theological doctrine as a space of knowledge/power. They seek to create alliances and networks according to a globalised logic for the benefit of Muslim women's rights, to debunk degrading stereotypes based on a false image of women and to counter the patriarchal discourse conveyed by fundamentalists and Islamists[38].

Asma Lamrabet, a major figure within Islamic feminism, who in 2011 was appointed as Director of the "Centre for Feminist Studies in Islam" within the Moroccan League of Theologians (*'Ulamâ*), is also the author of numerous publications on the question of women and Islam. With regard to inequality in relation to succession grounded on verse 11 of chapter 4, she proposes that it be re-read in an egalitarian light that discards this verse in favour of verse 7 of the same chapter, which calls for equal shares between women and men. By acting in this way, she in some sense replaces the interpretative principle of "chronological repeal"[39] by the principle of "egalitarian repeal", whilst nonetheless remaining strictly rooted in the Koranic paradigm.

> *"The only verse that refers to a half share for the daughter is thus that under which the sister inherits one half of the amount due to her brother: Koran 4 ;11 'As far as your children are concerned, God requires you to give a boy an equal share to that of two girls'. (...) The solution is thus found in the Koran itself in this fundamental verse, which most serenely*

---

[37] Chikhaoui N., *op. cit.*, March 2009.

[38] *Ibidem.*

[39] According to an orthodox Sharia logic, which vests the Koran with a legal significance, earlier "legal" Koranic verses are abolished by later verses in accordance with the chronological order in which they were "revealed", in the manner of a religious norm.

> *reassures us regarding its egalitarian approach to inheritance: 'One share (nassib) of the estate left by the parents or relatives falls to the male heirs; similarly, one share (nassib) of the estate left by the parents or relatives falls to the female heirs; and irrespective of the significant of the inheritance, complying with this quantity requirement is an obligation (nassiban mafroudan)' [Kùoran 4; 7]"* [40].

Having courageously and publicly taken this position in favour of equality in relation to succession, justified by a religious argument based in Koranic verses, in 2018 A. Lamrabet was forced to resign from the League of Theologians, which was clearly dominated by conservatives. In our view, this episode illustrates the limits to different readings of scripture (a majority patriarchal and a minority feminist) when dealing with women's rights. And it is reiterated once again that this issue should be freed from the religious domain and be treated as a matter of citizenship and public freedoms.

7. Conclusion: proposition of a framework for distinguishing between laical feminism, secular feminism and Islamic feminism

To conclude this article, it is important to recall that, in the Maghreb, laical and secular feminists have their roots, both historically and sociologically, in the associative movements emerging from civil society that have combatted all forms of discrimination against women (creation of refuges for the victims of physical abuse, etc.), whilst making collective political claims in favour of gender equality throughout all areas. Islamic feminists are often academics working under their own initiative, who develop their ideas at international congresses and symposia, examining religious texts and devising feminist interpretations, which they publish in particular on social networks with the aim of debunking patriarchal interpretations of orthodox and ideological Islam.

As regards the reference points used, it is interesting to propose a framework for distinguishing among the three groups of actors, namely: laical feminists, especially in Tunisia, refer exclusively to universal human rights (CEDAW, etc.), considering the separation between state and religion to be a *conditio sine qua non* for achieving full equality throughout all areas. In other words, they call for unconditional laical equality between the sexes in a manner *detached* from religious considerations. Secular femi-

[40] Lamrabet A., *L'héritage, relecture des versets*, available at http://www.asma-lamrabet.com/articles/l-heritage-relcture-des-versets/.

nists in Morocco invoke the primacy of universal human rights in conjunction with religious arguments, which they deploy – as is necessary in Morocco – from an egalitarian perspective in order to call for reforms to the Family Code. In other words, they call for secular equality between the sexes conditioned by an *instrumentalisation* of the religious sphere. Finally, Islamic feminists such as Asma Lamrabet invoke the primacy of religious texts read in an egalitarian perspective, affording only secondary importance to human rights, calling for an "Islamic equality between the sexes", which is often nuanced, and conditioned by the need for religious justification as a basis for its legitimacy.

Finally, as a citizen, it appears to the author that the emergence of Islamic feminism, in a similar manner to Jewish and Christian feminisms, represents a subversive act in religious terms as Islamic feminists reject male religious power using the instruments of religion itself. This may genuinely lead to an egalitarian form of Islam based on actual scriptural criticism and the abandonment of patriarchal foundations. However, Islamic feminisms, most of which for the moment are only calling for nuanced Islamic equality, have quickly reached their limits. In effect, they are both calling for an egalitarian reinterpretation of scripture (which remains locked in a conflict between different interpretations, within religious and political spheres that are dominated by patriarchal interpretations) and also seeking to replace patriarchal – majoritarian – verses and *hadîth* with egalitarian – yet minoritarian – verses and *hadîth*. As such, they quickly come up against a major difficulty owing to the fact that the theological status of scripture has not yet been officially and publicly questioned within Islamic contexts. Moreover, it would appear that outside the religious sphere – where they are able to engage in fruitful debates in particular with Salafist women are unconditionally endorse patriarchal Islam which regards them as inferior – the approach taken by Islamic feminists at family, social and political level is ultimately not relevant. It is essentially illusory to make modern claims (to equality, freedom, democracy, citizenship, etc.) based on mediaeval scripture that ignores these rights. The author takes the view – in line with laical feminists, in particular from Tunisia – that claims to equality within the public and private spheres that are grounded on a modern concept of full and unconditional equality must be brought into the domain of citizenship and public freedoms and freed from culturalist and "identito-religious" discourses that ascribe an inferior and different status to women.

References

Alami M'chichi H. (2010), *Le féminisme d'État au Maroc: jeux et enjeux politiques,* Paris, Éditions L'Harmattan.

Alami M'chichi H. (2014), "Les féminismes marocains contemporains. Pluralité et nouveaux défis", *Nouvelles Questions Féministes*, 2, 33.

Barkaoui A. and Bouasria L. (2013), "Les paradoxes de l'indigène. La voix d'une femme est une révolution", in *Printemps arabes, Printemps durables, revue des femmes philosophes,* 2-3, May.

Ben Achour S. (2012), "Féminismes laïcs en pays d'islam", in *La diversité dans le droit*, Tunis, *in Mziou K. (dir.), Mélanges: La diversité dans le droit*, Tunis, CPU.

Bessis S. (1999), "Le féminisme institutionnel en Tunisie", in *Clio. Histoire, femmes et sociétés,* 9, https://journals.openedition.org/clio/286?amp%3Bid=286&lang=en#.

Chafiq C. (2011), "Le piège du féminisme islamique", ed. by Domingues C., *Clara magazine,* 9 February.

Chikhaoui N. (2009), ""Féminisme islamique au Maroc", Paroles de féministes musulmanes", *L'autre parole*, 121, http://www.lautreparole.org/articles/298.

Collectif 95 Maghreb-Égalité (2005), *Guide to Equality in the Family in the Maghreb,* Bethesda Éditions Women's Learning Partnership for Rights, Development and Peace (WLP).

Dassetto F. (2014), "Le drame de l'islam contemporain", *La Libre Belgique,* 10 septembre, https://www.lalibre.be/debats/opinions/2014/09/10/le-drame-de-lislam-contemporain-ENDU57VWNVASJIJPSD6ZMOVOJI/?fbclid=IwAR0P7WG6ID-ucmMdegWcVT5akPnAaazkb2Dgpt3fDz0srjUnm39ySHRfYIY.

Dayan-Herzbrun S. (1998), "Féministe et nationaliste égyptienne: Huda Shaarawi", Figures d'intellectuelles, *Mil neuf cent,* 16.

El Bouhsini L. (2009), "Le féminisme au Maroc : histoire d'une évolution difficile", in Benradi M. (dir.), *Le Féminisme face aux défis du Multiculturalisme*, Université Mohammed V Rabat-Agdal, Faculté des Sciences Juridiques, Économiques et Sociales Rabat-Agdal, AFARD.

Entretien avec Wassyla Tamzali, realised by Sarah Morsi, https://e-mujeres.net/entretien-avec-wassyla-tamzali/.

Glacier O. (2007), "Le féminisme arabe", revue relation, n. 719, September, http://www.cjf.qc.ca/fr/relations/article.php?ida=664.

Haddad T. (1930), *Notre femme, la législation islamique et la société,* Tunis, Maison tunisienne de l'édition, (French translation in 1978)

Lamrabet A. (2012), "L'héritage, relecture des versets", in http://www.asma-lamrabet.com/articles/l-heritage-relcture-des-versets/.

Latifa Jbabdi, présidente de l'UAF, 'Nous ne devons plus tolérer le terrorisme intellectuel', interview by Khadija Ridouane, *Le Matin,* Casablanca, 15 juillet 2003.

Leïla Tauil revient sur le siècle de combat des féminismes arabes, interview with Mounira Elbouti, *Le Monde arabe,* octobre 2018 https://le monde-arabe.fr/15/10/2018/leila-tauil-feminisme-arabe-maroc-tunisie/.

Maréchal B. (2009), *Les Frères musulmans en Europe, racines et discours*, Paris, PUF.

Rhiwi L. (1997), "Revendications collectives des femmes du Maghreb/Cent mesures et dispositions pour une codification maghrébine égalitaire du statut personnel et du droit de la famille", in Preiswerk Y. and Thorndahl M. (dir.), *Créativité, femmes et développement,* Genève, Éditions IUED.

Rouadjia A. (2006), "La lutte des femmes laïques en Algérie", *Confluences Méditerranée*, 59, 4.

Tauil L. (2018), *Féminismes arabes: un siècle de combat. Les cas du Maroc et de la Tunisie*, Paris, Éditions L'Harmattan.

Chapter 8

ISLAMIST WOMEN'S MOBILIZATION AND AGENCY IN THE ARAB UPRISINGS AND THEIR AFTERMATH IN EGYPT

Erika Biagini and Paola Rivetti

ABSTRACT: *The so-called "Arab Spring" has brought about renewed attention to women as agents of social and political change in the countries of the North African region. Since then, a growing body of feminist scholarship has emerged addressing Arab women's mobilization in the revolutions and, more broadly, their role as social and political actors in struggles for women's rights and gender equality. A recurrent theme within this body of literature points to the renewed challenges that women faced in retaining the gains made during the period of mobilization in the aftermath of the revolutionary momentum, often described in the literature as an "Arab Winter". This narrative was paradigmatic of the unparalleled political gains made by Islamist movements after the Uprisings, who are believed to work to limit women's agency and rights in the region. Consequently, scholars have given less attention to the agency and political role of Islamist women in these events. This chapter fills this gap in the existing literature on women's mobilization by looking at Islamist women's role and agency in Egypt's uprising. In doing so, the chapter addresses the broader debates concerning women's agency in religious political movements, bringing attention to ideological and cultural constrains that limit participation, but also questioning the feminist value of their organizing. The chapter argues that, while it is true that Islamists have worked to limit women's agency and gains, we should shift the focus to the resilience of gender conflict and the development of feminist identities also in those movements believed to be impermeable to feminist organizing. Thus, the chapter challenges extant scholarship on women and the uprisings two grounds. First, it shows that Islamist women's agency and organizing can mobilize for feminist gains. Second, it demonstrates that feminist struggles that emerge in times of upheaval survive the post-revolutionary momentum.*

1. Introduction

Women were among the main participants of the wave of popular protests that swept across South West Asia and North Africa (SWANA) starting in late 2010, and which came to be known as the "Arab Spring". Women from all walks of life joined street protests in Tunisia, Morocco, Libya, Egypt, Syria and Yemen demanding social justice and regime change. Women partook in the protests as leaders and mobilizers, but their role was not limited to peaceful participation. Where peaceful demonstrations culminated into devastating civil wars, like in Syria for instance, women also joined their male counterparts in conflict as combatants (Gazzawi 2014). In 2011, under the pressure of protest movements the Tunisian President Zine El-Abidine Ben Ali and the Egyptian President Mubarak eventually stepped down, while the Moroccan King Mohammad VI vowed for comprehensive constitutional and democratic reforms managing to retain power, and others such as President Muammar Gadhafi was initially deposed and then killed on October 20, 2011, by the Libyan National Liberation Army in joint operation with NATO forces. These new political arrangements provided an initial sense of possibility for regime change in the region, but also brought an immediate backlash to the millions of women who made these events possible. As it usually occurs in times of revolution and conflict, revolutionary movements initially welcomed women's participation in the struggle but then demanded women to abandon the public sphere once again, at times violently (Pratt 2020 and 2013).

Since the uprisings, a growing body of feminist scholarship has emerged addressing Arab women's mobilization in the revolutions and, more broadly, their role as social and political actors in struggles for women's rights and gender equality (among others, see Pratt 2020; Hafez 2019; Allam 2018; Touaf, Boutkhil and Nasri 2017; Tadros 2016; Sadiqi 2016; Abouelnaga 2016; Khalil 2015; El-Said, Meari and Pratt 2015; Olimat 2013; Stephan and Charrad 2020). A recurrent theme within this body of feminist literature points to the renewed challenges that Arab women faced in retaining the gains made during the period of mobilization in the aftermath of the revolutionary momentum, often described in the literature as an "Arab Winter" (Feldman 2019; Grinin *et al.* 2018). This perspective aligns with a considerable body of literature emphasising the losses that women incurs by taking part in revolutionary struggles, due to the inherent patriarchal nature of nationalist and revolutionary movements (McClintock 1993, 1996; Enloe 1989, 1993, 2000; Mayer 2000; Bernal 2000; Peterson 2000; Cockburn 2000, 2007, 2013; Hale 2002; Omar 2004; Kaufman and Kristen 2010; Salhi 2010; Parker 2018; Yuval-Davis 1997; Ben-Shitrit 2016;

Olivius and Hedström 2019). As this literature suggests, nationalist and revolutionary movements are patriarchal in nature and consequently they tend to reproduce the patriarchal gender order that was in place before the struggle, leading to little or no tangible gains for the women who participate in it. While women may be able to play more equal roles as men during times of upheaval, these processes hardly ever result in more egalitarian arrangements for women in their aftermath. Women continue to be excluded from the political decision-making of post-revolutionary societies and, at times, their situation would be worsened by their participation.

In the case of the SWANA uprisings, the narrative of an 'Arab winter' was also paradigmatic of the unparalleled political gains made by Islamist movements in the post-Uprisings transitions (Kraetzschmar and Rivetti 2019), believed to work to limit women's agency and rights in the region (e.g. Tadros 2016). In this narrative, 'Islamist winter' got to replace 'Arab winter'. The international community, along with Arab societies' secular sectors, perceived Islamist electoral victories as a further setback for Arab women and gender equality in the region. Similarly to other contemporary religious-political movements globally, Islamists support a conservative gender ideology that attributes men and women different social roles based on what are believed to be natural differences between the sexes. They understand gender roles to be complementary, rather than equal, and attribute to women the primary duty of caregivers in the family and the community. Islamists have often supported gender policies that endorse and perpetuate women's subordination to men in the family and in society, and that limit women's involvement and participation in areas that reflect this gender complementarity. In several instances, Islamists have also advanced laws that discriminated against women in matters of reproductive, personal, and family rights (Brand 1998; Kocamaner 2018). With few exceptions (Tajali 2017, for example), the scholarship has paid little attention to the agency and political role of Islamist women in the events of the "Arab Spring", because Islamist women are not believed to be advancing a gender politics that is liberatory for women.

This chapter fills a gap in the existing literature on women's mobilization in the context of the uprisings by looking at Egyptian Islamist women's role and agency in the context of Egypt's 2011 Revolution[1] and its aftermath. In doing so, the chapter addresses the broader debates concerning women's agency in religious political movements, bringing attention to ide-

[1] It is contested whether the Egyptian uprisings that begun on the 25th of January 2011 can be termed a revolution; herein, we call it Revolution (Thawra) based on how the women we interviewed called it.

ological and cultural constrains that limit participation, but also examining the feminist value of their organizing. The chapter argues that, while it is true that Islamists have worked to limit women's agency and gains, we should shift the focus to the resilience of gender conflicts and the development of feminist identities also in those movements believed to be impermeable to feminist organizing. Thus, the chapter challenges extant feminist scholarship on Arab women and the uprisings two grounds. First, it shows that Islamist women's agency and organizing can mobilize for feminist gains. Second, it demonstrates that feminist struggles that emerge in times of upheaval survive the post-revolutionary momentum. The chapter does so by drawing at the case of Islamist women in Egypt in the aftermath of 25th of January Revolution.

2. The Muslim Sisterhood and Islamic Feminism

The Muslim Brotherhood (henceforth Brotherhood) was established in Egypt in 1928 in the Suez Canal city of Ismailia. Its founder, Hassan al-Banna, established the movement to challenge Western colonialism and to advance an alternative nationalist ideology that found inspiration in Islam for society's reforms (Gershoni and Jankowski 1995). Al-Banna believed that society's change could only be achieved if Muslims lived by the Islamic religion, morals and values. Women were involved in the Brotherhood since the very beginning because of their role as the main biological and cultural reproducers of the new generations (Yuval-Davis 1997, 2003; Yuval-Davis and Anthias 1989). Their inclusion in the Brotherhood, however, remained subordinated to the movement's goals and mission, meaning that their interests and demands as women acquired only second place before that of the movement. In addition, the Brotherhood's emphasis on women's position in the family, believed to be central to its political achievements, caused the movement to support a gender ideology that privileged the patriarchal family, male authority over women, and complementary gender roles (Badran 1991). It also dictated women's inclusion and position in the Brotherhood organization, limiting women to roles that were complementary and of support to those of men.

In the movement's early years, women contributed to the Brotherhood by spreading its *da'wa* (invitation to Islam) among their families and communities via charity and religious work (Karam 1998). Prominent Sisterhood figures were Labibah Ahmad and Zeinab al-Ghazali. Labibah Ahmed, who briefly held an honorary leadership of the Sisterhood in the 1930s, built on an Islamic nationalist discourse that involved women in the political struggle against British occupation based on the role they played in the family (Baron 2005, 189-213). She run her own journal, The Women's Awakening (al-Nahda al-Nisa'iyya) and a philanthropic women's association, the Society of Egyptian Ladies' Awakening (Jam'iyyat Nahdat al-Sayyidat al-Misriyyat), to promote her ideas and to foster women's participation in the struggle for Egypt's independence. She had a past as an activist that preceded that of the Brotherhood's establishment and only later she joined the movement to support the development of the Sisterhood branch in Cairo. Under her leadership the Sisterhood expanded as a philanthropic association, but Ahmad never advocated for the inclusion of women in the world of politics (Talhami 1996, 49). Zainab al-Ghazali also had an independent activist career before joining the Brotherhood. Initially, al-Ghazali was active in the Egyptian Feminist Union (EFU), a nationalist women's organization of secular orientations that originated as the women's committee of Egypt's secular-nationalist al-Wafd Party, led by the Egyptian feminist pioneer Huda Sharawi. However, in 1936 al-Ghazali left the EFU to establish her own organization, The Society of the Muslim Women (al-Sayidat al-Muslimat), because she believed that the elitist discourse promoted by the EFU prevented women from joining in mass as it did not appeal to them and their values. When al-Banna tried to co-opt al-Ghazali in the Brotherhood, al-Ghazali initially refused to maintain her independence, and only pledged her loyalty to al-Banna and the Brotherhood in 1948, when the movement was first dissolved by the Egyptian monarchy (Talhami 1996, 49-52). It was under the leadership of al-Ghazali that the Sisterhood's involvement in political activities expanded.

The Sisterhood's political role in the Brotherhood grew exponentially in the 1950s and 1960s, consequently to the movement falling under the repression of the regime of Gamal Abdul Nasser. The Brotherhood had supported the Free Officers Movement's coup d'état against the Egyptian Monarchy in 1952, hoping to play a leading political role in an independent Egypt, but Nasser soon grew intolerant of the Brotherhood and its politics, and repressed the movement as he consolidated its power (Gordon 1992; Mitchell 1993). With the arrest of thousands of male members, the Sisters emerged as the movement's powerhouse, as they became responsible of sustaining the Brotherhood's network, the prisoners and their families (Abdel-Latif 2008), as well as contributing to its ideological survival by acting as a bridge between the leaders in prisons and the members on the outside (Zollner 2007). The formal separation of the Sisters and al-Ghazali's society from the Brotherhood organization proved of strategic advantage because Nasser initially overlooked women's role in the Brotherhood's resistance, thus sparing the Sisters from a similar repression (Talhami 1996,

52). It also facilitated the building up of leadership skills among women, who were forced to step up into new roles to sustain the movement's continued existence. It was only in 1964 that Nasser closed down al-Ghazali's society and arrested her along with other fifty Sisters, mainly family members of key Brotherhood leaders (Abdel Hady 2011, 37).

In the 1970s, the Brotherhood took advantage of Sadat's tolerance towards Islamists to re-build its organization, but the Sisterhood never acquired a strength similar to that it had obtained during the Nasser's era. The Brotherhood's status as an illegal group since it was first banned in 1948 left it exposed to regime repression, granting the leaders grounds to deny the Sisterhood formal status in the organization and to exclude them from political activities as a protective measure (Abdel-Latif 2008, 11). The Brotherhood spent this decade to expand as a significant political and social force in Egypt once again, counting on the support of young activists members of the university Islamic movement (al-Jama'a al-Islamia) which it co-opted into its ranks to revive a tired organization (Al-Awadi 2014). While in the 1970s the Sisterhood's activism survived predominantly on the basis of women's individual initiatives, in the 1980s the university Islamic movement became an important venue for Islamist-oriented women to become politically active. A new generation of female university students, by then a significant majority of young Egyptians who had benefited from Nasser's free education policies, availed of the services that the Islamic movement provided in universities, in turn lending it support and credibility. Within universities, female students also participated in protest activities, testifying to the growing politicization of Egypt's university Islamic movement in the 1970s, and to the mobilization of women in its ranks (Talhami 1996, 53; El-Tohamy 2016).

By the 1980s, the young activists that the Brotherhood had co-opted into its ranks from the Islamic movement came to be known as the middle-generation leaders, or the reformist trend (al-Tayyar al-Islami), because of their moderate orientations and pragmatic attitudes towards political participation (Wickham 2013, 67-69). Several had rose up the ranks of the Brotherhood organization after pioneering the movement's expansion in Egypt's professional associations, student unions and its entrance in parliament. Islamist female activists benefited significantly from the programme of social and political reforms led by the middle-generation activists and from their advocacy for women's greater political participation (Wikham 2013; El-Ghobashy 2005; Biagini and Rivetti 2020). Jihan al-Halafawy, the first Sister to run for elections as part of the Brotherhood, competed for the medical board of Egypt's professional association in 1992, and was supported by the middle-generation leaders (El-Ghobashy

2005). In the informal spaces of the universities, female students also enjoyed greater leadership opportunities under the lead of the middle-generation activists, who radically altered the Brotherhood membership's requirements to emphasise political and activist skills as opposed to religiosity (Biagini 2017b, 123). Furthermore, and contrary to prevailing ideas, the gender segregation the Brotherhood adopted in university demanded women to take up leadership roles among other women to guarantee the execution of the organizations' agendas and goals, thus fostering women's sense of empowerment (Biagini 2017b, 122; see also Ababneh 2016a, 2009; Abbasi and Saeidi 2020).

From within such university-based informal spaces, the Sisters could develop independent organizing and leadership. Their skills and independence were not, however, welcome in the Brotherhood, as the Sisters could not enjoy equal opportunities in the organization. While in informal spaces women, along with more progressive male leaders, enjoyed greater freedom to run their own agenda, the Brotherhood organization rested under the control of the senior and more conservative leadership (Tammam 2011). This created a situation where, upon graduation, women who were politically inclined perceived a halt in their careers as activists upon entering the Brotherhood. Indeed, the movement channelled women to those fields of activism that it perceived more adapt to their gender, such as the education of children, the family and social outreach, while the leadership of political offices were considered as male domains. Thus, the hybrid nature of the Brotherhood movement as both a social and political organization allowed members to enjoy greater freedom in informal spaces, which remain crucial for the development of women's activism and gender demands, but also resulted in competing gender projects being carried out by the membership in the organization, where women experienced exclusion.

In the 1990s, the Egypt's political context changed and consequently did political balances within the organization. The Mubarak-led liberalization created opportunities for Islamists to participate politically and electorally, thus engendering internal demands – including by women – for greater pluralism and democratic reforms in the movement (El-Ghobashy 2005; Wickham 2013). The Brotherhood's access to institutional formal politics also revived old debates about its nature, as either a religious or political movement. This debate was crucial to strategize about participation. While the senior leaders aligned with al-Banna's view of Islam as a comprehensive system of religion and state thus rejecting the establishment of a separate party void of any religion mission, the middle-generation members advocated for the separation of the Brotherhood's religious and political project. According to them, the separation would have enhanced the

Brotherhood's popularity considering that now it had the opportunity to become fully and legally part of the institutional political system of the country. One of the requisites for parties' legalization was their secularity (Al-Awadi 2014, 82-83). The middle-generation also argued that separating the party from the Brotherhood organization was about making sure that the Brotherhood would have not fallen victim once again of the regime's brutal repression. They supported the separation of the Brotherhood's religious and political mission, with the latter residing in a legal party with separate goals and leadership (Wickham 2013, 205-228).

The middle-generation also wanted to revise the Brotherhood's position on women and women's role in the organization and society. The Brotherhood's conservative positions was damaging of the organization's appeal to the larger society, they argued. They campaigned within the Brotherhood to increase women's participation, mirroring the greater leadership roles that women got to play in the Egyptian society at large (Wickham 2013, 205-228; El-Ghobashy 2005). Although challenged by these younger generation activists, the senior leaders managed to resist meaningful reforms and cemented conservative positions on women's political roles. This is clear, for instance, in the Brotherhood's first position paper addressing women and political participation, issued in 1994. While it is argued that the organization has a duty to support women's political inclusion, it is also restated that women's primary role is within the family. Their primary responsibility is to embody and project traditional feminine qualities such as piety and modesty (Wickham 2013, 69-70). The same conservative positions are upheld in later documents, such as the 2004 Initiative for Political Reform, the 2005 and the 2007 Party Platforms (Abdel-Latif 2008, 1). As Tammam (2011) notes, the early and mid-1990s saw the consolidation of the conservative leadership in the Brotherhood organization, with conservative members successfully containing the challenge that the middle-generation activists had represented some years before.

Women were also part of the middle-generation that had tried to reform the Brotherhood. Since the 1990s, they availed of middle-generation leaders' support to establish a base of power upon which building leadership and political consensus. They partook in syndicates and parliamentary elections as candidates (El-Ghobashy 2005, 382), and used university campuses and informal spaces out of the control of the Brotherhood's leadership to push progressive opinions about women's participation and their role in the movement (Biagini and Rivetti 2020). This work resulted into the establishment of alliances and of support for the more progressive Sisters' criticism of the leadership. For example, when the Brotherhood published its Party Platform in 2007, which once again reinstated the exclusion of women from the presidency of the state, the Sisters and the Brothers alike criticised the leadership publicly on social media (Lynch 2007). Criticism focused on the exclusion of women from the organization's decision-making offices, their exclusion from the right to vote in internal elections, as well as on the educational curricula for women, which proposed an unrealistic model of women as only concerned with house duties, child rearing, and cooking (Al-Arabiya 2016).

As 2011 approached, internal debates on women and their political participation have continued. At the eve of Egypt's Revolution, the Sisterhood persisted in their demands of greater recognition of women's contribution to and role in the Brotherhood organization. However, while demands for change were rife within the membership, the leadership was in full control of the structures of the organization. To further strengthen their position of power in the face of the revolution, the conservative senior leaders took advantage of the 2011-12 electoral victories to exclude progressive members, sanitizing the organization and keeping it at a distance from the revolutionary transformations that were taking place in society.

3. The Sister and their role is in the 2011 Egyptian Revolution

When the popular protests against the regime of Hosni Mubarak broke out in Egypt on 25 January 2011, on National Police Day, the Brotherhood was late to join the Tahrir square movement. Despite the lack of the organization's official backing, Brotherhood and Sisterhood members had joined the protests in individual capacity. In the decade leading up to the uprisings, links had been established between the Brotherhood youth and the Egyptian revolutionary youth on the wave of the Kefaya movement and the university students' initiatives (El-Tohamy 2016).

In the early days in Tahrir, the Brotherhood youth played a leading role in defending the square against the attacks of the police forces together with the other revolutionary forces. In this phase the Sisters were also present and contributed to the struggle by securing the perimeter of the square, preparing food and organizing shelter and medication for the protestors (Farag 2012). This was a transformative experience for many of the Sisters in terms of gender politics. During the 18 days of the occupation of the square, the Sisters joined the struggle as citizens, refraining from putting forward specific gender claims as tactical move to create an inclusive space for all, including (and crucially for) women who are usually emarginated in the public sphere (Allam 2018; Tadros 2012, 2016). In the aftermath of the uprisings, however, the Sisters' role in the revolution and their contribution to the electoral victories of the Brotherhood gave them a greater sense of entitlement and legitimacy to demand access to decision-making power.

The demands of this younger generation of Sisters for greater inclusion, fair distribution of power and meaningful change were however manipulated by the Brotherhood in the post-uprisings period. After the Brotherhood's decision to establish the Freedom and Justice Party (FJP) on 21 February 2011, the movement included women in political offices to reciprocate their decades of contribution to the organization. However, the senior Brotherhood leadership in control of the organization, and then also the FJP, was very selective in picking the women to promote into political and leadership offices. Like it had occurred in the decades leading up to Egypt's uprisings, the Brotherhood leadership promoted women who aligned with its gender conservatism and who enjoyed family linkages with prominent conservative Brotherhood leaders, marginalizing the younger members and progressive women's voices (Biagini 2020; Biagini and Rivetti 2020). In the FJP's Women's Sections, the Sisters carried out the same activities that the movement had promoted for decades as primary women's domains, such as philanthropic undertakings for the poor, the promotion of the institution of the patriarchal family and women's motherhood role, and religious work.

The Sisters also partook in the election as candidates. In such formal spaces of political participation, the younger generation stood little to no chance to gain the backing of the senior leaders. The Brotherhood selected 46 women to compete in the 2011 parliamentary election, to meet the requirements of the new Parliamentary Election Law (PEL) passed by the Egyptian Security Council of the Armed Forces (SCAF), which required all parties to include at least one woman in each one of their electoral lists. The few Sisters placed in a winning position in the Brotherhood's lists included those who had already held a senior position in the movement's *da'wa* circles and who enjoyed family linkages with prominent Brotherhood male leaders, such as Wafaa' Mashhur, the daughter of the fifth Brotherhood General Guide Mustafa Mashhur and Azza al-Garf. These female candidates were known for their religious-conservative views. During the election campaign, the Sisterhood candidates promoted the FJP as a true advocate for women's rights and political participation, while fully committing to party's programme for women demanding the reform the Personal Status and Family Law (PSFL) in agreement with Islamic principles. The Sisters also portrayed the family as an institution damaged by previous amendments of the PSFL, which had led to late marriages, an increase in divorce rates and extra-marital relationships, and endorsed the promotion of Islamic values as the solution to these problems. Similarly to the Brotherhood organization, the FJP excluded women from internal elections and its decision-making bodies. In sum, as the first free and fair parliamentary elections in Egypt's history were approaching, the Sisters did not have a voice and representation in the political decision-making bodies of the FJP and the Brotherhood – apart from those Sisters who were allowed in by the grace of the male central leadership of the Brotherhood. During the elections, younger Sisters participated mainly as canvassers for votes. While they were included in the FJP's Media Committee because of their predisposition to new media technologies, their lacked a real say in the Brotherhood political decision-making.

The inclusion of Sisters (and Brothers, for the matter) holding progressive views remained limited both in the FJP and the Brotherhood. Only ideologically aligned Sisters, who were picked and selected by the senior leaders on the basis of piety and loyalty (Biagini 2020), gained some space in the two organizations. It is interesting to note that, while the context had greatly changed from Mubarak's authoritarianism to a post-revolutionary free political environment, the gender policies of and the quality of internal democratic mechanisms within the Brotherhood remained the same, effectively denying the Sisters a say on crucial political decisions that the movement took while in government.

4. The Muslim Sisters in the Informal Activist Circles

Egypt's open political environment of the post uprising period, albeit short and of a limited duration, invalidated the Brotherhood's secretive and nepotistic culture (Ardovini and Biagini 2021b). The Brotherhood's newly acquired legal status in 2011-12 meant that it no longer had reasons to refuse greater transparency and openness to its members, or to exclude women from politics to protect them from regime retaliation. Therefore, core Brotherhood principles that sustained its organizational cohesiveness and collective identity, such as blind obedience and loyalty to the leadership, begun to loose traction among the membership. This was particularly true for the younger generations who already espoused more progressive views in terms of internal pluralism, the role of women and revolutionary action, and whose sense of entitlement to the leadership and decision-making of the movement had been boosted by the role they had played in bringing about the revolution and the Brotherhood/FJP's electoral victories.

While after 2011 the senior leaders at the helm of the Brotherhood organization brought no significant internal change to give space to the new and progressive voices, a considerable portion of the youth members begun to carve out spaces of their own to bring forward initiatives that distanced them from the Brotherhood on significant respects. Young Sisterhood members, for instance, have taken advantage of their already marginal status in the Brotherhood to operate under greater autonomy and initiate changes in their localities. They pushed for a change in the dress code, and the opening up to women of diverse political inclination. They also lobbied and successfully obtained their right to vote their own Sisterhood leaders, pushing forward a new generation of political cadres who held more progressive views in terms of women and their role in the movement and could support the young Sisters in their demands for emancipation (Biagini 2019).

Some of the young Sisterhood members also joined ranks with the Egyptian Revolutionary Youth who continued to protest against the rule of the military in Egypt's streets, while the Brotherhood turned its back on the revolution and prepared for elections. These members were a small minority, but their collaborations with leftists and revolutionary movements proved to be essential to the ability of the Sisterhood division to maintain a connection with Egypt's political groups whose voices were significantly silenced in the post-uprising period, because of the repression by the military and the exclusionary attitude of the Brotherhood once in government. This connection proved useful in the aftermath of the military *coup* that ousted the Brotherhood from government in July 2013. With the men in jail, the Sisters emerged as crucial actors of the Brotherhood resistance and their ability to work across diverse movements sustained their leadership in the repressive period.

5. The Radicalisation of the Sisterhood's gender politics after the 2013 *Coup*

The Egyptian military ousted the Brotherhood from government on 3 July 2013, amid mounting opposition against its rule. Disenchanted members interpreted the Brotherhood's ousting as a failure of the movement, which they attributed to its lack of political skills and its inability to set a coherent political project while in government. The young members who aligned with Egypt's revolutionary movement had since the uprisings been vocal against the decision of the Brotherhood to adopt a programme of gradual state reforms that unavoidably failed to challenge the SCAF's power and leadership in the post-uprising period (Ardovini 2020). Parallel to this, they had sought greater power-sharing with the senior leadership and, met with Brotherhood's resistance, had increasingly acted in greater autonomy from the movement (Biagini 2017a). Inevitably, when the SCAF ousted the Brotherhood and proceeded to arrest thousands of its leaders (Stork 2015), young members took the opportunity to lead the movement's resistance and to play roles previously denied to them, advancing a more radical political agenda against the regime (Fahmy 2015).

The repression of the Brotherhood stood as another significant experience for the Sisters who mobilised in resistance to it, and which, in addition to their involvement in the uprisings and their contribution to the Brotherhood's electoral victories, boosted a more progressive gender politics among the women involved. After the Brotherhood's ousting, young Sisterhood members also established their own women-only movements, sharing the Brotherhood youth's revolutionary ethos and advancing an increasingly autonomous political agenda from that of the senior Brotherhood leaders. This agenda more directly opposed the SCAF as well as the Brotherhood gradualist approach and gender conservatism. Initially, senior and younger Sisters operated under the banner of the Women Against the Coup Movement (Nisat did al-Inquilab – WAC), established in Rabaa al-Adaweya Square during the largest sit-in that the Brotherhood organized against the military intervention. In the meantime, other Brotherhood-led movements also emerged advancing specific causes such as the liberation of prisoners and claiming justice for the family of the martyrs. Up to a year after the Brotherhood's ousting, the WAC's main activities included organizing women's protests against the coup, awareness raising campaigns centred on state-led violence against women and hunger strike campaigns in support of Brotherhood prisoners in collaboration with human rights organizations and leftist activists (Biagini 2017a). However, when the Brotherhood senior leadership, along with some allied senior Sisters, attempted to establish their control of the WAC under the Revolutionary Coalition of Egyptian Women (RCEW), Sisterhood members of the Brotherhood university movement established separate mobilisation groups to retain their independence, sustain street protests and advance their revolutionary agenda (Biagini 2019).

Within these youth-led movements, the Sisters found a space to exercise leadership and also to collaborate with non-Islamist youth-led revolutionary groups, such as the Egyptian Revolutionary Youth, on common goals. While the primary objectives of their mobilization were to resist state repression and put an end to the military coup, the Sisters experienced resistance against their participation in street activism by conservative Islamist forces. Such opposition, along with the violence perpetrated by the state against them, boosted more progressive feminist demands among a young cohort of women members. Claims for greater bodily autonomy, for instance, became prominent among Sisterhood members of the Ultras Banat and Bint al-Thawra movements, subsequent to them experiencing state-led violence, including sexual and gender-based violence, and the simultaneous Brotherhood's attempts to abort women's awareness campaign on the issue. Indeed, when the young members took the matter into their own hands and begun to organize self-defense training for women to give them basic skills to defend themselves against security forces attacks, the Brotherhood criticised Ultras Banat and Bint al-Thawra activists for defying the Brotherhood's gender code around women's modesty, respectability and honour. Similar criticisms were raised by the Brotherhood senior leaders in jail against women's participation in protests activities when the Egyptian state intensified its use of violence against demonstrators (Biagini 2019). These experiences were significant for the Sisters because they fostered greater gender awareness among the young activists, nurturing a more radical critique of the Brotherhood's gender conservatism that reverberates in the Sisterhood's accounts in the current period of Islamists' demobilization.

After a period of intense Islamist mobilization, during which the Brotherhood had made no significant gains *vis-à-vis* the regime, by 2016 the movement risked severe internal splits unseen since the 1960s, whit some members self-proclaiming themselves to represent the organization and advocating for more radical revolutionary means (Willy 2021). The repression has costed the Brotherhood an estimated 40,000 political prisoners (Stork 2015), over a thousand of whom are stated to have been women (Biagini 2017a), thousands of members and supporters' lives (Human Rights Watch 2014), the freezing of its assets along with the closing down of its media channels (Mellor 2018), and a life in exile for thousands of its members (Ardovini and Biagini 2021a, Ardovini 2021). In response, the Brotherhood historical leadership has retrenched on a traditional pattern of self-restrain and isolation, focusing on limiting the damages caused by the repression and on gradually rebuilding the movement relying on *da'wa* activities, mostly from abroad (Ardovini, 2021). In Egypt, the repression exerted by the current regime of President Abdel-Fattah al-Sisi, the former army general that led the 2013 *coup* ousting of the Brotherhood, has made all expression of dissent as life-risk activity. Under these extremely repressive conditions, Brotherhood and Sisterhood members, along with Egypt's opposition movements, are finding it particularly challenging to mobilise.

Observers would however be mistaken to conclude that reduced or absent mobilisation in Egypt equates to the culmination of activists' demands for change or to the return to the status quo ex-ante the revolutionary momentum. Despite the restoration of authoritarianism, the revolution has been a "life-altering" experience for many of those who have taken part in it or lived one (see El-Chazli 2020), engendering a change in their subjectivity that cannot be erased with ease. In this new context, activists have adapted and have been creative in seeking new ways to continue to express the demands that have emerged in times of revolutionary struggle, often shifting to new venues to articulate them. Egypt's revolutionary youth, for instance, have responded to the traumatic experience of loss by focusing on those areas that are still under their control, such as their personal lives, establishing families, pursuing education and new careers (Matthies-Boon 2017), while the broader Egyptian feminist movement met the disappointment at the lack of meaningful gender reforms by challenging Egypt's patriarchal culture through cultural production (Allam 2018). Despite the increasing risk associated with authoritarian states' surveillance of the cyber space, the Internet has emerged as an important site where gender protests and conversations that would have one time taken place in public and social spaces, are being articulated among activists and citizens (Alhayek 2016).

Indeed, in the current period of demobilization, feminist demands that have emerged in the time of the struggle among some of the young members of the Egyptian Muslim Sisterhood have persisted. While women can no longer articulate their claims in the public sphere, debates concerning women's role in the Brotherhood movement continue to take place in informal spaces such as homes (Biagini 2019) and on social media (Mohamed 2020). Crucially, now that formal venues and the public sphere are banned for political activism, the private family sphere and personal relationships have become primary sites for the Sisters to advance gender change. The younger Sisterhood generations in particular, are taking this time of demobilization to reflect more deeply about their personal and marriage relationships, in ways that challenge the institution of the patriarchal family to grant women greater personal and financial autonomy (Biagini 2019), but also to pursue education and professional skills that they can put at the service of the organization in the future (Biagini 2021). This attention given to the individual and personal domains reflects a broader movement for change that persist in the Brotherhood amid its apparent immobility (Ardovini 2020; Ardovini and Biagini 2021b; Biagini 2021a). It constitutes a collective act of resistance based on individual efforts that point to the importance of focusing on the *longue durée* of the revolutionary struggle to assess the effects that individuals' experiences of participation in contentious activism has on their subjectivities, claims and politics, including gender politics (Rivetti 2015, 2020; Biagini 2019).

6. Conclusion

During times of revolutions, war, upheaval, ad repression, traditional gender roles become less rigid and it often happens that women play social and political roles that are usually reserved to men. In 'exceptional circumstances' in fact, women perform tasks that openly transgress the dominant gender order. This often leads them to gain greater access to spheres of society considered male domains. While scholars have observed this dynamic repeating itself across time and space, they have remained skeptical of the sustainability of such gender changes (for example, Ben-Shitrit 2016). Gender transgressions are necessary in exceptional circumstances – war, revolution, repression – because men are at the front, or in prison, or society goes through abnormal transformation of the ordinary, but they are only temporary.

As a fact, as the exceptional circumstances pass, things seem to go back to normal, meaning to traditional gender roles and expectations. The literature on gender and nationalism has documented the upsides and the downsides of women's participation in nationalist and revolutionary struggles, when in the aftermath of the post-conflict order women were pushed back in the kitchens (McClintock 1993, 1996; Enloe 1989, 1993, 2000; Mayer 2000; Bernal 2000; Peterson 2000; Cockburn 2000, 2007, 2013; Hale 2002; Omar 2004; Kaufman and Kristen 2010; Salhi 2010; Parker 2018; Yuval-Davis 1997; Ben-Shitrit 2016; Olivius and Hedström 2019). In Egypt too, while women were welcomed in the streets and in Tahrir Square as organisers and leaders, once the occupation was over they were again pushed out from the public sphere. It seems therefore that nationalist and revolutionary movements are as beneficial as damaging to women. They remain patriarchal in nature, and consequently reproduce the gender order in place before them, leading to little or no gains for the women who contributed to the cause. Although women may play equal roles to men during the upheaval, the result of such processes is never an egalitarian society. Women continue to be excluded from those who have a sit at the political table and, at times, they may even see their situation worsen in terms of personal and civil rights.

The case of the Egyptian Muslim Sisterhood, however, demonstrates that women's participation in revolutions and nationalist movements bear potential for the development and maturation of a radical gender politics. In Islamist movements supporting a nationalist agenda, the nationalist objective proves fundamental to women's ability to transgress gender boundaries in absence of situations of imminent threat or active conflict (Ben-Shitrit 2016). In addition, the fact that the majority of Islamist movements are in opposition to national governments and regimes in the region leaves them constantly vulnerable to threats of repression and violence. Under these circumstances, the exceptional circumstances necessary for women to transgress traditional gender roles are always present, and so is the potential for women to routinize such transgressive practices.

While the negative effects of female participation in nationalist struggles are undoubtedly real, scholars have also pointed out that nationalist and revolutionary movements can be fertile ground for the development of feminist identities at different latitudes, and that the two can have unexpected gendered intersections (Sunseri 2000; Vickers 2002; Alison 2003; O'Keefe 2013, 2017; Al-Ali and Tas 2018). In the SWANA region in particular, the emergence of feminist movements coincided with a strengthening of the demands of national liberation and the struggles for it (Badran 2016; Baron 2005), similar to what had happened in other post-colonial countries (Jayawardena 1986; Roy 2012). Today, as SWANA states remain in a situation of occupation, political repression and war (Haddad 2014), Islamist movements continue to provide opportunities to women for engaging in practices that empower them: to resist protracted occupation, conflict, and violence (Holt and Jawad 2013). Women's identities are inevitably transformed by this engagement, often in ways that suggest the development of a feminist identity and practice, albeit not necessarily in the liberal sense of the term. Furthermore, it is important to consider that, in most cases, feminist claims are not what spur revolutionary waves, although feminist identities precede, accompany, and protract well beyond revolutionary struggles (Badran 2016, 47). Feminist and new gendered subjectivities may survive in practices that are not necessarily outwardly political, and in spaces that are not essentially visible (Al-Ali 2014; Biagini 2021b). Revolutions are new beginnings, when identities and subjectivities are permanently transformed (Selbin 2010).

To conclude, it is important to emphasize that the achievement of gender equality and/or women's greater political inclusion at the outset of the revolutionary struggle is not conditional to the development of feminist identities. In other words, feminist identities do not only exist in contexts where gender equality and greater female participation in institutional politics are in place. On the contrary, it is often women's repeated experiences with marginalization after a political struggle to which they contributed significantly, that increases women's awareness of their status as gendered subjects, inducing women to reverse their efforts in more explicitly feminist activities. Islamist women are no different.

References

Ababneh S. (2009), "Islamic Political Activism as a Means of Women's Empowerment? The Case of the Female Islamic Action Front Activists", *Studies in Ethnicity and Nationalism*, 9, no. 1.

Ababneh S. (2016), "Troubling the political: Women in the Jordanian day-waged Labor movement", *International Journal of Middle East Studies,* 48(1), 87-112.

Abbasi Z. and Shirin S. (2020), "The fantastic politics of martyrdom: legacies of war and celestial spaces of women's empowerment in contemporary Iran", *International Feminist Journal of Politics*, 22(2), 280-288.

Abdel Hady F. (2011), *My Journey with the Muslim Sisters: from Imam Hassan al-Banna to Abd al Nasir's Prison [Rihlaty ma' al-Akhwat al-Muslimat: min al-Imam Hassan al-Banna ila Sugoun 'bd al-Nasir],* Cairo, Dar al-Shuruq.

Abdel-Latif O. (2008), "In the Shadows of the Brothers: The Women of the Egyptian Muslim Brotherhood", *Carnegie Endowment for International Peace*, available at https://carnegieendowment.org/files/women_egypt_muslim_brotherhood.pdf.

Abouelnaga S. (2016), *Women in Revolutionary Egypt: Gender and the New Geographics of Identity*, Cairo, American University in Cairo Press.

Al-Ali N. (2014), "Reflections on (Counter) Revolutionary Processes in Egypt", *Feminist Review*, 106, 122-128.

Al-Ali N. and Latif T. (2018), "Reconsidering Nationalism and Feminism: the Kurdish Political Movement in Turkey", *Nations and Nationalism* 24(2), 453-473.

Al-Arabiya, "Sisters seek to join the office of the Guidance Bureau and to participate in electing the General Guide: The First Women's Protest in the Egyptian Muslim Brotherhood Movement", 17 December 2007, available at http://www.alarabiya.net/articles/2007/12/17/43077.html.

Al-Awadi H. (2014), *The Muslim Brotherhood in Pursuit of Legitimacy. Power and Political Islam in Egypt under Mubarak*, 2nd ed., London-New York, I.B. Tauris.

Alhayek K. (2016), "ICTs, Agency, and Gender in Syrian Activists' Work among Syrian Refugees in Jordan", *Gender, Technology and Development*, 20(3), 333-351.

Alison M. (2003), "Cogs in the wheel? Women in the Liberation Tigers of Tamil Eelam", *Civil Wars*, 6(4), 37-54.

Allam N. (2018), *Women and the Egyptian Revolution: Engagement and Activism during the 2011 Uprisings*, Cambridge, Cambridge University Press.

Ardovini L. (2020), "Stagnation Vs adaptation: tracking the Muslim Brotherhood's trajectories after the 2013 coup", *British Journal of Middle Eastern Studies*, online first, 1-17.

Ardovini L. (2021), "The Muslim Brotherhood in Turkey after the 2013 *coup d'état:* organizational renewal in the diaspora", in Abdelhadi D. and Ramy A. (eds.), *Routledge Handbook of Middle East Diasporas*, Abingdon, Routledge.

Ardovini L. and Biagini E. (2021a), "10 Years On: New Contextual Factors in the Study of Islamism", *Middle East Critique*, 30(4), 411-429.

Ardovini L. and Biagini E. (2021b), "Assessing the Egyptian Muslim Brotherhood after the 2013 coup: Tracing Trajectories of Continuity and Change", *Middle East Law and Governance*, 13(2), 125-129.

Badran M. (1991), "Competing Agendas: Feminists, Islam and the State in 19th and 20th Century Egypt", in Kandiyoti D. (ed.), *Women, Islam and the State,* London, Palgrave MacMillan.

Badran M. (2016), "Creative Disobedience: Feminism, Islam, and Revolution in Egypt", in Sadiqi F. (ed.), *Women's Movements in Post-Arab Spring North Africa*, New York, Palgrave MacMillan.

Baron B. (2005), *Egypt as a Woman: Nationalism, Gender and Politics,* Cairo, American University in Cairo Press.

Bernal V. (2000), "Equality to die for? Women guerilla fighters and Eritrea's cultural revolution", *Political and Legal Anthropology Review,* 23(2), 61-76.

Biagini E. (2017a), "The Egyptian Muslim Sisterhood between Activism, Violence and Leadership", *Mediterranean Politics*, 22(1), 35-53.

Biagini E. (2017b), *A Revolution of Their Own. The Activism of the Egyptian Muslim Sisterhood and its Evolution since the Arab Spring (1928-2014),* PhD Thesis, Dublin City University, Ireland.

Biagini E. (2019), "Islamist Women's Feminist Subjectivities in (R)evolution. The Egyptian Muslim Sisterhood in the Aftermath of the Arab Uprisings", *International Feminist Journal of Politics,* 22(3), 382-402.

Biagini E. (2020), "Islamist Women's Activism under Morsi's Government (2011-2013). Political Inclusion, Gender and Discourse", *Egypte/Monde Arabe,* 21, 37-55.

Biagini E. (2021a), "Women and the Egyptian Muslim Brotherhood post-2013: Calls for Gender Reforms and Pluralism", *Middle East Law and Governance*, 13(2), 171-195.

Biagini E. (2021b), "What's Love Got to do With It? Women, the Muslim Brotherhood and Organizational Identity", *Partecipazione e Conflitto,* 14(2), 547-564.

Biagini E. and Rivetti P. (2020), "State Repression and Activist Organizing in Informal Spaces: Comparing Feminist Movements in Egypt and Iran", *MENA Politics Newsletter*, 3(2), 31-36.

Brand L.A. (1998), *Women, the State, and Political Liberalization: Middle Eastern and North African Experiences*, New York, Columbia University Press.

Cockburn C. (2000), "The anti-essentialist choice: nationalism and feminism in the interaction between two women's projects", *Nations and Nationalism*, 6(4), 611-629.

Cockburn C. (2007), *From Where We Stand: War, Women's Activism and Feminist Analysis*, London-New York, Zed Books.

Cockburn C. (2013), "Against the Odds: Sustaining Feminist Momentum in Post-War Bosnia-Herzegovina", *Women's Studies International Forum*, 37, 26-35.

El-Chazli Y. (2020), "Revolution as a Life-Altering Experience: The Case of Egypt", *Crown Centre for Middle East Studies*, https://www.brandeis.edu/crown/publications/middle-east-briefs/pdfs/101-200/meb136.pdf.

El-Ghobashy M. (2005), "The Metamorphosis of the Egyptian Muslim Brothers", *International Journal of Middle Eastern Studies*, 37(3), 373-395.

El-Said M., Meari L. and Pratt N. (eds.), (2015), *Rethinking Gender in Revolutions and Resistance: Lessons from the Arab World*, London, Zed Books.

El-Tohamy A. (2016), *Youth Activism in Egypt. Islamism, Political Protest and Revolution*, London-New York, I.B. Tauris.

Enloe C. (1989), *Bananas, Beaches and Bases: Making Feminist Sense of International Politics*, London, Pandora Press, Harper/Collins.

Enloe C. (1993), *The morning after. Sexual politics at the end of the Cold War*, Berkeley-Los Angeles, University of California Press.

Enloe C. (2000), "When Soldiers Rape", in *Maneuvers: The International Politics of Militarizing Women's Lives*, Berkley, University of California, 108-152.

Fahmy G. (2015), "The Struggle for the Leadership of Egypt's Muslim Brotherhood", *Carnegie Endowment for International Peace*, July http://carnegie-mec.org/2015/07/14/struggle-for-leadership-of-egypt-s-muslim-brotherhood-pub-60678.

Farag M. (2012), "The Muslim Sisters and the January 25th Revolution", *Journal of International Women's Studies*, 13(5), 228-237.

Feldman N. (2000), *The Arab Winter: A Tragedy*, Princeton, Princeton University Press.

Gershoni I. and Jankowski J. (1995), *Redefining the Egyptian Nation: 1930-1945*, Cambridge, Cambridge University Press.

Ghazzawi R. (2014), "Seeing the Women in Revolutionary Syria", *Open Democracy*, April 8, available at https://www.opendemocracy.net/arab-awakening/razan-ghazzawi/seeing-women-in-revolutionary-syria.

Gordon J. (1992), *Nasser's Blessed Movement. Egypt's Free Officers and the July Revolution*, Oxford, Oxford University Press.

Grinin L., Korotayev A. and Tausch A. (2019), "Introduction. why Arab spring became Arab winter", in *Islamism, Arab Spring, and the Future of Democracy*, 1-24.

Haddad Z. (2014), "How the Crisis Is Altering Women's Roles in Syria", *Forced Migration Review*, 47, 46-47.

Hafez S. (2019), *Women of the Midan. The Untold Stories of Egypt's Revolutionaries*, Bloomington, Indiana University Press.

Hale S. (2002), "Liberated, but not free: women in post-war Eritrea", in Meintjes S., Pillay A. and Turshen M. (eds.), *Aftermath: Women in Post-War Reconstruction*, New York, Zed Press, 122-141.

Holt M. and Jawad H. (2013), *Women, Islam, and resistance in the Arab world*, Boulder, Lynne Rienner Publishers.

Human Rights Watch (2014), *All according to Plan: The Rab'a Massacre and Mass Killings of Protesters in Egypt* https://www.hrw.org/report/2014/08/12/all-according-plan/raba-massacre-and-mass-killings-protesters-egypt.

Jayawardena K. (1986), *Feminism and Nationalism in the Third World*, London, Zed Books.

Kaufman J.P. and Williams K.OP. (2010), *Women and War: Gender Identity and Activism in Times of Conflict*, Sterling, Kumarian Press.

Karam A.M. (1998), *Women, Islamist and the State: Contemporary Feminism in Egypt*, Basingstoke, Palgrave MacMillan.

Khalil A. (ed.), (2015), *Gender Women and the Arab Spring*, Abingdon, Routledge.

Kocamaner H. (2018), "The politics of family values in Erdogan's new Turkey", *Middle East Report,* 48(3), 36-39.

Kraetzschmar H. and Rivetti P. (eds.) (2018), *Islamists and the Politics of the Arab Uprisings: Governance, Pluralisation and Contention*, Edinburgh, Edinburgh University Press.

Lynch M. (2007), "Young Brothers in Cyberspace", *Middle East Report*, 245, available at https://merip.org/2007/12/young-brothers-in-cyberspace/.

Matthies-Boon V. (2017), "Shattered Worlds: Political Trauma amongst Activists in Post-Revolutionary Egypt", *The Journal of North African Studies*, 22(4), 620-644.

Mayer T. (ed.) (2000), *Gender Ironies of Nationalism: Sexing the Nation*, London-New York, Routledge.
McClintock A. (1993), "Family Feuds: Gender, Nationalism and the Family", *Feminist Review*, 44(Summer), 61-80.
McClintock A. (1996), "No longer in a future heaven: nationalism, gender, and race", in Eley G. (ed.), *Becoming National: A Reader*, Oxford, Oxford University Press, 259-284.
Mellor N. (2018), *Voice of the Brotherhood. Da'wa, Discourse, and Political Communication*, London-New York, Routledge.
Mitchell R.P. (1993) [1969], *The Society of the Muslim Brothers,* Oxford, Oxford University Press.
Mohamed H.Z.H. (2020), *The Social Construction of Reality Through Facebook: Understanding Stories of the Egyptian Muslim Sisterhood During the Military Coup Era*, Master Dissertation, International Islamic University of Malaysia.
O'Keefe T. (2013), *Feminist Identity Development and Activism in Revolutionary Movements*, Basingstoke, Palgrave MacMillan.
O'Keefe T. (2017), "Mother Ireland, Get Off Our Backs': Republican Feminist Resistance in the North of Ireland", in Bosi L. and De Fazio G. (eds.), *The Troubles in Northern Ireland and Theories of Social Movements*, Amsterdam, Amsterdam University Press, 165-184.
Olimat M.S. (ed.) (2013), *Arab Spring and Arab Women: Challenges and Opportunities*, London-New York, Routledge.
Olivius E. and Hedström J. (2019), "Militarized nationalism as a platform for feminist mobilization? The case of the exiled Burmese women's movement", *Women's studies international forum*, 76, 102-263.
Omar K. (2004), "National symbolism in constructions of gender: transformed symbols in post-conflict states", *Seton Hall Journal of Diplomacy & International Relations*, 5, 49-68.
Parker A. *et al.* (eds.) (2018), *Nationalisms and Sexualities*, 2nd ed., New York-London, Routledge Revival.
Peterson S.V. (2000), "Sexing Political Identities/Nationalism as Heterosexism", in Ranchod-Nilsson S. and Tetrault M.A. (eds.), *Women, States and Nationalism: At Home in the Nation?*, New York-London, Routledge, 54-80.
Pratt N. (2013), "Egyptian Women: Between Revolution, Counter-Revolution, Orientalism, and Authenticity", *Jadaliyya*, May 6, available at https://www.jadaliyya.com/Details/28574/Egyptian-Women-Between-Revolution,-Counter-Revolution,-Orientalism,-and-Authenticity.
Pratt N. (2020), *Embodying Geopolitics: Generations of Women's Activism in Egypt, Jordan and Lebanon*, Los Angeles, University of California Press.

Rivetti P. (2015), "Continuity and Change before and After the Uprisings in Tunisia, Egypt and Morocco: Regime Reconfiguration and Policy-making in North Africa", *British Journal of Middle Eastern Studies*, 42(1), 1-11.

Rivetti P. (2020), *Political Participation in Iran from Khatami to the Green Movement*, Basingstoke, Palgrave McMillan.

Roy S. (2012), *Remembering Revolution: Gender, Violence, and Subjectivity in India's Naxalbari Movement*, New Delhi, Oxford University Press.

Sadiqi F. (ed.) (2016), *Women's Movements in Post-"Arab-Spring" North Africa* , New York, Palgrave MacMillan.

Salhi Z.S. (2010), "The Algerian feminist movement between nationalism, patriarchy and Islamism", *Women's Studies International Forum*, 33(2), 113-124.

Selbin E. (2010), *Revolution, Rebellion, Resistance: The Power of Story*, New York, Zed Books.

Shitrit L.-B. (2016), *Righteous Trangressions. Women's Activism on the Israeli and Palestinian Religious Right*, Princeton, Princeton University Press.

Stephan R. and Charrad M.M. (2020), *Women Rising in and beyond the Arab Spring*, New York, New York University Press.

Stork J. (2015), "Egypt's Political Prisoners", Open Democracy, March 6, available at https://www.opendemocracy.net/opensecurity/joe-stork/egypt%E2%80%99s-political-prisoners.

Sunseri L. (2000), "Moving beyond the feminism versus the nationalism dichotomy: an anti-colonial feminist perspective on aboriginal liberation struggles", *Canadian Woman Studies*, 20(2), 143-148.

Tadros M. (2012), *The Muslim Brotherhood in Contemporary Egypt: Democracy Redefined or Confined?*, London-New York, Routledge.

Tadros M. (2016), *Resistance, Revolt, and Gender Justice in Egypt* (Syracuse, NY, Syracuse University Press.

Tadros M. (2017), "Protesting Gender Discrimination from within: Women's Political Representation on Behalf of Islamic Parties", *British Journal of Middle Eastern Studies*, 44(2), 176-193.

Talhami G.H. (1996), *The Mobilization of Muslim Women in Egypt,* Gainesville, University Press of Florida.

Tammam H. (2011), "The Salafization of the Muslim Brothers", *Marased,* 1, 1-54.

Touaf L., Soumia B. and Chourouq N. (eds.) (2017), *North African Women after the Arab Spring. In the Eye of the Storm*, Basingstoke, Palgrave Macmillan.

Vickers J. (2002), "Feminists and Nationalism", in Dhuruvarajan V. and Vickers J. (eds.), *Gender, Race and Nation: A Global Perspective*, Toronto, University of Toronto Press, 247-272.

Wickham C.R. (2013), *The Muslim Brotherhood. Evolution of an Islamist Movement*, Princeton, Princeton University Press.
Willy V.J. (2021), *The Fourth Ordeal. A History of the Muslim Brotherhood in Egypt, 1968-2018*, Cambridge, Cambridge University Press.
Yuval-Davis N. (1997), *Gender and Nation*, London, Sage.
Yuval-Davis N. (2003), "Nationalist projects and gender relations", *Croatian Journal of Ethnology and Folklore Research*, 40(1), 9-35.
Yuval-Davis N. and Anthias A. (eds.) (1989), *Woman-Nation-State*, London, Palgrave MacMillan.
Zollner B. (2007), "Prison Talks: The Muslim Brotherhood's Internal Struggle during Gamal Abdel Nasser's Persecution, 1954 to 1971", *International Journal of Middle East Studies*, 39(3), 441-433.

Chapter 9

GENDER EQUALITY AND ISLAM: EXPERIENCES IN MOROCCO

Asma Lamrabet

ABSTRACT: *Gender equality is universally an uncompleted ideal and this issue transcends all cultures, ideologies, religions and societal structures. However, it is important to recognize that its implementation is much more difficult or even complex in societies where religion is lived as a hard-core identity, like Morocco, and where Islam remains a major and essential referential. Morocco has experienced two major reforms (Family Code 2004 and Reform of the Constitution 2011) which have had a beneficial overall effect on the legal status of women and this thanks to a political will coming from the highest spheres of the State but also to the deep and important struggle of the Moroccan secular feminists. However, it is clear that despite the positive impact of these two reforms on the symbolism of women's rights, the fact remains that their effectiveness within social reality has remained very limited if not insufficient compared to the aspirations of young people and to the societal metamorphoses in progress. This maintained juridical-political incompatibility, between laws and socio-cultural realities, constitutes in fact the crucial issue of gender equality and can only be resolved if we deconstruct this contradictory logic and also the confusing overlap between religious and socio-political realities. This is why we see today the importance of the deconstruction of traditionalist reading which is at the origin of the recurrent instrumentalization of religious discourse and this at all levels – official and ideological – and which impede any real approach to the issue of gender equality in a country like Morocco. The need for a reformist vision of religion on this issue is essential today because reforming the religion approach is simply reforming deeply the society and therefore constitutes a real and effective democratic issue.*

1. Introduction

Equality as a universal value inherent within the humanist principles of modernity, and as an alternative to a thousand-year-old sexual order, has still not been achieved globally. However, this objective is even more difficult to fulfil within societies dominated by religious sentiment.

Nonetheless, it is important to stress the distinction that needs to be drawn, even within the religious sphere, between the institutional-religious dimension (the locus of theological power, with all of its hierarchies and authoritative systems) and the spiritual-ethical dimension to religion (which pertains to the interior domain and the search for meaning). Within the former category, the thousand-year-long inequality is supported and consolidated by a patriarchal reading of religious scripture. As far as the spiritual dimension is concerned on the other hand, as is the case within all religions it often embraces egalitarian principles, although these are systematically marginalised and ignored by the male-dominated religious order.

Equality between men and women is thus more difficult to achieve within societies in which religion is a genuine foundation for identity, such as majority Muslim societies. One example of such a society is Morocco, where Islam is still a major reference point within constitutional law and an indispensable cultural marker [1].

This question, which crystallises the full range of contemporary socio-political tensions, is an extremely sensitive one. This is because it is not only an abstract question about women's rights but also a question about human rights. In other words, it is an eminently political question as it lies at the heart of current socio-cultural problems concerning for instance individual freedom, family law and in particular the duality, or even the persistent antagonism, between religious and universal values and principles.

2. Gender equality within contemporary Islam

Is it possible to speak of gender equality within a religion such as Islam today, and with reference to the current state of Arab-Muslim societies in general? It would be difficult to answer this question objectively quite simply because to ask Islam – or indeed to ask any other religion – to answer contemporary questions concerning gender equality would be to engage with an "anachronism". This modern conception of gender equality simply does not exist within orthodox and institutional Islam, just as it does not exist within other religious systems. However, an ethical and contemporary reformist reading of scripture can identify some scope for egalitarian ideas, which can make it possible to "imagine" and give tangible form to an egalitarian justice that is often apparent within the text of the Koran and

[1] Articles 1 and 3 of the Moroccan Constitution (2011 reform): http://www.sgg.gov.ma/Portals/0/constitution/constitution_2011_Fr.pdf.

yet has been unexplored or even ignored throughout centuries of patriarchal hermeneutic interpretations.

It should also be recalled that, with its philosophical inspiration in human rights, gender equality poses a genuine problem within majority Muslim societies, essentially on two levels. It is a problem first of all as this principle has been tainted by the traumas of the colonial political heritage and certain Orientalist narratives that debase Islam, which are still extremely vivid within the Muslim imagination. However, it is also a problem insofar as it clashes with an denied part of the religious tradition unconscious religious assumption that was forged, codified and legitimised by classical norms of classical Islamic jurisprudence, which remains wedded to the patriarchal model of the family and masculine authority, as sacred immutable principles.

The question of women within Islam thus represents the "weak link" within the Islamic tradition and tangibly reflects the *theological impasse within contemporary Muslim thought*. In fact, one cannot avoid noticing the yawning gap between the globalised social reality of Muslim societies and the archaic legal-theological discourse of most religious institutions, which have been incapable of formulating any legal alternatives to Islamic interpretations from the 9th and 10th centuries.

It is thus clear why the overall question of gender equality within Islam is repeatedly ***taken hostage*** by two extreme visions: the traditional, conservative vision resistant to any reform in religious thinking, and a "modernist" vision, which calls into question, or even rejects, any reference to religious doctrine, which is asserted to stand in opposition to universal values. This debate thus reveals a profound fissure as well as an ideological-political and theological polarisation within majority Arab-Muslim societies.

3. Key religious reference points

It is important first of all to clarify some concepts succinctly before proceeding with this discussion. Specifically, *what Islam is it that we are talking about*? Is it a socio-anthropological, historical, institutional, legal, Sufi, popular, rationalist, philosophical or political Islam? Does it concern the Fiqh, the Sharia or Islamic law? What about the prophetic tradition and the hadith? Islam is all of this. It is a multifaceted phenomenon and cannot be reduced to one single interpretative matrix or one single perspective. However, it must be noted that this diversity appears to have been reduced today to this ahistorical notion of an Islam that is fixed, abstract and monolithic.

It must also be recalled that, although there is no official clergy and there are no official religious institutions within Islam, throughout the history of Islamic civilisation a theological-political hierarchy has existed, which established itself several decades after the death of the Prophet, and which thus more or less institutionalised the religion. The exploitation of religion for political ends progressively increased with the co-opting of the ulemas, who rose to political power with the caliphs, but also with the codification of Islamic sciences under different dynasties during the 8th and 9th centuries.

In this respect it is important to clarify a number of terms relating to Islam, which arose within specific historical contexts, in order to be able to engage with the contemporary question of equality. A distinction must first be drawn between the different categories of Islamic tradition by reiterating that the text of the Koran alone is regarded as the primordial source of authority. This fundamental source has been canonised within Islam by almost universal consensus amongst most Muslim scholars [2].

It is also important to clarify briefly the extremely frequent confusion surrounding the concept of Sharia within Islam. Sharia [3], the etymology of which points to the word for "path" – i.e. that leads to the source – is cited twice in the Koran. With the development of Islamic civilisation and the expansion of religious sciences, this concept has been reduced to its legalist dimension (*ahkam*) at the expense of its much more important ethical dimension (*akhlaq*) within the Koran [4]. "*The term Sharia only has any meaning insofar as it is used*" and it has thus been used, depending on the different socio-political contexts within Muslim societies, as a basis for identity, political projects or activist movements [5].

---

[2] Owing to the large number of sources, precepts that are in some cases contradictory and above all the late codification, the "authentic" *Hadiths* or the tradition of the prophet (*Sunna*) are regarded as a source of norms which, whilst being important, are secondary in terms of their explanatory power and always complementary to the primary source, the Koran. For further details see: Merad Ali, "La textualisation de la Tradition", in Ali Merad (ed.), *La Tradition musulmane,* Paris cedex 14, Presses Universitaires de France, "Que sais-je?", 2001, 43-54 available at https://www.cairn.info/la-tradition-musulmane--9782130520740-page-43.htm.

[3] This concept can be found respectively in chapter 5, verse 48 and in chapter 45, verse 18. It is interesting to note that, in verse 48 of chapter 5, the term "Sharia" is not used specifically in relation to Islam, but rather that each Abrahamic religion has its own path: "*To each among you [i.e. Jews, Christians and Muslims] We have prescribed a law – shariatan – and a clear way – minhajan. If Allah willed, He would have made you one nation, but that (He) may test you in what He has given you; so strive as in a race in good deeds. The return of you (all) is to Allah; then He will inform you about that in which you used to differ*".

[4] It is thus rather a path that privileges the ethical aspect over the normative aspect. In the view of a majority of theologians, the latter aspect is limited to around 300 verses out of a total of 6,200 verses.

[5] Dupret B., *La Charia. Des sources à la pratiques, un concept pluriel*, Paris, La Découverte, 2014, 12.

Fiqh is also another equivocal Islamic concept, which is frequently rendered as "Islamic jurisprudence" or "Muslim law"[6]. In other words, it deals with interpretation and the rational inference, starting from religious texts, of laws or legal opinions (*istinbat alahkam*). It is, in a nutshell, the entire intellectual process by which the *fuqahas* (or jurisconsults) attempted during their respective historical epochs to establish specific legal rules based on the two principal sources, namely the Koran and the Sunnah, or the Prophet's way of life. *Fiqh* has progressively been built up as a body of Islamic norms and legal compilations were officially drawn up during the times of the Abbasid Caliphate (*'asr altadwin*). It is important to note here that *Fiqh* is still characterised by its plurality and the diversity of the legal opinions, or *fatwas*. This explains the existence of the various legal schools, *madhahib*, of which there were four within Sunnism during the 8th and 9th centuries[7]. *Fiqh* is thus a plural normative body, which has been socially and historically constructed. It is often confused with the Sharia owing to its sacralisation in the Islamic imagination. Whilst it is certainly an important dimension within the Muslim tradition, it was never regarded as immutable by its founders, having resulted from contingent human interpretations.

Thus, starting from the time when Muslim civilisation started to go into decline – and in particular during the colonial period, which was marked by the shock of encountering modernity – *Fiqh* crystallised and was reduced to its strictly codified and sclerotic legal dimension. Under colonial administrations it was reformulated under the name of "Muslim law" or "sharia", and construed as "Islamic law". In its first, original version, Fiqh was a code of ethics more than a legal system and the idea of codifying it and thus finally sacralising it within Islamic or divine law was completely at odds with its spirit[8].

This explains how the multiple attempts to reform the laws on personal status within Muslim countries have always clashed with this supposed sacrality of "Muslim law", which was regarded as equivalent to a divine law. However, today the key element to this Muslim law is in fact a hybrid law,

---

6 The term *fiqh* is derived from the root *ta-fa-qa-ha*, which means an effort at understanding and instruction.

7 The legal schools of Sunni Islam are respectively those of Imam Abu Hanifa, Shafii, Malik and Ahmed Ibn Hanbal.

8 See the excellent work carried out on this issue in the article: Dupret B. and Buskens L., "Introduction. De l'invention du droit musulman à la pratique juridique contemporaine", in Dupret B. (ed.), *La charia aujourd'hui. Usages de la référence au droit islamique*, Paris, La Découverte, "Recherches", 2012, 9-17, DOI: 10.3917/dec.dupre.2012.01.0009. URL: https://www.cairn.info/---page-9.htm.

which is not derived either from classical Fiqh or from western laws. It is in fact a legal compilation that draws together various interpretations of Islamic legal schools, and is also supplemented by articles from the Napoleonic Code as well as customary rules (*'urf*)[9]. In most Muslim societies, this Muslim law is often limited to questions relating to family relations, such as marriage, divorce or the rules of succession. These various family codes represent what may be termed as the last bastions of resistance by Islamic identity for traditionalists and the proponents of political Islam[10].

4. Reforms in Morocco

The reform of the Family Code in 2004 (Moudawana) without doubt constituted a major turning point in the history of women and the family in Morocco and triggered what may be termed the start of the "desacralisation" of Muslim law. This reform was the result of a fierce fight between conservatives (who represented a majority within Islamic thinking at that time) and the so-called "modernising" wing comprised mainly of secular, left-wing feminist associations. It should perhaps be recalled that it was thanks to the long battle and the feminist left-wing demands made by the "equality spring" coalition that these reforms could be adopted[11].

The polarisation of Moroccan society during this period between modernisers and conservatives, who were respectively for and against the reform of the Family Code, offers a graphic example of how religious considerations were heavily relied on in order to counter claims made by feminists at the time. Those who objected to the reform, who included Islamists as well as conservatives of all stripes, considered that the reform of the Personal Status Code represented a genuine attack on what they held to be sacred, and that this reform project was being piloted by an agenda of obedience to the West, the imported values of which were undermining tradition, the family and the identity of the Islamic *Ummah*. This standoff culminated in the organisation of two marches, one held in

[9] For references see above.

[10] This occurred during the reform of the Family Code in Morocco in the early 2000s when Moroccan Islamists rejected any reform of the old Personal Status Code, taking the view that it reflect the Sharia and was sacred in status.

[11] In 1992, the Union of Feminine Action launched a petition concerning the reform of the *moudawana* with the aim of obtaining a million signatures. See El Bouhsini L., "Une lute pour l'égalité racontée par les féministes marocaines", in *Rives Méditerranéennes, Récits de femmes en Méditerranée,* 2016, available at https://doi.org/10.4000/rives.5034, 121-133.

Casablanca by conservatives and the other in Rabat by those in favour of the reform. This is emblematic of a moment of social rupture, which was characterised by confusion, the ideological, political and affective exploitation of religious identity, fear, and the idealisation of a Code that was perceived as sacred, even though it was nothing more than one particular interpretation, amongst many, of legal sources exclusively from the Maliki school [12].

It was King Mohammed VI of Morocco (known as a fervent defender of women's rights) who, as Commander of the Faithful and as highest moral and religious authority in the country, was able to defuse the profound social crisis by setting up a multi-disciplinary royal commission including both conservatives and modernisers, which was finally able to reach a consensus on the reform of those laws that discriminated against women [13]. The consensus position was based on social reality, the goals of the Sharia as a philosophy of ethics as well as human rights

The 2004 reform was thus characterised by three main pillars: first of with regard to family responsibilities, thus repealing the old article that established the husband as the head of the family; secondly the empowerment of judges through the creation of family courts; and thirdly the protection of the rights of the child. Equality considerations also permeated other aspects of this Code, such as in particular the setting of the age of marriage at 18 for both men and women, and equal rights and duties for both spouses, as matrimonial protection (*wali*) is no longer mandatory for adult women [14].

The fact remains that, whilst this Code may have been revolutionary at the time, it still features a number of shortcomings, including in particular as regards legal protection for children, which is a right vested exclusively in the husband, in particular in the event of separation. Polygamy has been maintained, albeit subject to certain conditions. The question of the age of marriage is problematic as the exceptions, which are permitted subject to

---

[12] The reform was ultimately possible thanks to a consensus and a process of intense dialogue between the various social, political and religious actors in the country under the aegis of King Mohammed VI, who played a fundamental role in his capacity as *Amir al mou'minin* (Commander of the Faithful), and who thus had a religious legitimacy that enabled him to make the debate more dispassionate.

[13] Given his role as "Commander of the Faithful", representatives from Islamist parties were unable to dispute the King's mediation role and his proposal.

[14] It is also important to note other new features including: divorce as a basis for dissolving marriage becoming a right for both spouses (whereas under the traditionalist *Fiqh* it is a unilateral right of the husband), and divorce procedures being subject to control by the courts. Moreover, it is now possible to divide the assets acquired during the marriage following the married couple's separation.

review by the courts, have become the rule and a large number of underage girls still marry in Morocco.

In spite of all of this, the 2004 reform of the Family Code acted as a catalyst for a series of other reforms at various levels, resulting in greater equality between men and women. Examples include the reform of the Nationality Code in 2007, which granted mothers the right to pass on their nationality to their children, and above all the 2011 constitutional reform, with Art. 19 now providing, for the first time in the history of Morocco, for full equality between male and female citizens.

These two major reforms – the reform of the Family Code and the constitutional reform – have had an extremely beneficial effect overall on the legal status of women and represent tangible legal process compared with other countries in the region, other than Tunisia. In effect, these two reforms have been emblematic in terms of their philosophy of emancipating women and, despite some concepts that are now outdated, have made it possible to move beyond the traditionalist and discrimination conception of the family and of women.

However, it is important to acknowledge today that, despite their positive impact on the symbolism of women's rights, these two reforms are still proven examples of this dissonance between the law – which is certainly progressive compared in particular to other Muslim countries – and its low level of efficacy within social reality.

It should also be noted that Art. 19 of the new Moroccan Constitution of 2011, which for the first time in the country's history provided for full equality between men and women throughout all areas, is still subject to a condition laid down by that very Article of respect for the "permanent characteristics of the Kingdom" [15]. In fact, those permanent characteristics that "condition" equality include the stipulation laid down by the Constitution concerning "moderate Muslim religion". This begs the question as to what is intended by moderate Islam.

This "conditional equality" is a clear expression of the "overlaying" of two sentiments: the religious sentiment, which constitutes the basis for Moroccan family law, and the universal sentiment enshrined in the international conventions ratified by Morocco, which acts as the basis for the rights of Moroccans within the public sphere.

The situation thus involves a constitutional "legal duality", and it must

---

[15] Art. 1 of the Moroccan Constitution of 2011: The Nation relies for its collective life on the federative constants [*constantes federatrices*], on the occurrence of moderate Muslim religion, [on] the national unity of its multiple components [affluents], [on] the constitutional monarchy and [on] democratic choice. Art. 3: Islam is the religion of the State, which guarantees to all the free exercise of beliefs [*cultes*].

be acknowledged that certain religious "inequalities" condition equality in general, and that these religious inequalities are untouchable as they pertain to "permanent characteristics with sacred status". This ultimately consolidates, fuels and endorses the numerous contradictions existing between the law and the socio-cultural reality.

The legal-political incompatibility between the law and the socio-cultural reality is the key aspect to this issue, and can only be resolved after first deconstructing this contradictory logic and this confused intermingling of religious and socio-political realities.

Indeed, one might ask how equality should be conceptualised within the family sphere, within the laws that govern it and within the public sphere, when inequality between men and women within socio-cultural mentalities and imaginations is still a major structural given, having been fuelled by traditionalist religious and patriarchal discourse in which equality is perceived of as being inherently incompatible with religious sentiment, or even as an entirely Western intrusion.

It is thus clear that the laws are important, but the reform of the understanding and approach to religion is absolutely necessary if we want to change the mentalities which are the main structures that impede the compatibility between the two legal and religious referential and therefore to the establishment of a real culture of equality.

One possible approach could be to attempt to steer a third way between the traditionalist conservative viewpoint and the modernist one. This could specifically reconcile the ethical principles of Islam with the principles of universal rights, such that there is no major incompatibility between gender equality and religious sentiment in its ethical and spiritual dimension.

This issue lies at the heart of the problem of gender equality and of all the ambiguity surrounding it. Moreover, the questions that still need to be put will be crucial for the future consideration of this problem. Specifically, there is a question as to how this tension between the presence of two sentiments that appear to be diametrically opposed can be reconciled. Is there really any incompatibility or contradiction between religious sentiment and universal values? Is, as is often believed, that religious sentiment with which a majority of Muslims identify anti-egalitarian and discriminatory against women?

It would be very difficult to answer these legitimate questions either in the affirmative or in the negative as the answers depend upon how this religious sentiment is construed. However, the majority approach taken by clerics today is a literal, legalist and discriminatory approach, which is above all exploited politically. It is ultimately not religious sentiment itself that represents a problem, but rather how this religious sentiment has been exploited for socio-political ends throughout the centuries.

It is therefore in this sense that contemporary reformist, and in particular feminist interpretations seek to engage with this problem by deconstructing the *a priori* assumptions and the barriers to a reconciliation between contextualised religious sentiment and reappropriated universalism.

5. The alternatives proposed by new feminist and reformist readings

To start with, we must ask why a reformist vision of religious sentiment is necessary, rather than simply dispensing with the religious norm? First of all, this is the case quite simply because Islam remains an indispensable normative point of reference in most Muslim countries, both as a State religion and as a source of legislation. As such, reforming religious sentiment today means profoundly reforming society, and for this reason represents a major democratic challenge.

Another reason is the fact that it is always legitimate to propose alternatives based on one's own history, one's own memory and one's own cultural reference points, with all of their contradictions and indisputable riches, whilst at the same time remaining open to the contribution of universal human experience. A final reason is that – it must be repeated – the history of reformism is an integral part of the history of Islam. Since the revelation, the history of Islam has been one of plurality, and the constant rejuvenation of how it is interpreted and understood [16].

Resistance to any form of religious reform arose progressively between the 12th and 19th centuries, leading to the emergence of a kind of "historical lethargy", which inaugurated a period of decadence (*inhitat*) characterised by hostility to any innovation and a rejection of any effort to contextualise *ijtihad*.

Today there is a feminine dynamic – which certainly still has minority status – within the Muslim and Western world, which since the 1990s has been calling for a new interpretation of the sacred texts [17]. This ongoing

[16] The religious heritage of Islam is characterised by a variety of spiritual, philosophical and legal currents, ranging from the traditionalist *ahl al-hadith*, or strict adepts of tradition, to those who exercise their personal reasoning (*ahl alr'ay'*) and rationalist reformists (*Mu'tazila*, from the 8th century), as well as the rationalist school (Ibn Rochd), the mystical school (Ibn Arabi), and not forgetting the reformist *Nahda* around the end of the 19th and the start of the 20th centuries (Al-Afghani, Mohammed Abdouh).

[17] It is not possible to cite all of them, although I shall provide the names of the networks and the women involved in this work: the networks *Musawah* in Malaysia and *Karamah* in the United States, theologian academics such as the Pakistani Asma Barlas, the Anglo-Iranian Ziba Mir Hosseynni, the Afro-American Amina Wadud, the Egyp-

dynamic has been inspiring extremely important work on the deconstruction of most of the misogynistic religious interpretations, whilst at the same time proposing a new textual approach that is essentially ethical, egalitarian and innovative, in sharp contrast to the currently dominant legalistic and traditionalist approach. By reappropriating religious knowledge, one of the main steps made by these movements has been to denounce shortcomings and gaps within traditionalist religious discourse concerning the founding text of Islam.

Having had access specifically to textual sources, to religious knowledge and to theological tools and argumentation, these women have understood that it is not the ethical-spiritual dimension to Islam that has caused discrimination, but rather the various human interpretations that have built up within religious compilations, although also within mentalities that are averse to any female presence within the socio-political and theological spheres.

The work pursued by this generation of Muslim women, amongst whom I count myself, is a discourse that stresses the centrality and importance of the ethical-liberatory dynamic within an Islamic sentiment that has been revisited, historicised and contextualised.

The synthesis resulting from this work reveals that Islamic scripture is open to a just and egalitarian ethical interpretation, in opposition to the discriminatory framework established over centuries of theological and legal compilations.

For this reason, by ascribing priority to the reformist, feminist viewpoint it has been possible to rediscover this flexibility and these ethical benchmarks laid down by the Qur'an which had been marginalised by traditionalist readings, and which today are compatible with an interpretation that respects the universal values of equality, non-discrimination, justice and the dignity of women and men.

The alternative reformist methodological approaches are essentially focused on an ***ethical-spiritual approach*** that adopts a dual perspective rooted both in faith as well as in a rigorous, rational, academic approach to the holy text and its interpretative tradition.

Indeed, as Muslim women we assert the right to participate in the process of deriving meaning and religious knowledge, tasks that have until now been the exclusive domain of men. We endorse the postulate that asserts that the Qur'an s a sacred text has a consistent worldview and imparts the-

tians Omaima Abou Bakr and Mulki al Sharmani, the Moroccan Aicha el Hajjami, the South African Africaine Saydiya Shaikh, and the Lebanese Nayla Tabbara amongst others… See also our book on this work: Lamrabet A., *Women in the Qur'an: An Emancipatory reading*, 2016, Leicestershire, Kube Publishing limited.

ological, ethical and legal teachings that are profoundly interconnected, and moreover that ethical and legal issues cannot be detached from it, as the traditionalist majority interpretation asserts.

It is thus necessary to establish a new hermeneutical ethical framework with a view to proposing interpretations that promote equality between men and women. Specifically, it must be recalled that, in spite of the recent development that some researchers have termed the "ethical turn" within Islamic research, in particular in relation to *tafsir*, generally speaking no classical exegesis has used a systematic ethical approach as an interpretative method or independent discipline [18].

The history of classical Qur'anic exegesis shows that neither the classical commentators nor indeed Muslim jurists sought to construct any ethical theories rooted in the Qur' in spite of the fact that the sacred text is fundamentally and primarily ethical [19].

In order to be able to infer ethical and egalitarian meanings from within the text, we must change our interpretative paradigm. Accordingly, the new ethical approach applied to the question of gender relations has filled the gap of this "hermeneutic silence" in relation to those verses that concern equality, which were ignored and marginalised by classical commentators.

It is in this sense that the new approach would enable three different types of reading to be pursued at the same time:

- **A holistic reading of the text**: (*shoumoulya*) in order to re-establish the issue of women within the globality and universality of the spiritual message.
- **A purposive reading of the text** (*maqassidya*) still known as "*maqassid acharia*", or purposes of the Qur'anic way, which emphasises the spirit of the text above its literal provision.
- **A contextualised textual and inter-textual reading** (*siyakyah*): this enables all of the verses to be construed in the light of one another, taking account of the circumstances of revelation as well as historical context, and enables the etymological meaning of Qur'anic concepts to be clarified.

---

[18] Exegetical works tend to have been classified according to theological, legal, philosophical or Sufi schools of thought on the one hand, or according to the method of inferring meaning on the other hand, but not according to a coherent ethical system; see also *The Journal of Islamic Ethics*; Ghaly M., "A Pressing Demand and a Promising Field", *Journal of Islamic Ethics*, online publication 27 July 2017 available at https://brill.com/view/journals/jie/1/1-2/article-p1_1.xml?language=en.

[19] There are around 300 verses with a legal meaning (*ahkam*) out of a little over 6,600 verses in total.

This new approach thus highlights three major dimensions within the Qur'an:

- ***The ethical dimension***: the most predominant with its universal principles of the need for justice (*'adl*), equity (*qist*), compassion (*rahma*), probity (*taqwa*), love (*mahaba*), wisdom (*hikma*), solidarity (*ta'awoun 'ala al bir wa taqwa*) and protection of the oppressed (*mustad'afin fil ard*), and it applies to men and women without any distinction.
- ***The humanist dimension***: symbolised by the Qur'an concept of *însan*, whether man or woman. In effect, the Qur'an addresses itself to men and women in terms of their humanity above all. In most cases it is a theology of the human, which transcends gender, and calls upon human beings to display above all their most noble aspects, namely human dignity (*wa karamna baniadam*), the soul (*ruh*), reason (*'aql*), intelligence (*hikma*) but also human vulnerability (*khulika alinsan dai'fan*). The most important point here is to note that the text contradicts the argumentation reiterated many times within a number of discourses and interpretative compilations of the "vulnerability and inferiority of women" as an argument for endorsing the superiority of men.
- ***The historical-cyclical dimension***: this focuses on those verses that address the historical context of the time, as well as questioning or socio-cultural requirements from the time of the revelation. The verses relevant here essentially talk of wars and tribal conflicts, the spoils of war, slaves, and corporal punishment, and are considered to be obsolete today[20].

According to this methodology, it is possible to identify a total of between 55 and 60 verses that consider marriage, divorce, the roles of parents and their relations with children. When considered as a body, these verses on marriage and family relations are grounded on ethical values such as compassion (*rahma*), dialogue and compromise (*tashawur wa taradi*), reciprocal love (*mawada*), the common good (*ma'ruf*), respect for ethical limits (*hudud Allah),* protection for the vulnerable (*yatama wa mustad'afin*), justice and equity (*'adlwa qist*), generosity (*elfadl*) serenity (*sakinha*)...

Other feminist approaches have also made it possible to question masculinist approaches and thus to reverse the way in which the question of women is addressed, with the aim of "***de-patriarchalising***" **and** "***de-***

[20] These verses reflect the needs of the peoples of Arabia of the 7th century and focus on some of their existing practices, whilst framing them with ethical values. On the other hand, some of the norms and practices relating to marriage that existed at that time were corrected or abolished by the Koran, either by prohibition or by progressive reform.

***universalising*"** texts[21]. The aim is thus to reformulate classic Islamic norms, thereby questioning roles within representations and the construction of "Muslim masculinity".

It is thus necessary to study men and masculinity in order to provide an account of Islamic ethics, which was for a long time an ethical-normative system of thought, written ***by men and for men***. The "*însan*" human being – which can be either a man or a woman in the original message – is exclusively male within pre-modern and modern interpretative texts. It is in principal a man – generally Arab and white – who is "The" universal ethical subject with an idealised masculinity. Others by contrast, namely women and other men, who do not fall into this category are eternally subordinated and subservient.

These different approaches have thus made it possible to deconstruct numerous discriminatory interpretations against women that have been generated by patriarchal readings and falsely imputed to the Qur'an. Examples of this include the following:

The subordinate creation of the woman from a rib of Adam: a universal misogynist myth which is totally absent from the Koran, where the creation is entirely egalitarian without any suggestion of the subordinate creation of women. Men and women were created from one single and unique essence – *nafs al-wahîda* – which symbolises the equality of humanity and of men and women[22].

Lapidation and female circumcision: neither exists within the Koran, both having been developed later within Islamic jurisprudence.

The superior status of the husband: this is based on the notion of "*qîwama*", a Koranic concept implying the material responsibility borne by men. This concept was understood and interpreted within the Islamic *Fiqh* as an authoritarian power of men (*soulta)* over women based on the husband's legal duty to provide maintenance (*nafaq*a) in return for the wife's duty of obedience *(taa')*. However, the Koran does not contain any reference to material maintenance in return for obedience[23].

---

[21] This is argued by some Muslim academics such as the Egyptian Omaima Abu Bakr in her excellent article: "Turning the tables: perspectives on the construction of Muslim Manhood", available at https://www.researchgate.net/publication/274337068; see also Ayubi Z., "De-Universaling Malenormativity: Feminist methodologies for studying Masculinity in premodern Islamic Ethics texts", *Journal of Islamic Ethics*, 2020.

[22] Coran 4, 1.

[23] This legal postulate underlies the entire hermeneutical construct of the discriminatory patriarchal structure within the notion of family in Islam, and it is this notion

Polygamy: monogamy is the norm within the Koran. The possibility of polygamy was a contextual exception within the ambit of a patriarchal society that had been traditionally polygamist in order to protect the most vulnerable, including specifically widows and their orphans during times of war[24]. This exceptional permission is made conditional within the Koran on the almost impossible stipulation that the man must behave fairly and equitably in relation to his wives. However, within the Islamic *fiqh*, this permission *became* a timeless right of men.

The unequal sharing of the estate: this arises in particular with regard to relations between siblings. It should be recalled that women – in the same way as the elderly and children – did not have any right to inherit assets within the pre-Islamic tradition, as the criteria were based on the aptitude and material capacity of men in their prime years to take care of their families and to defend their tribes. With the advent of Islam, the right to inherit was extended in general terms to all persons, including in particular to women – with a half share for the sisters amongst their siblings – in spite of the fact that they did not fulfil the merit-based criteria of the age. It is by reference to this purposive philosophy that we can state today that – as they are heavily involved in the management of the household, the maintenance of the family and various material tasks – this rule on allocation should be reviewed in order to guarantee respect for this Koranic spirit that seeks to achieve justice and fairness. Within our context, granting an equal share to brothers and sisters means fulfilling these Koranic goals[25].

The criteria for evaluating men and women can be encapsulated not so much in terms of their biological difference, as is asserted by the patriarchal interpretation, but rather the ethics of their social and moral actions. This conclusion follows from Koranic concepts that stress equality between men and women through concepts such as the edification of human civilisation (*istikhlaf*)[26], the socio-political alliance between men and

---

that blocks any attempt at an egalitarian reading by clerics. See the academic study concerning this issue in Ziba Mir Hosseynni, Mulki al-Sharmany and Jana Rumminger, "Men in charge? Rethinking Authority in Muslim legal Tradition", *Oneworld Academic*, 2015.

[24] Coran 4;3 et 129.

[25] This measure must today be reviewed and re-interpreted with reference to the aims of justice pursued in the text as well as social changes, but also other Koranic concepts such as the importance of the will (*wassiya*), which have been marginalised by the *Fiqh*. For more details see Lamrabet A., *Islam et femmes : les questions qui fâchent*, Casablanca, En toutes lettres, 2017, and Benchekroun S. (ed.), *L'héritage des femmes en islam: l'exemple du Maroc*, Paris, Editions l'Harmattan, 2021.

[26] Coran 35; 39.

women *(a'wilya'a)*[27], doing good *(el amal el salih)*[28], moral integrity *(taqwa)*[29] and hard work (nassib fi aliktissab)[30].

6. Conclusion

In order to move beyond the duality and incompatibility between law and religion as regards the issue of gender equality in Islam, as is the case in Morocco, it will be necessary to reform the approach taken by clerics according to a new ethical dimension. This will make it possible to instil in future generations, through education, a fundamental notion, namely that their religious sentiment is an expression of an egalitarian and humanist culture and that it does not in any sense contradict universal values.

Today many men and women throughout the Muslim world are working to achieve this reappropriation of the ethical meaning of Islam. The reformist feminist dynamic currently underway has unfortunately only attracted minority support. However, it has taken on a monumental task involving the deconstruction of all patriarchal interpretations, and the results are now starting to be felt within the social realities of numerous Muslim countries, including in particular Morocco following the various reforms of the Family Code and the Constitution as well as calls for further reforms in future.

I believe that we are today living through an extraordinary age within the Arab-Muslim world. This age is certainly a difficult one and extremely fragile, but it is nonetheless full of hope. The hope is that it will be possible to open up a new space within the Muslim legal tradition, and to re-establish equality, pluralism, individual freedom and justice as the indispensable spiritual ideals of this religion.

References

Abu Bakr O. (2014), *Turning the tables: perspectives on the construction of Muslim Manhood*, available at https://www.researchgate.net/publication/274337068.

Ayubi Z. (2020), "De-Universaling Malenormativity: Feminist methodolo-

[27] Coran 9; 21.

[28] Coran 16; 97.

[29] Coran 49; 13.

[30] Coran 4; 7.

gies for studying Masculinity in premodern Islamic Ethics texts", *Journal of Islamic Ethics*.

Benchekroun S. (2021), *L'héritage des femmes en islam: l'exemple du Maroc*, Paris, Editions l'Harmattan.

Chiadmi M. (2006), *Le Noble Coran,nouvelle traduction francaise du sens de ses versets*, Lyon, Éditions Tawhid.

El Bouhsini L. (2016), "Une lutte pour l'égalité racontée par les féministes marocaines", *Rives Méditerranéennes, Récits de femmes en Méditerranée*, available at https://doi.org/10.4000/rives.5034, 121-133.

Dupret B. (2014), *La Charia. Des sources à la pratiques, un concept pluriel*, Paris, La Découverte, 12.

Dupret B. and Buskens L. (2012), "De l'invention du droit musulman à la pratique juridique contemporaine", in Dupret B. (ed.), *La charia aujourd'hui. Usages de la référence au droit islamique*, Paris, La Découverte, 9-17, DOI: 10.3917/dec.dupre.2012.01.0009, URL: https://www.cairn.info/---page-9.htm.

Ghaly M. (2017), "A Pressing Demand and a Promising Field", *Journal of Islamic Ethics*, available at https://brill.com/view/journals/jie/1/1-2/article-p1_1.xml?language=en.

Lamrabet A. (2016), *Women in the Qur'an: An Emancipatory reading*, Leicestershire, Kube Publishing limited.

Lamrabet A. (2017), *Islam et femmes: les questions qui fachent*, Casablanca, En toutes lettres.

Merad A. (2001), "La textualisation de la Tradition", in Merad A. (ed.), *La Tradition musulmane*, Paris, Presses Universitaires de France, "Que sais-je?". available at https://www.cairn.info/la-tradition-musulmane--9782130520740-page-43.htm, 43-54.

Mir Hosseini Z., Al Sharmani M. and Rumminger J. (2015), *Men in charge? Rethinking authority in Muslim Legal Authority*, London, Oneworld Academic.

Mir Hosseini Z., Al Sharmani M., Rumminger J. and Marso S. (2022), *Justice and Beauty in Muslim Marriage*, London, Oneworld.

Secrétariat Général du Gouvernement, Royaume du Maroc (2011), *La Constitution*, Direction de l'imprimerie officielle, Série Documentation juridique marocaine.

Chapter 10

ALGERIAN CITIZENSHIP BETWEEN THE PRINCIPLE OF EQUALITY AND FREEDOM OF ENTERPRISE

Leila Boussaid and Souad Ghaouti Malki

ABSTRACT: *The Algerian woman citizen has a historical asset during the fight against the colonizer, a cutting - edge fight which can only predispose her to the access and to the participation with the Algerian citizen to the management of the res publica in all its latitude and in its various components. Beside this historical asset, the socialist egalitarian logic has weighed with all its weight on the Algerian right from 1962 to 1989, that is to say during 27 long years. However, the Algerian legal texts, especially in public law, reflect a difficult dilemma between this effective and real achievement and the reluctance to fully translate the principle of equality. The first step will be to apprehend the egalitarian principle in the constitution, in the labor code and in the civil service law, in order to target in a second step, the political space itself as a fundamental ground of expression and participation.*

Introduction

This paper has been written against the highly singular backdrop of Algeria today. The country's political, economic and social climate is undergoing significant change, thanks to the peaceful, broad-based citizens' movement "Hirak" [1], which was launched on 22 February 2019 and over the following eighteen months spread throughout the country to 48 *wilayas* (provinces). It opposed the bid by President Abdelaziz Bouteflika (elected in 1999) for a fifth term in office, entirely rejects contemporary governance structures and above all aspires to build a new Algeria.

These claims include a desire to recognise the rightful place and legitimate role of Algerian women in the new social project.

Algerian women achieved progress in 2021 both in terms of the enshrinement in law of the **principle of equality** as well as **freedom of enterprise**.

A significant body of new draft legislation, including in particular the recent constitutional reform of 1 November 2020 [2], has been emblematic of this clear development.

This paper will first describe the halting development of the principle of equality within fundamental legal sources and in the reality of the political sphere, following which the second part will focus on Algerian women's freedom in the economic sphere, as terrain for the application of the principle of equality.

Freedom of enterprise is being encouraged by the government's new policies in particular on start-ups, and on small and medium-sized artisanal businesses, a space that has traditionally seen women entrepreneurs.

1. The principle of equality between the legal textual framework and the reality of hard figures

Having ratified no fewer than fourteen international conventions including, in 1996, Convention on the Elimination of All Forms of Discrimination against Women (CEDAW) [3], Algeria committed from the outset to incor-

---

[1] Hirak is the Arabic word for "movement".

[2] Referendum Law concerning the constitutional review adopted on 1 November 2020, promulgated by Presidential Decree no. 20-442 of 30 December 2020, Official Journal of the Republic of Algeria [JORA] no. 82.

[3] Ordinance no. 96-03 of 10 January 1996 approved without reservation the 1979 Convention on the Elimination of All Forms of Discrimination against Women (JORA no. 13/1996). Presidential Decree no. 08-426 of 28 December 2008 subsequently re-

porating the **principle of equality between men and women** into national law[4].

Algerian women thus participated in economic affairs and in public life in accordance with international standards, although paradoxically within the private sphere they were still subject to a Sharia-influenced Family Code, despite the Code's amendment in 2005[5].

Having occupied the public sphere extremely effectively throughout seven years of revolutionary struggles, Algerian women had made a historic achievement, acting as a vanguard paving the way for Algerian women's access to and participation in the management of the *res publica*, throughout its full breadth and in its various manifestations: public institutions, the public administration and employment in general. Alongside this historic achievement it is important not to overlook the influence of the Socialist egalitarian logic, which made its full weight felt on Algerian law over twenty-seven long years from 1962 until 1989.

Thus, having been embraced in both its Liberal and Socialist versions, the sacrosanct principle of equality was irreversibly and permanently incorporated into Algerian law, albeit after being modulated and adapted in line with existing socio-cultural limits.

1.1. The difficult path towards equality

We shall now consider the apprehensive attitude to the principle of equality and how it was addressed within subsequent constitutional texts, and later within the legislation governing elections, political parties and female representation within elected assemblies.

1.1.1. The recognition of the universal principle of equality within fundamental legal sources in Algeria from 1963 to 2021

Algeria has a legacy of no fewer than eight constitutions, and aside from the first constitution of an independent Algeria adopted by the Constituent As-

voked the reservation made in relation to Art. 9.2 of the 1979 Convention (JORA no. 05 de 2009).

[4] A decision of the Constitutional Council of 20 August 1989 refers to the principle of the integration of ratified conventions: "following ratification and publication, any convention is incorporated into national law in accordance with Art. 123 of the Constitution, [whereupon] the duly ratified convention acquires legal status superior to that of ordinary legislation".

[5] Law no. 05-09 of 4 May 2005 on the approval of Ordinance no. 05-02 of 27 February 2005 amending and supplementing Law no. 84-11 of 9 June 1984 laying down the Family Code, JORA no. 15/2005.

sembly (which was approved by a referendum held on 8 September 1963 and came into force on 10 September 1963)[6], as well as the 1976 Constitution[7] (promulgated by Ordinance no. 76-97 of 22 November 1976), all of the other constitutions were adopted according to the constitutional revision procedure.

1.1.1.1. *The 1963 Constitution*

Curiously, it would appear that the first Algerian Constitution paid more attention to the role of women than the others.

Specifically, recital 10 of the preamble states that "The revolution will be consolidated by... a social policy... to accelerate the emancipation of women in order that they may take part in the direction of public affairs and in the development of the country".

The fundamental objectives mentioned in Art. 10 include "the struggle against all discrimination, in particular discrimination based on race and religion".

Moreover, Art. 12 forcefully asserts in a peremptory manner the general principle of full equality between men and women, encompassing all rights and duties: "All citizens of both sexes have the same rights and the same duties".

1.1.1.2. *The 1976 Constitution*

This document entirely disregards women, both in the preamble and in the first three chapters[8], which deal with fundamental principles concerning the organisation of Algerian society; it is not until chapter four on fundamental freedoms, human rights and civil liberties that the last paragraph of Art. 39 prohibits "all discrimination based on prejudice based on sex, race or profession".

Although Articles 40 and 41 go on to assert the principle of equality before the law, they do so in extremely broad terms that cover people in general, and not women in particular.

Art. 42 of the Constitution is the only provision expressly dedicated to guaranteeing the political, economic, social and cultural rights of Algerian women.

This minimal level of attention to the role of women in the 1976 Consti-

---

[6] JORA no. 64 of 10 September 1963, 887 ff.

[7] JORA no. 94 of 24 November 1976.

[8] The first chapter concerns the Republic, the second Socialism and the third the State.

tution may be justified by the initial fundamentally egalitarian logic that permeated Socialist ideology that men and women are perceived and conceptualised together within the "asexual" whole of the Socialist citizen worker dedicated solely to the construction of the State.

1.1.1.3. *The amended Constitution of 1989*[9]

Breaking with the globalist concern of the 1976 Constitution, the 1989 Constitution took care for the first time to address Algerian women directly in Art. 30[10] as well as in Art. 31(2)[11].

However, it is curious to note that Art. 42 of the 1976 Constitution on women's rights was not retained.

1.1.1.4. *The amended Constitution of 1996*[12]

The assertion of the principle of equality before the law, already included within the 1989 Constitution, was carried over into Art. 29, as was also Art. 31. However, an important addition – resulting from the political crisis of 1989 and the years marked by terrorism – was made to the conditions applicable to the creation of political parties in Art. 42(3), which prohibits the establishment of political parties with a religious, linguistic, racial, sexual, corporatist or regional basis.

1.1.1.5. *The constitutional revision of 2008*[13]

This constitutional revision was distinguished by the fundamental contribution made by it to the political rights of women through the inclusion of a new Art. 31-bis: "The State works for the promotion of the political rights of women by increasing their chances of access to representation in elected assemblies".

Whilst being limited to elections to local and national bodies, this desire to promote female representation represented the first step in a clear development within subsequent implementing legislation, such as Organic Law no. 12-01 on the electoral system[14] and Organic Law no. 12-03 of 12

---

[9] JORA no. 9 of 1 March 1989.

[10] Art. 30: "The institutions shall have the purpose of ensuring equal rights and duties for all male and female citizens".

[11] Art. 31(2): "Rights and freedoms constitute a shared heritage of all Algerians, both men and women".

[12] JORA no. 76 of 8 December 1996.

[13] Constitutional Law no. 08-19 of 15 November 2008, JORA no. 63.

[14] JORA no. 1 of 2012, 8.

January laying down procedures for increasing opportunity of access by women to representation within elected assemblies [15].

In order to ensure full application to this Article, it provides that the arrangements governing its application are to be set out not in simple ordinary legislation but rather in an organic law.

This addition was considered to be a fundamental pillar of the revision, and to be just as important as the other changes made to the 1996 text. Provision was thus made for the constitutionalisation of Tamazight as a national language in Art. 3-bis, in addition to protection for the national flag and the national anthem by establishing the principle of their immutability (in Articles 5 and 178).

The 2008 revision established the principle that the President of the Republic could be re-elected without any restriction on term limits. Moreover, the presidency was reinforced by a new reconfiguration of the prerogatives of the executive, as the head of government was now nothing more than a prime minister, whose acts were subject to approval by the President, or were carried out in accordance with powers delegated by the latter [16].

This clarification needs to be made concerning the articles revised in 2008 in order to better assess the full weight of the new Art. 31-bis.

Moreover, from the entirely different perspective of freedom to form political parties, Art. 42(3) prohibited the creation of any political parties with a religious, linguistic, racial, sexual, corporatist or regional basis.

The principle of equality appears again in Art. 51 on access to State appointments and employment.

The public space of teaching and professional training is also open to **all citizens, both men and women**, in accordance with the principle of equal access (Art. 53). Finally, the right to work and its corollary the right to organise are guaranteed to all male and female citizens in Articles 55 and 56.

1.1.1.6. *The constitutional revision of 2016* [17]

A further step was taken in this revision with the addition of Art. 36, which for the first time enshrined the principle that the State must promote equality between men and women on the employment market in general terms.

---

[15] JORA no. 1.

[16] The internal restructuring of the executive is provided for in Articles 77, 78, 79, 80, 83 and above all 85 of the revised Constitution.

[17] Law no. 16-01 of 6 March 2016 in JORA of 7 March 2016.

Paragraph two of this Article specifies that the promotion of women must also be encouraged by the State in order to achieve "positions of responsibility in public institutions and administrations, as well as in enterprises".

However, paradoxically, this gigantic step forwards towards equality, as perfect equality, was not buttressed by the primary precondition for exercising equality rights, namely protection. In fact, it can be noted that the revised text makes no reference to protection for women in general terms; the lengthy Art. 72, which is comprised of no fewer than 7 paragraphs, conceptualises the family as a whole in which the State protects the rights of the child, as well as the vulnerable and the elderly, but disregards women, the central pillar of Algerian families. This gap would later be filled in the revision adopted on 1 November 2020.

1.1.1.7. *The constitutional revision of 1 November 2020*[18]

Art. 37 of the amended text refers not only to the principle of the quality of all citizens before the law, as enunciated in all of the previous constitutions, but now also expressly establishes a right to equal protection for that equality.

Above all Art. 40 guarantees Algerian women protection by the State, for the first time, against all forms of violence, in all places and under all circumstances in **the public sphere, at work** and in the private sphere.

It is important to clarify that, out of the seven points submitted by the President of the Republic to the committee of experts charged with drawing up the draft amendment, the priority issue was that of rights and freedoms.

The particular attention placed on the rights of Algerian citizens was consequently construed within this evolutionary logic of the confirmation of rights.

Having outlined how the universal principle of equality has been treated in the Constitution in the past, it is now essentially to consider how it has been implemented within legislation.

1.1.2. The implementation of the principle of equality within legislation

1. Law no. 90-11 of 21 April 1990[19] on labour relations enshrines and recalls the principle of non-discrimination in no fewer than four Articles:

---

[18] Presidential Decree no. 20-442 promulgating the Referendum Law, JORA no. 82 of 30 December 2020.

[19] This Law, enacted in 1990, was amended several times in 1991 (Law no. 91-29 of

- Art. 6 solemnly provides that workers have the right to protection against all forms of discrimination in holding a position, other than discrimination based on their aptitude and merit.
- Art. 17 outlaws any provision of a collective labour agreement or an employment contract that purports to establish any form of discrimination whatsoever between workers in relation to employment, remuneration or working conditions on the grounds of age or gender… and declares that any such provisions shall be null and void.
- Art. 84 calls on employers in a peremptory manner to abide by the principle of equality when setting pay.
- Art. 142 provides, as a rule of criminal law, for the imposition of a fine of between 2,000 and 5,000 DA in the event of any breach of Art. 17 that gives rise to any discrimination among workers upon appointment, when setting pay or in relation to working conditions; in the event of a repeat offence, the minimum penalty is increased from 2,000 to 10,000 DA and may be cumulated with a custodial sentence of 3 years.

However, according to a logic that seeks to over-protect women, the law contains two articles that depart from the principle of equality.

First of all, Art. 29 prohibits employers from using women for night work.

Second, Art. 141 punishes any breach of the provisions on the employment conditions of young female workers and women with a fine of between 2,000 and 4,000 DA.

It is important to mention that Ordinance no. 05-02 of 27 February 2005 laying down the Family Code amended Art. 19 on marriage certificates, granting the couple of the ability to protect the woman's right to work within a notarised contract drawn up either before or during the marriage; any violation of the terms set out in the marital agreement will then entitle the wife to apply for a divorce in accordance with Art. 53 of the Family Code. We shall now consider the principle of gender equality within the context of trade unions.

2. Law no. 90-14 of 02 June 1990[20] barely addressed the issue; only one single article, namely Art. 22, prohibits trade union organisations in ex-

---

21 December 1991), J.O.R.A, and later in 1996 (by Ordnance no. 96-21 of 9 July 1996). JORA no. 43 and in 1997 by the Ordinance of 11 January 1997. JORA no. 3.

[20] Law no. 90-14 of 2 June 1990 on the arrangements governing the exercise of the right to organise (JORA no. 23), as amended and supplemented by Law no. 91-30 of 21 December 1991 (JORA no. 68) and by Ordinance no. 96-12 of 10 June 1996 (JORA no. 36).

tremely broad terms from making provision within their statutes for, or from engaging in, any form of discrimination among members that is such as to interfere with their freedoms.

In its 2006 version, the Statute of Public Sector Workers dedicates only two Articles to the issue[21]. Art. 27, which is included among the "guarantees and rights of public officials", establishes the principle "that no discrimination is permitted among public officials on account of their opinions, gender, origin or any other personal or social characteristic".

Art. 74, on the recruitment of public sector officials, recalls the constitutional principle of equal access to public office and employment. However, evolution in the principle of equality has been apparent above all since 2012.

1.1.3. The specific treatment or "accommodation" of the principle of equality within the 2012 reforms

The Arab Spring, which continued throughout 2011 in some Arab countries such as Egypt and Tunisia, had the effect of triggering a series of legislative reforms in Algeria. These were approved by President Abdelaziz BOUTEFLIKA and announced in a speech given by him on 15 April 2011.

An analysis of the amendments made to the three fundamental laws[22] governing political action, namely the electoral law, the law on political parties and the law establishing the quota for female representation within elected assemblies, highlights a progressive slippage from the principle of full equality, as set out in the Electoral Code, towards the requirement for a certain proportion of women within the structures of political parties, and ending up finally with the quota solution.

1.1.3.1. *The organic law on the electoral system*[23]

A decoding of the terminology within the above law reveals that the three fundamental articles are targeted distinctly and separately at male and female citizens, as they are referred to one after the other, with the aim of achieving equal recognition and identification for the two sexes.

Art. 3 accordingly provides as follows: "**any male or female Algerian cit-**

---

[21] Ordinance no. 06-03 of 15 July 2006 laying down the General Statute of Public Sector Workers, JORA no. 46.

[22] These three organic laws were promulgated on the same day, 12 January 2012, in JORA no. 1 of 2012.

[23] Organic Law no. 01-12 of 12 January 2012 – JORA no. 1, 9.

izen who is over the age of eighteen on the day of the ballot who exercises his or her civic and political rights and is not subject to any of the grounds for incapacity provided for under applicable legislation shall be entitled to vote".

Art. 6 confirms this logic of separate but equal treatment by providing that "registration in the electoral register is a **duty for all male and female citizens** who fulfil the conditions laid down by law".

Art. 7 in turn insists that: "**any Algerian man or woman** who has never been included in an electoral register must apply for inclusion.

Having taken the precaution of solemnly "situating" the two categories of citizen at the outset, throughout the rest of the organic law comprising no fewer than 235 Articles, the legislature used **the sole generic, combined and unifying term "citizens"**. In the same spirit of non-discrimination, proxy voting is now limited to a closed list of six scenarios, thus eliminating proxy voting by the husband and head of the family on behalf of his wife and female daughters, a possibility provided for under Law no. 89-13 of 7 August 1989, which however resulted in abuses [24].

In effect, since Art. 53 of Organic Law no. 12-01 laying down the electoral regime now only permits proxy voting in the event of admission to hospital or confinement to the home, for the seriously ill or disabled, for those performing work outside their *wilaya* of residence or who are travelling for work, for university students studying outside their *wilaya* of origin, for citizens temporarily abroad and finally for members of the National People's Army, the National Security Service, the Civil Protection Service, the customs administration, as well as officials from the prison service and the municipal police who are working on the day of the election.

In addition, the procedure applicable to the grant of proxy vote is now organised more stringently as it may only be confirmed by a document executed before a judge or in this case the president of the administrative electoral committee in accordance with Articles 15 and 56 of Organic Law no. 12-01.

It is thus clear that this law has helped to reinstate full voting rights to women in Algeria by referring to them directly within the wording of the legislation and by requiring that they exercise their voting rights individually, by no longer facilitating the option of proxy voting.

However, the political and social reality inevitably led lawmakers to water down this principle of full equality within the most recent organic law on the organisation of political parties.

---

[24] Art. 54/2 of the 1989 electoral law had considerably expanded scope for voting by proxy, resulting in the practice of family voting.

1.1.3.2. *The organic law on political parties and the mixed regime of parity and proportionality*

Although Articles 10 and 11(9) of Organic Law 12-04[25] make provision along the same lines as the electoral law in terms of the primary choice in favour of the principle of equality, the provisions on the organisation of political parties contained in Articles 17 and 41 refer to the notion of a **representative proportion of women**, thereby establishing a mix between parity and proportionality.

Some political parties such as the National Liberation Front have moreover expressed reservations, arguing that the proportional mode of representation for women violates the principles of equality and parity. Art. 10 provides for **equality in relation to membership**: "Any male of female Algerian who is of legal age may join one single political party of his or her choosing and may relinquish his or her membership at any time". Art. 11(9) establishes as one of the goals of every political party the commitment to democratic action and the principle of rotation in power **as well as the promotion of women's political rights**.

The first modulation or accommodation of the principle of equality in terms of participation in political life is established by Art. 17(7) of Organic Law no. 12-04, which provides that there must be a representative proportion of women amongst the founding members of a political party. This requirement that there must be a representative proportion of women amongst the founding members is stipulated as a substantive rule, alongside the requirement of Algerian nationality, full enjoyment of civil and political rights, etc. Accordingly, failure to comply with it may constitute grounds for the Interior Minister to reject the memorandum of association of a political party following the review of the compliance with the law of the respective documentation[26].

Later, once the initial phase after the party's foundation has passed, Art. 41 of the Law also regulates the very operation of parties, requiring a certain proportion of women within their governing bodies.

According to a progressive and prudent approach that recognises the role of Algerian women in political action, Organic Law no. 12-04 is framed in general terms, and does not specify any further this representative proportion stipulated as a rule.

The government preferred to enact specific legislation, namely Organic

---

[25] JORA no. 02 of 2012, 9.

[26] An examination of the legal conformity of a declaration concerning the establishment of a political party is provided for in Articles 20 to 23 of Organic Law no. 12-04 on political parties.

Law no. 12-03, which lays down arrangements seeking to increase women's opportunities to access representation in elected assemblies. This law amounted to the second accommodation with the principle of equality, by applying the logic of quotas.

1.1.3.3. *Organic Law no. 12-03 and the rules on quotas*[27]

The new Art. 31-bis introduced by the constitutional revision of 15 November 2008 announced need for Organic Law no. 12-03, which specified the **minimum threshold** required for female representation within the different lists of candidates for elected assemblies at municipal, provincial and national level.

Art. 2 of the Law specifies a range, which varies between 20% and 50%, depending upon the number of seats in play.

- 20% of women candidates in at least 4 seats for the National People's Assembly;
- 30% for 5 seats or more;
- 35% for 14 seats or more;
- 40% for 32 seats or more;
- 50% for the seats of the national community resident abroad.

Art. 3 provides that the proportions **must be reserved** for female candidates in the order in which their names appear in the lists.

In order to ensure compliance with the minimum legal thresholds, Art. 4 provides that a declaration of candidacy **must** mention the candidate's gender in order to facilitate further checks, failure to pass which may be sanctioned by the rejection of the entire list[28].

Finally, with a view to encouraging the inclusion of women within candidate lists, the State may grant financial assistance to political parties depending upon the number of female candidates who are **elected** to assemblies[29].

It should be noted that the legislation on the participation of Algerian women in politics was applied almost immediately in the parliamentary elections held on 10 May 2012 to re-elect the National People's Assembly (the lower house of Parliament), and resulted in a significant advance in terms both of women candidates, **with 7,646 candidates out of a total of 25,800 (i.e. around 33%)**, as well as the number of women definitively

[27] JORA no. 1 of 2012, 39.

[28] According to Art. 5 of Law no. 12-03.

[29] According to Art. 7 of the above-mentioned Law.

elected, **with 145 women elected out of a total of 462 (i.e. 31.38%)** [30]. A comparison with Maghreb neighbours as well as with France confirms the progress achieved in this area. In Tunisia, 29% of the Constituent Assembly elected in October 2011 were women, or 63 out of 217 members, whereas Morocco had 17%, with 67 women out of 395 deputies. France for its part elected 107 women to the National Assembly out of a total of 577, or 18.54%.

Although it has been objected to by some political parties, Organic Law no. 12-03 resulted in the entry of a sizeable number of women into the partisan political arena, and their involvement above all in the drafting of legislation thanks to their membership of the Algerian Parliament.

It is interesting to note that the three Islamist parties from the Green Algeria Alliance coalition had a significant level of female representation, with 15 out of 47 deputies.

The overwhelming majority of the women elected defined themselves as sexist, or stated that they viewed their mandate exclusively as a means for defending women's rights. Most asserted their commitment to fulfilling their mission by stating their aim of occupying key positions within the National Assembly.

This revision of constitutional provisions and legislation has highlighted the repeated concern of successive governments to comply with all of the international conventions that have been duly ratified by the Algerian State and to act in accordance with international standards.

As a result, the principle of gender equality has been recognised, adopted, enshrined, recalled and valorised throughout all of the legal texts that make provision to regulate the public sphere and economic life.

However, political events occurring in 2019, expressing aspirations for greater freedom, new rules on impartiality, transparency and equality, and affirming more resolutely the role of women, will have a different impact on the participation of women both within elected bodies and also within institutions and the public administrations. It is now necessary to consider the practical effects of this recognition within the law and the adherence to this principle.

---

[30] Official figures from the Interior Ministry published in all daily newspapers on 12 May 2012.

1.2. The paradoxical reality of the figures

Following the popular rejection of the much-hated and misguided governance under the Bouteflika presidency over the twenty years from 1999 to 2019, the *Hirak* launched on 22 February 2019 called urgently for the amendments necessary to ensure the "clean and honest" election of a new President of the Republic as well as a new National People's Assembly.

A "commission for mediation and dialogue" was established, comprised of leading figures from civil society. It was charged in particular with contributing to the drafting of a new Electoral Code, which was enacted as Organic Law no. 19-08 of 14 September 2019[31]. Organic Law no. 19-07 on the National Independent Election Authority[32], which was to act as the principal guarantor of impartial and transparent elections, was promulgated in the same issue of the Official Journal.

Presidential elections were organised on the legal basis of these two organic laws, which led to the election of Abdelmadjid Tebboune as the new President of the Republic in December 2019. Shortly after his inauguration, he launched a process for a revision of the Algerian Constitution, with the revised text being approved by referendum on 1 November 2020. He also promoted the amendment of electoral law, which resulted in the enactment of Organic Law no. 21-01 of 10 March 2021[33].

Such an intense and repeated series of changes to the electoral law over such a short space of time – 2012, 2016, 2019 and 2021 – had quite a destabilising effect on the electorate, as the four texts had swung back and forth among the principles of equality, quotas and parity.

1.2.1. The number of women in elected bodies

The results obtained highlight the scale of improvements both in the number of women elected to Parliament following the application of the quota system in 2012, but also conversely the extent of the regression in 2021 with the application of the parity rule.

---

[31] JORA no. 55, 12.

[32] JORA no. 55, 6.

[33] JORA no. 17 of 2021, 8.

1.2.1.1. *The option for the quota system applied in 2012*

Table 1. The 2012 choice in favour of the quota system [34]

Year	Number of candidates	Number elected
1977	39 out of 783	9
1982	39 out of 840	04
1987	63 out of 885	07
1997	322 out of 7,749	11
2002	694 out of 10,052	24
2007	1,018 out of 15,134	30
2012	7,646 out of 25,800	145

Source: Mémoire de magister, Halim Laroussi.

The number of women elected in 2012 was practically five times as high as the number elected in the 2007 legislature. It is also interesting to review the figures based on the parties represented.

Whereas the parties that secured the largest cohorts of representatives in the parliamentary elections achieved a respectable score, with 68 women out of 221 for the National Liberation Front, 23 out of 70 for the Democratic National Party, 15 out of 47 for the Green Alliance, and 7 out of 21 for the Socialist Forces Front, a number of smaller parties performed even better, and in some cases exceeded the parity threshold.

The Workers' Party elected no fewer than 10 women out of 17 members, and the Algerian National Front returned 3 women out of 9 in total. However, it was the new and recently established parties that appeared to have embraced the principle of equality the most.

Table 2. Women elected to seven new parties

Party	Women elected
Union of Democratic and Social Forces (*Al Ittihad*)	2 women out of 3 candidates
National Republican Alliance (A.N.R.)	1 woman out of 3 candidates
Patriotic Republican Grouping (R.P.R.)	1 woman out of 2 candidates
Free Citizens' Movement (M.C.L.)	1 woman out of 2 candidates
Youth Party (P.J.)	1 woman out of 2 candidates
Algerian Radiance Party (P.E.A.)	1 woman out of 2 candidates
El-Karama Party	1 woman out of 2 candidates

Source: Doctoral thesis by Farid Debboucha.

[34] Figures obtained from the paper written by Laroussi Halim, *Analyse des élections législatives algériennes de 2007*, Master in Public Law – Ben Aknoun Law Faculty – University of Algiers 1, 2010 (written in Arabic).

Table 3. Summary of the number of female representatives within elected popular assemblies (National People's Assembly, people's provincial assemblies and people's municipal assemblies)

		Female candidates			Women elected		
		Number of candidates	**Total candidates**	**Rate**	**Number elected**	**Total elected**	**Rate**
National People's Assembly	2007	1,018	13,243	**7.68%**	30	398	
	2012	7,200	24,916	30.90%	146	462	**31.6%**
	2017	3,625	11,315	**32.13%**	120	462	25.92%
People's provincial assemblies (APW)	2007	1,564	21,591	/	133	1,960	/
	2012	5,046	18,421	26.95%	595	2,004	**29.69%**
	2017	9,200	12,559	**28.26%**	586	2,009	**29.24%**
People's municipal assemblies (APC)	2007	3,137	123,350	/	105	19,981	/
	2012	32,100	187,442	17.35%	4,122	24,891	**16.50%**
	2017	37,221	209,748	**17.75%**	4,142	24,876	**16.65%**

Source: Debboucha Farid, *Les fondements démocratiques de l'assemblée populaire communale*, doctoral thesis, January 2020, University of Algiers 1 (written in Arabic).

This Table 3 illustrates well the spectacular level of women candidates in 2012: 7,200 at a rate of 30.90% for the National People's Assembly, 5,046 at a rate of 26.95% for *wilaya* provincial assemblies and 32,100 at a rate of 17.75% for municipal assemblies.

In his analysis of the local elections held on 29 November 2012, A.K. Hartani presents a comparative table highlighting the increase in the number of women elected to both municipal assemblies and *wilaya* assemblies [35].

The figures were as follows for the respective municipal assemblies:

- 23 October 1997: 75 women were elected, comprising 5.8% of the total number;
- 10 October 2002: 147 women were elected, comprising 3.9% of the total number;
- 29 November 2007: 1.540 women were elected, comprising 9% of the total number;
- 29 November 2012: 4.120 women were elected, comprising 16.5% of the total number.

The figures for *wilaya* assemblies were as follows:

- 23 October 1997: 62 women elected, comprising 6.8% of the total number;
- 10 October 2002: 113 women elected, comprising 4.2% of the total number;
- 29 November 2007: 133 women elected, comprising 6.6% of the total number;
- 29 November 2012: 595 women elected, comprising 29.6% of the total number.

Having preciously oscillated between 3.9% and 9%, the rate shot up sharply to reach 29.6% in 2012.

A similar increase is apparent if the National People's Assembly is observed over the period 1962 to 2012:

- In 1962: 10 women were elected out of 194, i.e. 5.2% [36]
- In 1964: 2 women were elected out of 138, i.e. 1.4%;
- In 1977: 9 women were elected out of 261, i.e. 3.4%;
- In 1982: 4 women were elected out of 281, i.e. 1.4%;
- In 1987: 07 women were elected out of 295, i.e. 2.3% [37];

---

[35] Seminar in Algiers on 10 December 2013, 7-8.

[36] The elections held in 1962 were for the Constituent Assembly.

[37] The ten-year gap between the elections held in 1987 and in 1997 can be explained

- In 1997: 12 women were elected out of 380, i.e. 3.2%;
- In 2002: 24 women were elected out of 389, i.e. 6.2%;
- In 2007: 30 women were elected out of 389, i.e. 7.7%;
- In 2012: 146 women were elected out of 462, i.e. 31.6%.

Here too, the evolution in terms of female representation is striking, having passed from 1.4% to 31.6% in 2012[38].

This remarkable increase in the number of women elected to the National People's Assembly in 2012 was curiously halted following the application of the parity system introduced by Organic Law no. 21/01 of 10 March 2021.

1.2.1.2. *The new parity system applied from 12 June 2021*

In accordance with Art. 191 of the 2021 Organic Law, 8,305 women stood as candidates in party or independent lists.

Only 34 women were elected to a total of 407, representing a rate of 8.35%.

Male deputies totalled 373, or 91.65%.

This fall has been commented on and justified in various ways. Nadia AIT-Zai of the Equality Foundation[39] attributes this large fall to some of the exceptions granted by the National Independent Election Authority as well as the approval of lists that did not comply with the parity rule. She also suggests that the election campaign was rather lacklustre due to the health crisis, and that women were unable to occupy political terrain sufficiently, which may explain why voters did not choose the female candidates included in the list.

She states that the quota system had been a temporary, yet necessary, stating post: "The principle of parity cannot be introduced without first laying the groundwork... Parity is not something that can be decreed; it must be built up, it is an outcome"[40].

Political scientist Redouane Bouguerra from the University of M'sila takes the entirely opposite view, arguing that the abolition of the quota system was a wise and laudable decision.

by the cessation of the democratic process in 1992, the dissolution of the National People's Assembly and the resignation of the President of the Republic; a period of violence and terrorism prevailed from 1992 until 1997.

[38] All of the figures are contained in the thesis by Ghanem L., *Les droits politiques de la femme dans les Etats du Maghreb Arebe*, University of Algers, Faculty of Law, 2013 (in Arabic language).

[39] Nadia Aït-Zai is also Director of the Centre for Information and Documentation on the Children's and Women's Rights (CIDDEF).

[40] *Soir d'Algérie*, Wednesday 16 January 2021, 4.

"Today, even if female deputies might be much fewer in number than they were in the recent past, this matters little as the most important thing is to guarantee a fair electoral contest" [41].

Numerous analysts attribute the poor score on female representation achieved in 2021 to the novelty of the open list system adopted under the 2021 electoral law; information and awareness raising campaigns should have been conducted more intensively in advance with the aim of facilitating choice in favour of individual candidates, and no longer according to a logic of closed lists.

Another element contributed to this regression, namely the extremely low turnout in the parliamentary election, as recorded by National Independent Election Authority, of 23.03% of the electorate[42]. Out of a total electorate of 24,425,171 voters, only 5,625,324 cast a ballot.

Another factor was at play alongside this decline in numbers: it would appear that female candidates were chosen according to criteria such as intellectual ability, university education, competence and above all age, with young candidates being preferred in particular. Specifically, the National Assembly now includes 140 deputies aged under 40, representing 34%.

Graduates now total 305, or 74.94%. It may be hoped that, by combining age with university education, female deputies will be able to exert more influence both within the drafting of legislation as well as the task of controlling the executive.

In parallel with this see-saw evolution, as has been shown above within elected institutions, slow but sure progress has been apparent within the institutions and public administrations.

1.2.2. Distribution between women and men in access to employment

An analysis of figures published by the National Office for Statistics in November 2019 indicates relatively similar literacy levels between girls and boys at both nursery and primary school age with a slight increase at secondary school level.

- Nursery school: 48.8% of girls;
- Primary school: 47.8% of girls;
- Middle school: 47.9% of girls;
- Secondary school: 54.8% of girls, with 670,240 girls as against 552,433 boys.

---

[41] *El Moudjahid*, 16 June 2021, 5.

[42] Figures published by *El Moudjahid* on 16 June 2021, 3.

The imbalance in favour of girls starts at secondary level and becomes even more marked in higher education.

During academic year 1999-2000, there were 208,523 female students and 199,472 male students at university level, with women thus accounting for 51.1%.

In 2018-2019, the rate of female students increased to 62.5%: "within the space of 10 years, the total number of students of both sexes increased fourfold, whereas the number of female students increased fivefold" [43].

The proportion of women graduates in 2017 was 65.6%, and they also accounted for a majority of PhD awards with 52.5%. The comparative progression from primary school up to doctoral level shows that, following a slight predominance of boys at primary level, the trend switches to favour girls at higher levels.

However, once again, the inversely proportional relationship that is present within elected bodies is also apparent on the labour market.

Even though they graduate from university in larger numbers than men, Algerian women have poorer access to employment.

The overall proportion of women in employment has risen slowly from 15% in 2009 to 18% in 2019 [44].

Women in work only account for 18% of the total, and unemployed women make up 37% of the total unemployed. The following figures demonstrate the significant but slow progress.

- In 1977: 5.2%;
- In 1987: 8.1%;
- In 2001: 15%;
- In 2009: 16.8%;
- In 2019: 20.4%.

However, the percentage of women is higher in public sector employ ment, with a significantly higher proportion in national education, health and tertiary education.

In 2019:

- National education: 55.6% of women
- Health: 55.6% of women;
- Tertiary education: 37.3% of women.

---

[43] All of these figures were published in a special number of CIDDEF: *femmes algériennes en chiffres 2019*, 30 to 33.

[44] All of the figures provided have been obtained from the Algerian National Office for Statistics and were published in the CIDDEF review mentioned above.

The Finance Ministry absorbs 35.8%, and the Justice Ministry 31.4%. The Interior Ministry and local government bring up the rear in terms of female employment rates with 18.2%.

Numbers in employment are highest for those aged 25 to 34, with 561 female employees in 2019.

Aicha Kouadri, President of the association AFCARE (Association of Algerian Women in Middle Management) also provides figures for female employment levels:

- 13.2% in 1996;
- 10.4% in 2015;
- and 17.3% in 2019.

She notes that, in 2018, women are 61.42% of recruited positions within the public administration.

Finally, in a very recent study published in the journal *IDARA*[45], Essaid Taib assesses progress in the positions and roles of women in different Algerian governments. He reports that a total of 39 women have served in government: 26 as ministers, 8 as secretaries of state and one as a deputy prime minister.

However, he concludes that women have been marginalised within government both in terms of the nature of the governmental positions held as well as the nature of the functions performed.

Following this first stage during which the furthering of the principle of equality was solemnly asserted within the Constitution, although at the same time was held back by the reality of hard figures, within both elected bodies and public institutions, one must note that slow but certain process has been made in the application of this universal principle.

There is a question as to whether freedom of enterprise in the economic sphere, which was also affirmed in the last constitutional review of 1 November 2020, could make up for the limits identified within the public sphere.

2. Algerian women and freedom of enterprise

Within a liberal market economy, freedom of enterprise is a freedom guaranteed to all persons. This is not the case within planned economies, where the machinery of the economy is strictly controlled by the State. This distinction between the two economic models has lost significance in recent years, as the

[45] Essaid T., "La femme au gouvernement", *IDARA review*, 2020, 1-52.

system established by the USSR and other countries that subscribed to the same ideology has revealed its limits. Nowadays, liberalism has triumphed practically everywhere around the world, subject in some cases to limits of differing extents, with the State playing the role of regulator.

During the initial post-independence period, Algeria's governments favoured a socialist approach ("specific Socialism")[46]. The State held the economic reins in its hands, affording priority to the public sector, and leaving only a limited role for the private sector. Whether in the agricultural sector or industry, the State regulated the economy through national enterprises that pursued the dual objectives of profitability on the one hand and social wellbeing on the other hand (although it became apparent after a number of years that the latter had taken priority over the former). This choice, in addition to the dysfunctional outcomes that it caused, left little room for private initiative.

However, around the end of the 1980s Algeria made a radical shift, opening up its economy and adopting a Liberalist approach. At the same time, it promoted the privatisation of a large number of its companies, granting a more important role to the private sector[47]. However, private enterprises continued to follow certain patterns of behaviour inherited from the old system, and also had to deal with the burden of a bureaucratic administration. Despite the efforts made, private actors in the economy still largely responded to the State's priorities and were incapable of engaging with the challenges of a global economy in perpetual evolution and that had embraced the dictates of competition, including technical competition in particular. The State continued to be the main source of jobs, as the market was unable to absorb young and well-educated (although not always qualified) potential workers[48].

Following the crisis of 2008, which affected the entire country, Algeria was forced to make structural adjustments and to cut back on its ability to employ a significant share of jobseekers as a result of budgetary cuts. As it was no longer possible to mask the scale of unemployment, the private sec-

---

[46] See Hadjeres S., "Trois décennies de (socialisme spécifique) en Algérie", in Arzalier F. *et al.*, *Expérience socialistes en Afrique, 1960-1990*, Paris, Edition "Le Temps des Cerises", 2010, 129 to 148. Etienne B., Chapter VII – "Le socialisme algérien: du populisme au capitalisme d'Etat", in Etienne B., *Algérie, cultures et révolution*, Paris, Ed. Le Seuil, 1977, 193-226.

[47] Hamamda M.T., "Privatisation des entreprises publiques en Algérie", *Géo-économie*, 2011/1 (no. 56), 133 to 157.

[48] Feroukhid J., "Enseignement supérieur et marché du travail en Algérie", in Labaki B. (dir.), *Enseignement supérieur et marché du travail dans le monde arabe*, Beyrouth, Presse de l'IFPO, 2009, 60.

tor was now called upon to perform a leading role in this area. New businesses had to be set up, as their number was deemed insufficient for the economy to develop. In addition, setting up one's own business seemed to young people (as well as less young people) to be an essential step in a number of ways in gaining a foothold in the labour market.

Within this context, Algeria set up a variety of programmes with the aim of favouring the creation of businesses, with the support of international and regional institutions. As an objective for 2014 (2010-2014 five-year plan), Algeria set itself the goal of creating 200,000 businesses (medium-sized enterprises), which were to supposed to constitute a network for the productive economy. This target was not achieved[49]. On another note, two points should be made:

1. At present in 2021, government policy is aimed in particular at promoting start-ups as well as small and medium-sized enterprises[50]. The average business today is extremely small, and many qualify as micro-enterprises.
2. The proportion of women entrepreneurs is very low. Figures indicate that there are 394,000 in total (employers or self-employed)[51].

However, freedom of enterprise is guaranteed to all citizens in the same terms for both men and women. One might therefore ask why there should be such a low number of female business owners.

Before looking into reasons that might explain this situation, it is important:

- first, to set out the legal and institutional framework;
- secondly, to provide an overview of those sectors of activity in which female entrepreneurs are active.

2.1. The under-representation of women entrepreneurs and the legal environment

The legal and institutional framework might appear in certain respects to be favourable; however, it has not been capable of tangibly increasing the number of women entrepreneurs in Algeria. The facts speak for them-

[49] On the analysis of the constraints faced by SMES, see Kafia Berrah and Moussa Bourif, "La problématique de la création des petites et moyennes entreprises en Algérie", *Revue algérienne de développement économique*, 02-2015, 19 to 28.

[50] See the action plan of the Djerrad Government.

[51] See the ILO report (2017), *Evaluation nationale of développement de l'entreprenariat féminin en Algérie. Situation et recommandations.*

selves: women are under-represented at both national and regional level, and also under an international comparison.

2.1.1. The legal and institutional framework and the promotion of female entrepreneurs

2.1.1.1. *The regional and international level*

The Universal Declaration of Human Rights asserts the right to just and favourable conditions of work (Art. 23).

Although it does not deal specifically with entrepreneurship, this rights covers work in its totality; employment is covered by paragraph 2 of this Article.

ILO Convention no. 122 on Employment Policy enshrines the notion that States must pursue "an active policy designed to promote full, productive and freely chosen employment", and that this policy must "aim at ensuring there is work for all who are available for and seeking work" and that "such work is as productive as possible" (Art. 1).

The International Covenant on Economic, Social and Cultural Rights[52] also asserts this right to work for all persons. It also affirms the equality of all persons before the law, without any discrimination. Moreover, it is clearly stipulated that women and men must have equal rights (Articles 2 and 3), reasserting the principle already set out in Art. 2 of the Universal Declaration of Human Rights.

It should be pointed out that these texts were adopted at a time when the main concern was to combat unemployment on the one hand and to ensure worker protection on the other hand. However, it should be noted, insofar as is of interest for our present purposes, that each person must have the opportunity to work without any discrimination.

The CEDAW[53], which was adopted after these instruments, contains similar provisions, focusing on the rights of women, who have been found to lack them in various areas. This Convention establishes full opportunities for women to be able to earn an income that enables them to acquire a certain degree of autonomy. Other provisions of this Convention set out working conditions for women, without having to suffer from male sexism (equal pay, equal access to responsibilities and combatting harassment)[54]. Particular attention is dedicated to rural women.

---

[52] Adopted on 16 December 1966 by the United Nations General Assembly.

[53] The Convention on the Elimination of All Forms of Discrimination against Women was ratified by Algeria in 1996.

[54] Art. 11 ff.

The Millennium Declaration was a fundamental milestone in the history of the United Nations. This text sets out policy focuses for the 21st century. These include enhancing the autonomy of women, which is presented as one of the core objectives.

The acknowledgement at global level of the continuing inequalities within relations between men and women is now fully apparent. Moreover, the situation of extreme poverty experienced by a large proportion of the global female population has led the United Nations to fix Millennium Development Goals by 2015. Resolution 52-2 adopted by the General Assembly on 8 September 2000 focuses on the need to promote gender equality and to enhance the autonomy of women.

Within this perspective, a variety of international institutions have established vast programmes that grant financial and technical support to women to enable them to take their destinies into their own hands. These include, amongst others, the World Bank, the UNDP and the ILO.

Within the context of international cooperation, the Canadian International Development Agency (CIDA) and the EU have supported programmes with similar objectives.

2.1.1.2. *The national level*

The legal instruments reviewed above have had effects within the country: the Algerian Constituent Assembly included freedom of enterprise as one of the rights guaranteed to all Algerians in the Constitution.

Specifically, Art. 43 of the revised Constitution of 2016, and Art. 61 of the most recent revision of 1 November 2020 provide that the right to invest in, launch and run a business is a right guaranteed to all citizens.

Art. 32 provides that all Algerians are equal before the law and that any discrimination based, *inter alia*, on gender is prohibited.

However, one strand of the literature has played down the scope of these two provisions as the principle of equal rights for men and women is not clearly enunciated, as is required under the CEDAW (which has been ratified by Algeria). The inaccuracies and questions raised by Art. 2, which provides that Islam is the religion of State, leaves space in which inequality before the law and unequal treatment is permitted and accepted.

Whilst the provisions of the Constitution that mandate equality between women and men in the political arena as well as the right to access responsibilities and decision-making positions are regarded as progress on the road towards equal rights between men and women (Articles 35 and 36), by contrast the notion of parity does not appear to apply to economic affairs. For instance, Art. 35 (2020) provides that the State must undertake to remove all obstacles that imped the exercise by citizens of their rights. This provision leaves broad room for manoeuvre on account of its vague and imprecise nature.

Whereas equality between men and women is clearly established within the fields of education and health, and even at work, the same does not also apply to the legislation governing the variety of activities necessary in relation to investment or the production and marketing of goods. However, it must be stressed that women are not excluded from these areas, which thus confirms that men and women have equal rights in this area.

Given the principle of freedom of enterprise, the public authorities adopted schemes intended to promote the creation of new businesses.

Throughout the 1990s, Algeria experienced a period of political instability, which had indisputable consequences for the economic and social life of the country. A growing share of the population fell into poverty, which included essentially women. The Social Development Agency (*Agence pour le Développement Social*, ADS) was set up in 1996 in order to deal with this problem. Its goal is to promote the creation of small or even micro-enterprises through recourse to micro credit. It should be noted that numerous programmes of this type have been implemented throughout various countries in Africa, Asia and Latin America. Entrepreneurship is regarded as an instrument for combatting poverty, no longer by calling for international official development assistance (ODA), which fosters a spirit of dependency, but rather by stimulating initiative and creativity.

Women have been particularly affected by these programmes as they constitute the majority of the population living under the poverty threshold. The same holds true in Algeria. Women are often dependent upon men, or on their fathers or brothers before they marry. After marrying, they fall under the protection of their husbands. The various programmes launched by the ADS have enabled women who are isolated, or who bear sole responsibility for a family, to access micro credit with a view to setting up their own businesses, even if these are extremely small. The financing of entrepreneurial activity through micro credit is not provided exclusively to women, but also to men.

A number of other arrangements support the ADS.

The National Agency for the Management of Micro Credit (*Agence Nationale de Gestion du Micro Crédit*, ANGEM) was established in 2004 and its aim is in particular to combat unemployment and casual employment in urban and rural settings by favouring self-employment, working from home as well as craft and artisanal activities, in particular amongst the women. It offers two forms of financing:

- The first is the grant of interest-free micro credit directly by the ANGEM for the purpose of purchasing raw materials.
- The second consists in the grant of loans by a bank and the ANGEM at the time a business is set up in order to purchase minor items of equipment and an initial stock of raw materials, and also in order to pay the costs necessary in order to launch the business (triangular financing: ANGEM – bank – promoter).

The National Unemployment Insurance Scheme (CNAC) was established in 1994. Its aim is to guarantee a fixed income to the unemployed, who have now become more numerous (or at least more visible on account of the new economic policies adopted by Algeria at the end of the 1980s). Alongside the benefits it pays out to the unemployed, it also supports the creation of businesses by providing financial support, as well as technical assistance to improve the viability of businesses.

As for the National Agency for the Promotion of Youth Employment (ANSEJ), its mechanism is distinguished by the level of the amounts allocated to the investments required for new businesses. The process, which is lengthier, also involves banks. The bank's opinion plays a major role in the decision over whether or not to grant a loan[55].

Since 2020, the programmes presented by the new government have contained measures aimed at achieving hydrocarbon independence. These include the elevation of business to a special position.

Within this context, a particular focus is placed on female entrepreneurship. This goal is confirmed by the CARDEL programme, which calls for the participation of women and young persons in particular at local level. It thus recommends the integration of all actors, including in particular women, into economic and social life.

Although this equality within the socio-economic domain cannot be disputed on a legislative or regulatory level, the fact remains that the under-representation of women amongst the entrepreneurial class is a fact that cannot be questioned in view of the existing data.

2.2. Under-representation of female entrepreneurs within Algerian society

Before providing an overview of the position of women in the entrepreneurial class, it is important to clarify what is meant by "enterprise".

---

[55] Plans are being drawn up to change this body with the aim of achieving the creation of more viable and profitable enterprises, as until now the "social" nature of these enterprises has been the dominant consideration.

2.2.1. Legal and economic aspects of the enterprise

First of all it should be pointed out that there is no legal definition of the notion of enterprise. Existing definitions are derived from economics. However, lawyers do indeed use them in various areas of the law (commercial law, tax law and business law).

An enterprise is defined as an entity comprised of three elements:

- A body of assets and resources. Assets should be understood as tangible assets (machinery, vehicles and other means of transportation, goods, etc.) as well as intangible assets (patents, accounts receivable, etc.). Human resources comprise the totality of the workers carrying on activity relating to production, transformation or marketing.
- The entity must have a for-profit purpose, which sets it apart from non-profit entities from the world of associations.
- The entity has a group of managers whose task is to manage it according to arrangements and procedures in such a manner that it achieves its objectives.

An enterprise may be set up by one individual, or a group of people, either men or women, or both.

This economic definition underscores the great diversity of the enterprise: the nature of an enterprise's activity varies depending upon the sector of activity. Enterprises can also be distinguished by their size. Some of them are small, or even micro-sized, at the time they are created. A large number of them will stay this size, whilst others will evolve and grow by expanding their business into new geographical areas or diversifying from their initial activities. Finally, they may be wound up by their managers, if they decide to put an end to their activities, or also in the event of their death. An enterprise may "die" as a result of its insolvency, i.e. its inability to continue trading taking account of the poor results recorded by it.

Setting up a business requires certain skills or qualities, such as imagination and a spirit of initiative. One must also be willing to take risks and know how to manage them.

From the legal viewpoint, these enterprises come in different legal forms, ranging from the EURL (single-member enterprise with limited liability) to various other forms of company.

Moreover, the person or persons wishing to set up a business must have legal capacity, and must be of legal age (being of an age and having mental capacity that enables him or her to manage the business). They must not have received any criminal convictions for particular crimes or offences such as theft or fraud, embezzlement, or the passing of uncovered cheques

(Law no. 04-08 of 14 August 2004 on the conditions applicable to the conduct of commercial activities).

Following this brief introduction providing an overview of the condition of the entrepreneur, we must now consider the problem at issue in this paper: the under-representation of women amongst business leaders.

First of all, it should be pointed out that Algeria is not alone in being affected by this issue. In effect, the same observation could be made at global level, as only one enterprise out of every three in the world is led by a woman. However, there are significant regional disparities, as is apparent from the following figures[56]:

- East Asia and Pacific: 47%;
- Europe and Central Asia: 33%;
- Latin America and Caribbean: 50%;
- Middle East and North Africa: 23%;
- South Asia: 18%;
- Sub-Saharan Africa: 29%.

2.2.2. Algerian women in businesses

According to statistics from 2018, there are around 150,000 female business leaders (excluding professional services and agriculture) out of a total of more than 1.96 million, corresponding to a share of 7.6%[57], which is not in fact a bad score when compared to the rest of Africa and the Arab world.

Algerian women in charge of companies are more present in the craft sector than in others. The craft sector includes all activities the object of which is the manual production of goods for marketing. Work is considered to be manual where it involves the usage and (or) exploitation of manual expertise. It is possible to use an instrument such as an engine or any other tool, provided that it does not alter the manual nature of the work, with the result that the product is not industrial in nature, i.e. there is no mass production.

Algerian law[58] defines craft activity as any activity involving manual creation, transformation, restoration, maintenance or repair, or the provision of predominantly manual services that is carried out... as the principal and ongoing object of the business... whether from a fixed location or on an

[56] Source: business surveys. Data obtained from the World Bank's gender equality data & statistics.

[57] According to statistics, the association SEVE cited by El Watan of 18 November 2019.

[58] Ordinance no. 01-96 of 10 January 1996 laying down rules to govern craft and artisanal activities.

itinerant basis... in the areas of craft work, artistic craftsmanship, the production of goods and the provision of services.

It may be carried out individually, within the ambit of a cooperative or within an enterprise.

Women are represented in large numbers in this sector for a variety of reasons.

2.2.2.1. *Carrying on activity of this type requires little or no education, and does not require a high level of training, which means that illiterate women are able to perform the work*

For a large number of them, carrying on craft activity is (at least at first sight) particularly easy as they already have the necessary expertise, either through training or having been handed down through the family. Pottery making, weaving and wickerwork are moreover activities that women have traditionally performed within the home. These goods tend to be produced in order to satisfy self-consumption requirements, and not in order to obtain income from their marketing. Other food products – "homemade, made by hand" – are of particular interest nowadays, thanks to growing demand at local and even international level. Economists speak of niches where the marketing of these products may be profitable. Finally, other manual activities that have recently attracted a large number of women include dressmaking and apiculture.

2.2.2.2. *The availability of financing*

Artisan women benefited very early from the ADS financing mechanisms, with the support of the ANGEM, referred to above.

Although numerous artisan women are involved in activities within an increasing variety of areas, they are still not becoming business leaders. A large number of them are active in the informal sector, some of them voluntarily but others out of necessity, despite the financial mechanisms put in place[59].

Overall, it is possible to distinguish between four general groups:

- Women involved in craft activity, who earn money from it on an informal basis. They work on an occasional basis during periods in which the family does not earn sufficient income. This economic activity is not visible, as the women work from home and their products are marketed informally (for instance through family and friends).
- Women who carry on craft activity in the home, whilst also establishing

[59] See the study published by CREAD (in conjunction with the Konrad Adenauer Foundation) entitled: *L'entreprenariatféminin en Algérie, uneréalité en construction.*

or joining sectoral associations. These associations also have a cultural aspect. Their activity is more visible within society, as their products are openly available and presented to the public at cultural or trade events. Usage of an association framework is becoming more widespread, and women are also becoming more widely involved in e-commerce. It should be noted that associations have a non-profit purpose (Law no. 12-06 of 12 January 2012 on associations), even though the products of these women involved in craft work are marketed. Women within this group generally have a certain level of education and often live in urban or semi-urban areas where their products fulfil specific needs (dress-making, embroidery, traditional baking).

- Women who exploit their expertise, whether acquired traditionally or through "modern" training within the ambit of a cooperative. These women organise and share costs such as expenses relating to the purchase of raw materials, and the tools necessary for their activity. They benefit from financial support via the ANGEM or other support put in place under the various local development programmes promoted by the EU or other bodies such as the CIDA (Canadian International Development Agency), or the German cooperation organisation GDZ.
  The products of these activities are presented at trade fairs where they can be sold.
  Women, in this case, are part of a formal framework. As a result, the legal existence of their commercial activity is clearly identified and their visibility in the public space becomes undisputed. It should be noted that the risk is borne by the lending body. However, if they demonstrate that they are capable entrepreneurs, women end up developing their businesses further. This is because the aim of the programmes put in place by the various institutions is to ensure their autonomy as they establish production procedures and standards in the first instance, after which they go on to master distribution networks and marketing techniques. They differ from women involved in craft work who opt in favour of an association framework. Whilst these women are more visible in the public sphere, they do not clearly establish the commercial nature of their activity, at the same time avoiding any risk.
- Finally, the last category is comprised of artisan women who, by developing their activity and diversifying or reinforcing it, end up creating a micro-enterprise. As they have the status of craft workers and are subject to the laws and regulations applicable to craft work, they benefit from the same rights and the same obligations as men, who are also represented in large numbers in the craft sector (copperware, jewellery)[60].

[60] See the law on artisanal activities, cited above.

In actual fact, only women included in the fourth category should be regarded as entrepreneurs. Nonetheless, the other categories are still important. They represent the different phases through which women must pass in order to set up a business. The first category have demonstrated a spirit of initiative in breaking with the traditional domain of domestic work and focusing on activities that had previously been confined exclusively to the family setting and to the satisfaction of its needs. The second category represents a shift to the public sphere where the women are in fact visible, but do not bear any risk (the risk is not simply economic but also social).

Finally, the last group of artisans reaches the stage where the spirit of initiative and the management of risk are issues that are have been recognised and mastered, or at the very least accepted. It should be added that these elements are necessary in order for an enterprise to be created and to continue in existence. By reinforcing their initial activity, these craft workers develop, diversity and eventually promote it. Some level of assistance is required in order for these micro-enterprises to survive (training, tax breaks, etc...). These women generally have a certain level of education, experience of the world of work, as well as a spirit of innovation and creativity. They do not appear to be present in particularly large numbers.

As large numbers of women are investing in the craft sector, the situation is gradually evolving. Increasing numbers of women are investing in sectors such as training and the environment. They are even starting to set up their own businesses in the agricultural sector, although are still present in very low numbers. The percentage of women who have invested in the agricultural sector is 4.5% for ANSEJ projects and 11.5% for CNAC projects (2016)[61].

One of the reasons for this development appears to have been the appearance on the labour market of female graduates or holders of other advanced qualifications who are unable to find employment (which is an issue for all young Algerians, including both men and women). They have chosen in increasing numbers to invest in sectors that reflect their specialist expertise. However, taking account of competition on the market due to insufficient demand, a large number of them must retrain for sectors that offer greater opportunities. The privileged areas towards which women have traditionally gravitated (medicine, pharmacology, the bar, etc.) have started to become saturated and have become less attractive (it should be noted that these enterprises are not subject to the provisions of commercial law, but rather to civil law).

A distinction can be drawn between three sectors of economic activity: primary, secondary and tertiary. The first covers agriculture, pasturing and

[61] ILO Report, cited above, 35.

fishing. The second covers all industrial activities, specifically those related to the production and transformation of goods. Finally, the third encompasses all services, trade, banking, insurance, etc.

Women are present above all in this last sector. They are much less involved in the secondary sector, and even less in the primary sector.

This distribution can be explained first of all by the fact that the service sector offers more opportunities for the creation of jobs. It should nevertheless be noted that large businesses are led by men, and women are generally limited to small and micro-enterprises. It should also be pointed out that, in some enterprises apparently created by women, the owners are in actual fact nominees as the business is managed by the husband or another family member (such as the father or a brother).

Despite these comments, it is possible to note an expansion in the involvement of women in this sector. The businesses in which female entrepreneurs are represented in the highest numbers include training, cleaning, beauty services and fashion. Activities related to the environment are attracting increasing numbers of women. Accordingly, the percentage of women who have invested in the services sector is 16.3% for ANSEJ projects and 17.1% for CNAC projects (2016) [62].

The primary and secondary sectors are dominated by men. Agriculture and fishing are traditionally male activities. It is difficult for women to enter these sectors, and to survive within them. However, some women take the plunge and embark on a new adventure in this area.

The increase in the number of women who set up their own businesses can also be explained by the establishment of the ANSEJ, which appears to attract men and women alike who, according to available figures, appear to benefit in equal numbers. Another financial mechanism that is capable of promoting the creation of businesses is the CNAC.

Overall, these mechanisms have not achieved the desired results, taking account of the number of enterprises that have not seen the light of day and that have been unable to survive.

Finally, the growing presence of women amongst the entrepreneurial class is due to the emergence of new professions in which men have been unable to impose their dominance. Sectors that are so to speak "virgin", such as the environment, telecommunications and tourism are all areas in which men and women enter into competition, essentially in consideration of their respective skills.

The new policies adopted by the public authorities since 2020 with the aim of promoting start-ups (creation of a minister with responsibility for

---

[62] ILO Report, cited above, 35.

start-ups) provide young women with opportunities to set up their own businesses, in the same way as young men, by drawing on their knowledge and expertise in the field of computing.

Data currently available points to a see-saw type evolution. Following a significant increase in the number of businesses set up by women during the 2000s, figures have been falling since 2010[63].

It cannot be denied that the number of female business leaders in Algeria has not increased sufficiently. This is both having regard to the international instruments ratified by Algeria, and also taking account of the mechanisms put in place to promote entrepreneurship in general. This situation can be explained by reference to a variety of reasons.

Conclusion

This research has highlighted the slow integration of the principle of equality into the public sphere as well as into economic life.

The legal formalism forced by the introduction into the Constitution and into legislation of the principle of equality and freedom of enterprise, as well as accommodations such as the quota system or the principle of parity, have not resulted in immediate and compelling outcomes.

The historic achievement made by Algerian female combatants during the war of liberation were incapable, on their own, of overcoming the social hindrances and obstacles to the full application of these two principles.

This difficulty in adaptation is not specific to Algeria, but is also present in numerous other States in the Mediterranean region.

Very recent attempts to replace the parity system with the quota system have in effect demonstrated its limits.

However, a slow and very progressive evolution would be the best guarantee for fulfilling the principle of equality on a stable and lasting basis. On the other hand, the pace at which the principle of freedom of enterprise is applied could be stepped up in view of its goal of furthering equality in other areas.

References

Berrah K. and Bourif M. (2015), "La problématique de la 256reation des petites et moyennes entreprises en Algérie", *Revue algérienne de développement économique*, 2.

---

[63] See the ILO report on women entrepreneurs, cited above.

Etienne B. (1977), "Le socialisme algérien: du populisme au capitalisme d'Etat", *Algérie, culture et revolution*, Paris, Ed. Le Seuil.

Feroukhi J. (2009), "Enseignement supérieur et marché du travail en Algérie", in Labaki B. (dir.), *Enseignement supérieur et marché du travail dans le monde arabe*, Beyrouth, Presse de l'IFPO.

Ghanem L. (2013), *Les droits politiques de la femme dans les Etats du Maghreb Arabe,* University of Algers, Faculty of Law.

Hadjeres S. (2010), "Trois décennies de (socialisme spécifique) en Algérie", in Arzalier F. *et al., Expériences socialistes en Afrique, 1960-1990*, Paris, Edition "Le Temps des Cerises".

Hamamda M.T. (2011), "Privatisation des entreprises publiques en Algérie", *Géo-économie*, 1, 56.

Laroussi H. (2010), *Analyse des élections législatives algériennes de 2007*, Master in Public Law, Ben Aknoun Law Faculty – University of Algiers 1, (written in Arabic).

TaÏb E. (2020), "La femme au gouvernement", *IDARA review.*

Chapter 11

GENDER EQUALITY IN POLITICAL PARTICIPATION IN LIBYA: THE TRANSITION'S CONTROVERSIAL ASSESSMENT *

Jinene Limam

ABSTRACT: *This article traces the recent path of the political participation of women in Libya. It discusses some key actions that were taken to promote the equal participation of women, focusing on the national legal framework and the political participation of women in practice. Openness to comparative experiences and best practices that ensure better representation of women will be useful in this context.*

The article should under no conditions be understood as an assessment of the political participation of women in Libya. Rather, it seeks to identify challenges and concrete lessons learned with regards to the equal participation of women in politics with a view to providing guidance to different stakeholders and civil society on measures they can take in concert to promote full and effective participation by women in political life. An overview of different approaches that aim to reinforce women's political participation highlighted that most interventions with evidence of success operate at multiple levels and employ multiple strategies.

It identifies some key actions that were taken to promote the equal participation of women, focusing on the national legal framework and the political participation of women in practice. Comparative experiences and best prac-

---

* Acronyms: ARP: The Assembly of the Representatives of the People; CCMCE: Central Committee for Municipal Council Elections; CDA: Constitution Drafting Assembly; CEDAW: United Nations Convention on the Elimination of All Forms of Discrimination against Women; ECOSOC: Economic and Social Council; GNC: General National Congress; HNEC: High National Elections Commission; HoR: House of Representatives; IDEA: International Institute for Democracy and Electoral Assistance; IFES: International Foundation for Electoral Systems; ICCPR: International Covenant on Civil and Political Right; IPU: Inter-Parliamentary Union; LPDF: Libyan Political Dialogue Forum; NCA: National Constituent Assembly; NDI: National Democratic Institute; NGO: Nongovernmental Organization; NTC: National Transitional Council; SDGs: Sustainable Development Goals; UN: United Nations; UNDP: The United Nations Development Programme; UN ESCWA: Economic and Social Commission for Western Asia; UNSMI:L the United Nations Support Mission in Libya; UN: Women United Nations Entity for Gender Equality and the Empowerment of Women.

tices that ensure better representation of women will be useful in this context.

Since the 17 February 2011 revolution, Libya has been engaged in a bumpy, violent, and unfinished transition. In this context, the situation of women's rights is particularly problematic insofar as women are not only discriminated against in practice and in law, but their situation has clearly deteriorated during the transition phase. Indeed, the structural obstacles to women's access to their political, socio-economic, and cultural rights have been amplified and aggravated by the resurgence of violence and the rise of militias, tribal leaders, and fundamentalist groups. Some rights recognized to women under the regime of Gaddafi (1969-2011) have been challenged since 2011.

At the same time, the transition allowed for a debate on the status of women and their rights, and women participated in the uprising and formed civil society movements to demand their inclusion in the various transition processes. The issue of women's rights was on the agenda during the drafting of legal texts (electoral laws, draft constitution) and peace agreements. Since elections of General National Congress (GNC) in 2012, quotas as special measures were adopted to ensure women's participation in the new formal elected bodies at national and local levels. However, the results of the several elections suggest women are generally elected for reserved seats and are less likely to be elected when running for open seats. Women are also more vulnerable to security concerns. Indeed, political setbacks and protracted conflict since the revolution served to restrict the participation of women and have led to a rolling back of political gains for women experienced particularly during the GNC elections in 2012. Libyan women are seriously underrepresented in the formal elected bodies and other governing bodies and political process. The underrepresentation of women reflects the discrimination faced by women in public life – of which political violence against women is one of the worst manifestations.

The gap between the political rights enshrined in the legal framework and the political participation of women in practice persists. Women continue to face multiple economic, social, institutional, and cultural obstacles that severely limit their participation in public life, and particularly in government positions.

Weakness of political parties. – 7. Gender mainstreaming. – 7.1. Gendering the constitutional/legal language. – 7.2. Equality and prohibition of discrimination. – 7.3. Equality in political rights and special measures. – 7.4. Eliminating violence against women. – 8. Conclusion.

1. Background and context

Gender equality in political participation is a cornerstone of democracy. It is also associated with peace, stability, and the long-term success of transition to democracy. Most international treaties [1], social studies, and even modern universal insights, agree that both men and women should have equal rights and opportunities to participate fully in all aspects, and at all levels of political processes.

Gender equality in decision-making is to be viewed in the context of whether, or not, women are in the position to make or influence public decisions on the same footing as men. Indeed, if more women are political decision makers, they can create stronger alliances with each other to advocate gender-responsive laws and policies.

The 1995 Beijing Platform stressed that equality in decision-making is integral to the advancement of women's rights and that women's equal participation in decision-making is not only a question of simple justice or democracy, but also a necessary condition for women's fundamental rights to be taken into account.

The UN Secretary General's report to the commission on the Status of Women for the Sixty-fifth session 15-26 March 2021 [2], recommends "to implement international and national commitments and norms, including through temporary special measures, create more enabling environments and institutional systems, reduce violence against women in political life and strengthen the voices of women, who face multiple forms of discrimination". This statement is intended to reach equality in participation and decision-making in public life.

Globally, women's participation in the political life is still limited. Indeed, it is often more challenging for women to access and exercise these rights, more so, in Libya, a country in which the society is deeply rooted in overly conservative views based on outdated traditions and religious mis-

---

[1] UN, ICCPR, Art. 25(b); UN. CEDAW, Art. 7; African Charter on Human and Peoples' Rights, Art. 13 (1).

[2] Economic and Social Council, Commission on the Status of Women, *Women's full and effective participation and decision-making in public life, as well as the elimination of violence, for achieving gender equality and the empowerment of all women and girls, Report of the Secretary-General*, E/CN.6/2021/3, Sixty-fifth session, 21 December 2020, https://undocs.org/E/CN.6/2021/3 (accessed on 28 November 2023).

conceptions[3]. This is something common in many societies, although in greater proportions in the Arab and Muslim societies.

Women in Libya were largely marginalized under Gaddafi regime, although they played a frontline role in the success of the February 17, 2011, revolution. Following the revolution, women led civil society movements and began to advocate for opportunities for meaningful inclusion in Libya's emerging political transition[4].To win support, women advocated gender equality with popular revolutionary ideals, such as democracy as there is no democracy without equality. However, since 2011, Libya has been engaged in a bumpy, violent and unfinished transition. Indeed, the exaltation of the days of protest and triumph of the revolution has given way to multiple challenges to the construction of a nation-state and the transition to a democratic regime in Libya. These include ephemeral and failing public institutions, internal armed conflict with diffuse militia, territorial fractures, the resurgence of tribalism, the rise of religious extremism, and a declining economy...

In this context, the situation of women's rights is particularly problematic as women are not only discriminated in practice and in law, but their situation has clearly deteriorated during the transition phase. Indeed, the structural obstacles to women's access to their political, socio-economic, and cultural rights have been amplified and aggravated since 2011 by the resurgence of violence and the rise of militias, tribal leaders, and fundamentalist groups. Some rights recognized to women under the regime of Gaddafi (1969-2011) have been challenged since 2011. Women's rights are indeed a divisive issue that lies at the heart of political positioning and ideological conflicts between conservatives and liberals; those who are committed to the universality of human rights and those who challenge this paradigm of universalism of human rights and propose a relativistic and particularistic approach to human rights.

Nevertheless, the transition has enabled a debate on the status of women and their inclusion in the various transition processes. Women's rights

---

[3] Bugaighis, W., "Prospects for women in the new Libya", in *Handbook of Arab Women and Arab Spring*, ed. by Olimat M.S., London, Routledge, 2013, available at https://www.routledgehandbooks.com/doi/10.4324/9781315858661-8, (accessed on 1st December 2023).

[4] Langhi Z., "Gender and state-building in Libya: towards a politics of inclusion", in *The Journal of North African Studies*, 19, 2, 2014, 200-210, available at https://www.tandfonline.com/doi/abs/10.1080/13629387.2014.881736 (accessed on 25 November 2023); Hweio, H., *Libyan women and revolution : a study of the changes in women's political and social roles during and after the Libyan revolution*, Graduate Research Theses & Dissertations, 2016, 3798, available at https://huskiecommons.lib.niu.edu/allgraduate-thesesdissertations/3798 (accessed on 25 November 2023).

issues were on the agenda during the drafting of legal texts (electoral laws, draft constitution) and peace agreements. In 2012, electoral law for the GNC adopted a closed-list zipper system, requiring political parties to alternate sexes on their candidate lists and to place a woman candidate at the top of half of their lists. Learning from Tunisia, the Libyan quota required both horizontal and vertical zippering, but only applied to political parties; 80 of 200 seats[5]. For the next elections, this measure was abandoned in favor of reserved seats for women. But the results of the elections held in Libya since 2012 suggest women are less likely to be elected when running for open seats and more vulnerable to security concerns.

In times of significant societal upheaval, such as political transitions from autocracy to democracy, particularly in context of armed conflicts, constitution drafting processes represent an opportunity for citizens and the state to renegotiate the social contract that binds them and to define their common vision for a fairer society. There have been efforts to make these processes more inclusive and participatory.

On 29 July 2017, Libya's Constitutional Drafting Assembly (CDA) formally adopted a draft constitution but the constitution has not yet been put to a referendum. A 25% women quota was adopted in the Constitution draft as temporary measure to ensure female representation in Libya's next parliamentary elections. But the draft constitution is very insufficient in terms of guaranteeing and protecting women's rights.

In late 2020, the Libyan Political Dialogue Forum (LPDF) was launched to reunite the country by establishing a new national government and forging a path towards elections. Based on the UN Security-Council 2510 (2020), which endorsed the conclusions of the international Conference on Libya in Berlin, the United Nations Support Mission in Libya (UNSMIL) facilitated the first round Libyan Political Dialogue Forum (LPDF) from 7 to 15 November 2020 in the Tunisian capital. The LPDF brought together 75 participants Libyan women and men representing the full social and political spectrum of the Libyan society. The LPDF agreed to allocate 30 percent of leadership positions in the Government to women.

[5] Doherty M. (2012), *Libyan Women in the 2012 National Elections*, Conference on Women's Participation in Public Life, Politics, and Decision-Making, UNDP, Tunis, 29-30 October 2012, National Democratic Institute, available at https://www.ndi.org/sites/default/files/Doherty_Libyan%20Women%20in%20the%202012%20National%20Elections_October%202012.pdf (accessed on 1 December 2023).

2. Research objectives and methodology

This article aims to understand and analyze the transition processes undertaken in Libya since 2011 from a gender sensitive perspective, focusing on the women's representation in politics and the impact of their inclusion. It seeks to document and analyze the women's political participation in Libya, including their contributions and the obstacles to their full participation. Based on both national and international references in analysis and assessment, the article explores avenues for change to enhance women's political participation and support women's rights in Libya.

At the methodological level, the article builds on the most important legal texts resulting from the transitional processes. Furthermore, it is drafted based on an analysis of the legal framework and political environment in which Libyan women face their challenges, to highlight the main challenges women, face in accessing political structures, and to identify appropriate strategies to overcome these challenges, to promote gender equality in the political arena in Libya.

It explores also existing literature on comparative transitional processes and draws on references, research, and reports that have covered the political participation of women in other countries.

It also sheds light on the processes through the eyes of some actors. Five interviews have been conducted with women activists, academics, and political stakeholders[6]. Some of the interviewees have requested to remain anonymous and thus the option to add a list of respondents in an annex of the study has been waived. Beyond the interviews, this paper will try to capture the important contributions made by women outside of the formal process; some of the statements were taken from workshops and training sessions conducted by the author of the study and organized by UNDP for women candidates in 2012 and 2014 and during the drafting constitution process in Libya.

This article seeks to explore these central questions in the following chapters: Does the new legal framework guarantee an effective political participation of women?

---

[6] Interviews were conducted in July and October 2021 with Azza Kamel El Maghur (Libyan lawyer and feminist activist), Ramadan Eltweger (rapporteur for the CDA), Amal Al Obeidi (Researcher and Academician in Political Science), Khawla Jouili (lawyer and member of the women lawyers' union), Jazia Shaitir (feminist activist and university professor in Benghazi), Fatma Chenib (feminist activist, former judge and currently a lawyer in Tripoli), Abdelbari Chanbarou (former minister of local affairs), Leila Lefi (head of the women's support and empowerment unit), and Soulef Guessoum (head of the UNDP project on women's political participation in Libya - 2011-2012 and currently Senior adviser for UN Women).

How did women carve out their roles in the political arena?

What influence did women civil society organizations have on the different transitional processes?

What gendered challenges did women face?

What lessons can be learned from the comparative experiences which adopt more inclusive approaches?

3. Legal framework analysis

The legal framework in Libya continues to be problematic on the level of politics and gender with issues that still need to be tackled. But to have a better understanding of the current situation of gender equality in Libya, and to identify the constraints and obstacles that need to be addressed, it would be useful to take first a look at the historical background of women's political participation in Libya [7].

3.1. 1951-2011 Era

On 7 October 1951, Libya's 'Independence' Constitution was brought into the light, a few months prior to Libya's formal declaration of its independence on 24 December 1951, as a constitutional and hereditary monarchy under King Idris El-Sanussi. The 1951 Libyan Constitution set out some democratic features related to protection of specific rights [8].

Article 11 of the 1951 Libyan Constitution states that "Libyans shall be equal before the law. They shall enjoy equal civil and political rights, shall the same opportunities and be subject to the same public duties and obligations, without distinction of religion, belief, race, language, wealth, kinship, or political or social opinion". Article 12 states that "Personal liberty shall be guaranteed and everyone shall be entitled to equal protection of the law". The government focused on education and development and strived to establish a democratic culture based on respecting on the rule of law as well as respecting citizens' rights.

---

[7] See Vandewalle D.J., *Libya Since Independence: Oil and State-building*, Ithaca, Cornell University Press, 1998; Bugaighis, W., "Prospects for women in the new Libya", in *Handbook of Arab Women and Arab Spring*, ed. by Olimat M.S., London, Routledge, 2013, available at https://www.routledgehandbooks.com/doi/10.4324/9781315858661-8, (accessed on 1 December 2023).

[8] DRI, *Assessment of the 1951 Libyan Constitution according to international standards,* 2012, available at https://constitutionnet.org/sites/default/files/dri-ly-bp28-1951_libya_constitution.pdf (accessed on 28 November 2023).

Since 1964, Libyan women gained the right to vote and to participate in political life[9]. They earned that right through organized civil mobilization. In 1954, the Women's Renaissance Society of Benghazi was founded, to become the first women's NGO in Libya. Later in 1957, another Women's Society was formed in Tripoli, and formed the Women's Union of Libya[10]. Libya had held parliamentary polls in 1964 and 1965 and no women participated as candidates.

Following Gaddafi's military coup of 1969, the Libyan Constitution was abolished by the Constitutional Declaration in 1969[11], which was soon abandoned for many arbitrary declarations, finally being all overshadowed with Gaddafi's Green Book which became the foundation of the laws of Libya. The absence of a constitution that establishes and protects citizen's rights, and the marginalizing of the role of law, led to the setting up of an authoritarian regime. After a period of experimentation, in 1971 Popular Congresses were created to replace instruments of government, quickly followed by a system of local, regional and national parliaments termed the Arab Socialist Union. Women were largely excluded from participation in politics under Gaddafi's regime. Political parties were banned by the monarchy then under Gaddafi regime. Civil society organizations were also banned[12]. Women's limited participation under Gaddafi is attributable not only to the lack of political space available to women, but also due to the tainted public perceptions of the few women who penetrated Gaddafi's inner circles[13].

However, during this period Libya had made some progress towards the achievement of equality between women and men in the areas of education, health, Labor Law 12/2010, and social security, and legal protections such as divorce and custody rights. Law no. 1&0 of 1984 regulating marriage and divorce was amended by Law no. 9 of 1993 to prohibit polygamy without the written consent of the first wife and authorization from the court, which was a step towards the complete abolition of polygamy. Arti-

---

[9] United Nations Economic and Social Commission for Western Asia (UN ESCAWA), *Women's Political Representation in the Arab Region*, 2017, 9, available at https://www.unescwa.org/publications/women%E2%80%99s-political-representation-arab-region (accessed on 26 November 2023).

[10] Interviews with Azza Kamel El Maghur and Jazia Shaitir.

[11] Constitutional Declaration Of 1969, available at https://security-legislation.ly/latest-laws/constitutional-declaration-of-1969/ (accessed on 26 November 2023).

[12] Except for a few hand-picked associations, including the Aisha Gaddafi charity foundation, run by Gaddafi's daughter.

[13] Bugaighis W., *op. cit.*

cle 37 of the Law revokes all rulings based on the principle of *nushuz* (recalcitrance of the wife), which shall be considered null and void [14].

Libya ratified International Covenant on Civil and Political Rights on 15 May 1970, International Covenant on Economic, Social and Cultural Rights on the same date, Convention on the Elimination of All Forms of Discrimination against Women on 16 May 1989 with a general reservation and Optional Protocol to the Convention on the Elimination of All Forms of Discrimination against Women on 18 June 2004. In 1995, Libya withdraws its general reservation to the Convention but it formulated specific reservations to article 2 concerning the right to inheritance and article 16, paragraphs (c) and (d) regarding marriage and divorce. Libya did not enter any reservations to the International Covenant on Civil and Political Rights, which also requires equality between women and men in these areas.

3.2. The constitutional declaration of the transitional stage 2011

The National Transitional Council (NTC) was a coalition of rebel leaders set up at the beginning of the revolution. The roadmap for the post-revolution transition to full democracy was outlined in the 2011 Constitutional Declaration, issued in August 2011 whilst the country was still in the throes of the revolution. The Constitutional Declaration includes few specific references to gender: Article 5 Protects motherhood and article 6 guarantees Equality before the law, enjoyment of equal civil and political rights, same opportunities and be subject to the same public duties and obligations without discrimination due to religion, sect, language, wealth, sex, kinship, political opinions, and social status, tribal or eminent or familial loyalty.

Part 2 (Articles 7-15) deals with Rights and Public Freedoms. Article 7 provides that Human rights and freedom shall be respected. The State shall commit to joining international and regional declarations and charters …. This could provide enhanced protection to women. This chapter as well as the others is drafted in gender-neutral terms and it is not particularly focused on gender equity.

[14] Committee on the Elimination of Discrimination against Women, Concluding observations of the Committee on Libyan Arab Jamahiriya, Forty-third session 19 January-6 February 2009, CEDAW/C/LBY/CO/5, available at https://documents-dds-ny.un.org/doc/UNDOC/GEN/N09/227/84/PDF/N0922784.pdf?OpenElement (accessed on 29 November 2023).

3.3. Electoral laws

In early January 2012, the NTC's Election Committee released a draft election law for public comment. The law largely ignored political parties and established a majoritarian system in which individuals would compete for election to the GNC. Article 1 of the draft law stated that "the National Congress consists of two hundred (200) members chosen by direct and free elections, where a ten percent quota of the total number of members of Congress is reserved for women, unless the number of women candidates does not reach the ten percent quota." [15].

Almost immediately the draft was decried by political parties for failing to include them and for women's rights activists for the vaguely worded quota language. Some women activists worried the article was imposing a 10% maximum for women's membership in the GNC. The concept of special measures to ensure women's participation was largely debated. The controversy over quota is reflected in political spheres and in broader public opinion. Several fault lines quickly appeared in this debate. One set of concerns arose around whether a quota rule was necessary or appropriate. One point of view held that reserving seats for women would subvert their authority; women would be better off if their seats were won based on merit alone. For others, it undermined the principle of equality for which women had fought [16].

On the other hand, women's rights associations and feminist activists have defended the need for a quota to guarantee a threshold for the political representation of women in GNC. They wrote letters to the NTC Election Committee, organized lectures, and media commentary by prominent women academics, protested in front of the NTC and prime minister's offices, and held a national "Day of Anger" on February 2 to demand revisions to the electoral law including a 30% quota for women [17].

In February, the NTC Election Committee released a revised version of the election law that introduced political parties into the equation (80 of the 200 seats were reserved for political party lists, while 120 were to be contested by individual candidates), as well as new special measures for women's participation. Article 15 of the final election law adopted a closed-list zipper system, requiring political parties to alternate genders on their candidate lists and to place a woman candidate at the top of half of their lists. The zipper system is

[15] National Transitional Council, Draft Election Law, January 2012.

[16] Interviews with Azza Kamel El Maghur, Jazia Shaitir Amal Al Obeidi, and Fatma Chenib.

[17] Bugaighis W., *op. cit.*

widely considered to be among the most advantageous special measures available to ensure that women are elected. In requiring both vertical and horizontal zippering, Libya's election law drafters endeavoured to learn from the experiences of neighbouring Tunisia, in which a vertical zipper system was used for the election of National Constituent Assembly in 2011.

When the Constitutional Declaration was issued by the National Transitional Council in 2011, it mandated the General National Congress, once elected, to appoint the 60-member body that would draft Libya's new constitution, the Constitutional Drafting Assembly (CDA)[18]. However, an amendment to the Constitutional Declaration just prior to polling on 7 July 2012 stipulated that the Constitutional Drafting Assembly should be directly elected rather than be appointed by the GNC[19].

The General National Congress appointed a legislative committee to draft the electoral law for the Constitutional Drafting Assembly, which included three General National Congress members as well as representatives from Libya's principal districts. The electoral legal framework was finalized between July and September 2013, Law no. 17/2013[20]. According to this law, Constitutional Drafting Assembly is composed of 60 members[21], 20 from each of the three Libyan provinces: Tripolitania (the west), Cyrenaica (the east), and Fezzan (the south)[22]. Consistent with Libya's historical disinclination towards political parties[23], legislators demonstrated a marked preference for majoritarian voting systems, employing both first-past-the-post and single non-transferable voting. A complicated electoral system resulted, in which women were allocated six reserved seats[24], or 10% of the

---

[18] UNDP, *UN Women, Report on Electoral Gender Mapping of Libya*, 2014.

[19] The Third Constitutional Amendment was issued by the National Transitional Council on 5 July 2012 but was found unconstitutional by the Supreme Court due to lack of quorum. On 9 April 2013 a similar amendment was passed by the General National Congress.

[20] Law no. 8/2013 (adopted 28 March 2013) establishes HNEC as a permanent body; the Board of Commissioners was appointed less than a month later on 21 April 2012 (Decision 40/2013).

[21] Libyans elected a 55-member assembly to draft a new constitution. There were supposed to be 60-members, but violence inhibited the ability to hold elections in certain parts of the country.

[22] The 20-20-20 distribution was stipulated in the Second Constitutional Amendment of 10 June 2012.

[23] Libya banned political parties shortly after the 1952 elections, the first following independence.

[24] Art. 6 of the Constitutional Drafting Assembly Electoral Law (Law no. 17 of 20 July 2013).

Constitutional Drafting Assembly. Key elements of the system included[25]:

1. Each of the three Libyan provinces is divided into several main districts, sub-districts and in some cases local districts.
2. Each province has two reserved seats for women representatives:
   - In the western region, the reserved seats were allocated to two sub-districts within the main district of Tripoli. The reserved seat is voted for in a separate ballot by the constituency of each concerned sub-district, and the woman candidate with the majority of votes wins the reserved seat.
   - In the eastern region, the reserved seats were allocated to two groups each composed of two main districts. In each case, the reserved seat is voted for in a separate ballot by the constituency of the two main districts, and the winning woman candidate replaces the winner of the general contest in the sub-district in which she is registered as a candidate.
   - In the southern region, the reserved seats were allocated to two sub-districts. In each case, the reserved seat is voted for in a separate ballot by the constituency of the sub-district, and the winning woman candidate replaces the winner of the general contest in the local district (ward) in which she is registered as a candidate.

As for the House of Representations (HoR), elected on 25 June 2014 to replace the GNC, Article 18 of the law provides that 16% of seats are reserved for women[26]. All candidates are competing in a First Past the Postor Single Non-Transferable Vote system in 13 electoral districts that are further divided into 75 sub-constituencies. Candidates for reserved seats for women will compete in 27 of the 75 sub-constituencies.

Political entities were not allowed to submit lists in the HoR elections as opposed to GNC elections, where lists were elected under a proportional representation (PR) system. Candidates in this election ran as individuals, as per Law no. 10/2014 on the Election of the Council of Representatives during the Transitional Period, which states: “The individual electoral system, based on the single non-transferable vote, shall be used for the election of the Council of Representatives”.

---

[25] UNDP, *UN Women, Report on Electoral Gender Mapping of Libya*, 2014.

[26] The lawyer and feminist activist Azza Kamel Maghur was part of the group of experts who contributed to the drafting of this electoral law. In an interview for this study, she explained that the 16% quota was the result of long negotiations and that she had to fight hard to obtain this quota, however modest.

At local level, many municipal council elections were held between 2012 and 2014. These local elections resumed in 2018 and continue throughout 2019, 2020 and 2021 until all municipal councils are in place[27]. The Ministry of Local Government drafted the Local Administration Law no. 59/2012, which was endorsed by the NTC and later enacted by the GNC in 2013. This law and the Council of Ministers Decision 130/2013 established the institutional structure of local government and thematic areas of competency for municipal councils[28].

A total of 120 municipalities have been established in Libya pursuant to Law no. 59/2012. Articles 7 and 9 of Law no. 59 provide that each municipality will have a council elected by its citizens for a four-year term. Each municipality is one constituency.

According to Article 26 of Law no. 59/2012 and Article 32 of its Executive Regulation 130/2013, municipal councils consist of:

- Five members in municipalities with a population of 250,000 or less and seven members in municipalities with a population of more than 250,000.

In addition, municipal councils include:

- A woman and
- A person with a disability, “from the revolutionaries” if possible.

This means that each municipality will have either seven or nine municipal council members directly elected, depending on the population of the municipality and including the reserved seats for women and revolutionaries with disabilities.

The councilors then elect the mayor from within the council membership.

In January 7, 2019, the Presidential Council (PC) of the Government of National Accord issued Decision 18/2019, which introduces some changes on the electoral system, but it maintained the seats reserved for women.

---

[27] IFES, *Elections in Libya 2020: Municipal Elections Frequently Asked Questions, September 2020*, available at https://www.ifes.org/sites/default/files/migrate/ifes_faqs_elections_in_libya_2020_municipal_elections_september_2020.pdf (accessed on 29 November 2023).

[28] Interview with Abdelbari Chanbarou.

3.4. The draft Constitution (2017)

On 29 July 2017, CDA formally adopted a draft Constitution with the support of over two thirds of its members. At the time, the CDA's achievement was a breakthrough and many Libyans and international partners hoped that it could pave the way to a resolution of Libya's crisis[29]. Although a new conversation on Libya's long-term constitutional future[30] may follow after the Libyan Political Dialogue Forum (LPDF), it is crucial to raise awareness of some of the draft's merits and weakness regarding gender equality in political participation.

The assessment of the CDA's preliminary draft (2014) from gender perspective (and citizenship rights) was based on women's demands for the CDA, which is an outcome of a process lasting several months during 2014 and 2015 and engaging women's representatives from various groups and locations in Libya. This process was facilitated by UN institutions in Libya and based on international good practices and standards[31].

---

[29] Al-Ali Z., *Libya's final draft constitution: A contextual analysis*, Stockholm, International IDEA, December 2020, available at https://constitutionnet.org/sites/default/files/2020-12/Libya%20analysis%20-%20Zaid%20Al-Ali%20%28December%202020%29%20%28English%29.pdf (accessed on 29 November 2023).

[30] Regarding the 2017 draft Constitution, Zaid Al Ali in his above-mentioned book states a number of key issues that will have to be addressed. First is whether the 2017 draft constitution should still be under consideration or if it should be abandoned altogether. Currently, it appears that the draft is still considered to be the only viable basis for the country's future and as a result this paper will not consider possible alternative approaches. Second is whether the draft should be maintained entirely in its current form or if it should be amended, a fair question given that the text was adopted more than three years ago. The third question that will have to be addressed is how and when the draft constitution should be adopted.

[31] https://unsmil.unmissions.org/libyan-women-articulate-demands-constitution (accessed on 2 December 2023).

Table 1. Comparative table of Libyan Women's Demands for the Constitution and the CDA initial draft of the Constitution (2014)

Topic	Women's Demands	Initial Draft Constitution
Rights and Liberties and Provisional Measures	"The State shall commit to guaranteeing the rights and liberties acquired by women as well as taking all necessary measures to support and promote them".	Art. (50) Support of Women's Rights "The State shall support and care for women, enact laws that ensure their protection, promote their status in society, eradicate negative culture and social customs that detract from their dignity, prohibit discrimination against them, ensure their right to representation in general elections, and open opportunities to them in all fields. The State shall also take the necessary measures to support the acquired rights of women".
Equality and non-discrimination	"Male and female citizens are equal before the law. They shall have equal enjoyment of civil, political, economic, social and cultural rights as well as equal opportunities without discrimination based on race, gender, language, origin or any other basis. It shall also ensure equality among them in duties and common obligations in accordance with the provisions of the Constitution".	Art. (7) Citizenship Male and female "Citizens shall be equal in and before the law. There shall be no discrimination therebetween. All forms of discrimination for any reason, such as ethnicity, color, language, gender, birth, political opinion, disability, origin, or geographical affiliation, shall be ***prohibited*** in accordance with the provisions of this Constitution".
Representation of women in political elected Councils.	"The State shall commit to taking necessary measures to ensure a representation of women not less than 45% in all elected councils, in addition to ensuring the fair representation of women in cultural components seats. The legislator shall commit to adopt an electoral system that guarantees such percentage of women representation".	Art. (184) Special Provision for Women: "Any electoral system shall guarantee a quota for women of twenty-five percent of the total seats in the House of Representatives and local councils for two electoral terms, taking into consideration the right of women to run as candidates in general elections". Art. (40) Right to Vote and Run for Office Every citizen shall have the right to vote in referendums and vote

continued

		and run for office in free, fair, transparent, and equitable elections where all citizens are equal in accordance with the law. Eligible citizens may not be prohibited to vote except by a judicial ruling.
Representation of women in the executive authority and decision-making positions	"The State shall commit to representing women in the government as well as political, administrative and diplomatic decision-making positions with a percentage not less than 45%".	Art. (16) Equal Opportunity "Equal opportunity shall be guaranteed for male and female citizens. The State shall take the necessary measures to achieve the same". Art. (17) Holding of Public Posts "The holding of public posts for all Libyans shall be based on the criteria of eligibility and merit. The law shall determine the salaries of employees in accordance with criteria of competence, responsibility, professional hierarchy, and the needs for a decent life".
Representation of women in political parties and civil society	"The State shall commit to take the necessary measures to ensure the representation of women in leadership structures in parties and unions".	Art. (41) Freedom to Form Political "Parties Every citizen shall have the right to choose his political leanings. The State shall guarantee the freedom to form political parties based on national unity, transparent funding, and rejection of violence and hate speech. Every citizen shall have the right to join such political parties or withdraw therefrom without any discrimination whatsoever". Art. (43) Right to Participation "The State shall guarantee for citizens and civil society organizations in their field of activity the right to democratic participation by submitting petitions or legislative proposals in accordance with a regulatory law issued for such purpose".
Gender-sensitive language	"The masculine form in the constitutional text refers to males and females alike".	A variation between the use of masculine gender and the engendering of language: For example,

continued

		Art. 7 of the draft constitution states that: "male and female citizens shall be equal in and before the law [...]". Art. 16 states that: "equal opportunity shall be guaranteed for male and female citizens. The State shall work towards taking the necessary measures to achieve this". However, there is no engendering of Art. 17 that relates to positions of decision-making and leadership: "assuming public posts among all Libyans shall be based on the criteria of merit and eligibility...". If feminine gender is mentioned in some provisions but not others, authorities such as judges that are charged with the enforcement of the constitution may use this as a pretext to exclude women from provisions that stipulates rights.

Source: UNSMIL, UNDP and UN WOMEN, *Libyan Women's Demands for the Constitution* (2014).

Equality and non-discrimination are guaranteed for male and female citizens, and therefore, this general article (Article 7) may be used as a basis for claiming equality between women and men for any right or freedom.

However, the initial draft (2014) and the final draft Constitution (2017) fall short of women's expectations and demands. The establishment of Islamic Sharia as the source of legislation (Article 6) opens the way to legal insecurity and possible restrictions on women's rights, as they will be interpreted by the legislature, the executive, and the judiciary, within the framework of Islamic Sharia law and not according to the universal reference framework of human rights. Sharia's place within the Constitution is among the problematic provisions that still must be addressed[32].

---

[32] International Commission of jurists and Libyan Women's Platform for Peace, *Libya: Advancing women's human rights in the constitutional reform process*, Webinar, 19 May 2021, available at https://www.youtube.com/watch?v=BhiZl7eWEFQ (accessed on 1 December 2023).

As for the question of the right of Libyan women married to foreigners to transmit their nationality to their children, the draft is silent on this issue, leaving it to the legislator to decide, considering the public interest, national security, the preservation of demographics and integration into society.

Furthermore, the draft constitution is seriously deficient in terms of guarantees and protection of women's rights. No commitment has been specifically made to combat violence against women, particularly in post-conflict situations and reconciliation process[33].

The inclusion of specific measures to ensure better gender representation is a divisive issue. The debate inside and outside CDA was centered on whether a quota provision would be best placed in the constitution or electoral law and with what percentage. A 25% quota has been adopted in the draft constitution (2017) as a special provisional measure to ensure the representation of women in the next legislative elections. According to article 184 of the chapter on "transitional provisions", "any electoral system shall guarantee the representation of women by 25%of the seats in the House of Representatives and in the local councils for a period of two electoral cycles". The proposed rate and the timeframe for implementing quotas are likely to limit the effectiveness of such a measure.

The unblocking of the constituent process is one of the objects of the Berlin Process and the LPDF roadmap to ensure sustainable peace and stability. Following several discussions for a 30 per cent quota, in June 2022 the House of Representative and the High State Council (HSC) endorsed a 25% quota for women in all elected bodies including the Senate under the constitutional framework. However, according to the latest draft of the constitutional amendments 12 and 13, the quota was decreased to 20%[34].

4. Women's political representation

Since the close of 2011, men and women in Libya have had the opportunity to participate in several elections: national legislative elections for the General National Congress, held in July 2012; local council elections (between 2012 and 2014) and (between 2018 and 2021), the elections of CDA, on 20 February 2014 and the HoR on 25 June 2014.

---

[33] The draft (2017) provides for a general commitment "to protect dignity [...], to prevent all forms of violence and to combat torture" (Article 34, "Human Dignity").

[34] United Nations, UN Libya Results Report, 2022, available at file:///C:/Users/jlima/Downloads/2022_libya_annualresultsreports_v007%20(1).pdf (accessed on 1 December 2023). this is file in the computer, not accessible to the reader.

Different quotas were applied to guarantee women's political representation. Although the February 17, 2011 revolution catalyzed a shift in public perception toward the potential advantage of women's political engagement, women's political participation remains very limited. This trend is amplified when it comes to the executive branch and the political peace process, which reflect both an extremely weak representation of women as political decision makers.

4.1. Women's representation in national and local legislatures

July 7, 2012, witnessed the first free elections in Libya, to elect the members of the GNC, Libya's interim legislative authority. The HNEC stated that 2,865,937 voters were registred, equal to 82 percent of the estimated 3.5 million eligible voters. Women made up 45 percent of registered voters[35].

These elections attract votes from 1.77 million Libyans, 39% of whom were women (more than 687,000 voted)[36]. Studies conducted following the election showed that this was mainly due "to lack of permission to vote from male family members, dependence on male family members for mobility in public (even in cases where men supported women voting), insufficient information and, specifically in the regions of Cyrenaica and Fezzan, political opposition to the elections"[37].

In total, there were 625 Women candidates of 3,708 candidates across both majoritarian and proportional representation systems (17%). 545 women candidates ran on political entity lists, of 1,207 candidates (45%); 32 of them were elected. 85 women candidates ran as individuals, of 2,501.

Women candidates were active during the three-weeks' campaign preceding the July 7 vote. Many party and independent candidates made appearances in local and national press, printed posters, and leaflets, convened community meetings, and went door to door with their campaign

---

[35] The Carter Center, *General National Congress Elections in Libya. Final Report*, Atlanta, 2012, p.5, available at https://www.cartercenter.org/resources/pdfs/news/peace_publications/election_reports/libya-070712-final-rpt.pdf (accessed on 3 December 2023).

[36] UNDP, *UN Women, Electoral Gender Mapping of Libya*, Report 2014.

[37] See Gender Concerns International, *Gender Election Monitoring (GEM) Mission Libya General National Congress Election 7 July 2012 Final Report*, available at https://www.genderconcerns.org/pdfs/Final%20Report%20GEM%20Mission%20Libya_Gender%20Concerns%20International_English%20version%20(1).pdf (accessed on 3 December 2023).

teams to meet and persuade voters[38]. The United Nations Development Program (UNDP) ran series of campaign workshops targeting both independent and political party candidates[39]. Several Libyan women's organizations also held training for women candidates, including the Libyan Women's Forum (LWF) which ran campaign skills workshops in partnership with the Tunisian Center for Arab Women Training and Research (CAWTAR) for independent women candidates.

33 women were elected to serve in Libya's GNC, 32 winning on party lists (out of the 80 seats reserved for parties)[40] and one independent candidate[41] (out of the 120 seats allocated for independents). Women comprise 16.5 percent of the GNC's membership.

Several factors explain this relatively good result, including the horizontal and vertical zippered system for political party lists. Given that 32 of the women who were elected to the GNC were competing on party lists, the quota played a decisive role. However, the fact that only one woman was able to succeed when running independently highlights a key challenge for the women's political participation.

Participation of Libyan women in the CDA elections was lower than in previous elections held in 2012. Women were allocated 6 reserved seats[42], (10%) of the CDA. The CDA elections[43] saw that out of 1.1 million registered voters, 449,501 were women. The rate of women's registration for these elections (41%) was lower than the previous elections (45%). This may have been related to the nature and requirements of the new voter registration system used for these elections[44]. In this election, only 64 out of the 649 (9.9%) registered candidates were women. Fifty-four of these

[38] Interview with Soulef Guessoum.

[39] For example, workshop entitled "Introduction on women political participation" held by UNDP in Tripoli 10 May, Benghazi 11 May 2011.

[40] Former interim Prime Minister Mahmoud Jibril's party NFA won 39 of the 80 party seats, with 19 of those seats going to women. The Muslim Brotherhood affiliated JCP took 17 seats, with 8 of those seats going to women. The other parties are the Wadi Alhayat Gathering for Democracy and Development, the Labbayka Watani Gathering, the Conglomeration of National Parties, and the National Moderate Trend.

[41] Amnah Tkhikh succeeding in her constituency in Bani Walid.

[42] Art. 6 of the Constitutional Drafting Assembly Electoral Law (Law 17 of 20 July 2013).

[43] Figures provided by UN Electoral Support Team in Libya (UNSMIL/UNDP).

[44] The Carter Center, *The 2014 Constitutional Drafting Assembly Elections in Libya: Final Report*, Atlanta, 2014, available at https://www.cartercenter.org/resources/pdfs/news/peace_publications/election_reports/libya-06112014-final-rpt.pdf (accessed on 3 December 2023).

women contested the seats reserved for female candidates (6 seats), while another contested one of the seats reserved for the Tebu, but no women win in the general seats. Regarding the number of women who voted on Election Day, only 170,541 women voted of 511,259 voters (33%) [45].

According to the findings of a focus group published in January 2014, men and women generally supported the idea of women as candidates, but few of those surveyed said they would vote for a woman at this stage [46]. On the other hand, women outside CDA have been involved in the constitutional process as members of civil society and as engaged citizens.

Women were seriously underrepresented in the peace and transition processes around the world, but their participation has been increasing since 1990.

Table 2. The percentage of women and their representation in the drafting committees or constitution amendment committees and commissions

State	Mechanism	Total number of members	Number of females	% of female representation
Tunisia (2014)	Elections	**217**	**58**	**29%**
Morocco (2011)	Appointment	**19**	**5**	**27%**
Egypt (2014)	**Elections**	**50**	**5**	**10%**
Libya (2014)	**Elections**	**60**	**6**	**10%**
Jordan	Appointment	**10**	**0**	**0%**

Source: Draji I., Elsadda H. and Klibi S., *Comparative Study on Constitutional Processes in the Arab World A Gender Perspective*, Paris, Euromed Feminist Initiative EFE-EFI, 2017, 45, available at https://www.efi-ife.org/en/pdf-detail/94701-comparative-study-constitutional-processes-in-the-arab-world-a-gender-perspective (accessed on 25 November 2023).

The House of Representations (HoR) was elected on 25 June 2014 to replace the GNC. Of the 200 seats, 32 seats are reserved for women (16%).

At the local level, only 10% of the municipality councils 'members are women. The municipality councils are the main unit of local administration responsible for providing services to citizens. The municipality oversees es-

[45] UNDP, *UN Women Report*, 2014.

[46] Building a Better Libya Together? Perspectives of Men and Women on the Political Engagement of Women. UK Embassy/DCA/1Libya, page 158, finding 14.

tablishing and managing public utilities related to urban planning, organization, buildings, health and social affairs, water, lighting, sanitation, roads, bridges, local transportation, public hygiene, gardens, public recreation areas, real estate, public markets and construction permits for tourism and investment projects[47].

4.2. Women's participation in executive offices and political dialogue

In 2011, the National Transition Council (NTC), which is supposed to represent all Libyan cities, had 98 members, some temporary and some permanent, however out of 98 members the NTC only had 2 women as members[48]. Salwa Boughaigis, a prominent women's rights activist appointed as a Benghazi representative to the NTC, resigned from the council over frus-

[47] Art. 27 of Law no. 59/2012 states the powers of the municipal councils:
- Oversee the implementation of legislation and directives related to municipal affairs and follow up on work progress in accordance with the legislation in force;
- Oversee the administration of the municipality and its activities; follow up on the execution of the decisions thereof and oversee the work progress in municipal branches and localities within its jurisdiction;
- Propose municipal regulations;
- Propose and implement the budget; determine the expenditure priorities within the municipality; follow up on the disbursement and its conformity with the legislation in force; approve the final account of the municipality;
- Invest, develop and advance municipal resources to improve the quality of local services; grant initial approval for investment and charity permits;
- Propose the allocation of approved investment credits;
- Propose the imposition, modification, exemption and abolition of fees of a municipal character, determine the collection process and collect the fees;
- Follow up on development projects in the municipality; submit reports to the provincial council; handle small and medium projects within the municipality's jurisdiction; conduct feasibility studies;
- Follow up on the activities of executive units and assess their performance and the proper execution of work in the municipality;
- Provide localities with necessary administrative and technical units to perform their functions and assist with financial support to localities whose resources are not sufficient to meet their needs, within the limits decided by the council;
- Propose partnerships with other municipalities in the province to establish or manage other business or utilities; and
- Other functions vested in the municipality by laws and the executive regulation of those laws.

[48] National Transitional Council, *Libya: Members of The Transitional Council*, 18 June 2012, available at https://en.wikipedia.org/wiki/National_Transitional_Council (accessed on 1 December 2023).

trations with the lack of opportunity to influence decision-making. "They did not want to listen to anything I had to say. They just wanted a woman to stand there and smile in the pictures", said Boughaigis[49].

The post revolution governments did not adopt any serious programs to encourage and ensure women's participation, as proven by the lack of real female representation in governmental bodies.

In addition, the membership and leadership of Libyan political parties were dominated by men. Many of these groups paid lip service to the importance of women's participation, but rarely followed through by elevating women to leadership positions. Instead, some parties developed women's auxiliaries with vaguely defined mandates, while others recognized the organizing potential of women and dispatched groups of women party members to conduct neighbourhood surveys in eastern cities[50].

With the expansion of conflict in Libya in 2014, women turned to be divided along the political strata and along the different regions. In 2015, women participated in the peace process negotiations that led to the political agreement signed on 17 December 2015[51].

In November 2015, UNSMIL, the Swiss Federal Department of Foreign Affairs and UN Women Regional Office of Arab States organized the first conference for Libyan women in Montreux, Switzerland, to develop their Minimum Agenda for Peace. The conference convened a geographically and politically inclusive spectrum of 38 Libyan women. Libyan women managed to reach a consensus that resulted in the Libyan Women's Minimum Agenda for Peace. The overall objective of the agenda is to "enhance the role of Libyan women in peace building and social peace". The agenda has seven key strategic objectives covering the security situation, the situation of displaced persons and migrants, violence against women, the role of media, the economic situation of women, the role of women in transitional justice and reconciliation, and women's political participation including in the constitutional process.

After years of civil war, discussions of the Libyan Political Dialogue Forum (LPDF) started in Tunis on 9 November 2020 under the auspices of UNSMIL. The LPDF comprised 75 representatives, including 17 women, from all Libyan regions and political and social constituencies, as well as

---

[49] Salwa Boughaigis in an interview with NDI, April 5, 2011. Three years later, Ms Bughaighis was killed hours after she had cast her vote in Libya's parliamentary elections.

[50] Bugaighis W., *op. cit.*

[51] *Libyan Political Agreement as signed on 17 December 2015*, available at https://unsmil.unmissions.org/sites/default/files/Libyan%20Political%20Agreement%20-%20ENG%20.pdf (accessed on 3 December 2023).

from the House of Representatives (HoR) and the High State Council (HSC)[52].

The participation of women to peace process is very important. Indeed, when women are included, parties are more likely to reach an agreement and the resulting peace is more likely to endure. In fact, a peace agreement is 35 percent more likely to last at least 15 years if women participate in its creation[53].

After positive consultations and discussions, the participants of the LPDF agreed to resolve the current political deadlock by resuming the political process aiming at holding presidential and parliamentary elections on 24 December 2021. The LPDF adopted on 15 November 2020 a political roadmap "For the Preparatory Phase of a Comprehensive Solution" which identifies the main features of this political process.

Among the Governing Principles of the Roadmap is the emphasis of "full equality of all citizens, men and women, in rights and responsibilities of citizenship as per the Constitutional Declaration and international conventions ratified by the Libyan State. All authorities shall protect these rights and obligations" (Article 2).

The LPDF agreed to allocate 30 percent of leadership positions in the Government to women (Article 5)[54].

The new interim Prime Minister Abdelhamid Dbeibah appointed five women among 31 government posts, including the minister for justice and the minister for foreign minister, having backtracked on promises that 30% of ministerial posts would go to women and then faced a backlash[55].

5. The key role of the civil Society

Although heterogeneous, the Libyan civil society, which was set up after

---

[52] https://unsmil.unmissions.org/unsmil-announces-results-lpdf-vote-presidency-council-members (accessed on 3 December 2023).

[53] Draji I., Elsadda H. and Klibi S., *op. cit.*

[54] Art. 5 on the Structure of the Executive Authority during the Preparatory Phase: "In the formation of the Government of National Unity, competency, merit, and fair representation of the political and geographic diversity shall be taken into account; participation of cultural components shall be guaranteed, and the importance of real representation of women and youth shall also be taken into consideration. The representation of women shall be no less than 30% of leadership positions of the Government (ministers or deputies)".

[55] Hyde M., "Libya gets new unified government as corruption allegations swirl", in *The Guardian*, 2021, available at https://www.theguardian.com/world/2021/mar/10/libyan-parliament-approves-unity-government (accessed on 3 December 2023).

the revolution[56], has been trying to play an educational role and an advocate role in defending women's rights and encouraging women to participate in decision making[57]. Libyan NGOs have led this mission with the collaboration with international organizations that led to courses and seminars fitting each period and its needs, "starting from medical and aid organizations at the beginning of the revolution, moving on to management structuring and leadership, and finally reaching civil and political collaborations concerning such topics as the elections and the constitution"[58].

The NGOs' activities focused on promoting civic education and human rights including spreading awareness on women's rights. Campaigns, seminars, protests, flyers, and of course the media were the tools and channels used to encourage women to participate in the election process, whether as voters or as candidates. Civil society organizations worked also on legal framework reforms on electoral laws and the constitution draft process.

5.1. Influencing electoral law

The role of women in the transitional period is crucial, and it is paramount that the new legislature and government begin to take concrete, substantive measures to ensure that woman's participation increases.

In November 2011, two prominent women's organizations, the Voice of Libyan Women and Attawasul, convened Libya's first national women's conference and worked with activists from throughout Libya and the diaspora to draft recommendations to promote women's inclusion in the transition[59].The High National Elections Commission (HNEC)was urged by civil society to put forth more efforts proactively to promote the participation of women, both as voters and as candidates.

Civil society's potential and effect was highlighted in the event of the zipper system presented in the second draft of the election law, which was later amended, as a result of the great struggle by activists. Originally, the first draft of the election law secured a 10% quota for women in the 200 seat Congress. Women organizations started advocating through social me-

---

[56] Interviews with Azza Kamel El Maghur, Jazia Shaitir Amal Al Obeidi, and Fatma Chenib.

[57] Countless independent organizations and groups have been formed throughout Libya to help promote and defend women's rights. This 'movement' needs more support and more organization to focus their effort and maximize their results, yet, it remains a good start.

[58] Bugaighis W., *op. cit.*

[59] *Ibidem.*

dia, petitioning, and reached out through the media for a larger quota [60]. Eventually, and through negotiations and panels, they endorsed the zipper system for parties only, which hold 80 seats. The other 120 seats are for independent candidates, and no quota for women was applied to them.

The elections on 7 July 2012 were an achievement that holds several testimonials to the efforts of civil society. The mobilization of women's associations has been less striking in subsequent elections as the security situation has deteriorated.

5.2. Participation in the constitution drafting processes

It has become widely accepted that the success of the constitutional process in general, mainly depends on respecting the criterion of inclusive participation and transparency in all stages of the constitutional process.

The security conditions as well as the chaotic internal and external factions at war, made it difficult for NGOs to reach and communicate with the CDA [61]. Not only did the war stand in the way of guaranteeing a participatory dimension of the constitution drafting process, it also hindered guarantees of transparency. For these same security reasons, it became extremely difficult for civil society observers, their representatives and journalists to attend the Committee's sessions even though they were entitled to do so. This made it difficult to access accurate and clear information concerning the development of the Committee's activities.

Despite all these difficulties, a workshop was organized for women human rights activists under the patronage of the UN Support Mission in Libya, UNDP, and UN WOMEN in the presence of a number of Libyan Parliament and constitution drafting committee representatives. The workshop was held in Cairo in November 2014 aimed at reviewing and assessing the draft prepared by the CDA and to submit a list of recommendations on the subject matter. The aim was to assess and review the draft in light of women's rights and in pursuance of the international treaties and conventions ratified by the Libyan State [62]. Another workshop was organized for

---

[60] Although many activists called for a larger quota to protect women's right to participate, especially in the current social state of extreme conservatism, others did call for the negation of the quota completely, claiming a quota of any kind would limit women's potential to grow, and called for a zipper system to be applied to party lists but with the current state of Libyan women, and with the overly conservative society, quota, would seem as a better approach to 'safeguard' women's right to participate at this time rather than risk losing it altogether.

[61] Interviews with Azza Kamel El Maghur, Khawla Jouili, Jazia Shaitir.

[62] Interview with Ramadan Eltweger.

the same purpose in Tunisia in January 2015 with the participation of 30 women activists to follow up on the outcome of the recommendations they had submitted to the constitution drafting committee from the Cairo workshop. They also drafted alternative proposals to the CDA.

The principal issues that women prioritized for the constitutional text varied significantly along political, ideological, religious, geographic, and socio-economic lines. But women understood the importance of this process and that without specific, constitutionalized guarantees of their fundamental freedoms and participation, their voices would not be heard in future debates on other issues that affected their lives. Participants therefore prioritized what they viewed as the most fundamental and achievable freedoms, such as foundational gender equality before the law and in law. They have also strongly advocated for quotas to guarantee gender equality in political participation (45% quota for elected and appointed responsibilities).

However, the fact remains that even with this step forward, women are still facing great obstacles, both on the political field, and the social field.

6. Gendered challenges to women's political participation [63]

A Series of studies on gender and politics led by feminists has focused on the ways in which women's issues, concerns, and participation are excluded from the public political arena because of the division between the public and private spheres, on the one hand, and the language and politics of universal political rights, on the other [64]. As public and the universal have both historically been masculine, women have been systematically excluded from the political arena.

This gender discrimination is intensified within the Libyan context due to a violent and disarticulated political life. The atomisation of society and the fragmentation of the State raise a serious problem in terms of the accessibility and intelligibility of norms, their systematisation, the articulation of their sources and the predictability of decisions [65].

---

[63] The drafting of this chapter is largely based on interviews conducted with Azza Kamel El Maghur, Ramadan Eltweger, Amal Al Obeidi, Khawla Jouili,, Jazia Shaitir ,, Fatma Chenib, Abdelbari Chanbarou, Leila Lefi, and Soulef Guessoum.

[64] Brown G.W., McLean I. and McMillan A., *Concise Dictionary of Politics and International Relations*, 4th ed., New York, Oxford University Press, 2018, 231.

[65] Libyan women have been the target in the West and in the East of discriminatory restrictions on their right to travel abroad, by requiring authorisation from a male family member. On this subject, see Human Rights Watch, *Libya: Discriminatory Restriction*

In addition, the political influence of male dominated groups, such as tribes and militias, increases the marginalization of women in politics.

6.1. Missing or ineffective measures to eliminate discrimination against women in political and public life

Although quotas are instituted to guarantee a minimum number of seats for women, the implementation of the quota system has led to limiting women's representation to reserved seats. This is a real problem for two reasons: firstly, the quota is low; it doesn't enable effective representation of women. Secondly, women who have tried to run for open seats generally fail.

The adoption of the quota system was not accompanied by an awareness-raising effort by the authorities, hence the extent of confusion and misunderstanding. Indeed, some worried the quota requirement created a perception that women were included on electoral lists wholly to satisfy the law, not because of their expertise or capacity as political actors.

6.2. Violence against women in public life threatens women's participation

In communities where women chose to mobilize and participate in political activities, some were discouraged and even threatened. As elected officials, female assembly members also faced similar gendered double standards. As women, they were not considered legitimate political actors, but when they fought to be taken seriously, they are not perceived as good women, because they are behaving like men.

Women also faced personal attacks because of their participation. They are targets of harassment, assault, and insults either directly or through social media. In Libya, there is no specific law to combat violence against women.

Women's campaign posters were more likely to be defaced and destroyed than those of male candidates. Female candidates were also more vulnerable to security concerns while campaigning and had less access to financial resources than their male counterparts[66].

Since 2014, violence against women has reached significant levels, as evidenced by the murders of activists, women involved in politics, lawyers,

---

on Women. Order in Eastern Region Requires Male Guardian for Travel, 2017, available at https://www.hrw.org/news/2017/02/23/libya-discriminatory-restriction-women (accessed on 1 December 2023).

[66] UNDP, *UN Women Report*, cit.

and media personalities: this is the case of MP Fariha Al-Barakawi, lawyer Hamida Al-Asfar and Hanan Al-Barassi[67]. Women's rights activists and female politicians are regularly the target of defamation and intimidation campaigns in the media and on social networks, and in most cases, these acts go unpunished. Some activists have had to cease their activities and withdraw from the political scene under threats[68].

6.3. Stereotypes and social norms constrain women's participation in political life

In general, political women face misgivings related to their capacity and competencies; these however were driven by the internalization of social and cultural norms related to politics as an exclusively male affair. Women in politics also struggled to reconcile their identities as political actors and as caregivers in their families. Long hours of political responsibilities made it difficult for women to also fulfil "their duties" at home.

Within political institutions and processes, women were not necessarily viewed as legitimate political actors by the society and even by their peers, despite their ample presence and participation.

In Libya, women in politics face more problems as result of social conservatism and tribalism. NDI's qualitative research revealed that while Libyans were broadly supportive of women playing roles in public life, there was significant disagreement over what type of engagement is best suited to women. Some participants in a study conducted in November 2011 were uncomfortable with women playing a leading role in politics and thought high-level positions were inappropriate or would conflict with women's responsibilities to their families[69].

In a research study conducted in May 2012 participants were asked to share their opinions on women as candidates and whether they would vote for women. There was resistance among both women and men participants, some of whom claimed that women were too emotional to adequately handle the stresses of political life or too beholden to family responsibilities to be effective in politics[70].

Even where women succeed in getting a seat at the table, other barriers

[67] Working Group on Women, Peace, and Security, available at https://www.womenpeacesecurity.org/region/libya/ (accessed on 3 December 2023).

[68] Interviews with Azza Kamel El Maghur, Ramadhan Ettouijri, Jazia Shaitir Amal Al Obeidi, and Fatma Chenib.

[69] Doherty M., *op.cit.*

[70] *Ibidem.*

persist; entrenched male-dominated power structures and discriminatory attitudes concerning women's roles in politics often undermine women's influence; some women elected are viewed with little political credibility. In addition, some of the elected women are conservative and had not been advocates for women's rights during the discussion of constitutional chapters[71].

Extremist movements, who adhere to ultra-orthodox interpretations of Islam, require stricter enforcement of Islamic law according to their own distorted notions, which especially affect the empowering of women. Extremism potentially poses a threat to women's rights and freedoms because of their endeavor to impose their misogynistic point of views on society. The same finding applies to the tribes, which remain patriarchal and misogynistic social structures[72].

6.4. Lack/weakness of political support

The old regime eliminated any political life or engagement. The absence of traditions and political practices has made women's efforts harder. The nomination process of candidates within the political parties in Libya was not transparent according to women candidates who attended the workshops organized by UNDP in 2012. Many of participants did not even know their classification within the candidates' list. Also, participants indicated that many political parties nominated women at the top of the list in the regions where they have little chance to win.

During GNC elections, while women candidates on party list received support from their parties, the independent women candidates contended with more difficulties in financing than their party-affiliated counterparts, but both groups faced additional challenges. Some women were reluctant to appear in print or televised media and used symbols or drawings on their pamphlets, so as not to anger more conservative social elements who claimed that publishing pictures of women was un-Islamic.

Women candidates related also serious difficulties[73] in communicating with voters/citizens and putting their photos on posters and flyers; in mobility due to traditions and to security issues related to the proliferation of arms, limited access to the media, limited confidence and time, lack of en-

[71] Interviews with Azza Kamel El Maghur, Ramadhan Ettouijri, Jazia Shaitir Amal Al Obeidi, and Fatma Chenib.

[72] Interview with Azza Kamel El Maghur, Ramadhan Ettouijri, Jazia Shaitir Amal Al Obeidi, and Fatma Chenib.

[73] Workshop organized by UNDP in 2012 for women candidates to GNC elections in Tripoli, Sabha, Benghazi.

couragement of women from the political parties or families, radical discourse that present men as better leaders than women...

6.5. Weakness of political parties

The political parties are fundamental frameworks to express the various views, needs and expectations of all segments of society in democratic countries. The representation of women in the leadership structures of political parties is a prerequisite to ensure effective participation of women, as well as representation of women demands in all frameworks and political forums.

The period of democratic transition is usually characterized by the liberation of political activity.

In Libya, this resulted in a new legal framework with Law no. 29 (2012) on the right to establish and join political parties, and an intense surge in the number of formed political parties. Most of the parties founded in 2012 lack grassroots members as well as their limited territorial expansion and their weak structure. These political parties are short-lived and most of them have disappeared since the electoral Law of HoR forbidden the participation of political entities.

All these factors contributed to deepening the lack of political structuring. The events show an attempt to find alternative channels of political participation that emanate from other social components (tribes, militias, families...). But these alternatives are dangerous for the establishment of a state and widely marginalize women's participation.

7. Gender mainstreaming

Gender mainstreaming is a comprehensive approach where gender is taken into account in staffing, policy, and implementation in a wide variety of contexts. The terminology was first proposed as policy in the international arena in the 1985 Third World Conference on Women in Nairobi, Kenya, and formally featured in the policy conclusions of the 1995 Fourth World Conference on Women in Beijing. Gender mainstreaming has become since a mainstay of national and international bodies looking to address gender equality[74].

A gender sensitive Constitution combines the establishment of the rule of law, equality between women and men and respect for the human rights

[74] Brown G.W., McLean I. and McMillan A., *op. cit.*, 231-232.

and dignity of both women and men alike. It adopts gender sensitive language and wide-ranging gender equality provisions. This step is crucial as Constitution is considered the "supreme law" of the state and the core source that trumps other legal rules.

The advantages and disadvantages of universally applying one standard of mainstreaming, the inefficiency of some efforts at implementation, and how to apply gender mainstreaming either substantively or procedurally are challenging issues for states [75]. Being a divisive issue, Women's rights are at the centre of political and ideological conflicts between conservatives and liberals. Resistance to the principles of gender equality and non-discrimination in the universal sense is well entrenched in conservative societies, based on a stereotyped view of the roles of women and men. Politically, this tendency is reflected in claims for cultural relativism [76] in human rights, legitimising the inferior status of women based on religious and cultural considerations [77].

Although social, political, and cultural contexts are different, a gender sensitive constitution is framed by norms and standards that are grounded in the universality and indivisibility of the human rights of women and men [78].

First, these criteria consecrate the close link between democracy and gender equality in rights, duties, and principles of non-discrimination towards women. Second, they suggest formal measures such as engendering the constitutional language, and the procedures that guarantee and protect women's rights to address discrimination and exclusion. Moreover, they point at the contents that are to be consecrated to achieve such a gender sensitive constitution.

7.1. Gendering the constitutional/legal language

The purpose of gendering the Constitutional/legal Speech in all the subjects is to achieve a major pedagogical function, through engraving women's rights in the minds and stimulating their participation in public affairs. This principle is essential to deny any opportunity to interpret the constitutional text in a manner that leads to the exclusion of women from the guarantees contained therein concerning the rights and liberties.

The gendering of the constitutional rhetoric can also make the issue of

---

[75] See Freeman M., *Human rights*, 4th ed., Cambridge, Polity press, 2022.

[76] For the definition of cultural relativism, see Brown G.W., McLean I. and McMillan A., *op. cit.*, 136-137.

[77] See Ferrari A. and Toronto J. (ed.), *Religions and Constitutional Transitions in the Muslim Mediterranean. The pluralistic Moment*, New York, Routledge, 2017.

[78] Draji I., Elsadda H. and Klibi S., *op. cit.*

equal citizenship present in the collective imagination and contribute to raising awareness of women conditions and the need to support and promote their rights for the public at large.

The Moroccan constitution appears to be highly engendered. It talks in many articles about "male and female citizens" (Articles 6, 7, 14, 15, 16, 19, 27, 30, 31 and 38)

> Article 19: "*The man and the woman enjoy equally the rights and freedoms of civil, political, economic, social, cultural, and environmental character, enounced in this Title and in the other provisions of the constitution [...]*".
>
> Article 30 on the political rights reads: "*All the citizens [feminine] and the citizens [masculine] [...] are electors and eligible. The law includes provisions for encouraging equal access to women and men to elective functions*" [79].

The lack of gender sensitive language in a constitution is not the only issue. Problems also arise where constitutions have engendered some, but not all provisions. In the first category, the rights of women are clearly ignored. In the second category, such rights may be ambiguous and confusing. Consequently, if feminine gender is mentioned in some provisions but not others, authorities such as judges that are charged with the enforcement of the constitution may use this as a pretext to exclude women from provisions that stipulates rights. The shifting use between engendered language and masculine gender is indeed problematic, especially in the absence of a comprehensive article that establishes equality between women and men or between [female] citizens and [male] citizens in the rights, freedoms, and duties.

7.2. Equality and prohibition of discrimination

A gender sensitive Constitution shall recognize not only equality before the law but also equality with regards to rights, freedoms and obligations.

Among the constitutions that have adopted such a formulation, we can quote:

> Article 9 of the South African Constitution [80]: "*1. Everyone is equal before the law and has the right to equal protection and benefit of the law.*

[79] https://www.constituteproject.org/constitution/Morocco_2011.pdf?lang=en (accessed on 3 December 2023).

[80] https://www.gov.za/documents/constitution/constitution-republic-south-africa-04-feb-1997 (accessed on 3 December 2023).

2. Equality includes the full and equal enjoyment of all rights and freedoms. To promote the achievement of equality, legislative and other measures designed to protect or advance persons, or categories of persons, disadvantaged by unfair discrimination may be taken".

Article 23 of the Tunisian Constitution[81]: "*all citizens, male and female, have equal rights and duties, and are equal before the law without any discrimination [...]*".

Article 19 of the Moroccan constitution acknowledges that "*the man and the woman enjoy, in equality, the rights and freedoms of civil, political, economic, social, cultural, and environmental character [...]*".

The principle of non-discrimination rises to the level of the general principle that applies to all the recognized rights in the constitution. The principle of non-discrimination is established in the International Covenant on Economic, Social and Cultural Rights and in the International Covenant on Civil and Political Rights. What is important in the formulation of these articles is that they provide for the principle of non-discrimination and show the aspects that should not be grounds for discrimination (sex, race, religion, language ...). The non-discrimination aspects are listed so that the list remains open to prevent interpretations that can allow discrimination on grounds not provided for therein.

The principle of non-discrimination in the rights between men and women set forth in several compared constitutions where it occupies a prominent position. The wordings, talking about the principle of non-discrimination and showing the banned aspects of discriminations, deemed the best for what they offer in terms of guarantees safeguards against any form of discrimination.

Among the constitutions that have adopted such a formulation, we can quote:

Article 14 of the Spanish Constitution[82]: "*Spanish are equal before the law without any discrimination based on birth, race, sex, religion, opinion or any other status or special or social circumstances*".

Article 9, paragraph 3 of the South African constitution: "*The state may not unfairly discriminate directly or indirectly against anyone on one or more grounds, including race, gender, sex, pregnancy, marital status,*

[81] https://legislation-securite.tn/law/105339 (accessed on 3 December 2023).

[82] https://www.senado.es/web/conocersenado/normas/constitucion/detalleconstitucioncompleta/index.html?lang=en#t1 (accessed on 3 December 2023).

ethnic or social origin, color, sexual orientation, age, disability, religion, conscience, belief, culture, language and birth".

7.3. Equality in political rights and special measures

It is obvious that society in general and specifically the Arab-Islamic societies, suffer from many cases of gender inequality which may, if the law is enforced evenly on everyone, lead to a further deepening of the social disparities between men and women. Thus, equality will truly mean the fact of being offered equal chances, which would require special measures and actions to improve the rights, opportunities and access to resources and responsibilities of women in order to compensate for structural gender imbalances and overcome exclusion of women in public and political space.

The temporary special measure cannot be considered as discrimination, given that it seeks to eliminate an existing discrimination through legal actions[83].

A great number of Constitutions acknowledge the equal political rights of women. They dedicate articles that support the participation of women in public life and in holding senior administrative and political positions. Many Constitutions have established the principle of temporary special measure, for its importance in achieving real equality between men and women.

Constitutions vary in terms of their wording and mechanisms adopted to acknowledge equality between women and men in political rights.

Among the constitutions that have adopted such a formulation, we can quote:

Article 19 of the Constitution of South Africa: "*1. Every citizen is free to make political choices, which includes the right*

a. to form a political party;

b. to participate in the activities of, or recruit members for, a political party; and

c. to campaign for a political party or cause.

2. Every citizen has the right to free, fair and regular elections for any legislative body established in terms of the Constitution.

3. Every adult citizen has the right

---

[83] Many international texts go along with this principle, including Art. 4, paragraph 1 of the Convention on Eliminating all Forms of Discrimination Against Women which provides: "Adoption by States Parties of temporary special measures aimed at accelerating de facto equality between men and women shall not be considered discrimination as defined in the present Convention, but shall in no way entail as a consequence the maintenance of unequal or separate standards; these measures shall be discontinued when the objectives of equality of opportunity and treatment have been achieved".

> *a. to vote in elections for any legislative body established in terms of the Constitution, and to do so in secret; and*
> *b. to stand for public office and, if elected, to hold office*".

> In Morocco, Article 30 stipulates: "*The law provides the provisions of [a] nature encouraging the equal access of women and men to the elective functions*".

Article 19 establishes the Parity Principle, as a procedure aiming at promoting women's participation in public life. It creates a constitutional body that is independent and in charge of ensuring parity. It seeks to fight all forms of discrimination, in accordance with Article 164.

In a similar context, the Tunisian Constitution also provides for parity between women and men:

> Article 51 of the Constitution (2022) (*ex* Article 46 of the Constitution (2014) states that "*The state guarantees the equality of opportunities between women and men to have access to all levels of responsibility in all domains. The State shall guarantee the parity between women and men in all elected assemblies*".

Despite the importance of inserting parity in the Constitution, it falls short of the expected equal opportunities for electoral jobs. In Tunisia Since 2011[84], majority voting[85], has been replaced by List proportional representation (List PR). Parity between men and women was introduced for candidate electoral lists. The same electoral system was adopted for the legislative election by the Organic Law no. 2014-16 dated May 26th, 2014, on Elections and Referenda. *List PR involves each party,* electoral coalitions or independent candidates *presenting a list of candidates to the electorate in each multi-member electoral constituency. The lists receive seats in proportion to their overall share of the vote in the electoral district. Winning candidates are taken in order of their position on the lists. The system used to calculate the allocation of seats after the votes have been counted is Largest Remainder Method without threshold.*

The list is closed, the number of candidates in each list should be equal to the number of seats allocated to the relevant constituency and the order of candidates on the list is fixed without deleting or changing the ranking of candidates[86].

---

[84] Decree-law No. 2011-35 dated May 10th, 2011, on the Election of the National Constituent Assembly.

[85] Since the independence, this system had enabled the ruling party to win most of the seats in elected councils and contributed to a great extent to the marginalization of the opposition parties in terms of political representation at the local and national levels. The opposition parties were not able to enter the Parliament until 1994 after the electoral code was amended by introducing a measure of proportionality to the voting system.

[86] According to Articles 22 and 108 of Law no. 16 of 2014.

The electoral list should establish parity between men and women in a rotated pattern between them in the lists of candidacies-vertical parity. Any list that is not compliant to this condition is disqualified. In the 2014 legislative elections, women candidates represented 47% of all candidates, but only 12% of all lists were headed by women. The rate of elected women increased, and according to Inter-Parliamentary Union (IPU) ranking based on the number of female MPs in 2017, the number of female MPs in the ARP elected in October 2014 was 68 out of a total of 217, amounting to 31.34%. This puts Tunisia ahead of all Arab countries, which average at 18.2%, and puts it above the international average, which is 23.5% [87]. After the resignation of a few MPs appointed to ministerial positions, the representation of women in the Tunisian parliament further increased to 78 female MPs which amounted to 35.9% [88]. It is worth noting that the increase in the percentage of female representatives on the national scale is primarily due to the two main political parties, Al-Nidaa' and Ennahda, winning more than one seat in many constituencies.

In the 2019 legislative elections, the number of women deputies in the ARP decreased significantly. 49 women out of 217 were elected which represent 22.6% [89]. This decrease can be explained by the limited number of lists headed by women, which did not exceed 14%. In addition, the large number of the lists and the tight competitiveness between them, led to a decrease in the number of lists winning more than one seat in an electoral constituency. All these indicators point to a lack of genuine conviction in parity by most parties and other political actors.

Article 51 of the new constitution adopted by referendum on 25 July 2022 maintains the State's various commitments to women's rights, including parity. However, the new legislative electoral law (Decree No. 2022-55, 15 September 2022) has introduced radical changes regarding the electoral system, by replacing proportional representation with the two-round majoritarian system and by establishing 161 single candidate electoral districts. In addition, the new law makes no mention of any type of system for women's quotas. As a result, the rate of women in parliament decreased in the December 2022 elections to 16.2 % [90].

Other Constitutions do not limit equal opportunities to electoral jobs but go beyond it to cover all the public responsibilities.

According to Article 10 of the Constitution of Rwanda [91]: "The State... commits itself to upholding the following fundamental principles and ensuring their respect: ... 4° building a State governed by the rule of law, a

[87] http://archive.ipu.org/wmn-f/world.htm (accessed on 3 December 2023).

[88] https://data.ipu.org/women-ranking?month=6&year=2019 (accessed on 3 December 2023).

[89] https://data.ipu.org/women-ranking?month=12&year=2019(accessed on 3 December 2023).

[90] https://data.ipu.org/women-ranking?month=11&year=2023 (accessed on 3 December 2023).

[91] https://www.constituteproject.org/constitution/Rwanda_2015 (accessed on 3 December 2023).

pluralistic democratic Government, equality of all Rwandans and between men and women which is affirmed by women occupying at least thirty percent (30%) of positions in decision-making organs".

Table 3. Women in Parliaments

Rwanda: Chamber of Deputies **Ranking as of 1st November 2023: 1**	
Quota and reserved seats Legal source	Art. 75 of the Constitution: " 24 women elected by specific electoral colleges in accordance with the national administrative entities At least thirty percent (30%) of Deputies must be women". Art. 109 of Organic Law 03/2010/OL of 18 June 2010 governing presidential and legislative elections
Number of members	80
Women	49
Percentage of women	61.3%
South Africa: National Assembly **Ranking as of 1st November 2023: 15**	
Voluntary political party quota Legal source	ANC Constitution, Art. 6(1)
Number of members	399
Women	182
Percentage of women	45.6%
Tunisia: ARP **Ranking as of 1st November 2023: 141**	
Electoral quota for women Legal source	Art. No quota
Number of members	154
Women	25
Percentage of women	16.2 %

Source: Interparliamentary Union, *Monthly ranking of women in national parliaments*, 1st November 2023, https://data.ipu.org/women-ranking?month=11&year=2023.

7.4. Eliminating violence against women

Violence against women in all its forms whether material, sexual, moral, psychological, economic, political… constitutes one of the main obstacles for women participation in the public sphere and political competition. Thus, there has been a growing awareness in recent years of the potential power of more progressive legislation in changing social norms around gender-based violence.

International conventions and declarations are important, not least because they have provided specific definitions of what constitutes gender-based violence, but they have served to set standards not only globally, but in national legislation.

> The 1979 Convention on the Elimination of All Forms of Discrimination against Women ("CEDAW") was a major step forward in establishing key rights for women and has to date been ratified by 189 States[92]. CEDAW outlawed "discrimination against women in all its forms" (Article 2) and obliges States "to take all appropriate measures, including legislation, to modify or abolish existing laws, regulations, customs and practices, which constitute discrimination against women" (Article 2, f.).
>
> But the Convention did not explicitly prohibit violence against women. Subsequent recommendations issued by the CEDAW Committee, which oversees States' compliance with the Convention, have explicitly defined "discrimination" to include violence against women. Specifically, the Committee's General Recommendation No. 19 (1992)[93] broadly defines discrimination to incorporate gender based violence including physical, mental or sexual harm or suffering, threats of such acts, coercion, and other deprivations of liberty.

Several regional instruments prohibit gender-based violence. The Protocol to the African Charter on Human and Peoples' Rights, on the Rights of Women in Africa, also known as the Maputo Protocol, prohibits gender-based violence as part of women's rights to life, integrity and security of the person, and dignity. Article 1 defines violence against women as including "all acts perpetrated against women". The Maputo Protocol addresses violence against women in many of its provisions and establishes legal obligations.

Security Council Resolutions on Peace, Security, and Women 1325,

---

[92] Convention on the Elimination of All Forms of Discrimination against Women, Status of ratification interactive dashboard, available at https://indicators.ohchr.org (accessed on 1 December 2023).

[93] UN Committee on the Elimination of Discrimination Against Women, Convention on the Elimination of All Forms of Discrimination Against Women, General Recommendation no. 19, (1992).

1820, 1888, and 1889 address women's role in peace-building, and sexual violence against women in conflict.

Over the past three decades there has been a tidal wave of countries introducing gender-based violence legislation. However, few countries have enacted specific laws covering violence against women in the political life, although it is increasingly recognized as an issue that undermines women's presence in politics. Latin America has been at the vanguard of this global discussion. In 2012, Bolivia became the only country in the world to criminalize "political violence and harassment against women"[94]. Other countries have incorporated aspects of political violence into their general laws on violence against women. This is the case of the Special Comprehensive Law for a Life Free of Violence for Women of El Salvador, which incorporates, as an expression of violence, the mockery, discredit, degradation, or isolation of women in different spheres, including spaces of political or civic participation. In its definition of institutional violence, the Argentinean Law for the Integral Protection of Women includes violence against women perpetrated in political parties, unions, business organizations, sports, and civil society[95].

In Tunisia, Article 51 of the Constitution (2022) (*ex* Article 46 of the Constitution (2014)) provides that: "The state shall take all necessary measures in order to eradicate violence against women". Law no. 2017-58 of August 11, 2017 on the elimination of violence against women in Tunisia includes key elements from the United Nations Handbook for Legislation on Violence Against Women[96]. *It adopts* a comprehensive legislative approach, encompassing not only the criminalization of all forms of violence against women and the effective prosecution and punishment of perpetrators, but also the prevention of violence, and the empowerment, support, and protection of survivors. It recommends that legislation explicitly recognize violence against women as a form of gender-based discrimination and a violation of women's human rights. The Law includes a comprehen-

---

[94] This pioneer Law has inspired the Inter-American Model Law on the Prevention, Punishment and Eradication of Violence against Women in Political Life drafted within the framework of the Organization of American States (OAS).

[95] Organization of American States, *Inter-American Model Law on the Prevention, Punishment and Eradication of Violence Against Women in Political Life*, 2017, available at https://www.oas.org/en/mesecvi/docs/LeyModeloViolenciaPolitica-EN.pdf (accessed on 1 December 2023).

[96] United Nations, *Handbook for Legislation on Violence against Women,* New York, 2010, available at https://www.un.org/womenwatch/daw/vaw/handbook/Handbook%20for%20legislation%20on%20violence%20against%20women.pdf, (accessed on 1 December 2023).

sive definition of gender-based violence, including physical, sexual, psychological, economic and political violence.

The political violence is defined as: "any act or practice based on gender discrimination whose perpetrator aims to deprive or prevent women from exercising any political, partisan or associative activity or any fundamental right or freedom". Article 18 mentions that "Is punished by a fine of one thousand dinars whoever commits political violence. The penalty is increased to six (6) months of imprisonment in case of recidivism" (Article 3).

8. Conclusion

There are many steps to be taken to bring unity and peace to the country on the one hand and to build democratic and sustainable institutions on the other. This process of change cannot be achieved without considering women as true partners in the promotion of peace, peaceful dialogue, and the reconstruction of the national state. This perspective of egalitarian participation must be concretized at the level of the legal and political system put in place by the new Libyan authorities. For this to happen, profound reforms are needed in legal norms, public policies, and social representations. Reform initiatives to promote women's rights are supported by the United Nations system and the European Union in Libya. These include support for an agreement on the constitution, the electoral law to increase the quota of women's representation, a law on combating violence against women, a national action plan for the implementation of Security Council Resolution 1325 "Women, Peace and Security", gender institutionalization, and capacity building on gender equality for the various stakeholders (public institutions, private sector, media, civil society). However, these different projects should not be based on constitutional and institutional mimeticism but should be motivated by a desire for reform on the part of the national elites and supported by the citizens.

General References and Reports

Al-Ali Z. (2020), *Libya's final draft constitution: A contextual analysis*, Stockholm, International IDEA, available at https://constitutionnet.org/sites/default/files/2020-12/Libya%20analysis%20-%20Zaid%20Al-Ali%20%28December%202020%29%20%28English%29.pdf (accessed on 5 December 2023).

Allen M. (2016), *Constitution Assessment for Women's Equality*, Stockholm,

International IDEA, available at https://www.idea.int/publications/constitution-assessment-womens-equality (accessed on 29 November 2023).

Brown G.W., McLean I. and McMillan A. (2018), *Concise Dictionary of Politics and International Relations*, 4th ed., New York, Oxford University Press.

Bugaighis, W. (2013), "Prospects for women in the new Libya", in *Handbook of Arab Women and Arab Spring*, ed. by Olimat M.S., London, Routledge, available at https://www.routledgehandbooks.com/doi/10.4324/9781315858661-8, (accessed on 1 December 2023).

Cats-Baril A. (2022), *A Guide to Being an Effective Advocate for Gender Equality*, Stockholm, International IDEA, available at https://www.idea.int/sites/default/files/publications/a-guide-to-being-an-effective-advocate-for-gender-equality-CAWE1.pdf (accessed on 29 November 2023).

Doherty M. (2012), *Libyan Women in the 2012 National Elections*, Conference on Women's Participation in Public Life, Politics, and Decision-Making, UNDP, Tunis, 29-30 October 2012, National Democratic Institute, available at https://www.ndi.org/sites/default/files/Doherty_Libyan%20Women%20in%20the%202012%20National%20Elections_October%202012.pdf (accessed on 1 December 2023).

Draji I., Elsadda H. and Klibi S. (2017), *Comparative Study on Constitutional Processes in the Arab World A Gender Perspective*, Paris, Euromed Feminist Initiative EFE-EFI, available at https://www.efi-ife.org/en/pdf-detail/94701-comparative-study-constitutional-processes-in-the-arab-world-a-gender-perspective (accessed on 25 November 2023).

Ellena K. and Brown A. (2019), *Beyond Constitutional Reform to Elections Libya Electoral Legal Framework Analysis*, Arlington, International Foundation for Electoral Systems, available at https://www.ifes.org/sites/default/files/libya_electoral_legal_framework_analysis_november_2019.pdf (accessed on 26 November 2023).

Ferrari A. and Toronto J. (ed.) (2017), *Religions and Constitutional Transitions in the Muslim Mediterranean. The pluralistic Moment*, New York, Routledge.

Freeman M. (2022), *Human rights*, 4th ed., Cambridge, Polity press.

Hamrouni S. (2012), *Equal Citizenship in Tunisia: Constitutional Guarantees for Equality between Citizens*, New York, International Peace Institute (Project Arab Forum for Citizenship in Transition), available at https://www.ipinst.org/images/pdfs/women-and-constitution-tunisia-english1.pdf (accessed on 27 November 2023).

Hart V. (2003), Democratic Constitution Making, Washington, DC, United States Institute of Peace, SpecialReport; no. 107, available at https://peace

maker.un.org/sites/peacemaker.un.org/files/DemocraticConstitutionMaking_USIP2003.pdf (accessed on 15 November 2023).

Hennette-Vauchez S., Pichard M. and Roman M. (ed.) (2014), *La loi et le genre. Etudes critiques de droit français,* Paris, CNRS ed.

Houlihan E. (2020), *Women Constitution-Makers: Comparative Experiences with Representation, Participation and Influence*, First Annual Women Constitution-Makers' Dialogue, Edinburgh 2019, Stockholm, International IDEA.

Hweio, H. (2016), *Libyan women and revolution: a study of the changes in women's political and social roles during and after the Libyan revolution*, Graduate Research Theses & Dissertations, 3798, available at https://huskiecommons.lib.niu.edu/allgraduate-thesesdissertations/3798 (accessed on 25 November 2023).

Langhi Z. (2014), "Gender and state-building in Libya: towards a politics of inclusion", in *The Journal of North African Studies*, 19, 2, 200-210, available at https://www.tandfonline.com/doi/abs/10.1080/13629387.2014.881736 (accessed on 25 November 2023).

Limam J. (2018), "Les rebelles libyens: de la révolte à l'Etat défaillant", in Hatem M. (ed.), *Transitions arabes. Révoltes, gouvernance et géopolitique, Association tunisienne d'études politiques*, Tunis, Nirvana, 57-74.

Mekki N. (2014), *Tunisia: Equality in Gender and Constitution*, New York, International Peace Institute (Project Arab Forum for Citizenship in Transition), available at https://www.ipinst.org/images/pdfs/FACTReport-Gender_Constitution-English-September2014.pdf (accessed on 27 November 2023).

O'Reilly M., Ó Súilleabháin A. and Paffenholz T. (2015), *Reimagining Peacemaking: Women's Roles in Peace Processes*, New York, International Peace Institute.

Important links and documents

Constitue Project, available at https://www.constituteproject.org/constitutions?lang=en&status=in_force&status=is_draft (accessed on 1 December 2023)

Economic and Social Council, Commission on the Status of Women (2020), *Women's full and effective participation and decision-making in public life, as well as the elimination of violence, for achieving gender equality and the empowerment of all women and girls, Report of the Secretary-General*, E/CN.6/2021/3, Sixty-fifth session, 21 December 2020, available at https://undocs.org/E/CN.6/2021/3 (accessed on 28 November 2023).

Gender Concerns International (2012), *Gender Election Monitoring (GEM) Mission Libya General National Congress Election 7 July 2012 Final Report*, available at https://www.genderconcerns.org/pdfs/Final%20Report%20GEM%20Mission%20Libya_Gender%20Concerns%20International_English%20version%20(1).pdf (accessed on 3 December 2023).

Human Rights Council (2015), *National report of Libya*, Universal Periodic Review, A/HRC/WG.6/22/LBY/1, Thirty-sixth session, 5 May 2015, available at https://documents-dds-ny.un.org/doc/UNDOC/GEN/G15/089/43/PDF/G1508943.pdf?OpenElement (accessed on 1 December 2023).

Human Rights Council (2015), Re*port of the Working Group on the Universal Periodic Review - Libya*, A/HRC/30/16, Thirtieth session, 22 July 2015, available at https://documents-dds-ny.un.org/doc/UNDOC/GEN/G21/000/74/PDF/G2100074.pdf?OpenElement (accessed on 1 December 2023).

Human Rights Council (2021), *National report of Libya*, Universal Periodic Review, A/HRC/WG.6/36/LBY/1, Thirty-sixth session, 18 August 2020, available at https://documents-dds-ny.un.org/doc/UNDOC/GEN/G20/211/92/PDF/G2021192.pdf?OpenElement (accessed on 1 December 2023).

Human Rights Council (2021), *Report of the Working Group on the Universal Periodic Review Libya*, 5 January 2021, A/HRC/46/17, Forty-sixth session, 22 February-19 March 2021, available at https://documents-dds-ny.un.org/doc/UNDOC/GEN/G21/000/74/PDF/G2100074.pdf?OpenElement (accessed on 1 December 2023).

Inter-Parliamentary Union (IPU) (2023), *Women in parliament in 2022 The year in review,* Geneva, available at https://www.ipu.org/resources/publications/reports/2023-03/women-in-parliament-2022 (accessed on 1 December 2023).

Libyan Political Dialogue Forum, available at https://unsmil.unmissions.org/libyan-political-dialogue-forum (accessed on 1 December 2023).

Organization of American States (2017), *Inter-American Model Law on the Prevention, Punishment and Eradication of Violence Against Women in Political Life*, available at https://www.oas.org/en/mesecvi/docs/LeyModeloViolenciaPolitica-EN.pdf (accessed on 2 December 2023).

Oxford Constitutions of the World, available at https://oxcon.ouplaw.com/home/OCW (accessed on 29 November 2023).

The Carter Center (2014), *The 2014 Constitutional Drafting Assembly Elections in Libya: Final Report*, Atlanta, available at https://www.cartercenter.org/resources/pdfs/news/peace_publications/election_reports/libya-06112014-final-rpt.pdf (accessed on 03 December 2023).

The Carter Center (2012), *General National Congress Elections in Libya. Final Report,* Atlanta, available at https://www.cartercenter.org/resources/pdfs/news/peace_publications/election_reports/libya-070712-final-rpt.pdf (accessed on 3 December2023).

The Central Committee for Municipal Council Elections (CCMCE) (2018), available at https://www.facebook.com/ccmce/ (accessed on 1 December 2023).

The High National Elections Commission (HNEC), available at https://hnec.ly/ (accessed on 1 December 2023).

Réseau Euro Med France (2021), *Libye, une histoire heurtée, un présent énigmatique, une société engagée*, Cahier n. 7 du Réseau Euromed France, available at http://www.euromed-france.org/2021/03/24/cahier-n7-ref/ (accessed on 1 December 2023).

Chapter 12

WOMEN AND POLITICAL PARTIES IN CONTEMPORARY TÜRKIYE

Jean Marcou

ABSTRACT: *After having been presented for a long time as a reference within the Muslim world, as far as the status of women is concerned, Türkiye today is regularly perceived as a country where women's rights are questioned and where the emancipation inherited from the Kemalist period is threatened. This perception is based on a certain number of tangible observations: the worrying situation of the level of violence against women (harassment, domestic violence, feminicides...), persistent difficulties encountered by the latter in accessing positions of responsibility, and even outright declarations by prominent political leaders (starting with Recep Tayyip Erdoğan himself) rejecting the claim of male-female equality, in favor of the traditional idea of complementarity, the religious inspiration of which is most often claimed. The current lack of involvement of Turkish women in the political life of their country is particularly surprising, given that they have voted since the 1930s and have often been considered the first beneficiaries of the modernization reforms initiated after the advent of the Republic. Their situation is nonetheless particular within the Muslim world, and it will be appropriate to try to define it first, before entering into the heart of the matter and examining their place in political parties, in order to finally consider the main challenges, they are facing in contemporary Türkiye.*

Having been presented for a long time as a something of an exemplar within the Islamic world as regards the status of women, today Türkyie is frequently perceived as a country where women's rights are called into question and/or the emancipation inherited from the Kemalist period is under threat. This perception is based on a number of tangible factors: worrying levels of violence against women (harassment, domestic violence, feminicide...), the persisting difficulties encountered by women in accessing positions of responsibility, or even outright declarations by prominent politicians (starting with Recep Tayyip Erdoğan himself) rejecting claims to equality between men and women, harking back to the traditional idea of "complementarity", for which religious inspiration is often claimed.

The current very low level of involvement of Turkish women in the political life of their country is particularly surprising if it is considered that they have had the right to vote since the 1930s, and have often been regarded as amongst the primary beneficiaries of the modernising reforms launched following the establishment of the Republic. Their situation does not stand out particularly within the Islamic world, and we must attempt to describe it in greater detail before entering into the details of the issue and examining their role within political parties. This paper will then conclude by considering the main challenges facing them in today's Türkiye.

1. Women in Türkiye: a special case in the Islamic world?

Women started to come to prominence and to assert claims during the final stages of the Ottoman Empire in the 19th century within the context of modernisation movements that sought to halt its decline. During the *Tanzimat* period[1], women originating from various communities throughout the Empire, including in particular from the middle and upper classes, built on this Ottoman liberalism and sought to break out of the domestic straightjacket by accessing education. Journalists, or in some cases novelists such as Zafer Hanım or Fatma Aliye (whose portrait features today on the Turkish 50 lire note[2]), started to make their voices heard. This movement later consolidated itself during the Second *Meşrutiyet* (1908-1912)[3], which saw a proliferation of women's associations, and also after the end of the First World War when the Turkish nationalist movement came to light, leading to the rejection of the Sèvres Treaty and the outbreak of the war of independence. In particular, during protests held in May 1919 against Istanbul's occupation by the allied powers, the novelist and militant feminist Halide Edib Adıvar was one of the figureheads of the fledgling movement.

The proclamation of the Republic (1923) and the modernisation reforms implemented during the 1920s and 1930s accelerated these changes, which then reached their high point. The most important step was without

---

[1] Between 1839 and 1876, under the reign of several sultans, attempts were made to stem the decline of the Ottoman Empire by adopting legal, administrative, tax, educational and even constitutional reforms.

[2] On this issue, cf. Marcou J., "La polémique provoquée par la présence de Fatma Aliye sur les billets de 50 TL tourne au boycott", *Blog de l'OVIPOT*, 8 February 2009, available at https://ovipot.hypotheses.org/772.

[3] This was the second period of constitutional monarchy, which saw the re-adoption of the Ottoman Constitution of 1876 following the Young Turks' revolution in July 1908. It was characterised by attempts to establish representative government as well as major social turmoil, with a proliferation of parties, associations and newspapers and the emergence of feminist movements.

doubt the adoption of a Civil Code in 1926, as it provided for equality between men and women, marking a break with the personal status based on religion on which women had previously been dependent. This secular civil law continue still guarantees Turkish women full citizenship rights, which is something of an exception within the Islamic world. Over the following decade, women were granted the right to vote, initially in local elections (1930) and later also in national elections (1934). This led to the election of 18 female deputies to Parliament in 1935. The regime was however dominated by one single political party, and it goes without saying that these members of Parliament were very rigorously hand-picked. However, at a time when many European countries (starting with France) still only allowed men to vote, the reform nonetheless caused a sensation. Turkish women thus appeared to have had their demands addressed by Kemalism.

However, Şirin Tekeli has clearly shown the limits of this success, as in a number of ways the Kemalist regime sought above all to exploit women in order to achieve its own objectives[4]. By implementing these spectacular changes in the area of women's rights, the aim of the new political class was to highlight the success of a modern Türkyie that aspired to become part of "civilisation", i.e. to adopt westernised habits. The new Turkish woman was thus encouraged to cast off the veil[5], to go to the theatre, to dance with her husband, to pursue an advanced education, or even to work. People celebrated Keriman Halis Ece, a young Turkish woman who won the title of Miss Universe in 1932, and Mustafa Kemal Atatürk himself adopted seven daughters, one of whom became a fighter pilot and another the President of the Turkish Historical Society. In tangible terms however, the actual facts painted a less rosy picture. Early militant feminists who sought to create a political party at the dawn of the Republic, even before the future single Kemalist Party was founded in 1924, were prevented from doing so and the Turkish Women's Union (which they were allowed to set up) quickly fell under external control, and was invited to dissolve itself ten years later on the grounds – as stated by leading figures in the regime – that feminist claims had been satisfied and an association of this type no longer had any reason to exist.

Paradoxically, the democratisation of the single party system in the

[4] Tekeli Ş., "Les femmes: le genre mal-aimé de la République", in Vaner S., *La Turquie*, Paris, Fayard, 2005, 251 to 281.

[5] Whilst the Kemalist regime enacted legislation concerning men's clothing, in particular banning the wearing of the fez, it was less prescriptive as regards women's clothing. As such, a prohibition on the wearing of the headscarf was not introduced in general and absolute terms, but only for certain women (judges, public officials members of Parliament...).

wake of the Second World War barely improved the position of Turkish women. During the second half of the 20th century, female representation within Parliament was often lower (less than 2%) than it had been during the Kemalist period (4.5%). At the same time, it should be noted that the urbanisation of Turkish society resulted in a decline in the number of women in work. Those who had previously worked in the countryside often became housewives after moving to the cities, as such excluded from the economy and only performing casual or informal work.

With an employment rate for women over the age of 15 of 34%, Türkiye was ranked in last place of all OECD countries in 2019 (as against an average figure of 63%)[6]. It has often been complained that the AKP has been unable to achieve any improvements on this score despite the spectacular economic development during the decade after the year 2000, as well as improvements in the level of women's education. Türkiye has in fact caught up with developed countries in terms of literacy rates for young women (100%) as well as adult women (93%)[7], whereas in the early 2000s more than 20% of all women were still illiterate[8]. However, significant inequality between girls and boys persists as regards access to secondary or higher education, and strong regional disparities are still apparent on this score. The number of young girls entering college in the south eastern Kurdish provinces is still low (often less than 20%) compared to levels in the more developed parts of the country (+80%). In the 1980s by contrast, Ayşe Öncü observed that Turkish women were particularly well represented within the advanced white collar professions (lawyers, doctors, university staff, researchers, journalists, etc.), in some cases in greater numbers even than in western countries[9]. This Kemalist legacy – a result of the social benefits available to elites – has subsequently continued. Thus, in 2009, 36% of all researchers were women in Türkiye, as against only 27% in France[10]. Thus, whereas women accounted for 44% of Turkish university staff in 2018, only three of them were rectors at the country's 111 public universities[11].

[6] Jégo M., "Les femmes turques réduites à la précarité", *Le Monde*, 23 May 2019.

[7] Cf. Figures regularly published on the UNESCO website: http://uis.unesco.org/fr/country/tr.

[8] Tekeli Ş., *op. cit.*, 266.

[9] Öncü A., "Turkish Women in the Professions: Why so many?", in Abadan-Unat N. (ed.), *Women in the Turkish Society*, Leiden, E.J. Bril, 1981.

[10] Source: OECD Report for 2009.

[11] "Only three out of *11* state rectors are women in Turkey", *Hürriyet Daily News*, 9 January 2018.

Overall, although in terms of female education and activity Türkyie is still therefore struggling to rival OECD countries, on the other hand it compares very favourably with the rest of the Islamic world. However, figures aside, it must be concluded that it is above all the law that sets Türkyie apart in this respect, including in particular the fact that there is genuine secular citizenship based on a civil code and a system of civil courts.

2. Women in Turkish political life

If there is one area in which women from other Muslim countries have nothing to envy in Türkyie, it is participation in political life. Türkyie currently occupies 119th place within the world classification of the number of women in national parliaments, behind Tunisia (30th), Algeria (65th), Pakistan (100th) and even the United Arab Emirates (84th) or Saudi Arabia (105th)! The situation has however improved somewhat since 2015, following the entry into Parliament of a sizeable contingent from the Kurdish party HDP [12].

Four major political families have been represented within the Grand National Assembly of Türkyie since the 2007 general election: conservative-Islamists (AKP), Kemalists (CHP), nationalists (MHP and *İyi Parti*) and Kurds (HDP). Before the most recent parliamentary elections in 2018, the electoral law was amended in order to allow parties to conclude agreements among themselves. This led to the emergence of two alliances: the Popular Appliance (*Cumhur ittifaki*), including the AKP and the MHP, and the National Alliance (*Milli ittifaki*), in which the CHP and the *İyi Parti* are dominant. Although it is still legal and represented within Parliament [13], the Kurdish party HDP has thus been marginalised and relegated to a position outside the system's traditional machinery. The parties in power accuse it of being in cahoots with the PKK, whereas opposition forces attempt to attract its voters, whilst however refusing to conclude an official alliance with it. Following the 2017 constitutional amendment, the traditional Turkish parliamentary regime changed into an authoritarian presidential system highly centralised around Recep Tayyip Erdoğan as an individual.

---

[12] Kadiri G., "Les femmes entrent en force au parlement turc", *Le Monde*, 9 June 2015.

[13] In March 2021, an application seeking to ban the HDP was rejected by the Constitutional Court. Cf. "Top court returns indictment aimed to ban HDP", *Hürriyet Daily News*, March 31, 2021. In Parliament, the HDP now has 55 members, although a dozen of them are currently facing prosecution, which may result in their imprisonment.

The under-involvement of women, already noted above, has also continued following the establishment of this personalised presidentialism. It should be pointed out that in Türkyie (as in France moreover), no woman has ever served as Head of State, and only one (as is moreover the case for France) has ever headed a government (Tansu Çiller, from 1993 to 1996). As far as female ministers are concerned, they have hardly been more numerous; generally each government only has one or two, and they are most often responsible for social or family affairs. In the spring of 2021 following the resignation of Ruhsar Pekcan as Trade Minister, Recep Tayyip Erdoğan's ministerial team was left with only one woman (Derya Yanık) at the Ministry for Families and Social Affairs. She shocked public opinion in May 2021 when commenting that the increase in conjugal violence rates in Türkyie during the Covid-19 lockdown was "tolerable" [14]. As will be seen below, women's involvement in political parties is hardly more significant.

The majority party in power, the AKP (*Adalet* ve *kalkınma partisi*) headed by Recep Tayyip Erdoğan, which has 295 members of Parliament including 53 women (or 17.9% of the total number of AKP members) in the Parliament elected in 2018, has a highly patriarchal vision of society. This party, which does not officially define itself as formally Islamist, has nonetheless drawn on the legacy of the Turkish Islamist movement, and has attracted most of the voters who previously supposed Turkish right-wing conservative parties (which non longer, or barely, exist today). Its conception of the status of women and couples is thus highly traditionally and is inspired by religion. Although the party has not declared that it is systematically hostile to women's rights, the philosophy that dominates its notion of female emancipation draws more readily on complementarity than on equality. Against this backdrop, it will come as no surprise that women are viewed above all as wives and mothers, a perception which is often reasserted and accepted by female members of Parliament themselves from the majority party [15]. For his part, Recep Tayyip Erdoğan has frequently expressed his concern regarding sex before marriage (in particular in university halls of residence [16]). Moreover, being troubled by Türkyie's low birth rates, he does not miss any opportunity to remind Turkish women that they

[14] Nazlan E., "Why Women are calling to only female cabinet member to resign", *Al Monitor*, 27 May 2021.

[15] Tremblay P., "How female politician in Turkey's ruling party help strengthen patriarchy", *Al Monitor*, 4 January 2021.

[16] Marcou J., "Turquie, la polémique de la mixité des logements étudiants détrône celle du port du foulard islamique", *OVIPOT blog*, 9 November 2013, available at https://ovipot.hypotheses.org/9506.

must have at least three children. However, since Turkish women have the right to vote and the AKP has always adopted a highly pragmatic (or one might way even opportunistic) approach, his pronouncements are often marked by ambiguity. Whilst stressing the importance of the work done by housewives, the regime concedes that women will have to work in order for the country to develop economically. Moreover, where appropriate, he does not fail to celebrate Turks' educational or economic achievements. In addition, the party still maintains an important women's branch (*Kadın Kolları*), the militancy of which has enabled women wearing the veil to access universities and some other institutions or professions that had previously been inaccessible to them (Parliament, the judicial system, the police...). It has thus achieved part of its success by embracing this resurgence by underprivileged women over those from the middle and upper classes, who as noted above are over-represented within the white collar professions; indeed, this rivalry is even apparent within Turkish sitcoms [17]. However, it is not certain that the AKP still benefits from this favourable image, in particular with the younger generations.

The Turkish nationalist family is now comprised of two rival formations: the Nationalist Action Party MHP (*Milliyetçi Hareket Partisi*) founded in 1958 by the iconic general Alparslan Türkeş, which has been led since his death in 1997 by Devlet Bahçeli, and the Good Party (*İyi Parti*) founded by Meral Akşener. This split in 2017 was caused both by objections to the sclerotic direction of the MHP, as well as its decision to ally with the AKP, in particular in order to enable the latter to amend the Constitution for its benefit by transforming it into a presidential system, after which it went on to win the next presidential and parliamentary elections held in 2018. Whilst the stance taken by women from this political family is in some senses very similar to that promoted by the AKP, as both are dominated by a patriarchal philosophy, it differs essentially in that it is more nationalist than religious. Here, Islam is regarded as a constituent element of Turkish identity, more than as a religion setting out a genuine paradigm for living. Nationalists have not been systematically opposed to the veil, and even promoted the constitutional amendment in 2008 that allowed women wearing the veil to attend universities. The fact remains that most nationalist militants do not wear a veil and the new *İyi Parti* defends a different position as regards women's rights. This difference is rooted in the more open

[17] In particular in *Bir Başkadır,* one of the most recent Turkish series to be released on Netflix, of the two main female characters, one has recently moved to Istanbul, whilst the other is a psychiatrist with a middleclass background. Cf. Skyvington E., "*Bir Başkadır* sur Netflix: quatre raisons de regarder cette série sur les fractures de la société turque", *Télérama*, 14 January 2021.

nature of this dissident nationalist grouping, which is moreover led by a woman (Meral Akşener) and includes militants originating on the one hand from the moderate arm of the MHP and on the other hand the more nationalist positions within the CHP. Women are accordingly very well represented within this party (3 women out of 43 MPs in 2018) than they are in the MHP (5 women out of 49 MPs); moreover, these figures confirm more generally that women are present in the lowest numbers within the parties from the nationalist bloc

Considering the comments made above concerning the history of the Republic, it will come as no surprise that women's issues are important within the Republican People's Party CHP (*Cumhuriyet Halk Partisi*). This is the party that today claims the Kemalist mantle, even though it also considers itself to be social democratic [18]. It is nonetheless surprising that, with 18 members elected out of 146 in 2018 (corresponding to 12.3%), the CHP has a lower rate of female representation than the AKP. This phenomenon clearly reflects the difficulties encountered by women in becoming involved and achieving recognition in Turkish political life, even where they are active within parties that cite the defence of women's rights as one of their primary concerns. Fundamentally, the CHP seeks above all to defend the Kemalist heritage of a laical civil and criminal law. However, it does not shirk back from becoming involved in current debates (education, abortion, forced marriage of children, women's employment…). Moreover, over the last few years, women in the CHP have often taken spectacular initiatives in attempts to make their voices heard in Parliament. In December 2019, they notably performed the anthem by the Chilean feminist group Las Tesis in Parliament [19] in a protest against sexual and sexist violence [20]. Another memorable incident occurred when, during discussion of the wording of the 2017 constitutional reform, Ankara MP Aylin Nazlıkaya, handcuffed herself to the rostrum in Parliament, provoking a barrage of arguments concerning the sexism prevailing within Parliament itself [21]. However, at the time of these events, this MP was no longer a member of the CHP, having been previously expelled (although was later readmitted

[18] The CHP is also a member of the Socialist International, just like the German SPD, the British Labour Party or the French Socialist Party.

[19] "Women lawmakers perform 'La Tesis' in Turkish parliament", *Hürriyet Daily News*, 15 December 2019.

[20] Gomez F.-X., "Le violeur sur ton chemin: le slam féministe du Chili à la conquête de la planète", *Libération*, 2 December 2019.

[21] Nazlan E., "Unchain my vote: handcuff and sexism in Parliament", *Hürriyet Daily News*, 21 January 2017.

in 2019). The CHP's problem is therefore still how to expand its electorate and to address women from the lower classes, amongst whom the AKP is still extremely influential. It has implied in particular a relaxation of the more traditional laical symbolism (for example, an end to the Kemalist party's systematic opposition to the wearing of the veil).

It is clear that the classical feminism of the CHP is now being challenged by the new approach pursued by the Democratic People's Party HDP (*Halklaren Demokratik Partisi*). This left-wing party influenced by libertarian municipalism, sets itself apart from the previous Kurdish parliamentary parties in that it also seeks to argue the case of the downtrodden throughout the Republic, thus also including women. This promise has in part been kept, if it is considered that the HDP has the highest proportion of women in Parliament (25 members, comprising 37.3% of the total of 67 elected in 2018). Moreover, it applies a policy of systematic equality in relation to the occupancy of its leading positions. As a result, it currently has two co-presidents, one of whom is a woman (Pervin Buldan) and the other a man (Mithat Sancar). Aside from the Kurdish electorate, this approach has enabled it to attract a left-wing Turkish electorate, in particular in the cities, which is weary of the CHP's traditionalism. One of the challenges that thus confronts the HDP is the need to reconcile this bold conception of the place of women with the still highly patriarchal Kurdish society.

3. Contemporary issues

To complete this overview of the respective positions of political parties in relation to feminism in Türkyie, it is now necessary to examine the main issues currently facing women. Parties are not generally the main actors, and developing issues risk throwing up surprises, especially in a society that is evolving at pace.

The first issue currently confronting women is the erosion of the gains made by them as a result of the evolution of the Turkish political system, and in particular its increasing rigidity. During its second decade in power, the *AKP* has in fact backtracked on the more liberal initiatives that had in some respects marked its first decade in government. This phenomenon, which is apparent in relation to democracy, the rule of law, the approach to the Kurdish question, has also manifested itself in relation to the position of women. It has led in particular to a decisive change in tone on the part of political leaders, who have openly proclaimed their attachment to macho patriarchal values, or called into question previously acquired rights. Thus, in May 2012, Recep Tayyip Erdoğan branded abortion as "murder"[22], comparing it to the Uludere airstrike[23], before going on to opine that equality between men and women ran "contrary to human nature"[24], that family planning and contraceptives could not be accepted by Muslim families[25] or that, at the risk of shocking, in every woman he saw above all a mother[26]. This clear change in official rhetoric on the official rights of women has been accompanied by specific initiatives. In 2012 the AKP attempted (unsuccessfully) to reduce the legal period during which abortion is permitted (which has been legal in Türkiye since 1983 during the first ten weeks of pregnancy). In 2016 it attempted (again unsuccessfully) to enact legislation providing for the abandonment of any prosecution of a rapist who accepted to marry his underage victim. In 2017 legislation was adopted enabling muftis to celebrate civil marriages. In 2021, Recep Tayyip Erdoğan issued a decree stipulating his country's withdrawal from the Istanbul Convention Action against violence against women, signed within the ambit of the Council of Europe.

The second issue in this case is whether women will be able to retain their capacity for mobilisation and dissent that they have often deployed in order to defend their rights or to protest against intolerable situations. As has been noted by Şirin Tekeli, "the status of women has been a privileged issue within Turkey's process of modernisation", and this has resulted in the consolidation of an active feminist movement, which has made itself heard effectively on various occasions over the last decade, despite the growing authoritarianism. In July 2014, comments made by Deputy Prime Minister Bülent Arınç suggesting that women should avoid laughing too loudly in public "so that they always maintain their decency" sparked off a process movement, which saw thousands of women to post content on so-

---

[22] Perrier G., "Recep Tayyip Erdoğan, gardien du vagin des femmes turques", *Le Monde*, 29 May 2012.

[23] In December 2011, a bombing raid by the Turkish air force caused the deaths of more than thirty Kurdish villagers involved in smuggling on the Turkish-Iraq border. The raid aroused strong emotions throughout the country and a number of controversies concerning the responsibility of the Turkish army. On this comparison, cf. Marcou J., "Les débats et les manifestations provoquées par le projet visant à restreindre le droit à l'avortement prennent de l'ampleur en Turquie", *OVIPOT blog*, 5 June 2012, available at https://ovipot.hypotheses.org/7450.

[24] Cf. Jégo M., "L'égalité des sexes est contre nature, estime le président turc", *Le Monde*, 25 November 2014.

[25] "Monsieur Erdoğan exorte les musulmans à bannir la contraception", *Le Monde*, 31 May 2016.

[26] Berkani M., "Turquie, pour Erdoğan, 'la femme est avant tout une mère'", *franceinfo*, 31 May 2016.

cial networks showing them guffawing with laughter[27]. Following the particularly heinous death in February 2015 of a young student, Ozgecan Aslan, after being attacked on a minibus in Mersin, women carried her coffin at her funeral, in defiance of traditional religious custom. At the same time, in Istanbul men demonstrated in the streets in skirts and dresses in a show of solidarity, branding the initiative on social media as *#sendeanlat* (tell me about it you too). These protests also particularly resonated. In 2012, following several weeks of demonstrations, the AKP was forced to withdraw its draft legislation on the reduction of the period during which abortion is permitted. In 2016, it was once again forced to withdraw draft legislation according to which any man who raped a girl could avoid punishment by marrying her. To date, these have been the only two cases since the AKP came to power in which it has shrunk back in the face of pressure from the streets and public opinion. On the other hand, the demonstrations held following the announcement concerning the withdrawal from the Istanbul Convention did not prevent Recep Tayyip Erdoğan from pushing through these plans, even though this in turn resulted in further controversy concerning the President's legal powers to decide himself by a simple decree that Türkyie should withdraw from an international commitment of this type.

Due to this questioning of women's capacity to mobilise in order to put an end to the erosion of their rights, it is necessary to consider one final issue. This concerns specifically the effects on the status of women of the rapid social transformations that are being witnessed today in Türkyie. Following two decades in power, opinion polls show that Recep Tayyip Erdoğan and the AKP are now being seriously challenged by one segment of public opinion. Many experts are asking in particular how the new generation will vote[28], given that it is not really attracted by the lifestyle proposed to it by party bosses[29]. Moreover, it is certainly not "this devout generation" which political chiefs think they can create[30]. Worried about its future due to rapidly rising unemployment rates[31], in Türkyie too, just as

[27] Tremblay P., "No laughing matter: social media mocks AKP's fight for chastity", *Al Monitor*, 30 July 2014.

[28] Yilmaz Ç., "Generation Z to hold key of Turkey's future as millions of new voters set to cast ballots in 2023", *Hürriyet Daily News*, 19 July 2020.

[29] Sharp Kenan B., "Turkey's ruling party blunders at youth outreach", *Al Monitor*, 26 October 2020.

[30] Tremblay P., "Why can't Erdogan win over generation Z", *Al Monitor*, 10 July 2020.

[31] Tokyay Me., "Youth unemployment reaches alarming level in Turkey", *Al Monitor*, 2 February 2021.

elsewhere, this Generation Z is sensitive to environmental issues, gender problems and freedom of information on social networks. Although a recent tendency amongst leading women within the AKP to stop wearing the veil has been observed, there is no doubt that the party in power will find it increasingly difficult to strike a balance between its conservative vision of the status of women and the silent evolution of Turkish society, which is becoming increasingly less tolerant of harassment, violence and feminicide. The protest movement triggered by the country's withdrawal from the Istanbul Convention clearly did not prevent it from happening. However, it resulted in a convergence of the interests of laical feminists and Islamic feminists. Moreover, some opinion polls have suggested that a majority of the public objects to the withdrawal from this international commitment[32]. It is thus not certain that the daughters of the new urban dwellers that swept the AKP into power twenty years ago will make the same choices as their mothers when they are soon due to vote for the first time in their lives.

References

Scientific articles

Öncü A. (1981), "Turkish Women in the Professions: Why so many?", in Abadan-Unat N. (ed.), *Women in the Turkish Society*, Leiden, E.J. Bril.

Tekeli Ş. (2005), "Les femmes: le genre mal-aimé de la République", in Vaner S., *La Turquie*, Paris, Fayard, 251-281.

Articles from sites or online magazines

Berkani M. (2016), "Turquie, pour Erdoğan, 'la femme est avant tout une mère'", *franceinfo*, 31 May.

Marcou J. (2012), "Les débats et les manifestations provoquées par le projet visant à restreindre le droit à l'avortement prennent de l'ampleur en Turquie", *Blog de l'OVIPOT*, 5 June.

Marcou J. (2013), "Turquie, la polémique de la mixité des logements étudiants détrône celle du port du foulard islamique", *Blog de l'OVIPOT*, 9 Novembre.

Nazlan E. (2021), "Why Women are calling to only female cabinet member to resign", *Al Monitor*, May 27.

[32] Zaman A., "Outrage at violence unites women across Turkey's ideological divide", *Al Monitor*, 19 August 2020.

Sharp Kenan B. (2020), "Turkey's ruling party blunders at youth outreach", *Al Monitor*, October 26.
Skyvington E. (2021), "*Bir Başkadır* sur Netflix: quatre raisons de regarder cette série sur les fractures de la société turque", *Télérama*, 14 January.
Tokyay M. (2021), "Youth unemployment reaches alarming level in Turkey", *Al Monitor*, February 2.
Tremblay P. (2014), "No laughing matter: social media mocks *AKP*'s fight for chastity", *Al Monitor*, July 30.
Tremblay P. (2020), "Why can't Erdogan win over generation Z", *Al Monitor*, July 10.
Tremblay P. (2021), "How female politician in Turkey's ruling party help strengthen patriarchy", *Al Monitor*, January 4.
Zaman A. (2020), "Outrage at violence unites women across Turkey's ideological divide", *Al Monitor*, August 19.

Articles from the daily press

Gomez F.-X. (2019), "Le violeur sur ton chemin: le slam féministe du Chili à la conquête de la planète", *Libération*, 2 December.
Jégo M. (2014), "L'égalité des sexes est contre nature, estime le président turc", *Le Monde*, 25 Novembre.
Jégo M. (2019), "Les femmes turques réduites à la précarité", *Le Monde*, 23 May.
Kadiri G. (2015), "Les femmes entrent en force au parlement turc", *Le Monde*, 9 June.
Perrier G. (2012), "Recep Tayyip Erdoğan, gardien du vagin des femmes turques", *Le Monde*, 29 May.
Yilmaz Ç. (2020), "Generation Z to hold key of Turkey's future as millions of new voters set to cast ballots in 2023", *Hürriyet Daily News*, July 19.

Chapter 13

THE STRUCTURAL INEQUALITIES IN LAWS AND PRACTICES AND THEIR IMPACT ON WOMEN'S AGENCY IN LEBANON: THE LONG BATTLE FOR GENDER EQUALITY

Rita Chemaly

ABSTRACT: *The article explores the main discriminations faced by women living in Lebanon, mainly the structural inequalities. From a holistic perspective the social barriers, are scrutinized from a gender lens. The author provides an overview of steps forward for gender equality and highlights main obstacles still hindering women's agency in a country lacking a civil code regulating personal status matters, such as marriage, child custody, divorce, inheritance, and is instead relying on multiple separate personal religious-based status laws with their own courts. Citizenship and equality between all citizens are analyzed. The paper offers a mapping of the laws related to Lebanese and resident women and being discussed by the Lebanese Parliament between 2019 to 2022. It is developed using a combination of methods mainly a comprehensive literature review and desk compilation of most recent published reports by various entities such as official public institutions and CSOs. Women living in Lebanon long battle towards their rights are described in this article with the latest progress made.*

issue of incapacity to contract a civil marriage in Lebanon and the challenges faced by those who opt to contract a civil marriage outside of Lebanon.

1. Introduction

Lebanon has made some positive strides on gender equality from 2017 to 2019 especially in some sectors mainly the strategic and normative framework related to gender equality. As per the latest official Universal Periodic Review 2021 (link) shows, Lebanon has made a breakthrough related to passing a law criminalizing sexual harassment in the workplace and in the public spaces. (Karam 2020). This amendment came after the progress that was made to reform discriminatory legal provisions against women that was led by women rights organisations, for more than a decade in Lebanon, mainly in the framework of the "Wayn Baadna" campaign, the long road ahead, (NCLW 2011). In a nutshell, this amendment came after reforms in the legal framework happened on the legislative front in a slow pace, giving women some of the bits and pieces of the rights they were advocating for. In 2011 Parliament repealed article 562 of the Penal Code to abolish what were called the "honor crimes" and in April 2014, it adopted for the first time in Lebanon Law number 293 criminalizing domestic violence, as well as increased the maternity leave period to 10 weeks instead of 49 days in the labor law and the laws related to public servants. Other advancement on law level, was made in 2015 when the Lebanese Parliament abolished article 522 that previously exonerated a perpetrator of rape from punishment if he married his victim. Nevertheless, despite some advancement on legal reforms that happened during the last decade, numerous legal, institutional, and mainly cultural barriers persist which hinder women's attainment of their full human rights mainly on the level of personal status laws that are still patriarchal and in favor of men in the families, on the level of political participation and on the level of role distribution within households. "The measurement of women's agency poses numerous challenges, including multi-dimensionality and context-specificity" (Qutteina, Al-Khelaifi and Yount 2019). "Women's autonomy has long been a central concern for researchers examining the social position of women in developing countries". (Agarwala and Lynch, 2006). Regarding the measurement of women's agency, this article will be concentrated on the legal normative framework in Lebanon, and take some case studies in specific topics to cover the subject of women's agency in Lebanon, and the various social, political and structural biases that need to be mitigated to ensure autonomy and equity on various levels for women living in Lebanon.

2. Main key policy initiatives taken by the Lebanese government framing women's rights in public policies

Important efforts have been undertaken by civil society actors, international organizations and other government entities to ensure gender equality and empowerment of women (World Bank and UN Women 2021). In 2012, the 10 years national strategy for women in Lebanon was adopted as a first public policy that is sectoral, with a clear action plan and strategic objectives aiming to put the main demands of civil society organizations in a policy framework that governmental institutions, parliament and CSOs can work to attain.

The yearly reports that were published on the implementation of this strategy and its action plan, clearly highlights the will of the women machinery to conceive public policies based on data gathered from various entities whether national CSOs and Ministries and International donors and funders as well as UN agencies leading projects in the country for women's rights.

Another step forward on the policy level was made in 2019, when the Government adopted the 1325 UNSCR national action plan, highlighting the need to amend discriminatory articles in laws, and work on consolidating women's role in the public sphere. "The Path to a Fair and Inclusive Society Through the Women, Peace and Security Agenda" 2019-2022, was an innovation as various law articles still discriminating against women were included in the normative framework of the action plan adopted by the government. (NCLW 2019).

Despite progress to date and policies and strategies drafted on various national governmental level and on the level of municipalities, Lebanon continues to suffer from severe gender inequality. According to the World Economic Forum's Gender Gap report for 2021, Lebanon has one of the highest overall gender gaps in the world (World Economic Forum 2021). Lebanese women's voices are still excluded, silenced and even marginalized in settings and processes such as the public sphere, labor market, personal status law systems, political decision-making and representation, and, peace and security affairs (Charrad 2010). Women's rights and entitlements in Lebanon, continue to fall victim to the patriarchal and confessional political system. Lebanese women still experience discrimination in marital and family relations as well as citizenship rights (Human Rights Watch 2020).

The progress towards women's agency have so far failed to breakdown the structural cultural barriers and deep-rooted discrimination faced by Lebanese women. That is why improvement shouldn't be mistaken by empowerment, and Lebanon still have a long way to go in promoting gender equality and in challenging gender hierarchies and structures of inequality that are deeply rooted in the system as well as in the norms and values of the society.

This chapter will rely on locally driven knowledge published by various national public and civil entities in order to explore the discriminations and structural inequalities faced by Lebanese women. The chapter also recommend the steps forward to advance gender equality and promote Lebanese women's agency.

3. Methodology and research overview

This paper aims at identifying main structural barriers facing women's agency in Lebanon. The approach used maps some laws and draft bills having an impact on gender in Lebanon in 2022, and based on the discriminatory laws and practices against women agency highlights with facts and numbers the needed actions.

This chapter was developed using a combination of methods mainly a comprehensive review of most recent published reports since the latest official CEDAW report presented by the Lebanese Republic until 2022.

The reports gathered and used as background material are about laws, and draft laws prepared, presented and recorded by various entities such as official public entities as the National Commission for Lebanese Women (NCLW), members of parliament, parliament committees, the government and or by National Civil entities preparing draft laws and regulations such as CSOs (Institutional: Academic, CSOs) and individual consultants.

The methodology used entails, a comprehensive literature review providing an overview of the existing laws in brief, and main status for amendment needed. The desk review aims to support in the design of needed advocacy efforts to perform the amendments requested by public authorities.

The research is based on extracting data from secondary resources such reports conducted and published by the national women machinery (NCLW) stated above, as well as by United Nations bodies such as UN Women, UNFPA, ESCWA, UNDP, ILO. The main resources used are stated in the specific bibliography below.

In addition to these reports, additional data and information were added from studies, reports and papers issued by local or international organizations as shadow reports, background documents, policy briefs, or studies performed by a various spectrum of civil social organizations.

Regarding the timeframe scrutinized, it is important to note that this chapter maps some of the laws presented since 2019 to 2021 with a very brief overview of main laws amended since 2011 pertaining to women rights, and present main case studies pertaining to women's capacity to exercise agency in public sphere and in high level decision making processes, the citizenship rights, vulnerable groups capacity to exercise agency under an abusive system, the case of foreign domestic workers, and the incapacity to exercise agency under religious laws and patriarchal social practices discriminating between men and women and between Lebanese women themselves.

2019 as a specific date, was chosen because it covers the latest national reports on Women's rights presented by the Lebanese Government, whether for the Beijing platform of action, and or to the CEDAW international committee as mentioned before for the National official CEDAW report. 2019 is also the date of the beginning of the implementation of the National Action Plan on UNSCR1325, adopted by the Lebanese government in September 2019, with a specific part related to laws amended, entitled the normative framework.

All the laws presented before this date have already been extensively studied and various mapping including what needs to be amended were published by national official entities or national and international civil society entities and academia. Some of the main reports produced before 2018 related to laws and regulations were stated in the part related to resources. (Karam, Bouakl, Chemaly and NCLW 2014).

The main official reports that were used are from various official reports by National Women machinery, UN agencies and CSOs related to laws mapping in Lebanon stated in the references part below. As per the above, a listing and identification of main legal reforms and amendments needed was performed. Main tipping point for change can be highlighted regarding women's agency in Lebanon and the main structural barriers women are facing when dealing with their main rights at work, within the family sphere or in the public sphere. The below segments of the article aim to understand if women in Lebanon are really empowered and do they have the ability to exercise choices? Empowerment "...incorporates three interrelated dimensions: resources (defined broadly to include not only access, but also future claims, to both material and human and social resources); agency (including processes of decision making, as well as less measurable manifestations of agency such as negotiation, deception and manipulation); and achievements (well-being outcomes)" (Kabeer and Naila 1999).

4. Women participation in the public and political sphere, the structural barriers and the prevalence of holistic discrimination by societal norms

The role and effective position of women in politics and the participation of women to the public sphere is clear in Lebanese and international legislations. The Lebanese Constitution in its Art. 7 is clear, it guarantees equality between men and women without any distinction. The Convention on the Elimination of All Forms of Discrimination Against Women CEDAW, ratified by Lebanon in 1996 encourages in its article 4 the State to adopt strict measures, more specifically "temporary special measures" aimed at increasing women representation in the bodies whose members are elected or nominated, in all areas of the public life. This was also validated by the World Conference on Women in Beijing in 1995, the International Covenant on Political and Civil Rights, the United Nations Security Council Resolution 1325/2000 on Women, Peace and Security, Resolution 1820/2008 and Resolution 2122/2013 urging the countries to strengthen the presence and participation of women in the negotiation and mediation commissions aiming at ending armed conflicts and establishing civil peace. Recently, the "2030 Agenda for Sustainable Development" has put equality back on the table of the national public policies, with an action plan adopted in September 2015 during the United Nations summit, comprising 17 sustainable development goals, of which Goal 5 is directly linked to the gender and equality between men and women. The 10 years National Strategy for women in Lebanon has also confirmed the need to have non-discrimination regarding women's political participation. More than that, the latest public policy adopted in Lebanon in 2019, which is the UNSCR1325, clearly confirms in one of its pillars the need to increase women political participation in various public spheres. Some of these texts are binding, others are not. But whether binding or not, it is up to the Lebanese State to take measures granting women a vital place in politics. The political and social "culture" of the country is displayed by factors such as the social and public role of female citizens. The main question remains: where do Lebanese women stand in regards to power and how can we measure the effective participation of women in the decision-making processes in Lebanon?

In other words, is the democracy in Lebanon really participative and egalitarian for all its citizens mainly women? Does it grant women their main rights for them to be able to participate in the public domain?

The withholding of dominant or "leadership" roles in society, particularly in elected and appointed bodies (ministerial portfolios, General Directors, Embassies, Commission, negotiation committee…) shows to which degree the patriarchy pervades the political culture and how the Lebanese State needs to reinforce the inclusion of all, women, youth and other marginalized communities in its public spheres, through its policies as well as practices.

5. Figures, measures and examples of social exclusion in the political and public sphere in Lebanon:

In facts, Lebanese women have obtained, following various mobilizations, the reform of the electoral law in 1953, enshrining their political rights. But given the various sectarian and geographic quotas existing in Lebanon, it is hard for Lebanese women to break the circle of male domination in politics. As Geha highlights it, "Lebanon's politics of representation are shaped by a century-old system of power-sharing among its recognised sects. This sectarian-based representation in national institutions is conducive to a form of leadership that emanates from clientelism, and from the father-figure or protector of the sect. We know from decades-old research and testimonials of women that this system not only favors men but is built on men. Consider the alliance of religious courts, led by men, with political parties, led by men. Both of these finance and foster a political system that functions, undemocratically, only when the men agree." (Geha 2020).

6. Spotlight on inequalities in women's representation and gender equality

6.1. Women in parliament, systematic structural barriers

It wasn't before 1963 when a woman was elected without vote at the Parliament to succeed her deceased father. During the 2009 legislative elections, of 587 candidates only 12 were woman, and only 4 were elected at the Lebanese Parliament. The May 2018 legislative elections underline a significant improvement of the political participation in terms of candidacy: 111 in personal candidacies, 86 candidacies on lists in 2018, compared to 12 female candidacies in 2009 and 38 in 2013 when the elections did not take place. The results of the 2018 elections expressed a modest number of 6 elected among 128, despite the proliferation of national awareness campaigns. Lebanon remains far behind in the international ranking. In 2022, as for women's representation in the Lebanese parliament, there has been a clear decline, with only 8 women elected in the parliament out of 128. As the quota for women was not adopted in the electoral law adopted in 2017, and many lists did not include women.

Political parties did not work hard to appoint women candidates on the electoral lists, preferring to choose known male candidates who could bring them more votes. As a result, the representation remains highly unequal in the parliament. Let's take a closer look at the numbers. Of the 1,043 candidates in 2022, 157 were women, or nearly 15%. But when the electoral lists were formed, only 118 women remained candidates on the lists, even though there were more lists than in 2018 with women candidates. In 2022, 38 lists had no women on them. And out of the 118 women candidates for the parliament, only 8 women managed to be elected. 4 of the elected women are part of the establishment and were supported by the traditional parties, the other 4 elected women were active and known in the protest movement of the October 2019 movement and are labelled as coming from civil society with reformist stands. The numbers at the parliament level, and in the national elections, indicate that women's agency in the Lebanese public sphere is not fully acquired as the system has been tailored in a way to exclude them if they are not part of main traditional political blocs. The will of various political entities to take action and nominate women on the lists was not fulfilled, political blocs and entities preferring to gain votes and ensure seats. Inclusion is still lacking as per the definition given in the Arab dictionary for elections (UNDP 2019).

6.2. National Commission for the Supervision of Elections, discrimination in nominations

The inequality between men and women was highlighted with the number of female candidates and elected women, additionally illustrated in the National Commission for the Supervision of Elections, a national entity created and aimed at supervising elections and which has only 2 women out of 11 members, which shows that Lebanon needs to make more effort for equality and women's agency.

6.3. Women in government, a scarce representation

In the cabinets, the representation of women is scarce; one female minister for the last government and none for the previous one. Even though various campaigns led by Lebanese civil society organizations with in parallel lobbying by international organizations repeated the need to have gender equality in cabinets formation. The social media platforms mainly twitter has witnessed campaigns led by CSOs and Ambassadors and UN agency representatives in Lebanon to have at least 50% gender representation. (Fiftyfifty 2022, Madanyat 2022). UN women issued a statement in this regard explaining in 2021, that having one women in the cabinet, "mirrors the strikingly low level of women's representation across political and public office in the country, with women currently occupying less than five percent of parliamentary seats and making up less than six percent municipal councilors".

Based on the facts presented, the main barriers for women to participate in the political and public sphere, are the structural inequalities hindering the women representation in cabinets during the most challenging time for Lebanon. These structural challenges are refraining women from breaking through the glass ceiling of social norms prevailing in Lebanon coupled with long-term patriarchal practices.

In a report Euromed women foundation, identify obstacles preventing women from participating in political life at three levels: "social factors such as cultural constructs, prevalent relationship patterns in Lebanon and the patriarchal society; Economic factors affecting women's political participation, particularly those related to electoral campaigns and "poverty among women" and their financial dependence; Political factors related to the prevailing political regime based on tribal, family and sectarian structures." (Euromed women foundation, 2017).

This shows that the reasons for women's poor representation in Lebanese politics are complex and far-reaching. The laws and traditions that are encompassed in a system of government based on patriarchal sectarian views and controlled by male political elites present a huge challenge to women entering the political sphere. This is of course in addition to the socioeconomic barriers to women's political participation that were deepened with the financial crisis that Lebanon has been living since 2019. Moreover, women who had some banking deposits lost them, whereas because of patriarchal practices, men have lost their deposits in banks but not their access to land or houses due to inheritance practices that favors the males of the family instead of the women.

The above evidently specifies that the social and economic status of women in society has a direct influence on their participation in political institutions and elected bodies.

6.4. "Manels" are the forms of the dialogues for reconciliation and national building, leaving women's role in the society on levels related to care work and households' scope

Other examples can be taken to show that since the 90's, women were put aside in main public decisions in the country. The "national dialogues" sessions have been initiated and organized by the political authorities such as political parties and government authorities; main leaders to decide civil peace, coordinate defense strategies and ensure the bases for national accord regarding Lebanon. Women are, up to this date, absent from these meetings which aim at deciding national priorities. The national dialogue meetings have established the foundations of the compromise in Lebanon, with the "Taef" agreement followed later on by the "Doha" agreement or the high-level sessions that took place in Lebanon for peace negotiations between various sects, or factions in conflict within the country. The problem is that all these meetings were manels. It means they are meetings, and conferences with only men, and disregarding women presence: the issues discussed and the suggested solutions during these manels without the participation of female citizens excluded from these reunions, risk not being suitable for women in Lebanon and being hindered by their lack of completeness and feel of ownership. (Chemaly R., *Gender Mainstreaming and Sustainable Development: Identifying biases and Managing Resistance*, ICT ILO, June 2022). After the Beirut blast of august 2020, the French President Emmanuel Macron visited Lebanon and organized a meeting with factions of all Lebanese political parties for them all to be held accountable and decide of the way forward for the country. The high-level meeting was a manel. Women as they didn't participate in them and voiced their concerns might not take them seriously neither educate others on owning their results. The role of women in the processes of the truth, reconciliation and reconstruction commissions must be a priority on the national level in Lebanon.

6.5. Women in municipalities, a better representation but still lacking parity and breaking down the motherhood wall in roles distribution

Municipal elections on the other hand show a slight advancement in women participation at the local level. The results of the municipal elections that took place in 2016 have shown a slight progress in the female participation rate in the municipal local decisions, from 4.7% in 2010 to 5.6% in 2016, with 680 women elected locally. This rate is surely not sufficient for a genuine inclusion of women in decision making at the local level, given all the work women can undertake, particularly in the framework of local reconciliation and mediation processes that did not systematically take place after the war and the various conflicts witnessed in Lebanon. Moreover, various studies and gender audits led on the municipal level showcased as a main barrier to women's agency "the sticky floor" biases. On the municipal level, women are mostly appointed on the social committees pertaining the image of the mother and their roles as mothers and care providers instead of appointing women in hard-core decision-making committees such as strategic and engineering committees.

6.6. Initiatives exist for mitigating biases hindering women political participation in decision making positions

Various initiatives were led by CSOs for the last decade to encourage women political participation. Most initiatives and activities were led in an empowerment perspective. These programs were led in parallel with a social movement that supports women political participation as a major cause. This movement is composed of national authorities, such as the National Commission for Lebanese Women, established by Law no. 720/1998 and had had the support of the Women's Affairs Ministry that was established in Lebanon in 2017 for a very short period of time. The movement was also supported by civil associations particularly NGOs that were gathered under the guidance of the national coalition "Women for Politics", formed in 2016. The demands were simple, particularly ensuring full social and political rights of the Lebanese women. Even if the establishment of a quota is not the dream solution for the gender equality, studies have shown however that this system allows women to access public affairs and decision-making positions. The civil society associations have claimed the establishment of a 30% quota system, a transitory and temporary system that might allow increasing the proportion of women in the Lebanese public life, particularly on the parliamentarian level. The common vision behind these egalitarian claims, as highlighted by the national women's strategy in Lebanon 2011-2021 consists in a public political sphere without a male domination, where women can also be completely established citizen actors. The marginalization and exclusion of women as a result of compromises and concessions, made because of a sectarian and patriarchal system, require patent measures and several action levels based mainly on amending electoral laws. Various bills and projects were submitted to amend the law for municipal elections and the law of national legislative elections with a quota for women. These project laws need to be brought up again and put on the political and public agenda. The 2017 law adopted for parliamentarian elections needs to be re-examined with measures that encourage mandatorily having a number of women on each list. Penalties can be thought of for list without women on them. Furthermore, ensuring the respect of the equality principle in all ministry's nominations, commission and delegation appointments is a needed step. The July 2022 political negotiations to appoint a new government are not taking into account gender equality. Even though women's right organization and activists visited the nominated government head that will nominate the ministers. (Lebanon's Feminist Civil Society Platform statement 2022) Pressure and momentum need to stay high by INGOs lobbying for fairer representation of all and full inclusion of women in all level of decision making specifically in time of crises.

In brief, the battle for an effective representation of women in decision making roles is long. Social norms, as well as political tractation are excluding women and keeping them out of the main political and public sphere decisions and roles and are creating a glass ceiling that is difficult to overcome in Lebanon. As described by Helou in 2001, "Women were denied their political rights either explicitly in electoral laws or implicitly by holding elections on the basis of electoral lists that did not have female voters on them yet." (Helou Marguerite, Al Raida, 2001). Therefore, temporary measures such as the quota in all legislations allow women, as an entity marginalized by the structure of the system, to access all areas of decision-making, administration and community service. This would ensure a better representation of women, one that would allow addressing gender issues and its various implications on the public life in the public debate, within entities such as the Government and the parliament.

Do women in Lebanon have the full ability to make their choices and act upon them? After understanding the place of women in the public sphere and the lack of women representation in high decision-making processes, we will check another example that we will use as a case study to understand women's agency in the context of Lebanon: the long battle for full citizenship rights.

6.7. Transmissions of nationality an identity factor excluding women from full citizenship rights

The Lebanese Nationality Law of 1925 gives a Lebanese man the right to transmit his nationality to his non-Lebanese spouse and children but denies Lebanese women the right to transmit their nationality to foreign spouses and children. Women can only grant nationality to their children if they are illegitimate according to the law. In Lebanon, a Lebanese woman married to a foreigner does not have the right to transmit her nationality to her husband or her children. However, a foreign woman who marries a Lebanese man can acquire it after one year of marriage. Art. 1 of the Nationality Law no. 15, dated 19 January 1925, stipulates that "every person born of a Lebanese father is considered Lebanese". According to this text, any person born of a Lebanese mother is not considered Lebanese. Nationality in Lebanon is based on blood ties, not on geographical soil ties. This law brings up the issues of discrimination against women and the principle of equality between men and women promoted by the Lebanese Constitution in its Art. 7. A law that leads us to question the status of the Lebanese woman as a citizen equal to the man. As nationality is the keystone of citizenship, Lebanese woman under this law, are considered "second class" citizen. As Joseph observed the "modern "nation-state" has mandated a masculine citizen". (Joseph, Suad 2010). The transmission of nationality is not a pure legal formality. The non-transmission of nationality to the children and husband of a Lebanese woman has important social consequences. It "discriminates against women married to foreigners, their children, and spouses, by denying citizenship to the children and spouses. The law affects almost every aspect of the children's and spouses' lives, including legal residency and access to work, education, social services, and health care. It leaves some children at risk of statelessness." (Human rights watch, 2018).

The children and husbands of Lebanese women are considered residents and not citizens and must obtain residence and work permits, and work to renew them every year. This is a costly and complicated operation with its heavy administrative paperwork, and slow with multiple appointments and interviews at the General Security in the presence of the children. The unity of the family is questioned and the risks of deportation increase. As for employment, it should be noted that as residents' husbands and children of Lebanese women, the choice of possible jobs to be exercised is limited; Belonging to unions, associations and orders, impossible. Some jobs are reserved for Lebanese holding a Lebanese passport.

In short, the transmission of nationality by Lebanese women is an essential right that allows Lebanese women to no longer be considered as "second class" citizens, and to give children and husbands access to social rights. The right to exercise a profession, the right to access public schools, to enrol in university as Lebanese citizens, the right to social security. While children born of Lebanese mothers and not holding another nationality are holders of a pass that must be regularly renewed and which does not give them access to the minimum social rights.

Progress is necessary and essential on the legislative level. Various draft laws to enforce gender equality and ensure the rights of all citizens were presented by multiple entities with the aim to give back to women their rights as citizens in an effort to modernize and put an end to discriminatory provisions and allow Lebanon to comply with international treaties ratified by it.

Until date, no progress was made on this front. Even though, Lebanon's National Action Plan on UNSCR 1325 calls for amendments to the Nationality Law to give equal rights to Lebanese women married to foreign spouses to transmit their nationality to their children. In its Concluding Observations, the CEDAW Committee noted its concern about the State party's reluctance to withdraw its reservation to Art. 9 (2) on granting women equal rights with men with respect to the nationality of their children. The Committee urged Lebanon to withdraw its reservations to Art. 9(2), repeal Decree No. 15 of 1925 on Lebanese Nationality and adopt legislation to ensure women's equal rights with men to pass on their nationality to foreign spouses and children [1].

In conclusion the right to transmit the nationality of women to their families as main factor for women agency, is still lacking behind demographic imbalances and sectarian fears. On December 12, 2011, the Lebanese Council of Ministers took the decision to grant emigrants the possibility of restitution of Lebanese nationality. A decision that could only be greeted with applause if it did not explicitly exclude Lebanese women. As it consecrated discriminatory practices against women and reinforced sexism and patriarchalism within Lebanese society. Political, confessional and demographic arguments are still challenging women's agency and full citizenship capacities.

In citizenship rights discriminatory provisions against women agency and capacities are highlighted in nationality law; A last example can be also analyzed in Lebanon with the lack of women agency of foreign domestic workers contracted in Lebanon. A woman's instrumental agency, is her ability to affect her life by having power to make choices and to control acquired resources (EIGE 2019).

7. Domestic work

Domestic workers mainly migrant workers, living in Lebanon, are facing exploitation and abuse by a complicated "kafala" system that is also coupled with impact of the economic crisis. Kafala means tutorship or guardianship.

[1] Concluding observations on the combined fourth and fifth periodic reports of Lebanon 2015, available at https://undocs.org/CEDAW/C/LBN/CO/4-5.

Treating the subject of women's agency in Lebanon needs to cover the main subject of migrant domestic workers living and working in Lebanon. The human rights violations in Lebanon, were sadly famous mainly with case of the "fairies" of many houses in the country that were exploited by a system that doesn't give them any right except the one of « flying » the house of their employers.

After the crisis, and the devaluation of the country's "Lira", many households had to make their domestic worker leave the house, as they couldn't afford paying their wages. A lot of foreign domestic workers were left alone on the road next to their embassies, without the price of a ticket home, and without being paid. "Repatriation had become a growing demand among migrant workers in Lebanon since the country's sprawling economic crisis began two years ago, particularly after hundreds were abandoned by their employers, tossed out in front of their consulates, often with no money, food or even their official documents" (Ramadan Tala 2021). The lockdown, coupled with the crises in Lebanon increased the exploitation system that existed. Lebanon for various workers "has become a purgatory" where they are stuck, not being able to leave, or send wages to their families back home, or even have a decent job.

In Lebanon before the crises, a confluence of factors has resulted in the country attracting thousands of immigrant women workers, who seek to earn enough money to support their families back home. Lebanese women who used to stay at home to take care of the household and educate their children were pursuing higher education and taking up positions of responsibility outside the family sphere to help in breadwinning; these few factors mean that, as in many countries with a growing young population, there was a growing need for a workforce to help with domestic tasks. So, fleeing the extreme poverty of their villages, many women and girls from Ethiopia, Sri Lanka, the Philippines, Madagascar, Nepal, or Bangladesh, embarked for Lebanon or other countries of the Arab world, in order to ensure their families a dignified life; often ignoring the prohibitions of their country of origin to come and work in certain countries labelled as dangerous. A glaring example of the role and space that domestic workers play in the households that were being built in Lebanon, is the appearance in the architectural plans of many real estate developers of "maids rooms", spaces limited to 2 square meters at best, often behind the kitchen. Even on the plans of small two-bedroom apartments, the "maid room" and its toilet remained one of the must-haves of an apartment for sale; because in Lebanon, as in the Gulf countries, the domestic worker lives at the employer's home, where she is "placed" there by an employment agency, she then depends on the "kafala" system or sponsorship of her employer, who thus becomes her individual guarantor. Often, as denounced by international and national civil society organizations, workers are unaware of their rights. Upon their arrival to Lebanon, servitude and exploitation awaits them in the homes of their employers. Often for fear of detention, deportation or physical punishment, they do not file a complaint. Moreover, these immigrant domestic workers are excluded from the Lebanese labor code (article 7), and are therefore not protected against abuse by any type of Lebanese legislation. This exception is denounced by the National Campaign Wayn Ba'dna (the long road ahead) conducted by various associations that was led by the National Commission for Lebanese women. The form of "modern slavery" begins with the confiscation of passports, the prohibition of going out, endless work days, weeks without leaves, and in most cases, the non-payment of salaries, which are often lower than the minimum wages established by the state.

The development of a national policy to protect the rights of foreign migrant workers remains a priority. Ratifying and bringing Lebanon into compliance with ILO Convention 189 on decent work for domestic workers is a must. The monitoring and evaluation of recruitment agencies and their methods and ways of dealing with immigrant women is also a must, together with the sensitization of the Lebanese households that will receive these immigrants, to their rights, and to their respect as human beings with a different and not lesser culture.

8. Personal statuses and practices and social norms limit Lebanese women's capacity to exercise their agency

8.1. The incapacity to exercise agency under religious laws and patriarchal social practices

Through the examples of women political participation, followed by discrimination in nationality rights, and the exploitation and abuse of vulnerable communities mainly foreign domestic workers working in Lebanon, we tackled how women's agency in Lebanon is not comprehensive. The latter continues in the field of personal status. Women's capacity as citizen is tied to the one of their family, the father's name is always prevalent in Lebanon, and while registering in the civil register, the daughter is linked to her father registry, unless married; the wife is tied to her husband register record. In case of divorce, the daughters are "linked back" to their father's registry.

Women's lack of agency and capacity to decide how to act with their resources and their rights is linked to the lack of a unified civil code considering all citizens as equals. Because of a lack if a unified civil code, Lebanese women can't open bank accounts to their children without the consent and the signature of the father. Making women uncapable to decide upon and act with the resources they acquire. The Constitution in its articles 9 and 10 gives religious sects the authority to govern legislation pertaining to the private sphere of the family. This is one of the major discrimination facing women in the multiple personal status laws that do not guarantee women's rights. And which allow under the current system, for various religious sects to apply different laws on issues related to divorce, heritage, child custody, adoption and marriage age and rights. The confessional system recognizes 18 religious communities with their laws on personal status that deal with marriage and its consequences and are handled by different religious courts run by each community. Druze, Shiite and Sunni citizens each apply different interpretations of sharia (Islamic principles of jurisprudence). And the Orthodox and non-Orthodox Christian communities apply different versions of canon law. Most of these laws tend to favor the rights of men and stress patriarchal values. This system of different courts results not only in unequal application of the law when it comes to men and women, but also amongst Lebanese women themselves. For example, a catholic Lebanese woman has different rights than a Shia Lebanese woman, which are different than a Sunni Lebanese woman. Sunni and Shia courts allow men to enter into polygamous relationships, while Druze and Christian courts do not. Divorce is prohibited in Catholic courts, whereas it is permitted in Sunni, Shia, Druze and Christian Orthodox courts. Sunni laws allowed recently for maternal child custody to be increased until 12 years old. Noting that after divorce in Shiite courts, women can keep their daughters until they turn seven and their sons two only, after which time they have to be raised by the father's family. Women's rights are limited in custody in personal status laws and the rights of men are recognized as the peremptory moral and financial guardian of their children.

8.2. The revolving issue of incapacity to contract a civil marriage in Lebanon and the challenges faced by those who opt to contract a civil marriage outside of Lebanon

Those who opt for civil marriages outside of Lebanon face another challenge. Many personal status laws disallow marriages if one person in a couple is from a different religious community. And because there is no civil marriage in Lebanon, many religiously mixed couples are obliged to travel to neighbouring countries like Cyprus or Türkiye to marry. Pursuant to Art. 25 of Decree no. 60/1936, the couple's marriage is recognized in Lebanon but governed by the civil law of the country where it was conducted – a legal headache for Lebanese judges who must therefore be familiar with the civil code of the country where the marriage was conducted in order to resolve any legal issues. Various attempts to institute one civil code pertaining to the status of the individual, even as an optional measure, have failed due to a political and social system based on confessional power-sharing. The latest draft law prepared by KAFA, clearly stipulates equality between men and women as far as marriage is concerned and at the spouse's discretion. KAFA advocates that all Lebanese people be subject to the same personal status laws, which guarantee women the same rights and obligations in marriage, inheritance, divorce, alimony and custody afforded to men under the Lebanese Constitution and gender-sensitive international agreements. A unified civil code on personal status would put an end to existing inequalities between men and women, and among Lebanese women of different confessions.

To conclude, in this chapter we mapped the efforts performed by the state national women machinery to tailor public policies and action plans framing women's rights and strategically pushing for further equality and less discrimination in the legal framework and in social norms. But these policies if not followed in parallel by clear actions by various sectors of the society such as unions, political parties, organizations, change will remain weak and ink on paper. In parliament the amendments and voting for laws is a very slow process, advocacy and lobbying activities need to take place to expand women's agency on the highest levels, while ensuring that on the agenda the bills amendments are stated. The main case studies and examples showcased how women are still facing manels, glass ceilings by societal norms and patriarchal practices. Nationality rights in Lebanon remain highly discriminatory and incapacitate women from transmitting their citizenship to their families. Personal status laws run by various religious courts as permitted in the constitution are still hindering women's rights and the road is paved by challenges and structural barriers to amend discriminatory provision and their impact on daily practices such as opening simple bank accounts and registering children in the civil registry census. The structural inequalities in laws and practices have a strong impact on women's agency in Lebanon: the long battle for gender equality is still ahead.

References

Accumulation and Agency, https://documents1.worldbank.org/curated/en/789321635270783493/pdf/The-Status-of-Women-in-Lebanon-Assessing-Women-s-Access-to-Economic-Opportunities-Human-Capital-Accumulation-and-Agency.pdf. Link accessed in November 2023.

Agarwala R. and Lynch S.M. (2006), "Refining the Measurement of Women's Autonomy: An International Application of a Multi-dimensional Construct", *Social Forces*, 84, 4, June, 2077-2098, https://doi.org/10.1353/sof.2006.0079.

Amnesty International (2016), *Lebanon: 'I want a safe place': Refugee women from Syria uprooted and unprotected in Lebanon*, available at https://www.amnesty.org/en/documents/mde18/3210/2016/en/, link accessed in October 2023.

Chemaly R. (2011), "Lebanon: civil society mobilized for equal rights", *Common Ground News Service.*

Chemaly R. (2018), "The Implications of the Political Participation of Women in Lebanon, a Culture of Inclusion and Reinforcement of Special Measures: an Imminent Priority for an Effective Role", Supplement of UNDP Peace building initiative, Published on Monday 6th of August 2018 with *Annahar*, *L'Orient-Le Jour* and *The Daily Star.*

Chemaly R. (2022), *Gender Mainstreaming and Sustainable Development: Identifying biases and Managing Resistance*, Turin, ICT ILO, June.

Country Profiles on Migration (2015), Statistics on Labour Migration in Pacific-Asia, available at http://www.ifrc.org/Global/Documents/Asia-pacific/201505/Map_Infographic.pdf, link accessed in March 2017.

Cruz A. and Klinger S. (2011), *Gender-based violence in the world of work: overview and selected bibliography*, Geneva, International Labour Office-ILO, available at http://www.ilo.org/wcmsp5/groups/public/---dg reports/---gender/documents/publication/wcms_155763.pdf, link accessed in October 2023.

Geha C. (2020), *Lebanese Women and the Politics of Representation*, available at https://www.arab-reform.net/pdf/?pid=9118&plang=en.

Global Migration Data Analysis Centre (2017), "Migrant deaths and disappearances worldwide: 2016 analysis", *IOM*, 8, March, https://publications.iom.int/system/files/pdf/gmdac_data_briefing_series_issue_8.pdf.

Helou M. (2001), "Lebanese Women and Politics: A Comparison between Two Field Studies", *Al Raida*, available at http://alraidajournal.com/index.php/ALRJ/article/view/544/542.

Hunt E. (2016), "Migrant women isolated and vulnerable to domestic abuse, study finds", *The Guardian*, available at https://www.theguardian.com/

society/2016/dec/09/migrant-women-isolated-and-vulnerable-to-domestic-abuse-study-finds, link accessed in November 2023.

ILO (2013), *Domestic workers across the world: global and regional statistics and the extent of legal protection*, Geneva, International Labour Office-ILO, available at http://www.ilo.org/wcmsp5/groups/public/---dgreports/---dcomm/---publ/documents/publication/wcms_173363.pdf, link accessed in November 2023.

International Labour Office, ILO Regional Office for the Arab States (2016), *A study of working and living conditions of migrant domestic workers in Lebanon: "intertwined: the workers' side"*, Geneva, ILO, available at http://www.ilo.org/wcmsp5/groups/public/---arabstates/---ro-beirut/documents/publication/wcms_524143.pdf, link accessed in March 2017.

International Organization for Migration (2009), *Working To Prevent And Address Violence Against Women Migrant Workers*, available at https://publications.iom.int/system/files/pdf/gender_report.pdf, link accessed in November 2023.

Jones K. and Ksaifi L. (2016), *Struggling to survive: Slavery and exploitation of Syrian refugees in Lebanon*, available at http://freedomfund.org/wp-content/uploads/Lebanon-Report-FINAL-8April16.pdf.

Joseph S. (2010) "Gender and Citizenship in the Arab World", *Al-Raida Journal*, 8-18, available at http://iwsawassets.lau.edu.lb/alraida/alraida-129-130.pdf

Jureidini R. (2009), "Irregular Workers in the Labour Market: the case of trafficked migrants and refugees working as domestic workers in Egypt", paper presented at the "Migration and Development: Building Migration into Development Strategies" conference at the Development Research Center at the University of Sussex, Royal Society, London, April 28-29, 2008 by Forced Migration and Refugee Studies Program, American University in Cairo, *International Journal on Multicultural Societies*, 11, 1, 75-90, can be downloaded from Academia.

Kabeer, N. (1999), "Resources, Agency, Achievements: Reflections on the Measurement of Women's Empowerment", *Development and Change* 30.3, 435-64, doi: 10.1111/1467-7660.00125.

Karam C., Abou-Habib L. and Ghanem M. (2020), "Influencing Policy through Research: The case of sexual harassment law in Lebanon", *CIBL for Women*, https://www.aub.edu.lb/cibl/news/Pages/The_case_of_sexual_harassment_law_in_Lebanon.aspx.

Karam F., Bouakl C. and Chemaly R. (2014), "Women rights in Lebanese legislation", *NCLW/UNFPA publications*, December, Collaborative publication, in Arabic, available for free download online at www.nclw.gov.lb, the link to download the full version of the study in Arabic.

Khatib L. (2008), "Gender, Citizenship and Political Agency in Lebanon", *British Journal of Middle Eastern Studies*, 35(3), 437-51, available in *JSTOR*, http://www.jstor.org/stable/20455620, accessed November 2023.

Meaker M. (2017), "Syrian refugee children reduced to selling on Beirut's streets to feed their families", *The Guardian*, available at https://www.theguardian.com/global-development/2017/jan/25/syrian-refugee-children-selling-beirut-streets-lebanon-support-families, link accessed in November 2023.

Mixed Migration Platform (MMP), (2017), "Mixed Migration Monthly Summary Middle East", Situation Report January, available at https://reliefweb.int/report/world/middle-east-mixed-migration-monthly-summary-january-2017 link accessed in November 2023.

Qutteina Y., Al-Khelaifi B. and Yount K. (2019), *Meanings of Women's Agency: A Case Study from Qatar on Improving Measurement in Context*, available at https://doi.org/10.1080/21534764.2019.1649828.

Save the Children (2016), *Every Last Girl*, available at http://www.savethechildren.org.uk/sites/default/files/images/Every_Last_Girl.pdf, link accessed in November 2023.

Spencer R. *et al.* (2015), "Gender based violence against women and girls, Displaced by the Syrian Conflict In south Lebanon and North Jordan: Scope of Violence and Health Correlated", *Alianza per la Solidaridad /AECID/UNFPA.*

Statistical Dashboard prepared by the Interagency Information Management Unit - UNHCR Lebanon, (2017 January).

The Institute for Women's Studies in the Arab World Lebanese American University (2010-2011), *Gender-Based Violence in the Arab World, Al Raida, IWSAW, LAU*, Issue 131-132, fall/winter, available at http://iwsawassets.lau.edu.lb/alraida/alraida-131-132.pdf, link accessed in October 2023.

The legal framework approved by the Lebanese Government in 2019 when adopting the National Action Plan on UNSCR 1325.

The National report on the implementation of the Beijing platform for action report 2019.

The Sixth periodic report on the implementation of the Convention on the Elimination of All Forms of Discrimination against Women CEDAW, NCLW, 2019.

The UPR 2021 presentation by the Lebanese government as for answering the discussion on the report and the received recommendations.

UNDP (2018-2019), *Arab Electoral Dictionary*, the full version of dictionary 323 pages, القاموس العربي للانتخابات | برنامج الأمم المتحدة الإنمائي (undp.org), the leaflet can be accessed through this link dictionary_leaflet.pdf (un.org), link accessed in October 2023.

United Nations Population Fund (UNFPA), United Nations Educational, Scientific and Cultural Organization (UNESCO), United Nations Children's Fund (UNICEF), Office of the United Nations High Commissioner for Refugees (UNHCR) or Save the Children International (SCI), (2014), *Situation Analysis of Youth in Lebanon Affected by the Syrian Crisis 2014*, available at https://reliefweb.int/report/lebanon/situation-analysis-youth-lebanon-affected-syrian-crisis, link accessed in October 2023.

Women's Access to Economic Opportunities, Human Capital Accumulation & Agency. Washington D.C.: World Bank, https://openknowledge.worldbank.org/bitstream/handle/10986/36512/The-Status-of-Women-in-Lebanon-Assessing-Womens-Access-to-Economic-Opportunities-Human-Capital-Accumulation-and-Agency.pdf?sequence=1also available at the link below.

World Bank and UN Women (2021), *The Status of Women in Lebanon: Assessing* Women's Access to Economic Opportunities, Human Capital.

INDEX

W

FSC
www.fsc.org
MIX
Papier | Fördert gute Waldnutzung
FSC® C083411

Kolibri 360 GmbH
Ferdinand-Jühlke-Straße 7
99095 Erfurt, Deutschland
produktsicherheit@kolibri360.de